جيمس مودرن أكاديمي
GEMS Modern Academy

THE MODERN
WORLD DEBATES 2019

THANK YOU

ADJUDICATORS

Women
Equality
Power

Women
Equality
Power
Helen
Clark

Selected speeches
from a life of leadership

ALLEN&UNWIN
SYDNEY · MELBOURNE · AUCKLAND · LONDON

Contents

Foreword

For many people a speech is something to endure before the main event—the entrée, if you like, before the main course.

Good speeches, however, can be the centrepiece. They are documents of a place and time; they encourage and they inspire. Truly great speeches can change the course of history.

Helen Clark put New Zealand on the world stage. Always the pragmatist, she was never afraid to say what she thought. That sometimes worked against her, but more often than not it garnered admiration and respect.

She often said, and continues to say, that having women in leadership positions not only sends a powerful message to other women but also changes societies' perceptions of gender roles and encourages girls to believe that no door is closed to them.

In many ways Helen opened the door for me. My generation grew up under her leadership. I was lucky enough to get a job in her office not long after I left university. Helen was wise, inspiring and provocative; she remains so to this day.

In 2008, in a speech to parliament, Helen said she was motivated by one goal: to secure the best possible living standards for all New Zealanders. Her vision of a sustainable and prosperous country, where inclusion and partnership was a given, is an enduring one.

I remember Helen saying in her valedictory speech (see page 231) that as a child she could never have imagined herself becoming prime

11

minister, because the politicians of that era were invariably elderly men.

When Helen entered parliament there was still such a thing as a 'gentlemen's club': the Members' lounge, where a billiard table was dominated by be-suited blokes. There were eight women MPs.

By the time she left parliament there were 40 women MPs. Helen broke the mould, and there is no doubt in my mind that she laid the path that I have benefited from.

It's pertinent here to reference a line in the speech I gave at the launch of the 2017 election campaign about how easy it is for leaders to come and go, but it's the really good leaders who leave something good behind.

Helen has certainly done that.

I hope you enjoy the book.

Rt Hon. Jacinda Ardern, Prime Minister of New Zealand
June 2018

Introduction

It is 2018, and around Aotearoa New Zealand, women are celebrating the 125th anniversary of winning the right to vote for all women, Māori and Pākehā alike. In 2019, we will commemorate several other milestones of significance. It will be one hundred years since New Zealand women won the right to stand for parliament. It will also be 20 years since we witnessed Helen Clark win the 1999 election to become New Zealand's first female Labour prime minister, and ten years since Clark became the first female head of the United Nations Development Programme (in 2009).

These moments in history are a result of the collective achievements of generations of women and the determination of individual women. And although New Zealand can claim three female prime ministers, negotiating the path to the pinnacle of political leadership remains a rare feat for women, both here and around the world.

Perhaps as a result, there continues to be considerable public fascination with the women who achieve these roles. They are seen as exceptional rather than the norm. Their popularity is sometimes greeted with astonishment, and their unpopularity is propagated as a reason why women should not be given the highest national office. This is never an extrapolation made about poorly performing men.

The rarity of seeing women in high office means that biographies and published interviews provide the public and scholars with invaluable insights into what is required by these remarkable women. This book is no exception. The selection of speeches given by Clark in parliament as an MP, cabinet minister and prime minister, and in her post-political career, highlights the range of issues she has championed for New Zealanders, for our region, and for women globally.

Clark recognises the significance of the Labour Party's long history in her maiden speech. Established in 1916, there has been no shortage of significant leaders of the Labour Party, including Michael J Savage. But also of note is that the party's first executive included two women, one of whom was Elizabeth McCombs, who went on to become the first woman elected to New Zealand's parliament in 1933. From the outset, Labour Party women demanded a voice, and the opportunity to organise separately, in ways that went beyond the traditional auxiliary function. Women-only branches were established throughout the country and these proved critical to the advancement of Labour women and their policy interests.

Indeed, in addition to the civil rights movement and the anti-Vietnam war protests, the women's liberation movement of the 1960s and 1970s resonated with many Labour women. They established the Labour Women's Council, and sought to revitalise what some thought was an elderly, male-dominated, conservative and sclerotic organisation.[1] Labour women, including Clark who joined the Party in 1972, were critical to the process of party reform that heralded a more diverse cohort of candidates, parliamentarians and policies of economic and social equality.

Up until this point, women's representation in the New Zealand parliament had been tokenistic at best. In the period between 1933 and 1946, only six women were elected, four of whom were Labour MPs. This trend of Labour proving the party more amenable to women's representation continued and, in 1981, the year that Helen Clark was elected for the first time, the percentage of women elected doubled—from 4.3 per cent to 8.7 per cent. As Clark herself says, this was a meaningful moment for women's representation, with her and two other new Labour women elected, doubling Labour's women's caucus from three to six. The advance of Labour women into parliament continued, a direct result of Labour women's activism, and the proportion of women in parliament reached 21 per cent by 1996. This comparatively 'high' percentage was considered a most unusual feat in political systems without proportional representation or gender quotas.

Research tells us that building a political career and winning the leadership in Westminster systems depends on hard work, resources, strategy and the stars being in alignment. It is necessary to gain selection to a safe seat or list position to ensure long-term incumbency; to build political capital within party executives and caucuses; to deliver practised performances and substantive outcomes in parliamentary committees and the debating chamber; and, for your party to win elections.[2]

However, we also know that political institutions are not gender neutral. There are gendered codes that underpin the practice and processes of candidate selection, campaigns, legislative work, cabinet careers and attaining executive leadership. Gender matters because in politics, as in other professions and walks of life, dominant cultural codes of masculinity and femininity persist. These order behaviour and attitudes in relation to the accepted rules of the game and what is deemed an acceptable career pathway in politics. Once these rules and norms become institutionalised, political actors—women and men—learn them, invest in them and make decisions accordingly.

We gain a glimpse through Clark's words of how she has managed to negotiate these (gendered) career requirements. Clark won the safe seat of Mt Albert in 1981, but only after running for local government (twice) and for the rural seat of Piako. She undertook considerable executive service for the Labour Party, and worked in a range of committees and portfolios, in government and in opposition. Thus, by embracing a wide range of parliamentary experiences, Clark ensured she was ready for a ministerial position.

Although she never held the Women's Affairs portfolio, Clark's consciousness of the importance of women's issues was raised early in her tenure as a parliamentarian. First, women in the community regularly raised their issues with her because she was a woman MP and, as a result, she came to see acting for women as a necessary part of the job. 'When I came here [the women in parliament] did feel there was a women's constituency that was genuinely underrepresented. Once you got the opportunity to be a Minister you set about righting a few wrongs of long standing.'[3] Secondly, when she entered parliament in 1981, Clark found herself isolated, treated with suspicion and hostility; in 1986 she publicly named 'sexist' members of Labour's male leadership team.[4]

Clark was only in opposition for three years before her party won government. She entered cabinet in 1987 and gained the deputy leadership late in 1989 after having served as Minister for Housing, Conservation and Health. However, the feminisation of political leadership that has become a feature of the New Zealand polity began in earnest in 1993 when Helen Clark became leader of the opposition Labour Party. This was no 'glass cliff' moment, where a party selects a woman as leader because their party is in crisis or decline. The glass cliff concept captures the idea that women become viable candidates only because such environments discourage men from contesting the leadership. Rather, Clark had built a solid, if not traditional, path to the leadership; her experience was sound, her support base was solid and it was a competitive battle. Despite the bitterness expressed by her opponents, attempts to undermine her as opposition leader, and low poll ratings, Clark remained resilient and led her party to a near victory in the first MMP election in 1996.[5] The 1999 election produced a historic moment for New Zealand and for Labour. For the first time, two women, Clark and Shipley, campaigned against each other as leaders of the country's two major parties.

A great deal of attention was paid to gender during that campaign and the unusual 'spectacle' of two women fighting for the top job. During this election, Clark's gender was discussed in almost a quarter of news stories focused on her, while for Shipley, close to a fifth of the stories contained some sort of gender reference.[6] Research indicates that gender stereotypes often lead to women being portrayed as less able to handle important policy issues like the economy and foreign affairs. To combat this, successful women demonstrate their capability by creating large and diverse policy agendas that span constituency interests, women's interests, and traditionally defined 'masculine' issues. This balancing strategy allows women to develop reputations for competence and leadership on a wide range of issues.[7] Such diversity was a feature of Clark's career, and she succeeded in serving nine years as prime minister, and became Labour's longest serving leader.

So why does women's representation matter generally, but also specifically in terms of women performing political leadership, as Helen Clark has done, both nationally and internationally? Feminist political scientists have offered convincing reasons.[8] The first relates to the idea of justice. If no systemic structural discrimination existed, the seats in our parliament would be randomly distributed between both sexes. That women have tended to remain numerically under-represented suggests that the system is one that advantages men. Getting more women elected can help to disrupt this advantage in several ways. We know that women who serve as political leaders often open the doors for more women to enter political hierarchies. They also present powerful symbols of inclusion for women by challenging the perception of parliamentary politics as primarily a 'man's game'. Moreover, the advent of women political leaders has been shown to boost women's political ambition and positively influence public attitudes about women's capacity for leadership.

The second reason speaks to the importance of expanding the range of policy issues that get debated as well as who participates in these debates. Although there is no fixed set of interests that belong to 'women', it is argued that women's experiences are sufficiently different from men's to warrant representation; particularly given they have seldom been addressed adequately in politics dominated by men. Indeed, it is precisely because interests are diverse, influenced not just by sex or gender, and often created through the process of debating and deliberation, that a case can be made for more women being present in both the parliament and cabinet.[9]

There can be no doubt that Helen Clark has reshaped New Zealanders' views on women and politics and the right of women to take up the mantle of political leadership. When she became Prime Minister in 1999, seven women were given ministerial positions, constituting 35 per cent of Clark's first cabinet, and women comprised at least 30 per cent of Labour's cabinets until 2008. Prior to this, women's inclusion in cabinet, the decision engine of government, had seldom reached 15 per cent. In 2008, National followed Clark's lead, with John Key's first cabinet comprising 30 per cent women, and women's inclusion in cabinet has not dropped below that level since. Alongside this, the overall representation of women in parliament grew to more than 30 per cent after the formation of the Clark-led government. While it is impossible to prove causality, it is likely that seeing Helen Clark, and her female cabinet colleagues, in government encouraged women to consider politics as a profession open to women of all political persuasions.

Indeed, Helen Clark attracted strong support from women voters across the political spectrum. Data from the New Zealand Election Survey reveals that from 1993 onwards, women became more likely than their male counterparts to vote Labour. In 1996, women's support for Labour and National was evenly split, but women were significantly more likely than men to support Labour (a gap of eight points). This support solidified and by 2005, more women were choosing Labour than

National. Studies also show that women were more likely than men to 'like' Helen Clark and this gap remained over her time as Prime Minister. Moreover, while Labour did not win in 2008, Clark's likeability rating among both sexes increased compared to 2005.[10]

It is likely that this support came in part as a result of Clark's demonstrable capabilities as a leader who produced stable coalition government, as well as her pursuit of policies that advanced women's material wellbeing. The latter is not always a straightforward task. When women enter the political executive they come up against an aspect of the 'leadership dilemma', whereby it becomes difficult for women leaders to openly pursue a feminist agenda, as national leadership requires the creation and representation of a national constituency. In addition, choosing to speak for women explicitly in making public policy can foster a backlash against gender equality claims. Certainly, some within the party had 'warned off' Labour women from representing women's interests, despite being supported by a strong women's party council and caucus. And during the 2005 election campaign, suggestions were made that Clark's cabinet was part of a broader 'feminist mafia' and should be voted out as a consequence.

Nevertheless, despite the potential electoral risks, Clark championed women's interests, as evidenced by some of the speeches here. In her portfolio of housing she established a new unit to deal with the rental housing needs of women, with research on Māori women's needs feeding into new funding commitments. After becoming Minister of Health in 1989, she oversaw the Nurses Amendment Bill which removed restrictions on midwifery practice and, as Minister of Labour, she was integral to the passage of Employment Equity Legislation in 1990, which (briefly) provided for equal pay for work of equal value.

When Clark became prime minister, women's policy was closely linked to the need to support women's economic independence, through early childhood services, out-of-school care, retirement savings reform and paid parental leave. The framing of these 'choices' for women was couched within a discourse of serving the 'national interest' by Clark and her leadership team: that is, contributing to economic growth, prosperity and moving New Zealand 'forward' as a highly skilled, innovative economy. This strategic way of acting is a form of substantive representation by stealth, and led to specific policy gains for women.[11]

Clark's term as prime minister ended at the 2008 election, after which political journalist Colin James heralded the re-emergence of the male establishment in the corporate and political spheres.[12] He also highlighted a residue of misogyny among New Zealand voters, suggesting some voters felt considerable discomfort at women's roles as political leaders. Clark vacated the Labour leadership gracefully, and set her sights on international policy leadership. There has been a growing trend for political leaders to leave office at a younger age than in times past. In part, this is connected to the fact that, for an increasing number of parliamentarians, politics is a first rather than second career. This was the case for Clark, and by leaving national politics in her fifties, she gave herself the opportunity to construct a post-political career of significance within the United Nations. This decision reflects a broader transformation of politics from being a craft (with its connotations of slowly acquired, abiding skills peculiar to that trade) to a profession built on deep knowledge of policy, administration and good governance.[13] Knowledge that is valued by, and valuable to, international organisations grappling with complex global challenges.

A focus on increasing women's representation in politics and the increased representation of women's voices and wellbeing within our parliament is one way to measure the significance of Helen Clark's political life. But another 'true' test of women's acceptance and influence within political elites is the extent to which these women leaders are able to capitalise on their leadership posts as 'progressive stepping stones to greater political influence'.[14] With her appointment to the UNDP, her commitment to advancing the lives of women and girls in the developing world, and her candidature for the role of UN Secretary General, we see Helen Clark has done just that. She has capitalised on her experience, her knowledge and her capacity to influence in ways that have impacted the lives of many beyond New Zealand. Kate Sheppard, Harriet Morison[15] and their suffragist sisters would no doubt be most satisfied with the result of their labours.

Professor Jennifer Curtin
Politics and International Relations
Director, Public Policy Institute Te Whare Matea Tātari Kaupapa
University of Auckland

1   Margaret Shields, 'Women in the Labour Party during the Kirk and Rowling Years' in M. Clark (ed.), *Three Labour Leaders*, Victoria University of Wellington Press, 2001; Margaret Wilson, 'Women and the Labour Party' in M. Clark (ed), *The Labour Party after 75 years*, Victoria University Press, 1992.

2   Jennifer Curtin, 2008. 'Comparing Pathways to Power: Women and Political Leadership in New Zealand', in Paul 't Hart and John Uhr (eds), *Public Leadership. Perspectives and Practices*. Canberra: ANU EPress.

3   Clark cited in Janet McCallum, *Women in the House: Members of Parliament in New Zealand*, Cape Catley Press, 1993, p. 150.

4   Clark cited in V. Myers, *Head and Shoulders*, Penguin Books, 1986

5   Linda Trimble, 2017. *Ms. Prime Minister. Gender, Media, and Leadership*. Toronto: University of Toronto Press.

6   Ibid, p. 70.

7   Mary Layton Atkinson & Jason Windett. (2018). Gender Stereotypes and the Policy Priorities of Women in Congress. Political Behavior. 10.1007/s11109-018-9471-7.

8   Anne Phillips, *Engendering Democracy*, (Cambridge: Polity Press, 1991); Anne Phillips, *The Politics of Presence*, (Oxford: Oxford University Press, 1998).

9   ibid.

10 Jennifer Curtin (2014). From Presence to Absence? Where were women in the 2011 election? In J. Vowles (Ed.). *The New Electoral Politics in New Zealand* (pp. 125–139). Victoria University of Wellington: Institute for Policy Studies.

11 Jennifer Curtin 2008, 'Women, Political Leadership and Substantive Representation: the Case of New Zealand' *Parliamentary Affairs*, 61 (3) 490–504

12 James, Colin, 2010. '2008: The last baby-boomer election', In Stephen Levine and Nigel Roberts (eds), *Key to Victory. The New Zealand General Election of 2008*, Wellington: Victoria University Press.

13 Paul Strangio (2008), 'The Retiring Premiers: A New Style of Leadership Transition,' in Paul 't Hart and John Uhr (eds), *Public Leadership. Perspectives and Practices*. Canberra: ANU EPress.

14 D.L. Baer, 2003, 'Women, Women's Organisations and Political Parties, in S. Carroll (ed.), *Women and American Politics. New Questions, New Directions*, Oxford University Press, p. 135–36,

15 Labour rights activist Harriet Morison was Vice Chair of the Tailoresses Union in Dunedin and was a passionate advocate for the right to vote as well as the need to ensure better pay for women. Members of the Tailoresses Union were to provide over a third of the signatures on the suffrage petitions in 1891.

Maiden Speech
to Parliament

Parliament, Wellington
27 April 1982

Helen Clark first entered local politics in 1974, and was elected to parliament in 1981 as the representative for the Auckland electorate of Mt Albert, a position she held until her resignation in 2009. T he Prime Minister at the time was Robert Muldoon, Leader of the National Party. The Mt Albert area is notable for having produced three Labour prime ministers: Michael Joseph Savage (1935–40), Helen Clark (1999–2008) and Jacinda Ardern (2017–).

I enter the House proud to be the member for the Mt Albert electorate. Mt Albert has long given its loyalty to the Labour cause, and I was honoured and deeply privileged to be elected its representative at the 1981 general election.

I pay tribute to my predecessor, the Hon. Warren Freer, who served the electorate and New Zealand well for an outstanding 34 years. His interest in and work for the people of Mt Albert will long be remembered, as will his achievements as a minister in the reforming Third Labour government. I extend my thanks to him for his support and encouragement, and I wish him well in his retirement from politics.

These days Mt Albert is coming to be regarded as an inner-city electorate. Its boundaries have changed greatly with time. As a result of the last boundary redistribution in 1977, Mt Albert expanded to include one-third of the former stalwart Labour electorate of Grey Lynn— destroyed by the Representation Commission. At that time, the close-knit community of Point Chevalier came into the electorate and the boundary extended up along Great North Road to include all of Western Springs and a good deal of Arch Hill. The electorate continues to include the greater part of Mt Albert City, with its communities of Kingsland, Morningside, Sandringham, Mt Albert and Owairaka.

The settlement of the Mt Albert area began the best part of a century ago, when the area was broken up into small blocks and farmlets. Closer settlement spread around the turn of the century, and its impact can still be seen today in the workers' cottages and modest villas of the Kingsland– Newton area. The modern Mt Albert electorate, however, owes much of its character to the pioneering work of the first Labour government and its extensive state-housing programme. Throughout Sandringham, Owairaka, Mt Albert proper and Point Chevalier stand the solid houses built by the state in that period. Many of those who settled in those state houses in the late 1930s and early 1940s still live there in strong communities with good facilities. Labour made housing in Mt Albert a priority by taking the initiative and building fine homes in which people could afford to live. It saddens me, therefore, to see today a housing crisis in this same area.

As in most parts of Auckland, house and rent prices have soared beyond the reasonable reach of working people. The government's lack of a housing policy now adversely affects those who have cared for their state houses with pride over three or four decades. In recent weeks my telephone has run hot with elderly people ringing in distress to tell me that, while their national superannuation has increased, their state-house rentals have increased even more, leaving them worse off than they could ever have expected to be. They look forward, as I do, to the return of a Labour government, which will make its priority housing for the people, and not profits for property speculators and moneylenders.

The welfare of the elderly is an important concern in my electorate.

More than one in five of our local population—well above the Auckland average—is over the age of 60. Generally the facilities for the elderly are good in our established community, but there is no doubt that those who live on national superannuation alone are finding life more and more of a struggle. The steep rises in government charges for postage, telephones and transport, and the price increases on basic foodstuffs, such as milk and butter, have hit them hard. The threat of a wholesale shift from direct to indirect taxation, contained in the government's recent McCaw report, will mean further and severe cuts in the standard of living of the elderly and, indeed, of all low-income households.

The Mt Albert electorate is also characterised by considerable ethnic diversity. People from all parts of the world have made their homes there. Many of them are new- and first-generation New Zealanders, particularly those from the Pacific Islands. I welcome the contributions they have made to the community, and the support they have given, and the life they have brought to local schools and organisations. Like migrant groups the world over, however, they were the first to suffer the effects of recession, and now of prolonged economic depression. What is more, opportunities are scarce when their young people seek to enter the workforce, and disillusionment about their human worth sets in. Youth unemployment is a genuine concern in my part of Auckland, and I fear its effects on those immediately crushed by it, as I fear a society that can tolerate it.

Reference to the Mt Albert electorate would be incomplete if I did not mention the new constituency that has developed for Labour in the suburbs closest to town. Inner Auckland has become a highly desirable area in which to live in these days of high transport costs. Those who might once have chosen to build in the outer suburbs are now setting up their households closer to their places of work in the city. Among the new influx of residents are many skilled and professional people who add another dimension to the community and its associations. They care for the neighbourhood and are fighting to preserve its residential character against further commercial encroachment. Their interest in the Kingsland–Newton area will help greatly in its preservation for future generations.

For most people in my electorate the past few years have brought falling living standards. Although gross incomes may have kept up more or less with inflation, real wages have not. Taxation slices heavily into average and below-average income today. Then, out of that reduced net income, our people must pay even more for their daily needs. Rents are up, mortgage interest rates are up, and so are food prices and government charges across the board. Free, quality public education is fast becoming one of those memories of the good old Labour days, as is adequate public healthcare. The proposed cuts in government expenditure are set to carve even deeper into the most essential welfare-state provisions. Consider, for example, the suggested charge on prescriptions. That is a miserable measure designed to tax the sick.

It is a basic tenet of my philosophy that a society can be judged on how it treats its weakest members—the sick, the disabled, the young and the elderly. Attacks on social provision for any of those cannot be defended in any humane society. Labour's concern has always been for the poor, and for those struggling on the margins of society. We do not seek as our first priority to make the rich richer and the powerful more powerful. Those who believe that is what the aim of government should be could not support us. Our party was founded on concepts of social justice and equality. It was founded by working men and women who could see from the experience of their daily lives the injustice of prevailing social conditions. They set out to change their society to ensure that the resources of the community were more fairly distributed, so that every member of the community could share in the wealth that the community had created.

That is the essence of the Labour Party's philosophy. The Labour philosophy sees the state rather differently from the way in which a conservative philosophy sees it. We believe that the state must act to correct the imbalances in our society that favour the rich and powerful. The conservative position is the laissez-faire posture. 'The less the government does, the better,' they say, and 'Let the market sort the matter out.' We know that if the market is left to sort matters out social injustice will be heightened, and suffering in the community will grow with the neglect the market fosters. The law of the unregulated market is, in the end, the law of the jungle, where only the strongest can survive. We have seen all too much of that in New Zealand in recent times, and the law of the jungle has helped the process along.

My objectives for, and demands of, the government are relatively simple. They centre on the right to work, and to be adequately housed, the need for better living standards, for access to healthcare at a price everyone can afford, for free and quality public education, for recognition of the rights of minorities, and for tolerance and social peace within the community. All those objectives, though simple, seem very far from realisation for the people I represent. There is an immense job of social reconstruction to be done—a job that can begin only when a Labour government committed to social change and equality is elected.

If Labour's objectives are to be met, a strong economy is required. That strong economy is not an end in itself; it is a means to an end. A strong economy produces the wealth to fund our social objectives, to employ our people, to house them and to give them the means to live in dignity. A strong economy must enable us to do those things, or else it has failed in its central purpose. In the past two years the major economic debate between Labour and National has focused on the direction in which to steer our economy. The National government has campaigned for a strategy based on think-big projects. That so-called strategy for growth was in itself a novel idea, coming from the government at the end of six years that averaged almost no economic growth at all. Given the present level of casualties decimating the think-big projects, the next three years may well produce not growth, but shrinkage. Even if thinking big had lived up to its promise of producing growth, it would have been growth of a distorting and dubiously beneficial kind. No planning has been done to ensure that the rewards of high-risk and heavy public investments are distributed throughout the community.

Growth on the model prescribed would be achieved only at an enormous cost to the people, and with dangerous distortions for the economy. There may well be profit in it for multinational companies greedy to exploit our resources. There may well be high wages for the relatively few workers to be directly employed. But there will be too little for the unemployed up and down the country who desperately need work. Insufficient investment capital will be left to put into the key productive and social areas of our economy, which are at present crying out for it. We delude ourselves if we believe that the government will have gained revenue from taxing the profits of the multinational investors. They know better than to make a profit that might be taxable in any country, and they are adept at using transfer pricing and other mechanisms to launder their gains through sister companies in other parts of the world.

There is an alternative to that doomed think-big strategy. Labour has always stood for development. The development we promote will be development that benefits first and foremost the people of the country. It will be balanced development across the regions. It will be balanced development across a range of products and sectors. Above all, it will be development that brings jobs, and thereby confers immediate benefit on the people we represent. It will be a development and growth-for-jobs strategy.

In developing this economy, and in producing more wealth for the community—which is a primary objective—New Zealand needs to build on its own resources and skills. Our primary industries have as-yet-untapped potential. So do our well-educated people. Renewed investment programmes in the primary areas of the economy, backed up by planned marketing and promotion, will reap real and lasting rewards. Our manufacturing sector plays a significant role in providing employment in our towns and cities. Its future is uncertain at present.

A number of secondary industries have been under study by the Industries Development Commission, whose byword 'restructuring' has become, in the experience of many, an acid synonym for unemployment. Most of our industries have one inherent limitation in that they produce for a small market and cannot, without exporting, effect economies of scale. Our industry pays above-subsistence wages, unlike many of its international competitors for which near-slave wages are the norm. Those factors all unavoidably contribute to raising a range of New Zealand prices even though we are nowadays a lower and lower wage economy. But the multiple benefits our industries bring for employment, for expression of our capacities, our knowledge and our initiative make their retention essential to New Zealand's existence as a modern economy and an independent society.

Currently, the government is setting its sights on developing a closer economic relationship with Australia. Negotiations have been proceeding for some time, although by and large they have been shrouded in a mixture of double-talk and secrecy. We are now told that an agreement may be reached in June. Given the lack of information available about the shape of the likely agreement, there is considerable suspicion and foreboding about what its contents may be. No one, of course, is opposed to expanding trade, and certainly not to profitable trade with Australia. But if the ultimate objectives of the proposed closer economic relations are to establish an uncontrolled zone of trade between Australia and New Zealand, that is a different matter altogether.

The world's strongest economies do not expose themselves to such uncontrolled importation, and for very good reason. While Japan's economic strength is based on its industry, its agricultural sector, producing for the domestic market, still provides a source of income and a way of life for millions of its people. In New Zealand, while our agriculture and other primary industries provide the bulk of our export receipts, it is our secondary industries that have been the big employers of our people and the mainstay of the domestic economy.

Any move to foster closer economic relations with Australia has to take into account the effects on employment and the wider economy in New Zealand that will certainly result.

Indeed, when we read in the press that Australia's Deputy Prime Minister has come to demand an execution date for our structure of import licensing and export incentives at the same time as he represents the inherent advantages for Australia of being a going concern five times our size, we can see why the government hesitates to complete a policy that has already gone far beyond the limited intentions and benefits with which it began. The government started out to redraw the North American Free Trade Agreement (NAFTA), and has ended up by supping with a short spoon with a giant competitor. Can junior statehood be far behind? If it is not, at least conservative ministers will get into the habit of resigning, as the Westminster model of government intended they should when affairs for which they were responsible went awry.

I now turn to the current international situation, the prospects of disarmament, and the part that New Zealand might play in making disarmament a reality. The international outlook is gloomier than it has been for many years. Tension between the two major superpowers has escalated again at an alarming rate. The background note prepared by the Ministry of Foreign Affairs to mark Disarmament Week last year states that there is 'little cause for optimism about the prospects for disarmament'. It draws to our attention the view in the *Bulletin of [the] Atomic Scientists*, which in January 1981 'moved its famous clock to four minutes to midnight, signalling that in its opinion the world had moved closer to nuclear disaster'. By January of this year it may well have moved closer still.

In Europe, considerable public pressure for disarmament has grown over the past two years. It has been stimulated by the nuclear rearmament policies of both the North Atlantic Treaty Organization (NATO) and

Warsaw Pact alliances. NATO has taken the decision to deploy the new-generation nuclear missiles, the Pershing IIs, and the cruise. Similarly, the Soviet Union stock of SS-20 intermediate-range missiles is being rapidly added to. The relative strength of the two superpower arsenals is not easy to assess, but they appear to be near enough to parity. Each side possesses a formidable first-strike capacity. In addition, other minor powers in the nuclear league continue to deploy nuclear weapons of their own.

Powerful forces within each major superpower are pushing for a new drive to rearm.

The American Secretary of Defense, Mr Weinberger, wants to expand America's military budget and responsibilities worldwide. He has worked alongside his admirals and generals to haul every area of the globe into one more section of a universal front line. The Soviet marshals share a view similar to Weinberger's. The Soviet admirals similarly plough too many seas, though, fortunately, far from ours. It is almost as if there is an international conspiracy between the generals and admirals on both sides to keep us all on the brink, in order to promote the proliferation of their deadly playthings.

New Zealand's national interests stand completely opposed to any such competition. Yet slowly we in a hitherto peaceful Pacific are being drawn into the new era of heightened international tension. It is in that light that the Memorandum of Understanding negotiated recently between New Zealand and its major ANZUS ally, the United States, should be seen. Since 1965 New Zealand has had a co-operative logistics agreement with the United States to cover the provision of munitions and equipment from that country to New Zealand in times of peace. The significance of the new memorandum is that it is an extension of the 1965 agreement to cover supply in times of war. As Dr Korb—a high-ranking visiting American defence official—explained here in February, the memorandum adds specificity to the ANZUS pact, so if the parties decide to act we will not have so many road blocks to keep out of the way.

It is hard to resist the conclusion that the present government has taken concrete steps to prepare for our involvement in war. In an age when the ultimate weapons of destruction exist in abundance, it is long past the time when we need to reshape our ideas on defence.

We want no part of a nuclear war against which there is no conceivable conventional defence. One American authority wrote in the March 1981 *Bulletin of [the] Atomic Scientists*: 'In any nuclear war between the United

States and the Soviet Union missiles will go both ways. There is no way we can make the world more dangerous for them without also making it more dangerous for ourselves. The less secure the Soviets feel,' the bulletin said, 'the more they will be doing about it, and the less secure we will become.'

In the nuclear age, military hardware becomes an insecurity, not a security blanket. Nuclear-armed warships in our harbours make us a target rather than give us protection. Our only defence, long term, will come from the contribution we make as a country to the search for peace at the United Nations, in our region, and on a bilateral basis in the capitals of the world. New Zealand, in concert with other small states, should act towards that end at every opportunity. When we have a history of friendly relations with a superpower, as we have with the United States, we should use our influence to press for a moderation of international tension, and for progress on disarmament talks between the superpowers. But the perspectives of small states like ours must, in the end, be fundamentally different from the superpower perspectives, and we should be wary of their games. I call on the government to make every effort to ensure that New Zealand is well represented at the second special session of the United Nations on disarmament in June of this year. The government should publicise the aims and objectives of the special session in order to draw the attention of all New Zealanders to its importance. Disarmament will come about only when there is a universal conviction that it must. It will come about only after long and patient negotiations. I should like to see New Zealand, as a concerned state, play a leading role in fostering the international climate in which that will be possible.

I have spoken of the concerns of my electorate, the state's role in providing economic and social security for our people, the economic outlook, and the prospects for international peace. I believe that the philosophy of my party links those concerns. It is my hope while in this House to promote constructive solutions based on equity and social justice for the great problems that challenge us today. In so doing, I share my perspective as a woman, as a member of a farming family, as one who was fortunate to have educational opportunities, and as one now privileged to represent one of the finest electorates in New Zealand for the Labour Party. My greatest wish is that at the end of my time in this House I shall have contributed towards making New Zealand a better place than it is today for its people to live in.

Comments on Nuclear Testing in the South Pacific

Parliament, Wellington
28 April 1983

The French government carried out extensive nuclear testing in the South Pacific between 1966 and 1996, despite repeated international protest. In 1974, the Labour Government had sent two frigates to Moruroa Atoll in protest for a nuclear-free Pacific. Then in 1985, just two years after the following speech, the Greenpeace activist ship the Rainbow Warrior, *which was due to sail to the atoll to protest nuclear testing, was sunk while still at port in Auckland by two explosives placed on board by French intelligence service operatives.*

Many disturbing trends are emerging in New Zealand society. There is increasing violence. I believe that the long-term answers lie in social and economic reconstruction, in the rebuilding of the welfare state, and in the promotion of full employment and a caring society. The police do have a role to play in rebuilding New Zealand, yet the role that they are cast in by the government will, over time, work to tear our society apart by serving to heighten, rather than to diminish, existing tensions. These days, of course, the rigid views of the government must win out at all costs. Apartheid sport must be played in New Zealand to prove some obscure notion about freedom, at the risk of splitting open our society. The ritual Waitangi celebrations must take place, even if they do so behind barriers of riot shields and police.

Is that New Zealand the way we want it, or is there a better way?

Are New Zealanders not fed up to the teeth with that kind of confrontation and division, and are they not ready for a change geared around a new consensus?

Won't Rob's mob have to give way to the concern of decent citizens for social justice across the board? That is the clear message I take from the polls, and it is the clear message that Labour Opposition members are getting throughout the country. As the *Dominion* reported on 19 April in reference to his appearance at Eden Park with the royal couple, the Prime Minister may still 'prove a runaway success as a side show', but as a serious solution to the political, economic, social and moral crisis that New Zealand now faces he and his accomplices among government members should be immediately dismissed.

It is not just New Zealand's political leaders who are taking flight from reality these days. They have their counterparts at the highest level in other important nations. Just as I am struck by the inadequacy of the government's response to New Zealand's present crisis, so I am appalled at the inappropriateness of the response by major world leaders to the most critical issue confronting the international community—that of disarmament. I must say that Opposition members note with particular sadness the recent announcements by the socialist government in France concerning its increased spending on nuclear defence. Its four-year military programme announced last week gives clear priority to nuclear weapons. That is especially bad news for South Pacific nations like New Zealand, because it indicates a continuing commitment by the French government to further develop its own nuclear deterrent, and that means a continuation of the nuclear weapons testing programme at Moruroa.

It is pleasing to note that the Leader of the Opposition took the earliest possible opportunity to express the unanimous opposition of the New Zealand Labour Party to continued French nuclear weapons testing in the South Pacific. That message must be driven home to France—the message that all democratic political forces in the South Pacific deplore its nuclear weapons testing, and that that, indeed, is the unanimous view of all nations that take part in the South Pacific Forum. While the Labour Party is opposed to nuclear weapons testing by any nation, wherever it may occur, it is particularly concerned that it should be carried out in our region, in a colonial territory, by a colonial power operating from half a world away.

While I have singled out the French government for particular criticism, the continuing antics of the two major superpowers concerning their nuclear arsenals also warrant some comment. Each is engaged in a deadly game of blindfold bluff, each trying to perpetrate the fiction—and it is no more than that—that the other side has assumed nuclear superiority, and, therefore, that it poses a greater threat to security than before, and that massive expenditure to close the alleged gap is required.

The alleged nuclear gap has as much validity as Major Douglas's. It exists purely in the mind. An article in the influential British *Observer* of Sunday 27 March reported that the concept that the Russians were ahead of the Americans in the nuclear arms race was one that 'even the most hawkish American generals concede is nonsense'. Unfortunately, it is highly dangerous nonsense. It leads to the promulgation of the most fantastic plans for so-called defence. The 'Star Wars' scenario or Buck Rogers schemes announced by the American President a few weeks ago are the most fanciful yet.

Surely small nations such as New Zealand have a moral duty to voice their concern about the escalation of the arms race between the superpowers. Have we not the right to ask where all this arms expenditure has got us? Could anybody argue with any credibility that after 45 years of East–West rivalry and the expenditure of billions of dollars on nuclear weaponry any of us feel more secure than we did before it all started? I doubt it. The irony is that the more that has been spent on nuclear weapons the more insecure we have all felt. We have ended up frightening ourselves with the size and the power of the arsenals constructed to defend us, let alone those arraigned against us.

A few months ago a very influential report was published by an international commission formed to consider international security issues and headed by Mr Olaf Palme, who is now the Prime Minister of Sweden. The report, entitled 'Common Security', made the point that no nation's security can be guaranteed by the unilateral measures it adopts to defend itself. The report states that a doctrine of common security should replace what it calls the present expedient of deterrence through armaments. International peace, it states, must rest on a joint commitment to survival rather than on a threat of mutual destruction. I certainly agree with that. The Palme Commission advocates that all nations should adopt certain principles of common security as the basis for their own defence policies. States should recognise that all nations have a legitimate right to security, that military force is not a legitimate instrument with which to resolve disputes between nations, and that security cannot be gained through military superiority. The first consequence of military superiority is, of course, the insecurity felt by everyone round about.

The report states also that reductions and quantitative limitations on armaments are necessary for common security to be effective, and that linkages between arms negotiations and political events should be avoided. A small nation such as New Zealand should have little difficulty in recognising the sound common sense of those principles. We should also give our support to the proposals made by the Palme Commission for strengthening the United Nations.

When the United Nations was established, the Rt Hon. Peter Fraser, on behalf of New Zealand, pressed for it to play a strong role in guaranteeing collective security. Unlike the League of Nations, the new international organisation was to have teeth in that respect. It was envisaged that the United Nations would be able to rely on trained military units earmarked for United Nations service to deter wars and enforce peace, but, sadly, the cold war and subsequent East–West confrontations put paid to those early hopes, and the United Nations was left to play only a strictly limited role in peace-keeping.

The Palme Commission has proposed afresh that the United Nations should have at its disposal standby forces recruited from a wide base with adequate and automatic funding. It proposes in the first instance that the United Nations should commit itself to invoke collective security procedures whenever a border dispute threatens or provokes armed conflict between two or more Third World countries. The report states that Third World countries should commit themselves to settle disputes without interference from the great powers, which should resolve not to become involved. Invoking such collective security measures would not mean taking a position on the merits of any particular dispute, but it would mean that all nation states could be absolutely confident that the United Nations would tolerate no violation of territorial integrity. The certain knowledge that the United Nations would intervene would act as a deterrent to aggressors and diminish the tendency for small countries to look to great powers for protection.

Just as Peter Fraser did almost 40 years ago, it is now time for the New Zealand Government to join in fresh initiatives such as those proposed by the Palme Commission to enhance the effectiveness of the United Nations. It is time to bring issues of security under the umbrella of that organisation, and not to leave them to the whims of the superpowers, whose guarantees of protection are only ever offered if it is in their own interests to do so, and have little to do with profound respect for territorial integrity and independence.

Finally, I want to draw the attention of the House to the linkage that exists between the issues of disarmament and aid and development. While the major economies of the world bankrupt themselves to pay for increased defence budgets, the considerations of sharing out the world's resources more equitably, widening trade possibilities and raising living standards take a back seat.

In addition, in the present international recession it is easy for nations in crisis to cut back on aid spending in the belief that that cutback, unlike others, will not have domestic repercussions. If New Zealanders have a conscience they will not allow the government to get away with the shabby cuts it has made to its aid programmes. People should be aware that New Zealand's credibility as a donor country to the developing world has been seriously undermined by the massive cuts in its aid. In this, as in so many other aspects, New Zealand's image abroad has been seriously damaged by the government.

Consider that inflation and diminishing allocations have brought New Zealand's present aid commitment down to less than half of what it was under the Third Labour Goverment. In 1982 the aid commitment stood at only 0.22 per cent of the gross domestic product—light years and millions of dollars away from the internationally agreed target of 1 per cent. The downward trend is even more serious when one considers what has happened to the buying power of the New Zealand dollar in recent years. The government has tried to make a virtue out of its declining aid commitments by concentrating much of what is left on the Pacific. That has been done to the virtual neglect of almost all other potential recipient countries. The most savagely treated have been those on the African continent, where the level of New Zealand aid spending has declined by more than 97 per cent, from $1.27 million in 1980–81 to $35,000 in 1982–83.

The present government also concentrates its aid on those countries that follow a narrow capitalist model of development, and might be potential trading partners. In doing that, New Zealand is following its OECD partners. Officially they show scepticism about assisting those who want to follow policies of self-reliance—a model of development, it should be remembered, that has been extremely successful hitherto in the People's Republic of China. Just as increased economic aid abroad could do much to restore the shattered reputation of this country, so policies of economic construction at home could do much to rebuild the social consensus that the government has done so much to destroy.

I look forward after the next election to being part of the fourth Labour Government, which can commence that task—and it cannot happen a moment too soon.

Comments on Nuclear-armed Ships in New Zealand Waters

Parliament, Wellington
12 February 1985

This speech, made in parliament, comes just a few months before the infamous sinking of the Rainbow Warrior. *Public emotion was running high over New Zealand's nuclear-free status, and the government's responsibilities to its South Pacific neighbours.*

———

How would having nuclear weapons in New Zealand contribute to disarmament? It would do absolutely nothing for disarmament if this country were to be the willing host of the nuclear weapons of another nation. I believe that the government and the Prime Minister have taken a positive step towards implementing the policy that we went to the country with in the middle of last year—of ridding New Zealand of any contact with nuclear weapons. That policy has been applauded around the world.

The Leader of the Opposition asked if the government had a mandate for what it was doing. Of course it has. We had an election policy, and

I remind those listening of the four clear points that were outlined in the government's policy on the ANZUS alliance: to renegotiate ANZUS to ensure that it recognises New Zealand's non-negotiable, non-nuclear stance; recognises and encompasses our desire for a nuclear-weapon-free South Pacific; recognises New Zealand's desire to be in the treaty on an equal footing, having an equal voice in decisions; and, finally, recognises New Zealand's sovereignty.

Those four important points were well known to the electorate and reiterated at election meetings up and down the country, and we believe the country gave us the mandate for carrying the policy through.

This is not some fringe concern; it is a mainstream concern. The member for East Coast Bays has made that point again today. The Opposition is now isolated with Dr Sprott. The Opposition and Dr Sprott alone are defending the entry of nuclear weapons into New Zealand. Bob Jones and the New Zealand Party have welcomed the moves the government has made. It was interesting to see a few weeks ago that 15,000 to 20,000 Aucklanders came out to support the government's policy at 48 hours' notice. I challenge Dr Sprott to produce at 48 hours' notice 20,000 cheering New Zealanders to march for the entry of nuclear weapons into Auckland Harbour. I know he could not get them.

I call on the National Party to come in from the cold on this issue and to make New Zealand's moves towards disarmament bipartisan. It should get rid of that Cold War mentality and be big enough to admit that it has been wrong. The world is full of former prime ministers, generals and brigadiers who say that they were wrong to endorse nuclear weapons when they were in office. Let the Opposition be big enough to admit that it has been wrong in the support it has given to nuclear weaponry.

I notice that already some faint-heartedness is appearing in the stance adopted by members opposite. I have seen reference to a committee—chaired, I believe, by the member for Fendalton—that is examining the reasons for the National Party's fairly dismal urban vote in the election. It got one seat only in Christchurch, none in Dunedin, none in Hamilton, none in Wellington and a handful in Auckland. The committee believes that the National Party must reopen debate on issues such as its nuclear policy stance if it wants to win back the vital urban seats and regain the Treasury benches. It believes that the party's rigid stance on issues such as nuclear ships and South African sporting contacts was a major factor in its defeat at the election.

One has only to look at the opinion polls to see that the National Party is out of touch with the electorate. The committee has stated that the National Party is seen as failing to identify with urban voters and their idealistic desire to respond to challenges in the future. What those voters have heard today will do nothing to persuade them to come back.

Let me deal with another allegation made by the member for Tamaki— that somehow the government's policy might have the effect of creating a whole lot of vassal states of another power in the South Pacific. In 1976 the former Prime Minister of Australia, Mr Fraser, and the former Prime Minister of New Zealand [Mr Muldoon] went running around the South Pacific worried about the possibility that Tonga might become a vassal state of another power. Nothing more ridiculous than that a medieval, feudal kingdom like Tonga should become a vassal state can be imagined. I defy anybody to tell me of any state in the South Pacific that is going to give any succour to any policy of the Soviet Union. That is inconceivable in the South Pacific today.

I come back to the matter of relations with the United States. New Zealand has many American friends spread throughout the political spectrum in that country. The former United States Ambassador to New Zealand, Mrs Martindell, has spoken out in support of New Zealand's stand, as have many others, and as will many more. The American people have a sense of fair play. They have democratic values. They know that New Zealanders have fought alongside Americans for common values. We will continue to share those values. In the context of New Zealand's relationship of 150 years' standing with the United States, the issue of ship visits is a minor fly in the ointment. The American people know that, and will respond in a reasonable manner.

The government's intentions are clear: vessels that are nuclear capable will not be welcomed. However, if the government is convinced that a vessel is neither nuclear-powered nor nuclear-armed it will be welcomed. The Prime Minister has made it clear, and has left it open to the United States to request visits to New Zealand by vessels such as FFG7s of the Oliver Hazard Perry class, or other vessels in the United States Navy, but nuclear vessels will not be welcomed.

I refresh Opposition members' memories about the nature of a treaty. The 1983 defence review states that an alliance is the free association of countries with common but not necessarily identical interests. That describes the association between New Zealand and the United States.

The defence review points out that ANZUS brings together countries of very different scale but comparable outlook. It was recognised in the 1983 ANZUS Council communiqué that there may be varying views and perspectives between sovereign and independent nations. Such differences are a healthy reflection of diversity, and enhance rather than detract from the ANZUS alliance. The alliance has never meant that there will be total identity of interests, but allows for diversity. The defence review pays tribute to that interpretation and the government supports it.

The ANZUS alliance is not, and has not been, a nuclear alliance. We need only go back to the defence reports of the National government for reiteration of that view. The 1983 annual defence report, to which the former Minister of Defence, the former member for Taranaki, put his name, states, 'New Zealand is not a nuclear power and does not become one by association with nations that are. ANZUS is not a nuclear alliance.' As that report implies, the government is justified in considering ANZUS a conventional alliance. It is an alliance that does not rest for any alleged strength on nuclear weaponry.

We have heard over and over again today that members in the House are for nuclear war. I hope they are not. However, when one hears that Opposition members would have welcomed the USS *Buchanan* knowing it is nuclear-armed, in all probability, one can only ask what contribution that would have made to disarmament. It would have made none.

The Homosexual Law Reform Bill

Parliament, Wellington
16 October 1985

*The Homosexual Law Reform Bill, which was hotly debated,
had two parts: the first decriminalised consensual sex between
men sixteen and over, and the second would make it illegal to
discriminate against a person because of their sexual orientation.
The first part of the Bill passed narrowly (49 votes to 44), while the
second did not. The Homosexual Law Reform Act came into effect
in August 1987.*

————

I have supported the Bill from the time it was introduced into the House,
and I have done so for reasons similar to those expressed by the Minister
of Housing. Fundamentally, I believe that what people do in private by
way of consenting sexual behaviour should not be within the reach of the
criminal law. I strongly believe that what people agree to do in private is
no business of mine, or of anybody else, or of the law.

New Zealanders have traditionally enjoyed a great degree of personal
freedom, and that is as it should be when the rights of other people are

not infringed by the exercise of that freedom. I would not argue for absolute personal freedom to act without regard to the rights of others—no rational person would do so. However, the point about the practice of homosexuality is that when it occurs between consenting persons in private it infringes upon the rights of nobody else in society.

For a long time the New Zealand statutes have treated consenting homosexual activity as if it were such a heinous offence that it warranted the special attention of the law, and as if it in some way infringed upon the rights of others who are not so engaged. While it is true that homosexuality is regarded as an affront to the morality of a section of the community, it can in no way logically be turned into an argument that an affront to the morality of some should deserve criminal sanctions under the secular law of the land.

It is extremely important that when parliament passes judgment on the Bill it should make a clear distinction between what some people in the community regard as a sin and what is a fit subject for the secular law of New Zealand, and all that the enforcement of that law entails. Those who believe that homosexuality is a sin are entitled to hold that view, and I personally defend their right to hold it. What deeply concerns me—and has increasingly concerned me throughout the public debate that has followed the introduction of the Bill—is that some people would seek to have the law enforce their moral viewpoint on into the twenty-first century, as it has done for the past 100 years. I believe that by doing that we would carry on a serious injustice and would continue seriously to impair the civil liberties of a minority in society.

By world standards New Zealand has a remarkably free society. People here are free to practise any religious or ethical belief they choose, and are free to follow any political cause they choose. New Zealand has a free press—we often curse it, but we would not be without it. The *World Human Rights Guide* rates us extremely highly on all the criteria it uses to judge whether or not a society can be considered free, open and democratic. Along with countries such as Finland and Denmark, New Zealand enjoys a 96 per cent rating on that index of what constitutes a fair, open and democratic society. If the Bill is passed that rating will increase to 100 per cent.

The Bill removes the injustices that those who are seriously concerned with human rights regard as the one serious blot on our image. As it stands now, only New Zealand and Ireland in the Western world continue to regard male homosexuality as a criminal act. The British Act on which the law is based was changed almost 20 years ago, after the acceptance of the Wolfenden report on homosexuality.

It is time New Zealand took out of the statute book a law that was passed in the British Parliament 100 years ago and adopted into New Zealand law a year later. It was a law that was not intended to have the effect of totally outlawing male homosexual activity. It was put forward as an amendment by a member of the British House of Commons at the time to protect young boys from prostitution. The way in which the Bill was drafted—poorly and without thorough parliamentary scrutiny—led to the Commons actually outlawing all male homosexuality. It was a mistake then and I think 100 years is much too long to have lived with a mistake such as that on the statute book. Surely now, 100 years later, on the centenary of that event, we can take the step to remove that blot from our own statute book.

We have heard much debate in the House and in the public arena about the age at which it is appropriate to decriminalise consenting homosexual behaviour. At present there is no age of sexual consent whatever for men concerning heterosexual activity. At present the law imposes an age of consent only on women, and that age is sixteen. It is an arbitrary age. Before the 1880s the age of consent in New Zealand was twelve; it rose to fourteen, and later to sixteen in the 1890s. There is nothing preordained about an age of consent. It is an arbitrary judgment, arbitrarily fixed, and it varies widely across countries. The age of consent has no bearing on the age at which young people become sexually active. The age at which they become sexually active is more likely to be related to levels of sexual maturity and to peer group and lifestyle pressures.

If, however, there is to be an age of consent, the one for which we have settled as being appropriate for young women for about 90 years is logically the one we should now accept as appropriate for young men. I can see no logic in the argument being advanced by some that boys are more deserving of protection in that respect than girls are; nor do I see any evidence to suggest that an age of consent of sixteen for boys could lead to their being seduced and orientated to homosexuality against their will and before they have had a chance to make up their own minds. Those who argue that way are poorly informed about the nature of homosexuality.

We know that sexual preference and orientation are fixed rather earlier in life than sixteen years of age. No one quite knows why or how it is fixed. It is probably valid to describe homosexuality as a fundamental tendency in human behaviour that will show up among certain sections of populations across all cultures. Some people will be exclusively homosexual; others will be truly bisexual; many will have at least some, or occasional, homosexual experiences during their lifetime; but most will probably be exclusively heterosexual. Whatever we turn out to be, we probably have very little choice in the matter. Our sexual orientation will have been set early, and will be well established by the time we are sixteen years of age, which I submit is a fit age at which to establish the age of consent in the Bill.

I suggest that even occasional homosexual experiences—even seduction—cannot make a blind bit of difference to the fundamental sexual orientation of young men in our community. We are either predisposed to act in that way or we are not.

Some have suggested in the debate—and we have heard the case again tonight—that the community is not ready for decriminalisation at the age of sixteen, but that it might accept a higher age. The ages of eighteen years and 20 years have been put forward. I put it to those who have argued that way that we have a role as opinion leaders in the broader community and we have a responsibility to do what is sensible and logical and to persuade others of the reasons that sixteen years should, in all logic, be seen as an appropriate and sensible age of consent.

The report of the Department of Justice gives some weight to that argument when it states: 'Logic and principle would seem to support a uniform age of consent for both heterosexual and homosexual relations. In the absence of clear evidence that boys need a further period of protection in respect of homosexual acts, there is a logical difficulty in justifying a higher age of consent for homosexual acts'—I stress 'a logical difficulty'.

Others have suggested in the course of public debate on the Bill that decriminalisation of homosexual acts might lead to an increase in the numbers of homosexuals in the community. I believe that the evidence I have already alluded to shows that that view cannot be supported. People are either predisposed to homosexuality or they are not and the position of the law on the matter will not make one iota of difference. People cannot be recruited or seduced into permanent identification with homosexuality. What a change in the law may well do is increase the number of people in the community who are known to be homosexual.

It often amuses me when I hear people say that they have never met a homosexual. Almost certainly they have, but those people have not felt able to express the fact that they are homosexual, given the present state of the law in this country, which buoys up unfortunate public attitudes towards homosexuality. Many homosexual men and women repress their homosexuality because they are afraid to express it. For men it is a criminal offence to do so. For women it is seen by a vocal section of the community as offending against social norms. Many homosexual men and women lead secret and unhappy lives because they feel unable to express the way they are. Some of them came to the select committee the day I sat on it in Auckland and told us what it was like to grow up as homosexuals in a society in which legitimate expression of their homosexuality is denied.

We heard oral submissions such as the following from a male homosexual: 'As a teenager my life was confused, sad and frightening. At school there were no role models presented which had any relevance for me. My peers proved unmerciful at any suggestion that one's behaviour or sexual interest was anything other than that of a pattern determined by macho male role models of a type best exemplified by reference to film star heroes or famous rugby players. The total effect upon myself over an important formative period of my life was the development of an extremely negative self-image. Any list of adjectives I might have honestly used to describe myself would have included sinner, abnormal, dirty, wicked and perverted. Such was the influence of my peers, societal mores, the church and the education system.'

We heard similar evidence from a female homosexual who told the committee that through lack of information, confusion and social naivety as a teenager when she was brought up in a small country town she thought she was the only homosexual in New Zealand and that marrying and having a baby would cure her love for women. She told the committee, 'I do not want another generation with probably 10 per cent of its adult population so utterly miserable.'

Last week the member for Hauraki took exception to my statement in the House that the passing of the Bill would help to build a healthier social climate in New Zealand. I stand by that statement now, as I did then. I believe that society is far less than healthy when it represses fundamental aspects of the identity of some of its citizens. Society is not healthy when it sends overt messages to that minority that their behaviour is disgusting, abnormal and so perverse that it should be regarded as criminal. Society is not healthy when it forces on people secretive and closet lifestyles because of a fear of their expressing what they are.

I believe that society will be healthier when people acknowledge their differences, acknowledge that the preference of a minority is not a fit subject for legal or other persecution, and accept homosexuals as normal members of any community—as they are entitled to be accepted.

Finally, I come to the second section of the Bill, which would prevent discrimination against New Zealanders on the basis of their sexual orientation. Some members have told the House that while they accept the case for decriminalisation of homosexual acts they are still unsure about the second part of the Bill. I put it to them that the second part of the Bill, dealing with anti-discrimination measures, follows on naturally from an acceptance of the case for decriminalisation. If we accept homosexuality as a form of sexual practice that is normal for a minority and not deserving of criminal sanction, what then is the case for saying that others, presumably of a heterosexual orientation, should be free to discriminate against that minority? The rights of the minority in that case are thereby very seriously infringed.

I suggest that we will have made little progress if on the one hand we decriminalise, at whatever age, and on the other hand fail to take steps to discourage discrimination on the ground of sexual preference. It would be utterly wrong for the House in any way to imply, by failing to pass the second part of the Bill, that it is legitimate for employers or landlords to discriminate against people who are homosexual. There will, of course, be good and bad employees and good and bad tenants among homosexuals, but there is simply no case to be made for blanket persecution and discrimination against homosexuals because they are homosexual or for refusing to employ them on that basis or refusing to rent flats to them.

The experience with anti-discrimination legislation in New Zealand has been that over a period it has the effect of lessening prejudices against those likely to have been discriminated against before those laws came into effect. In the case of women, anti-discrimination legislation has helped to build a social climate in which it is accepted in the employment field, for example, that girls can do anything, and that they are fit to be employed across a wide range of occupations. Similarly, it has been found that legislation to prevent discrimination on the grounds of race and national or ethnic origin has helped to bring about a change in attitude and practice towards those minorities. I hope that, in the same way, if anti-discrimination provisions to protect gay people are enacted they will, in the longer term, lead to greater acceptance of them, their talents and the useful role they can play as citizens of a healthy society. On that basis I appeal to those who are still thinking of supporting the first part of the Bill on decriminalisation and not supporting the second part to think again. I support the Bill in its present form, as I believe the evidence before us and simple common logic compels each of us to do.

The New Zealand Nuclear Free Zone, Disarmament, and Arms Control Bill

Parliament, Wellington
12 February 1987

The New Zealand Nuclear Free Zone, Disarmament, and Arms Control Act 1987 officially established New Zealand as a nuclear-free zone. When the United States retaliated with the Broomfield Act, which downgraded New Zealand's status from ally to friend, Prime Minister David Lange responded that 'it is the price we are prepared to pay' for New Zealand remaining nuclear free.

———

The Opposition has outlined today what amounts to a 'Don't know, don't care, can't confirm' policy towards the entry of nuclear weapons into New Zealand. The Leader of the Opposition said that his party would work to re-establish the trust that would enable New Zealand to be an active member of the ANZUS alliance. That is a pure and simple code for the acceptance of the 'neither confirm nor deny' policy, which means acceptance of nuclear weapons coming into New Zealand. Let the House be clear about that.

Members opposite quoted the United States Secretary of State, Mr Shultz. He may well have said in very clear terms, 'No ship visits, no ANZUS!' He has also said very clearly that if a country accepts ship visits it must expect from time to time to get nuclear weapons on them. That appears to be acceptable to the Opposition.

The government, backed I believe by most New Zealanders, has said time and time again that it wants conventional ship visits and conventional defence within the ANZUS alliance. That is a valid interpretation of New Zealand's commitments under that treaty. It is not invalidated simply because the United States does not share the same view.

I take great pleasure in supporting the second reading of the Bill. It has been eagerly awaited by many New Zealanders, who take pride in seeing the government act to make their country nuclear free. The Bill fulfils an important pledge made by the Labour Party during the last election. The government has kept faith with that pledge by introducing the Bill in December 1985 and moving it through its various stages to the second reading today.

The public has had ample opportunity to debate and examine the Bill, and its general thrust is well supported. It was my privilege to chair the select committee that examined the Bill. Of the 1236 submissions that were received, 1225—about 99.1 per cent—broadly favoured the principles of the Bill. I am prepared to concede that more than 0.09 per cent of the population does not support the Bill, but it is significant that those persons care so little about the subject that they failed to make any effort to inform parliament of their views.

There was a similar pattern with the defence committee of inquiry. For the most part, the minority that does not share the government's general view on the issues could stir itself only to post in a simple newspaper coupon putting its point of view. The public may well wonder where previously unheard-of groups like the Plains Club suddenly found enormous amounts of money to place nationwide advertisements in newspapers asking people to oppose the government's policies.

The purpose of the Bill is to establish in New Zealand a nuclear-free zone and to implement in New Zealand a number of disarmament and arms control treaties to which New Zealand is a party. The treaties are listed in the schedules to the Bill, and have been mentioned by other members. The one of most concern to Members of Parliament is New Zealand's adherence to the South Pacific Nuclear Free Zone Treaty. I take pride, as many others do, in the fact that New Zealand has been in the forefront of those countries that have signed and promoted arms control treaties. New Zealand continues to promote a comprehensive test ban treaty. We want to see progress on chemical weapons conventions. When international agreement on such matters can be reached I am sure that members would want the Bill amended to include them, and I look forward to that day.

Enough countries in the South Pacific nuclear-free area have signed the treaty and ratified it so that it may come into force. New Zealand signed and ratified it late last year. Inclusion of the treaty in the Bill emphasises New Zealand's commitment to it, but I must join with other colleagues who have expressed concern that the United States has not seen fit to sign the treaty. The nations of the South Pacific Forum reached a consensus that a nuclear-free-zone treaty is what they want. They have gone out and asked the world's acknowledged nuclear weapons states to respect the treaty by signing the protocols. China signed this week. The Soviet Union signed, although one must record with regret that it signed with some reservations. Britain has yet to decide, but one hopes that its traditional friendly relations with the South Pacific will lead it to sign the protocols. France remains intransigent because of its present commitment to nuclear testing in the Pacific.

However, the main disappointment must be the attitude taken by the United States. It is an attitude that I do not believe is unanimously shared in Washington—and for good reason, because reasonable people in Washington recognise the very considerable care that was taken in drafting the treaty to devise a text that the United States could live with. Many would say that the South Pacific Forum countries bent over backwards to devise a test that was suitable to the United States. The treaty does not prevent the United States from undertaking any activity that it undertakes at present in the South Pacific, so what can explain its actions? One can only assume that the United States puts a higher priority on its relationship with France than it does on its relationship with countries in the South Pacific Forum. By coming out against the treaty the United States is endorsing the continuation of French testing in the region.

Secondly, I believe that the United States continues to see the proliferation of nuclear-free zones as detrimental to its security interests. That is very hard for us in New Zealand to understand, because we do not believe that an arms race in the South Pacific is in the interests of any country. It must be in our interests to limit nuclear conflict. I believe that a region such as the South Pacific, which is friendly to the West but which puts off limit the nuclear weapons of all nations, can be seen only as a stabilising force in world affairs. It is as much in the interests of the United States as anybody else to support and recognise that nuclear-free status, and I hope that, in time, that will come to be the point of view adopted in Washington. The Bill deals mostly with New Zealand becoming a nuclear-free zone.

As I have said, the Bill implements a very important pledge made by the Labour Party at the last election. The Labour Party has seen ANZUS as a conventional alliance that could accommodate a state party that was determined to keep its defences conventional. That remains the government's view. There is every reason to believe that that view is substantially in line with public opinion. New Zealanders have a very grave concern about nuclear war, and it was demonstrated clearly in the opinion survey conducted last year for the committee of inquiry on defence. In that survey 48 per cent of people polled said that nuclear war was a present worry to them, and 86 per cent agreed with the proposition that New Zealand should actively promote worldwide nuclear disarmament. I find that a staggeringly high figure. I am glad it is so high and that so many New Zealanders feel positively about the work their country undertakes for nuclear disarmament.

Let us consider the heart of the concern, which is where the Bill is focused. How can a state such as New Zealand—a small state isolated in the South Pacific—actually actively promote nuclear disarmament? It can do so by starting at home, and that is what the Bill does. By declaring our country a nuclear-free zone we give ourselves much more credibility in urging those countries that have nuclear weapons to do something about seriously negotiating their elimination. That remains the key motivation behind the Bill.

It is interesting to reflect on New Zealanders' response to last year's opinion survey about their views on the way in which New Zealand should actively promote nuclear disarmament. People were given a choice of options about how New Zealand should act. Nine per cent of them thought New Zealand should fully support Western allies and their nuclear capability. That seems to be about the position of the National Party. Twenty-nine per cent thought that New Zealand should go along with the Western allies and their nuclear capability, but still work for nuclear disarmament. I suppose that represents the position of some people in the National Party. Thirty-eight per cent favoured rejecting nuclear weapons for New Zealand's defence but contributing to conventional Western defence and working for nuclear disarmament. Twenty per cent felt so strongly about nuclear weapons that they wanted New Zealand to dissociate itself entirely from any alliance with countries that have nuclear weapons.

Similar findings can be found throughout the poll. The major thrust of that opinion survey was that New Zealanders want a nuclear-free future and they want their country to take a lead on such matters. It is the objective of the Bill to ensure that New Zealand leads public opinion and that New Zealanders have a nuclear-free future.

Details of the Bill have been raised in previous debates on it in the House. Clause 5 is a very important clause and makes it an offence for a New Zealander to manufacture, acquire, possess or have control over nuclear weapons in the nuclear-free zone, and an offence to aid and abet anyone else to do such things. It further makes it an offence for New Zealand citizens who are agents of the state to manufacture, acquire, possess or have control over nuclear weapons beyond the New Zealand nuclear-free zone and to aid and abet others to do so beyond the New Zealand nuclear-free zone. That clause is important, because it emphasises the government's determination not to have New Zealand engage with nuclear defence strategies.

[. . . detailed comments on specific clauses . . .]

In summary, I believe that the principles and objectives of the Bill are broadly in line with mainstream public opinion in New Zealand on the issues. Mainstream public opinion wants New Zealand to disengage from nuclear weapons strategies. It wants New Zealand to work actively for nuclear disarmament.

It remains a disappointment to many people that the National Party chooses to remain outside that broad mainstream. I note that recently in its propaganda the National Party has tried to portray itself as a party of peace. The Leader of the Opposition is on record as saying, 'I am committed to peace, and the National government I lead will direct its energies to that cause.' That does not square with the commitment the Opposition is making to return nuclear weapons to New Zealand, and few New Zealanders will be fooled by that. The Leader of the Opposition has also said, 'We do not consider the occasional visit of a nuclear-powered or possibly nuclear-armed warship of our allies breaches our commitment to a non-nuclear New Zealand.' Most New Zealanders think differently from that.

Even within the National Party a few brave souls struggle to put a different light on National Party policy. I wish the nuclear-free Nationals well. I have no desire for the Labour Party, the Democratic Party and the New Zealand Party to have a permanent monopoly on the development of nuclear-free policies for New Zealand.

The Smoke-free Environments Bill

Parliament, Wellington
17 May 1990

Almost 30 years after making the following speech, Helen would write in a column for The New Zealand Herald *that, 'One of my proudest achievements as a politician was sponsoring New Zealand's pioneering Smoke-free Environments Act [1990] when I was Health Minister.' The Act placed smoking restrictions on indoor spaces, banned smoking on public transport and established the Health Sponsorship Council to replace tobacco sponsorship of events and organisations.*

_____

I move that the Smoke-free Environments Bill be introduced. The Bill is undoubtedly the most important health legislation introduced by the government. It is one of the major planks in a strategy aimed at achieving a smoke-free generation in New Zealand. I am disappointed that there is so little support for that idea from Opposition members. The Bill will ensure that New Zealand takes its proper place in the global efforts against the death and suffering that are being caused by tobacco.

It is not a punitive Bill. It is not a Bill that outlaws smoking or penalises those who remain addicted to the drug or who just choose to smoke. It is a Bill that ensures that the rights of non-smokers are also recognised. The Bill aims to protect young people from being exposed to false images of tobacco as a healthy and desirable product. The Bill will create a social environment that encourages young New Zealanders to remain non-smokers and protects non-smokers from the effects of tobacco smoke. It will also set up a new health sponsorship council that is specifically established to promote health and healthy lifestyles through the sponsorship of sport, the arts and cultural or recreational events. It will provide alternative sources of funds for those groups currently reliant on tobacco.

The Bill raised much controversy, both for and against, before its introduction, but there can be no controversy about the need for steps to be taken to tackle the problems currently being caused by tobacco. Every year more than 4000 New Zealanders are dying from diseases directly attributed to their smoking of tobacco, and 273 of them do not smoke at all but are dying from other people's smoke. That clearly makes tobacco-smoking by far the biggest single preventable cause of death and chronic illness in New Zealand. There can be no controversy about the health consequences of cigarette consumption.

The most worrying issue is not simply that thousands of New Zealanders are dying from the drug; it is that the rate of uptake of the drug continues to be high among young people. Most of those people who become addicted to tobacco do so as teenagers. They begin smoking when it is seen to be a habit that is adult, glamorous, grown-up, cool or sophisticated. They start at an age at which parliament does not consider them capable of making mature decisions about many other significant aspects of their lives. They start long before they would be legally entitled to drink in a public bar. Many are smokers before we would allow them to obtain a driver's licence. Most of them are already addicted by the time we would give them the right to vote or before we would allow them to fight for their country.

Yet the decision to begin smoking is likely to have a much greater impact on their life chances nowadays than any of those other factors. One in four of all regular smokers will die prematurely from smoking. Despite that, we allow our young people to be subjected to hours and hours of tobacco promotion on television and to explicit advertising in all print media.

In the past we have not appreciated the full health consequences of tobacco consumption. There have been times when the production and sale of tobacco have been explicitly encouraged. Returned servicemen remind us that, during the war, governments provided soldiers with free cigarettes. For that generosity, many of them have paid a very high price in terms of appalling disease and early death. We do not have the excuse of ignorance now.

We know that tobacco contains more than 50 toxic and cancer-causing chemicals, and the list of diseases caused by its use is extensive, including not only lung cancer, bronchitis, emphysema and heart disease, but also stroke, arterial disease and cancer of the oral cavity. The use of tobacco products also contributes towards or is associated with cancer of the bladder, kidneys and stomach. In addition to those risks that can affect all who smoke, there are some further specific risks for women. The risk of a stroke is increased for a woman who smokes and uses oral contraceptives. Smoking is associated with diseases such as cancer of the cervix and osteoporosis. Those are the risks of active smoking.

It is also known that passive smoking is a significant cause of disease, and, in so far as it often occurs in the workplace, it must be considered as an important occupational health hazard. Passive smoking not only causes discomfort and irritation to the eyes, nose and throat, but it distresses asthmatics and increases the risk of lung cancer and heart disease in non-smokers. We know the costs and we must be prepared to take positive action to avoid them.

There is no monetary self-interest whatsoever for the government in the Bill. It does not save money. Studies carried out internationally show that reducing tobacco consumption can be costly for governments. Studies show that the reduction in revenue from tax on tobacco might well outweigh the savings in the Health vote. They show that because people would live longer the state would have a greater liability for superannuation payments. The government is not prepared to place those revenue benefits to itself above the health of New Zealanders. The government values the years of extra healthy living given to people because they do not smoke. It is appalled by the suffering, not just of those with smoking-related illnesses, but also of their families and friends who watch helplessly as lung cancer and emphysema take their toll.

It is the human costs and benefits of smoking that the Labour government is most concerned with. The Department of Health, and others, have worked actively for a long time to promote non-smoking. Education to warn the public of the effects of smoking is essential. It has had some success—tobacco consumption and rates of tobacco use have declined—but it is clear that those trends have not been uniform throughout our community, and that there are some groups among whom tobacco use is not declining significantly at all. Research shows that young people in New Zealand—those aged between 15 and 24—are taking up regular smoking more than at any time since records began in 1976. Nearly half the young people of that age group are or have been regular smokers. Almost as quickly as smokers die or quit, their ranks are rejuvenated. The trend is particularly noticeable among young women, for whom the percentage taking up daily smoking dramatically increased between 1976 and 1988. Among young people aged between 15 and 24, women smokers outnumber male smokers.

Tobacco use is also a major contributor to ill health among Māori, who have smoking rates and lung cancer rates approximately twice that of the non-Māori population—among the highest in the world for any population group. Deaths from lung cancer have now overtaken deaths from breast cancer among Māori women.

While those trends continue, it would be irresponsible to stand back and do nothing more than we are doing. Inaction on the issue would be as irresponsible as doing nothing in the face of any other public health epidemic. Those are the reasons that the government is introducing comprehensive legislation.

[. . . detailed provisions of Bill explained . . .]

In conclusion, the time for the Smoke-free Environments Bill has certainly come. It will be effective, and it will bring major benefits. Overseas evidence is that advertising bans do reduce tobacco consumption. Most important, the number of young New Zealanders who take up smoking is expected to fall. The provisions relating to workplaces and public places will work because the public wants them.

The Bill is not expected to work miracles on its own. It is part of a comprehensive strategy to bring down the national consumption of tobacco. The strategy includes educational measures and effective levels of taxation. The Department of Health will continue to be very active in promoting non-smoking through educational means. It will continue to produce leaflets and posters, liaise with the Department of Education on school-based activities, produce resources for smoke-free policies in the workplace, develop reports and discussion papers and promote publicity campaigns such as the 'Kick it in the Butt' one and the present 'Smoke-free Generation' campaign. It has enjoyed, and it is enjoying, the full support of area health boards in its efforts.

Education on its own cannot do the job. Experience here and abroad shows that a multipronged strategy is needed to succeed, and educational, fiscal and legislative strategies reinforce and complement each other.

The benefits of the Bill are clear. The public health will be greatly improved by effective measures to reduce the leading cause of preventable death in New Zealand. Hospital beds will be freed for people with less preventable diseases. Workers will benefit from breathing cleaner and less smoky air. Employers will benefit from having cleaner workplaces and workable policies on smoking in the workplace that establish clear guidelines on where and when people may smoke. Sports, arts, recreational and cultural groups will benefit from having access to health sponsorship consistent with their own objectives. Families will be able to enjoy sports, arts, recreation and culture free of incompatible tobacco disease messages. Children will grow up free of commercial pressure to smoke. With the Bill, the children of 1990 have a real chance of being the first true smoke-free generation.

The Employment Equity Bill

Parliament, Wellington
17 July 1990

The Employment Equity Act 1990, which addressed equal employment opportunity and pay equity for women, was short-lived. It was repealed just a few months after passing, when the government changed to National leadership under Prime Minister Jim Bolger.

———

The reasons for the Employment Equity Bill were thoroughly canvassed by government members during the committee stage. Put simply, government members believe that further considerable advancement for women in the workforce now needs legislation to help it along. The government believes that without legislation progress will not only be slow but will almost certainly be negligible. The Bill has been designed to help push aside those barriers that stand in the way of equality. They are not going to fall away of their own accord; they have never done so and they never will. That is why there is a history of parliament's legislating for advances for women.

I am one who believes that there would never have been equal pay in New Zealand had it not been for legislation.

[. . . interruption . . .]

I shall come to the question of the member for Clevedon in a moment, because I want to give the National government credit for introducing the Equal Pay Act in 1972. However, twelve years before that time the Labour government introduced equal pay for women in the state services. The general assumption was that the private sector would follow that progressive move and gradually introduce equal pay itself. Of course, twelve years went by and nothing happened. The National government did legislate for equal pay; I pay it due credit for that. However, I have to say that if in 1972 that government had applied the logic that Opposition members are applying to the Employment Equity Bill in 1990 it would never have legislated for equal pay.

Opposition members have consistently condemned the Bill through every stage—the introduction, the reporting-back debate, the second reading and the committee stage—as being unwarranted intervention in the market. Some wonderful phrases were heard from the member for Selwyn during the committee stage. She described the Bill as being 'crude collectivist intervention', and said that the Bill was the 'enemy of flexibility'. There could be no cruder intervention in the market than the Equal Pay Act. There could be no cruder intervention than an Act that stated that men and women who stood next to each other in the workplace should be paid equally.

What has changed in the logic of the National Party since 1972? The National Party has changed its spots on equality for women. I heard the member for Waipa make her sad speech a few moments ago. She said that the National Party had never opposed pay equity, but I say that the National Party has a very strange idea of the definition of pay equity. The member for Waipa welcomed with open arms the report of the committee convened by Margaret Wilson. When that report appeared in August two years ago she said, 'Now we have a wonderful report on comparable worth. The report is excellent and brilliant in theory.' That is the theory behind the Bill, I might add. 'The theory is excellent, and the National Party has always believed in it.' What happened to the member for Waipa? In December 1989, when the Employment Equity Bill was introduced, she said, 'the Opposition does not support the Labour Party's pay equity proposal in any shape or form'—a pay equity proposal that was based precisely on the theory and principles of the Wilson report. That is the kind of phoney argument that members have heard throughout the committee stage.

These days the National Party's old ideas about equality for women have been subordinated to 'new Right' dogma that states that there should not be intervention in the market. 'It does not matter who is being disadvantaged; do not intervene in the market'—that is the sacred chalice that cannot be hurt. It is a pity about women, and a pity that they are disadvantaged; nothing can be done about it because that would interfere with the purity of the market.

The government believes that the Employment Equity Bill is the natural successor to the Equal Pay Act, which is now almost 20 years old. The Bill deals with barriers that the Act could not deal with in the times of eighteen years ago. The Bill deals with barriers to opportunity for women in the workforce. It deals with the barriers to the skills of women in female-dominated occupations receiving fair recognition through fair pay. I now come to that part of the Bill on equal employment opportunities that was discussed during the committee stage.

Opposition members have not disagreed with the concept of equal employment opportunities. They like to think that they support that concept, but throughout the debate they have not come up with any practical proposal on how to advance it outside the provisions of the Bill. As has come through strongly in the debate throughout the Bill, progress on equal employment opportunities has been pitifully slow. A few moments ago the member for Waipa referred to the policy of the Employers Federation. I have consistently said that the Employers Federation policy on employment equity and equal employment opportunities is excellent. It is a very good policy, but the problem is that nobody takes any notice of it. That is the problem with leaving to voluntary action very important social advances such as equal employment opportunity measures—they do not happen.

There is now action in the state sector. There is action because the government legislated through the State Sector Act. There comes a time—as there came with equal pay—when those measures need to make their transition across to the private sector through legislation. That is happening in the Bill for equal employment opportunities for all groups that are disadvantaged in the workforce—not only for women, but for Māori, for Pacific Island people, and for disabled people.

The Bill requires action on equal employment opportunity. I am confident that under the legislation many more women will be found in positions of responsibility in workplaces throughout the country. Women are capable of taking responsible jobs on merit, but in order to progress they need encouragement and support. That is what equal employment opportunity programmes are about. However, it is in relation to the pay equity issue that the Opposition has shown its true spots. It hates pay equity; it loathes pay equity. It has opposed any concrete action to redress unfair pay for those women in occupations that are denied fair pay.

In the course of the debate Opposition members presented their own pathetic proposal—a proposal advanced at an earlier stage when they said that a National government would appoint an extra member to the staff of the Human Rights Commission. What would that staffer do? We were told that the appointee would identify practices and regulations that created barriers to employment equity, but would not have powers to implement findings, which would simply be tendered as advice to the government. That appointment would achieve absolutely nothing.

Government members know what the barriers are—the Bill deals with them. Other barriers are falling as women move into non-traditional occupations, as, thanks to the government, more women have access to quality childcare, and as parental leave provisions available under the law are taken advantage of. What else apart from those provisions and the provisions of the Bill could a staffer in the Human Rights Commission possibly tell us needed to be done to lower barriers to employment equity for women?

The problems are known. The time has come to act—not to set up phoney appointments that are not designed to achieve anything. What would happen if that staffer came to the almost inevitable conclusion that employment equity legislation was needed? No doubt the staffer would be brushed aside completely because that would constitute the unwarranted intervention in the market to which the National Party is completely opposed. It is sad that throughout the debate the Opposition has made it clear that it believes that employment equity can come about through deregulation of the labour market. I shall turn around on Opposition members the phrase used by them. To achieve pay equity in that way would be pay fraud. Pay equity will not come out of labour market deregulation; poverty will come out of it.

Comments on the Waitangi Day 1995 Protests

Parliament, Wellington
28 February 1995

Official events on Waitangi Day, which commemorates the signing of Te Tiriti o Waitangi in 1840, were particularly fraught during the nineties. Protest against the government's December 1994 proposals for addressing Te Tiriti claims reached a head in Waitangi on 6 February 1995: dignitaries were spat on, protest flags were flown at the Treaty grounds and the New Zealand flag was trampled at Te Tii Marae.

———

Reports from Waitangi on 6 February shocked New Zealand. The Opposition believes that it is important that this House reflect today on what happened, why it happened, and where as a nation we go from here. I say that because unless the issues that led to the fiasco at Waitangi are handled better, and unless we deal with the future of Waitangi Day in a mature way, divisions will be left in our society that will be very difficult to heal. I thank you, Mr Speaker, for the initiative you have taken to bring together political leaders to begin some discussion about what might occur on Waitangi Day in the future.

First, I think it would be useful to summarise what happened on Waitangi Day. I was there, as were nine colleagues from the Labour Opposition. There were also a considerable number of Ministers of the Crown. The day dawned fair and sunny, the waka went out on cue to escort the Governor-General to the shore, the Governor-General duly arrived at the wharf at Waitangi, and the official party proceeded off down the road and over the bridge to the national marae at Waitangi. There, a rather long wait ensued. It was not quite clear to those waiting why we were waiting, but eventually word came through that the seats we were to occupy were otherwise occupied while another debate was going on as to what would occur if and when we were admitted. Eventually the official party was admitted to the foreground of the meeting house.

Then began a powhiri the like of which I had never seen before and the like of which I hope never to see again. In the course of it there was the notorious spitting incident, trousers were lowered, and the New Zealand flag was trampled in the ground—such behaviour, of course, being unacceptable at any time and in any place and totally unacceptable on that occasion. Can I say that, in particular, it is unacceptable for the Queen's representative and the representatives of foreign governments to be subjected to verbal abuse. I found the heckling of Dr Weber, who spoke on behalf of the diplomatic corps, particularly reprehensible, as was the heckling of a senior Tūhoe kaumātua, John Turei, who spoke on behalf of the Governor-General.

It emerged that earlier in the day there had been an attempt to set fire to the historic Treaty House itself. Later in the day the Treaty House grounds were occupied, the New Zealand flags were ripped down and replaced with the protesters' flags, and it also appears that the seating for New Zealanders from all walks of life who had come to watch the naval ceremony in the evening had been tampered with.

So, in summary, these were ugly events. They left everybody present, I believe, deeply disturbed by them; disturbed because, I believe, they exposed to all of us an underlying fragility in our country. That fragility relates to the fact that 155 years after the signing of the Treaty of Waitangi the Crown and Māori are still in dispute about how to honour it. Until that fundamental issue is resolved a cloud will hang not only over the future of Waitangi Day but also over the kind of future we have as a nation.

It is fair to observe that protest is not new at Waitangi on Waitangi Day. The reasons for it have not changed over the years, either. The reasons have always been the Treaty grievances. The saddest thing to me about what happened on 6 February this year was that it felt like a regression to a state of affairs at Waitangi on Waitangi Day that had last prevailed more than a decade ago.

I went back to reports of what had happened on Waitangi Day in previous years. I went back at least as far as 1978; whether similar things happened before then I do not clearly recall. Maybe they did, and maybe they did not. But in 1978 a headline from *The New Zealand Herald* recorded 'Dissension fails to cloud ceremony'. Maybe dissension did not cloud the ceremonies in those days, but it was there. There was a small band of what the *Herald* described as 'Māori land rights demonstrators', who shouted protests in front of the Treaty House. A group of young representatives of Ngā Tamatoa quietly handed pamphlets to people outside the marae gates. The pamphlets asked when the Treaty would be given its true recognition so that Māori could once again stand tall. The pamphlets stated that in terms of the Māori people today, Waitangi Day was not a day of celebration but a day of mourning, the day the Queen's people broke their promises.

Then, moving on to 1980, the *Herald* headlined its report of Waitangi Day as 'Marae jostle sours Waitangi Day festivities'. On that occasion there was a jostling incident involving the then Governor-General, Sir Keith Holyoake, a former member of this House, who was pushed with some force and half fell. The member for Northern Māori at the time observed that it was regrettable that the marae had become the focus of politics.

Things heated up the following year in 1981. A headline stated, 'Waitangi marae is in uproar as police arrest eight protesters'. The police said they did it to prevent the protest disruption from becoming a full-scale riot.

The following year in 1982, the Governor-General, Sir David Beattie, was struck by missiles during the evening of the Waitangi Day celebrations, which were punctuated with violence. One of the objects was a golf ball, and the other was an egg. There were lines of policemen to ensure that the ceremony went ahead. The bags of everybody who went into the grounds were systematically searched.

In 1983 the headline was 'Police swoop on Waitangi: 99 protesters arrested'. And so it went on. In 1984 there was the incident of Sir David Beattie, as Governor-General, waiting to meet a delegation of protesters; and waiting and waiting, as the meeting never happened because the protesters would not accept that some of them, not all, should meet the Governor-General.

So that was the history up to 1984. At that time there was a change of government. The Labour government of the day decided to shift the focus of the national day ceremony away from Waitangi. Whether it returned there prior to 1990 I do not clearly recall, but in 1990 the Queen came to New Zealand, and Waitangi Day was marked—not without incident; I recall a pair of pants being thrown, or some such thing. But in the period from 1984 considerable progress was made in beginning to address the grievances that had led to that rumbling and dissent at Waitangi over the years. I believe that, in particular, the fact that claims under the Treaty going back to 1840 could be presented to the government and the Waitangi Tribunal was a very, very important step. I am not saying that the 1980s went smoothly as we tried to sort out these problems. It was a rocky road. There were issues that arose from corporatisation and asset sales, but a process was in place.

It is fair to observe that since 1990 that process has continued. So where did it go wrong and what lay behind what happened at Waitangi this year? I believe that in looking for answers we do not have to look very far beyond the government's latest proposals to settle Treaty issues. As I said in the debate in the House at the time the proposals were released, there is a lot of good in them and I believe that they are well intentioned in seeking settlement of long-standing grievances. But I said at that time that the proposals contained a fundamental flaw, and the fundamental flaw is to place a cap—the so-called fiscal envelope—on the overall settlement sum. I said then that that attempt would undermine what the government sought to achieve, and so it has proved to be. Māori reaction has been swift and it has been 'No'. The issue has simmered over the summer and prior to Waitangi Day, culminating in the very significant hui of 1000 Māori leaders and individuals at Turangi, which was convened by Sir Hepi Te Heuheu. Again, from that hui there was a resounding 'No'.

I do not think it helped that the resounding 'No' was greeted by some in the government with the response that the Māori present at Turangi had not understood the fiscal envelope proposal. I think they understood only too well. They understood that the fiscal envelope, the cap, was a non-negotiable item of the government's proposal; that, if Māori were to accept it, Māori would be pitted against Māori; and that the decision to impose the cap was not arrived at as a result of the partnership that the Treaty clearly implies.

Recently I saw reference to the comments made by the head of the Ngāti Porou rūnanga, Api Mahuika, who was reported as saying that the government had single-handedly developed the parameters for consultation, and iwi had been asked merely to react. There had been two partners to the Treaty, but now one partner was assuming a unilateral right to determine how the consultation should occur. That is how this matter is seen in Māoridom. Until such time as the fiscal envelope becomes a negotiable matter, there is little for Māori leadership to engage in dialogue with government about.

So there, I believe, is the background to what happened at Waitangi. I believe that Māoridom's leadership was marginalised, and I believe that that left the way clear for extreme elements to put on a show—and they did. We are all appalled by what happened, but we have to ensure that those appalling events do not distract us from the central issue, and the central issue is the future of negotiations between the Crown and Māori. I appreciate how difficult it is to change course on a policy after anarchic events like those at Waitangi, but I believe that the course must be changed.

I come to the issue that you, Mr Speaker, have convened a meeting on, and that is the future of Waitangi Day itself. Firstly, it would seem clear that until some agreement is reached in partnership with Māori on the process of settlement, it is very hard to see how official commemorations can take place at Waitangi. I believe that the same events would probably occur again, and that simply is not fair to the Governor-General and to foreign dignitaries. Further, I understand that the Prime Minister himself has no wish to see the ceremony conducted in a state of siege, with lines of police, and I certainly agree with him on that.

But what of the future? We have to decide—and I think it is up to this House to lead an informed public debate—a number of issues. Should we have a national day? Not everybody does. I am hard-pressed to think of a British national day. If so, which day should it be? For my part, I do not see how one can go past 6 February, the day on which the founding document of our country was signed, but that is something that can be legitimately debated. What should the national day—if we have one and if it is 6 February—be called? There have been suggestions of New Zealand Day. There have been suggestions of Waitangi Day. We need informed debate about that. Finally, how should the day—if we have it, wherever we have it—be commemorated? Should the events that led to the signing of the Treaty be the focus of the national day?

There are not any obvious and overwhelming answers to those questions, but I think it is important in today's climate that there is a debate that is informed, spreading out from this House, spreading out from the meeting that you, Mr Speaker, have convened, and that there should not be unilateral action on the future of Waitangi Day. I wonder whether, just as a committee was set up to look at the future of the honours system, this issue is also one on which a group of the good and wise should be convened to look at the options and to attempt to get some kind of consensus on the future of a national day for New Zealand.

Beyond that, I believe, is a more fundamental issue. That issue is what kind of nation we are to be. Are we to be a bicultural nation, or are we to be a divided nation where tangata whenua take no joy in the national day that we commemorate?

Response to Ministerial Statement on French Nuclear Testing

Parliament, Wellington
14 June 1995

*In 1995, France resumed nuclear testing in the South Pacific,
carrying out a series of tests in September and October, in spite of
a United Nations General Assembly treaty banning all nuclear
explosions which was to be signed the following year. This sparked
international protests, riots throughout Polynesia, and a threat of
suspension from the South Pacific Forum. The last nuclear test at
Moruroa Atoll took place in January 1996.*

———

This decision by France to resume nuclear testing in the Pacific is the
arrogant action of a colonial power. It is very important that New Zealand
speak out for those people who cannot speak out because they are the
subjects of that colonial power. We have a very important leadership role
in the South Pacific on this. It is entirely appropriate to freeze military
co-operation with France, as the Prime Minister has proposed. In his

response today I would like him to explore a little further whether that means the kind of exercise like Tasmanex, which has occurred between our two countries, is also to be put on ice until the abomination of French nuclear testing is gone.

But there is no question that this country must take strong action. France does not respect weakness. France is arrogant. There is a history of its arrogance in the South Pacific, and this is just the latest dreadful example of it.

Only in recent weeks we have seen the conclusion of the non-proliferation treaty conference in New York. At that conference France, like other nuclear weapons states, put up a pretence of being prepared to stop testing and move on. That was given the lie to when the Chinese resumed testing almost immediately after the signatures were on the document, and now within six weeks France has followed with this incredible action. There must be strong and co-ordinated action on it in the South Pacific. I would ask the Prime Minister whether in his conversations or the conversations of the Minister of Foreign Affairs and Trade with the Australians the prospect of the Australians also taking similar actions with regard to military co-operation has been raised. There is no question that if Australia joins us in this then that has great moral force.

I think the Conference on Disarmament is the right place to raise the issue multilaterally. Of course, the United Nations General Assembly is not in session, and that forum is not available to us. But we must use any forum we have to express our horror of this.

Perhaps in the Prime Minister's reply he could also consider the proposal I have made to send a frigate. I raise that because it has been done before. The Rt Hon. Norman Kirk sent a frigate to Moruroa in the early 1970s. It had a Cabinet Minister on board, and I will not suggest volunteers—I do not wish to make light of the occasion by suggesting names. A frigate going to Moruroa would certainly be a signal that our views now are as strong as they were in the early 1970s. If New Zealand can consider sending a frigate all the way to the Persian Gulf to patrol sanctions against Iraq then we can consider sending a frigate to Moruroa. This is a case of charity beginning at home.

So I join the Prime Minister in deploring this arrogant, colonial action by France. I join him in saying that military co-operation should cease. I want to know whether that extends as far as Tasmanex, and I would like the Prime Minister to respond positively on the issue of a frigate going up to the test zone, backing the brave action of the people on the *Rainbow Warrior*.

Remembering Princess Diana

Parliament, Wellington
2 September 1997

On 31 August 1997, Diana, Princess of Wales, was killed in a car accident in Paris. The sudden death of such a beloved public figure resulted in an international outpouring of grief, and tributes from senior political figures the world over.

It is with enormous sadness that I rise today to pay this tribute to Diana, Princess of Wales. On behalf of the Labour Party and its members in this House I extend our most sincere sympathies to princes William and Harry, to Princess Diana's mother, her brother and sisters and their families, the royal family and the people of Great Britain. Words cannot express the grief we feel at seeing a young woman like Diana struck down in the prime of her life in a horrible accident. Many of us over the past two days—and I freely admit to being one—have sat choked up in front of our television sets, overwhelmed by the sadness of what has happened. We feel the deep unfairness of a life ended in this way. We feel sorrow for the family. We think of those last terrible moments. In many ways it is as if we have lost a member of our own family, and, indeed, we have lost a very special member of the human family.

Although most New Zealanders, myself included, never met Diana, we feel as though we have done so because her life was always before us. Photographs of her were everywhere, her joys and sorrows were widely written about, and suddenly as the light has gone out on her life it feels as though a light has gone out in our own.

In the past two days Diana has been described in many, many ways. She was, as the *Daily Express* in London has stated, an icon for a generation. That perhaps explains the response, particularly of young people. I have reflected a good deal on what it was that made Diana special, and why her sudden death has touched the lives of so many people. She was, after all, an immensely wealthy woman who lived a life beyond the imagination of most of us. But what was special about Diana was that she was both willing and able to step aside from the privilege created by birth, marriage and rank, and communicate her feelings and her concerns about ordinary people and their problems.

In turn, the causes Diana championed benefited enormously from her compassion. She could explode myths where no public relations strategy could have succeeded, as she sat and touched the hands of people with AIDS, showing that such normal social interaction carried no risks. She touched lepers, helping break down the stigma of their disease. And so often she was seen comforting the dying and the relatives of the deceased, even as recently as last week in that visit to Bosnia, and this I know will never be forgotten.

What was special about Diana was that she communicated as a real person, with feelings, with humanity, and with her own problems. Her brief life took her from a sheltered upbringing through the fairy-tale wedding, the joys of the children, the disappointment of a failing marriage, bulimia, the constant intrusive scrutiny of her personal life and, finally, this awful tragedy. Diana was real, she was vulnerable, she made mistakes, and she had problems in common with many ordinary people.

Much has already been said about the role of the news media in this tragedy. News today that the chauffeur was well over the blood-alcohol limits for driving may mitigate that a little. But let it be recorded in this House that Diana the person was harassed beyond all reason and that her fear of, and the reality of, that harassment, were without doubt contributing causes to her death.

All of us in public life are conscious of the pressures of media scrutiny. We can only be thankful that in our own country, in general, a boundary is drawn between our public and our private lives. Diana did not enjoy that personal space. She was never left alone, and the consequences have carried a terrible penalty, and remind us all of our fragility under such pressure.

Throughout New Zealand many people have grieved for Diana over these past two days. I thank those church leaders who have arranged for special services of remembrance so that people can come together to express their love and respect for her. Diana's brother, Earl Spencer, said two ago that she is now in a place where no human being can ever touch her again. To the princess of the people, I say rest in peace.

New Zealand
in East Timor

Parliament, Wellington
17 September 1999

The Indonesian occupation of East Timor (Timor-Leste) lasted from 1975 until 1999, during which time the Timorese people were the victims of mass torture and violence at the hands of their occupiers. In August 1999, a UN-sponsored referendum was held and returned overwhelmingly in favour of East Timorese independence from Indonesia. New Zealand sent troops to the region as part of the International Force East Timor (INTERFET), an Australian-led multinational peace-keeping task force which operated in accordance with UN resolutions in East Timor from 1999 until the arrival of UN peace-keepers in 2000. At the time, it was New Zealand's largest overseas military deployment since the Korean War. East Timor officially became an independent nation in 2002.

The New Zealand Labour Party strongly supports New Zealand making a contribution to the peace-keeping force in East Timor. Our first thoughts today are for the men and women who will be representing New Zealand in East Timor and for their families. Everyone is well aware that our commitment of troops to East Timor involves real risks to those whom we are sending. No country ever takes lightly the decision to commit its men and women—and mainly young men and young women—to any kind of military activity overseas. In this case, however, our responsibility as New Zealanders is clear. It is to act to uphold the result of the ballot for independence in East Timor and to enable that small country to establish its independence. Clearly, that could not be achieved without the presence now of an international peace-keeping force.

I believe that most New Zealanders understand very well the background to the recent traumatic events in East Timor. East Timor was illegally annexed by Indonesia in 1975. An estimated one-third of its population was killed or starved to death in the next four years. East Timor was subjected to heavy military oppression by Indonesia, yet over those long, terrible 24 years, the desire of the people there for independence never died. Standing alongside the people of East Timor have been many people and organisations of conscience.

In that respect, today I pay a special tribute to the Catholic Church and its agencies, and to the outstanding figure of Bishop Carlos Belo, a Nobel Peace Prize winner, alongside Jose Ramos Horta. Without their constant faith, the attention of the world may well have been diverted permanently away from the cause of East Timor.

East Timor's chance for independence came with the crumbling of the old order in Indonesia, as we have seen over the past year on our television screens. We know that Indonesia itself is in a process of political transition. That process is far from stable and settled. Elections have been held and it is expected that a new president will in due course be elected. All eyes are on Indonesia now to assess whether the new civilian administration will be able to exert more control over its military than the present one of Mr Habibie seems capable of.

It is true that the interim President, Mr Habibie, has enabled an election on the future of East Timor to be held in the territory. However, it has been tragic that the Indonesian government, having given its word to the United Nations that it would maintain law and order both before and after the ballot, proved either unable or unwilling to do that. Historians will debate at length whether the United Nations was even wise to accept Indonesia's assurances of maintaining order in East Timor, given that lines of civilian authority in Indonesia are so weak, given that

Indonesia's military itself does not appear to have strong command and control systems, and given that that military has been highly resistant over the 24 years of occupation to allowing East Timor to embark on the route to independence.

In the run-up to the East Timor ballot there were indeed many signs that Indonesia would not be able to maintain law and order in the event of a vote for independence. I know that our colleagues from this parliament were well aware of that during the two weeks they spent in the territory. Notwithstanding those concerns, and a great deal of intimidation against the East Timorese, they went out in very great numbers, they voted decisively, and they showed enormous courage in even coming forward to vote in the circumstances.

The reaction since from the militia and from the Indonesian military itself has been quite simply monstrous. They have destroyed East Timor's infrastructure. Many people have been killed. And I would estimate that probably in excess of 200,000 people have been displaced. International pressure on Indonesia became overwhelming, and by last weekend that country agreed that the United Nations should indeed intervene.

The Security Council has acted speedily in resolving to support the rapid entry of a multinational force, in which we participate with pride, and to follow that through with a formal United Nations peace-keeping force. In readily agreeing to be part of that force we, as New Zealanders, demonstrate again our willingness to back the United Nations, our commitment to regional peace and security, and our commitment to see the ballot for independence in East Timor upheld.

The first task of the international force will be to establish a foothold and then to move progressively to extend its authority throughout the territory. Alongside that will be the efforts of the aid agencies to provide food and other badly needed humanitarian relief. The task ahead of the military in the United Nations—sanctioned force, the civilian aid agencies and friendly governments—is huge because this new small nation inherits the scorched earth left behind by the departing Indonesian occupiers.

There is a new civilian administration to be built from the ground up. There are massive needs for new housing and infrastructure. There are a couple of hundred thousand displaced people who need to be able to come home to safe conditions. And there will be many traumatised men, women and children who have seen acts of savagery committed against their families and their neighbours. It is going to be tough. It is going to be very tough indeed.

It is not yet clear whether Indonesia will continue to obstruct the movement to the independence of East Timor. I must say that reports from West Timor, where there are already well in excess of 100,000 refugees, are not encouraging. Oxfam today has called for diplomatic pressure to be placed on Jakarta, to enable relief agencies and human rights monitors to have access to the West Timor refugee camps. It is essential that those camps are demilitarised and that the safe return of refugees to East Timor is facilitated.

In the next few days as the New Zealand troops enter East Timor we know that they may well face resistance from the militia and from dissident units of the Indonesian army. I am confident that we are sending world-class professional soldiers who will acquit themselves well, whatever the challenge they meet.

There remains the medium- and longer-term issue of New Zealand's relationship with Indonesia. Both New Zealand and Australia have worked very hard on that relationship for decades. That did not stop Indonesia yesterday unilaterally abrogating its security agreement with Australia, and that is a matter of deep regret. The most optimistic view is that a new Indonesia will emerge from the transition to democracy and that in time better and more durable relations with New Zealand and Australia will follow. The more pessimistic view is that Indonesia may be in turmoil for some time, and that its evolution to more democratic government may be impeded by secessionist forces in other parts of the country.

I believe New Zealand has every interest in seeing Indonesia complete its transition to democracy, and in rebuilding its economy and society from the very harsh blow dealt to it by the Asian financial crisis. I trust that the strong message from this parliament today will be New Zealand's desire to be a good neighbour, to both a new Indonesia and to the new nation of East Timor. There is a long road ahead of both countries, one vast, the other very small. New Zealand stands ready to help as best it can in the interests of peace and stability in the region.

To the New Zealand servicemen and servicewomen who, in the next few days, will leave for East Timor, I say to them that parliament supports their mission and we have every confidence in their ability to acquit themselves very well on our behalf.

Official New Year's Day Address

Te Poho-o-Rawiri Marae, Gisborne
1 January 2000

As the year 2000 loomed people fretted about the Y2K bug, South Pacific nations vied to be the first to see the dawn of the new millennium, and a gaggle of skydivers were so eager to beat anyone else to seeing in New Year's Day that they threw themselves out of a plane over the international dateline, not far from the Chatham Islands. Gisborne, on the east coast of New Zealand's North Island, laid claim to being the first city in the world to welcome the dawn of the new millennium, and that's where Helen gave the following address on 1 January 2000.

E ngā mana, e ngā reo, e ngā iwi o te motu, tēnā koutou katoa.
Tēnā hoki koutou e te iwi o Te Poho-o-Rawiri Marae, i mihi mai nei,
  ki a mātou.

Distinguished guests, ladies and gentlemen, this new year carries even more significance. At midnight we farewelled the twentieth century and the second millennium. At dawn we saw the first light of the twenty-first century and the third millennium. Throughout the world at this time people are looking back, not just over the twentieth century, but over the entire past 1,000 years of human endeavour. Not only is our world unrecognisable from that of a thousand years ago, but also it is unrecognisable from that of one hundred years ago.

A thousand years ago Māori were, in historical terms, relatively new settlers in New Zealand, a forested land of spectacular beauty. On the Pākehā side of our heritage, the Norman conquest of England by William the Conqueror was still decades away.

A hundred years ago, Māori were a diminishing proportion of the population, ravaged by introduced diseases and the legacy of war, and overwhelmed numerically by a fast-growing settler community. New Zealand soldiers were in South Africa on their first overseas deployment. The motorcar, like much else we take for granted now, was a relatively new invention.

This last century has seen the world and New Zealand wracked by traumatic events.

World War One, often described as the last great imperial war, and certainly one of the most pointless and disastrous, signalled the end of an era. New Zealand's and Australia's participation as ANZACs at Gallipoli marked the beginning of a new post-imperial sense of identity for both our nations.

Russia's Bolshevik revolution, the Great Depression, the rise of Nazism and other forms of fascism and World War Two were all cataclysmic events. New Zealanders fought bravely in World War Two, with contributions like that of the Māori Battalion at Monte Cassino becoming etched forever in the nation's memory. The war in Asia ended with the nuclear-bombing of Japan and the dawn of an even more dangerous age. A line was drawn through Europe as communist governments were installed in its east. The Chinese Revolution of 1949 and the Korean and Vietnam wars all added to the tension.

The post-World War Two period also saw the European colonial empires dissolve. India gained its independence in 1947, followed by other British colonies and those of France, Holland, Belgium and, eventually, Portugal over the next three decades.

New Zealand has been touched in one way or another by all these events. Our families, Māori and Pākehā, were torn apart by wars, and many suffered greatly in the depressions of the 1920s and 1930s. Our response to hardship at home was the establishment of social security which survives, albeit in a battered form, to this day.

As a small, remote trading nation, New Zealand depends for its prosperity on a stable and peaceful world. We have been an active, committed member of the United Nations from its inception, and participated in many of its peace-keeping missions, including that presently in place in East Timor. Our thoughts are with our servicemen and women in East Timor as they spend this new year apart from their families and friends.

Since World War Two, more and more of our diplomatic and trading activity has focused on the Asia-Pacific region. We have also engaged in the great campaigns for nuclear disarmament and for a free and democratic South Africa.

Here at home, our country has changed enormously from the one I was born into in 1950, let alone that which my parents were born into in the 1920s. While much of our living is still derived from the primary industries, we are now a highly urbanised people. But we are finding it difficult to sustain First World living standards for all our people with what amounts to a Third World export profile. Transforming our economy on the basis of knowledge, skill and technology into one which delivers better living standards and more employment is probably the greatest challenge our country faces in the twenty-first century.

Two changes stand out for me above all others in New Zealand society.

The first is in the role of women. In my lifetime, women have come from holding almost no significant positions in our national life to holding many throughout government, the judiciary, the public and private sectors, the professions, the churches and community organisations. The glass ceiling has been well and truly broken.

The second is in the recognition and place of Māori. Truly a renaissance in Māoridom has occurred, with huge and positive implications for Māori and all other New Zealanders. In my childhood and teenage years, the Treaty of Waitangi was for Pākehā a largely forgotten document. Today it is at the centre of national debate about our future, and its constitutional significance is fully recognised. Claims pursuant to the Treaty have been settled and will continue to be settled. The path has often been difficult and uncertain. It has not always been well understood. But it is a path we must continue along. Article Three of the Treaty presents our country with great challenges. It guarantees Māori equal rights of citizenship. Yet great gaps have developed between Māori and other New Zealanders. Closing those gaps is essential if this nation is to be at peace with itself.

So where now for New Zealand in this twenty-first century and third millennium?

Ours is a young country with so much potential. While we have many achievements and many acts of individual brilliance to our credit, in many ways we haven't yet fulfilled our potential as a nation. We haven't done everything right, but we have the capacity to do so much better. And if we pull together as a nation we will.

We have choices before us. We can let our differences pull us apart. Or we can celebrate our diversity in ways which make us stronger. We can let the gaps between us grow wider, or we can determine to close them so we all move forward together.

I sense that, as we enter this new millennium, New Zealanders are yearning for a fresh start. We are mature enough to recognise where things have gone wrong—and we are talented enough to put them right if we have the collective will to do so.

My hope for the future is for a New Zealand in which every citizen feels they have a stake, and in which every citizen's humanity and dignity is acknowledged. Whether we be Pākehā, Māori, Pacific people or New Zealanders whose heritage is from other parts of the world, we are all in this together. Whether we be rural, urban or small-town dwellers, we all have a contribution to make. While our hopes for the future rest with the nation's children, we owe it to those who built this country to respect their contribution and ensure their security in old age. And we must value and support our families in all their many forms.

While change in our ways of life and our world have been so immense in the past century, the pace of change in the next century will be faster still. It is said that most of today's five-year-olds will be doing jobs which have not yet been invented. Keeping up with change is essential if our nation is to prosper. Education, research, science, technology and investment, built on a sound social infrastructure, truly are the keys to our future.

But it will be important, too, not to neglect the non-material aspects of our lives. The arts and culture feed the soul of our country. Through our talented and creative people we express our identity, and from their work we can all derive pleasure and enjoyment, as so many have from the performance of Dame Kiri Te Kanawa and the New Zealand Symphony Orchestra here in Gisborne this morning.

In a world which is globalising so fast, small nations like New Zealand are very vulnerable. If we wish to be more than cultural offshoots of Sydney, Los Angeles or London, then we will take steps now to protect, assert and affirm our unique identity as a nation, drawing on our strong indigenous Māori heritage, the cultures of the Pacific and the heritage of all other peoples who have contributed to the building of New Zealand.

In the course of economic development, New Zealand's and the world's environment has been greatly affected. Indigenous forest cover is a fraction of what it once was. More and more species face extinction. Glaciers are receding, and temperatures and sea levels are rising. Pollution is an ever-present problem. These issues must be addressed on a global scale. Yet while thinking globally we can and must also act locally to conserve the natural heritage we have for future generations to love and cherish.

My hopes for the future are simply expressed. Would it not be wonderful to live in a world where no child went hungry and homeless, where all communities experience peace and decent living standards and show tolerance towards others, where the environment truly is clean and green, and where affirmation occurs through cultural and creative expression?

Our contribution to that world can be made by overcoming division at home, by achieving steady economic development and sharing the gains, by our commitment to justice and fair play, and by our willingness to act as a good international citizen in all respects.

May our efforts as a small but concerned nation contribute to a twenty-first century which offers more peace and security to all people than did the twentieth century which we farewelled a few hours ago.

No reira, tēnā koutou, tēnā koutou, tēnā koutou katoa.

Waitangi Day Speech

Ōnuku Marae, Banks Peninsula
6 February 2000

On Waitangi Day in 1998, Helen (then Leader of the Opposition) appeared at Te Tii Marae but her right as a woman to speak during the pōwhiri was challenged. (Some iwi do not permit women to speak on marae, because of traditional Māori protocol.) Two years later, Helen was invited to join Ngāi Tahu celebrations at Ōnuku Marae, where she delivered the following speech. Afterwards, she was quoted in The New Zealand Herald *as saying, 'I think today Ngāi Tahu has shown what Waitangi Day can be.' Ōnuku Marae was the site where two Ngāi Tahu chiefs, Iwikau and Tikao, signed Te Tiriti o Waitangi on 30 May 1840.*

———

E ngā mana, e ngā reo, e ngā iwi o te motu, tēnā koutou katoa.
Tena hoki koutou e te iwi o te Ōnuku marae, i mihi mai nei, ki a matou.

My thanks go to Ngāi Tahu for their invitation and welcome here today. Our presence here at Ōnuku is a reminder to us all that the Treaty of Waitangi was signed not just at one place on one day but in many places on many days. For Ngāi Tahu here at Ōnuku that day was at the end of May in 1840. Governor Hobson dispatched Major Bunbury by ship to get signatures from the eastern and southern iwi. Bunbury did not do particularly well. Twenty-five days after leaving Russell he arrived off Akaroa with only six signatures. At Ōnuku on 30 May the rangatira Iwikau and Tikao signed. Across all of Ngāi Tahu only seven rangatira signed.

The rest is history. As is now well known and documented, the Crown failed spectacularly to fulfil its Treaty obligations to Ngāi Tahu over a very long period of time. The Crown itself took ownership over much of Ngāi Tahu's lands, leaving it as largely a landless people. The loss of its lands was a major assault on the mana, the identity and the status of the iwi.

But from the outset Ngāi Tahu kept its faith in the Treaty. Generations of Ngāi Tahu sought redress under its provisions. For generations they were knocked back, but in 1985 a new mechanism became available. The Fourth Labour Government legislated to enable Treaty claims to be made dating back to 1840.

Ngāi Tahu wasted no time in re-presenting its claim. It was formally lodged in 1986, and hearings followed in 1987 and 1989. In 1991 the Waitangi Tribunal reported very substantially in Ngāi Tahu's favour. Negotiations began and settlement was reached with legislation to enact it coming before parliament.

Given the history of the issue and the manifest injustice which the settlement sought to redress, it was inconceivable to me that parliament would not pass the Ngāi Tahu Settlement Bill. Labour, as the major opposition party, threw its weight behind the settlement. In so doing, Labour expressed its hope that, in years to come, oppositions of the future would not play politics with settlements reached in good faith between iwi and the government of the day.

Much has flowed from the Ngāi Tahu settlement and the process leading to it. The iwi has been empowered to take charge of its own destiny and to invest in its future and in its people. It is a significant player in the economy of the South Island and indeed of New Zealand as a whole.

Very important to me is the iwi's commitment to building the capacity of its people to lead in the future. Last year 460 tertiary students of Ngāi Tahu descent were assisted. Among them will be the future teachers, health professionals, community workers and business managers of the iwi. Among them, I hope, will be its philosophers and its wise men and women.

We are all aware that the Treaty settlement process has not always received a good press. We are all aware that there are still some in our country who seek to deride and question it. All I can say is that common justice demands that the settlement process continues, and that the positive outcomes achieved by Ngāi Tahu are indeed a beacon of hope for others going through that process.

Elsewhere many are yet to settle. There are some difficulties in determining who has a mandate to settle. Our new government will have to work in good faith to resolve those issues.

But there are also other steps we must take to honour the Treaty. While the 1990s saw some action to honour Article Two, the widening of the economic and social gaps between Māori and other New Zealanders undermined Article Three. And so in the first years of this twenty-first century and third millennium, our policies must also embrace the spirit of Article Three and work to close those appalling gaps. That is why I am establishing a new cabinet committee to focus on these issues.

The task before us is huge. There is a legacy of entrenched poverty, of second- and third-generation unemployment and under-employment, of poor health, bad housing and low educational achievement. Turning that around will not be easy or quick, but we have to make a start in the interests of all New Zealanders. Māori and Pacific peoples are a very fast-growing proportion of our population. It is in everyone's interests that all can share in the common citizenship that is our right in this country.

This year we mark the one-hundred-and-sixtieth anniversary of the signing of the Treaty of Waitangi. For much of that 160-year period the Treaty was, for Pākehā, largely a forgotten document. Settlers arrived in their many tens of thousands, and Māori became even more of a minority in their own land. The Treaty was honoured more in the breach than in the observance by governments. Certainly in my childhood and teenage years the Treaty did not figure prominently in our school curriculum or in any public debate.

All that was to change dramatically in the 1970s. The establishment of the Waitangi Tribunal was a small step forward. But I think, looking back, it was the land march and then the protest at Bastion Point which forced Treaty issues on to the public agenda. Treaty issues have been controversial, but as a nation I hope we continue to have the courage and the wisdom to deal with them.

Waitangi Day itself presents the opportunity to reflect on the nation we have been, and to dream of the nation which we could be. Our nation of today in effect began with the signing of that Treaty. It was signed so that two very different peoples could co-exist in one country. And, one way or another, we have. But we have changed a lot along the way. Many, many peoples now make up New Zealand, and all bring to it the richness of their cultures, heritage and languages as well. We have a challenge to celebrate that multiculturalism on the foundation of our biculturalism. Sir Tipene's wise words on the distinction between those who are here because of the Treaty and those who are here by right of the Treaty should be heeded.

In the end, Waitangi Day for me is a day when we can celebrate our nationhood. We can acknowledge the upside and the downside. We can take pride in the progress we have made and we can resolve to do better in the future.

I know that so often in the past Waitangi Day has brought images of discord and disunity, and not of unity and common purpose. In years gone by there has been good reason for that when the Treaty was so marginalised. As recently as 1995 the concept of the fiscal envelope for claims roused much anger in Māoridom. But I would like this millennium year to give us the opportunity to make a fresh start and to see the focus of Waitangi Day and surrounding days move to include all New Zealanders in a celebration of the richness and talents which make up our country today.

This weekend I have had an opportunity to do just that. I was yesterday at Tūrangawaewae with many thousands of others, enthralled by the dazzling performances of kapa haka groups from all over New Zealand who blend the traditional and the contemporary in their presentations. I was able to celebrate the Chinese New Year for the Year of the Dragon with many thousands in the Chinese community in Auckland. In Marlborough on Friday night, I opened a wonderful exhibition of local artists' work. Tonight I will be in Auckland to see the Warriors in the first big league match of the season, and I will take your good wishes to them for the game against Melbourne. So much is happening that is positive across our communities.

Waitangi Day has the capacity to draw us together, rather than drive us apart. Our people have a yearning to move on, put things right and accentuate the positive. That is the challenge before us in the twenty-first century. Central to that challenge will be the further steps we take to honour the Treaty, put right the wrongs of the past, and build a strong basis for our communities to continue to live and work alongside each other.

No reira, tēnā koutou, tēnā koutou, tēnā koutou katoa.

Address to The New Zealand Federation of Country Women's Institutes

Wellington
24 July 2000

Established in 1921, The New Zealand Federation of Country Women's Institutes provides community support and opportunities to women throughout the country. Helen, whose mother, grandmother and great-grandmother were all Women's Institute members, gave the following speech at the institute's conference in 2000.

My great-grandmother used to walk around three miles to the institute meetings, so much did the movement mean to her. My grandmother also was a foundation member of her local branch in Te Pahu in the Waikato. She used to go to the meetings on horseback with her youngest child. The meetings involved a day out and members took their lunches. In those days of bad roads and poor communications, women on isolated farms had little contact with other women. It is fair to say that they lived for those Women's Institute meetings and the contact and friendship the meetings made possible with other women.

My mother, who is here tonight, has been a member of Country Women's Institute for half a century. Mum has been a regular office holder in the institute and a full participant in its activities, including being a delegate to the national conference on at least five occasions. She often starred in its dramatic productions in Te Pahu. For my mother, like my grandmother, the monthly Country Women's Institute meeting was not to be missed.

The institute continued to be a place to meet other women, hear a speaker and catch up with what was going on in the district. It was a means for introducing new settlers in the district to others, and it was also an organisation which encouraged good works for others. The institute's motto—'For home and country'—has been enduring. It has supported women in their role as homemakers, it has fostered cultural and craft activities, and it has encouraged women to participate in community affairs and to take an interest in all aspects of our national life.

All these aims and activities are of course still relevant in the twenty-first century. More than ever women are involved in community affairs, public life and the workplace, but that does not mean that other aspects of our lives need be neglected. Women take their roles as parents very seriously, and homemaking is an important part of that.

As Minister of Arts and Culture, I also want to give my strong endorsement to the Country Women's Institute's support for arts, cultural and craft activities. Through them we each can express our creativity and our talent, and our appreciation for the things of beauty others create. It is interesting that research into how we New Zealanders spend our time outside work finds that more of us spend our time actively or passively engaged with arts, culture or crafts than we do with sport—yet these are aspects of our national life which have traditionally been undervalued and not well recognised.

This conference in [the] millennium year is the ideal opportunity for the institute to be looking ahead to the kind of role it can play in the twenty-first century. Your theme 'Today, Tomorrow, Together' is a forward-looking one.

Undoubtedly the Country Women's Institute and its branches have been affected by trends in rural society. Many fewer people live on farms these days, and many more women work full-time away from the farm and so are identified less with community activities within their district. On the other hand, regional New Zealand's economy is diversifying and bringing new, non-farm families into rural and small-town areas, particularly people engaged in tourism or the visitor industry in some way. Country Women's Institute has also for a long time been established in towns and suburbs.

So what of the future?

The community organisations which thrive in the twenty-first century will be those which adapt to meet the new needs and interests of their communities. That doesn't mean changing one's values, but rather adapting the way things are done to meet new needs. Only women themselves can define what it is they need from and can contribute to organisations like the Country Women's Institute.

I suspect that some of the needs which drove my grandmother to ride her horse to institute seventy years ago are still there today. Women at home with small children can feel very isolated. Country Women's Institute in the twenty-first century is still there as a place for friendship and fellowship. And, having established that friendship and fellowship, networks are established which can last a lifetime within communities, or as women shift to other communities knowing the structure of Country Women's Institute and what it has to offer.

I want to thank Country Women's Institute tonight particularly for its voluntary work. You have raised money for so many worthwhile causes— for medical research, for children, for a wide range of charities. Like so many other charitable and community organisations, your voluntary work helps keep our society ticking.

We all know that governments can do so much, but we can't do everything. Non-governmental organisations like yours provide that extra which really helps—and we thank you for that. You form a vital part of what we call 'civil society', and it and you are going to have a big role to play in the twenty-first century.

Thank you once again for the opportunity to say a few words.

I have pleasure in declaring your millennium.

Address to the State of the World Forum

New York, United States of America
5 September 2000

The State of the World Forum is a non-profit organisation that seeks to establish a global network of leaders, citizens and institutions, bringing them together annually for discussion and action on the issues confronting humanity. Its millennium conference in the year 2000 was timed to coincide with the historic United Nations Millennium Summit—at the time the largest gathering of government leaders in modern history. Helen spoke at the Forum about progress towards nuclear disarmament and the leadership role that New Zealand has taken on this issue.

———

Thank you for the invitation to participate in this opening session of the State of the World Forum. I have been asked to participate today as the leader of one of the seven nations in the New Agenda grouping which has taken a key role in pushing forward the agenda for nuclear disarmament. Our nations are a group of countries which cross the traditional North–South divide and have escaped the old straitjackets of the Cold War groupings of East, West and Non-aligned. We are Brazil, Egypt, Mexico, Ireland, Sweden, South Africa and New Zealand.

We came together in mid-1998 on a platform to inject new momentum into the pursuit of the total elimination of nuclear weapons. Support from the overwhelming majority of United Nations' members indicated that there was a new level of demand for action—and action now—by the nuclear weapons states to disarm. That action required, in the New Agenda countries' view, an unequivocal undertaking by the nuclear weapons states to the total elimination of their nuclear weapons, coupled with an undertaking to an accelerated process of negotiations delivering nuclear disarmament to which all states are committed under the NPT.

The New Agenda grouping set its sights firmly on the opportunity of the recent Nuclear Non-Proliferation Treaty (NPT) Review Conference to progress its agenda for a nuclear-weapons-free world. The pressure was on the five nuclear weapons states parties to breathe new life into the NPT, which stands as the cornerstone of arms control and disarmament.

The good news is they did respond. The five nuclear weapons states have agreed to make an 'unequivocal undertaking to accomplish the total elimination of their arsenals' in terms which heighten our hopes for future disarmament negotiations especially in the next five-year review period. The nuclear weapons states have agreed to a set of practical steps which go far beyond any earlier specific commitments. They include an agreement by the five acknowledged nuclear weapons states to provide more information on their nuclear capabilities and the implementation of disarmament agreements. They must also reduce their non-strategic nuclear weapons arsenals.

The five are also to take concrete measures to reduce further the operational status of their nuclear weapons systems. On 1 May they announced that none of their weapons remained targeted, but they have now promised to go further.

It was also agreed that nuclear arms reductions and disarmament are to be governed by the principle of 'irreversibility'. Where weapons are taken out of active arsenals and dismantled under disarmament agreements, they would not just be stockpiled and available for future reassembly, but rather would be rendered unusable forever. That should help lock in an end to the nuclear arms race.

Another encouraging result was the endorsement of the United States–Russian bilateral START process, including negotiations on START III.

To complement those efforts, the conference also agreed on the need for further unilateral efforts to reduce nuclear arsenals. The United Kingdom, France and China have accepted that they must in time join the largest nuclear weapons states in disarmament efforts.

Non-nuclear weapons states have been raising concerns about the option retained by Russia and NATO to use nuclear weapons in a first strike. There have also been worrying attempts to find a new role for nuclear weapons as a deterrent for chemical biological weapons. It was especially pleasing therefore to have the review conference agree that nuclear weapons should play a diminishing role in security policies.

The conference outcome was also designed to break the long-running stalemate at the Conference on Disarmament in Geneva. It has been told to get down to work on the 'cut off' negotiations to end the production of fissile material for nuclear weapons. It must also begin formal talks on wider issues of nuclear disarmament.

Finally, the Review Conference endorsed the moratorium on nuclear testing in the period before the coming into force of the Comprehensive Test Ban Treaty, thus strengthening the norm which we have urged Pakistan and India to meet.

It is fair to say that New Zealand and its New Agenda partners did not achieve all that we jointly wished at the NPT Review Conference. There is still, for example, no set time for progressing the measures agreed to at the conference, although progress will be monitored over the five-year review period. And some of the new commitments are explicitly or implicitly conditioned on developments which could yet prove negative.

Among these are the United States' proposals for a national missile defence system and the extent of opposition to it—most significantly from Russia and China, themselves nuclear weapons states. Russia has threatened to tear up the START I and II treaties, and walk away from START III negotiations, if its concerns about US missile defence are not addressed. China is worried that a US missile shield will render its smaller nuclear force irrelevant, and may respond by new efforts to enlarge its arsenal.

New Zealand's concern about deployment of the National Missile Defence System is that it could retard or even unravel nuclear disarmament efforts. We believe that front-line defence against the delivery of long-range missiles of weapons of mass destruction lies in:

- strengthened implementation of the Nuclear Non-Proliferation Treaty and its supporting regime

- full implementation of the Chemical Weapons Convention

- an effective verification regime for the Biological Weapons convention

- and on strict control on access to missile technology and components.

The Nuclear Non-Proliferation Treaty contains the obligation to negotiate nuclear disarmament. New Zealand strongly cautions against any act which could bring current bilateral and multilateral efforts to a halt, and harm existing arms-control treaties. While all countries have a stake in global security, we believe that the most powerful nations have a special duty to act with care and prudence, and with a strong sense of responsibility for the consequences of their actions.

Notwithstanding these concerns, we do believe that the NPT Review Conference broke new ground. The outcome exceeded expectations, invigorating the NPT at a time when pervasive pessimism about the nuclear disarmament agenda threatened to weaken the treaty's credibility and play into the hands of the nuclear proliferators.

This is obviously not a time for complacency. Implementation of the new NPT commitments is likely to take time. There will be obstacles. The nuclear weapons states will want progress to be dictated by their assessment of their own security environment. Current military doctrines foresee the retention of nuclear arms well into the future. Unfortunately, commitment to rapid reductions in nuclear stockpiles is not strong.

New Zealand will continue to play a leadership role on these issues. Disarmament and arms control initiatives must be constantly pushed, and we will keep pushing. New Zealand will continue its strong involvement in the New Agenda efforts at the United Nations and in the Conference on Disarmament in Geneva to ensure that there is follow-through on NPT commitments.

But the efforts of a small nation like New Zealand and its New Agenda colleagues on their own are not enough. All countries must fulfil their commitments to the elimination of weapons of mass destruction. Public opinion worldwide must be mobilised again as it was in the 1980s. Non-governmental organisations must play a vital role, working alongside committed governments.

I know that the State of the World Forum has been active in this area for many years. You supported the Six Nation Peace Initiative in the 1980s in an early effort to stimulate a change of mindset in the last years of the Cold War. The Middle Powers Initiative is the newest network supporting the New Agenda governments, and it has a wealth of expertise and experience in the field of nuclear disarmament.

Civil society organisations are demonstrating that they are more effective than ever. The Ottawa Convention banning landmines was driven by the work of many NGOs which forced governments to tackle what they thought was unachievable. New tools, such as the internet, break down traditional barriers between people, and help mobilise public opinion not just nationally but internationally.

The world must not retreat to the days when the doctrine of nuclear armament and deterrence seemed unchangeable. Perhaps our greatest challenge is complacency. We must take the opportunities that are available in this new century of globalisation to prevent a renewed nuclear arms race and to work for disarmament. We all have a stake in the security of the twenty-first century, and we must all work together to eliminate the dangers posed by weapons of mass destruction as we strive to free our world from the fear of the catastrophe of war.

I would like to conclude my remarks by commenting on why a small nation like New Zealand, so remote from major conflicts, takes these issues so seriously and involves itself so wholeheartedly in the multilateral systems offered by the United Nations and other international agencies.

In the 1970s, 1980s and 1990s, New Zealand took a number of unilateral initiatives for nuclear disarmament. We went so far as to declare ourselves nuclear-free as a nation. We did so because of our belief in the immorality of nuclear weapons and because we knew that nuclear war would be a catastrophe for our planet.

Perhaps as a small nation without enemies, in a benign strategic environment, we have had a greater freedom to raise these issues. But what we also know is that our individual actions must be backed up by the dedication to hard, slow, painstaking work at the multilateral level. Every state, large and small, has a voice. It is up to each nation how it uses that voice. We choose to use ours to call for strong, binding rules and conventions to make the world a safer, healthier, more socially responsible and prosperous place in which to live.

No nation can achieve all these outcomes on its own. But together we can. This must be our hope as an international community of peoples in the twenty-first century.

Achieving Equality in New Zealand

St Andrew's on The Terrace, Wellington
3 April 2001

St Andrew's on The Terrace describes itself as 'a lively and active faith community' with a commitment to creating a just and peaceful world. In 1991, St Andrew's officially declared itself an 'inclusive church', meaning it would welcome all people, no matter their beliefs, class, race or sexual orientation. Helen gave the following talk as part of a series of lunchtime lectures hosted by the church.

Thank you for the invitation to participate in this series of lunchtime addresses on the broad theme of achieving equality in New Zealand. The desirability of achieving greater equality is certainly one of the cornerstone beliefs of the Labour–Alliance government.

Nobody pretends that it is an easy objective.

Market forces let loose on New Zealand in our recent past did lead to inequality deepening at a faster rate in our country than almost anywhere else in the Western world. Others have suggested, and I agree, that New Zealand, a small, vulnerable and geographically isolated economy, which had long had the 'quest for security'—as Dr W.B. Sutch termed it—central to its policy framework, was probably the worst place in the world to launch into neo-liberal excesses and experiments.

Yet that happened here, and we must now deal with the consequences.

In the years of aberration, our economy and social policies were turned upside down and inside out, leaving broken communities, families and individuals in their wake. The disturbing statistics which now confront us on crime and family violence and the return of infectious diseases previously well under control should shock us all.

None of that can be changed overnight, and our government has never claimed that a magic wand was at hand. But what we are about is a new beginning, a fresh start and the necessary steps in a new direction. We acknowledge the problems. We don't run away from them, nor do we pretend they are not there. We do as much as we can in the short term, within the limited tax base and underperforming economy we have inherited. With our eyes firmly fixed on a better medium- and long-term outcome, we are working to put in place the foundation for something better, fairer and more sustainable for the future.

At this point, it is worth defining the notion of equality which forms the backdrop to our thinking. Personally I do not consider uniformity of income to be the goal. It is neither realistic nor do I think it desirable. There is for most of us a desire to be rewarded in some way or other for our efforts. But, having said that, there is deep in social Christian and social democratic philosophy a belief that we are each other's keepers and that we have a responsibility to each other.

Applied to government and to how the powers of the state are exercised that does lead us towards policies which redistribute in the broader public interest, and top up the income and life chances of those who would otherwise fall to an unacceptably low standard of living. The aim of that redistribution should not be to sustain people at a bleak level of subsistence which leaves them without any hope. That, in effect, was the outcome of the social policy changes of the 1990s. Rather, I think the aim should be to enable all to live at a level which enables each to participate in society around them. The concept of participation brings us closer to how I think the concept of equality can be more usefully defined.

In the old New Zealand which brought Seddon's Liberals to power in the 1890s, and Michael Joseph Savage's Labour to power in the 1930s, there was a strong egalitarian streak. Jack was as good as his master. These days we must of course add Jill into the equation as well. That was the New Zealand I was born into in 1950. It was far from perfect in that, just as Athenian democracy did not extend beyond a privileged few, so seldom were the rights of women, Māori, ethnic minorities, people with disabilities or homosexual New Zealanders acknowledged in 1950s New Zealand.

One of the challenges of subsequent decades has been to extend and promote the rights of all groups in society, and now, in the post neo-liberal era, to reclaim that old egalitarian streak for the twenty-first century.

My concept of equality, then, centres on the notion of equality of citizenship and equality of opportunity. The full rights of citizenship should be denied to no New Zealander. For me, those rights include the right to fair treatment, the right to opportunity to reach one's full potential, and the right to security when one is unable to sustain oneself.

Then, alongside the rights of citizenship go the responsibilities of citizenship. We each have a responsibility to contribute to the maintenance of the society, to its institutions, infrastructure and well-being, and we have the responsibility of sustaining ourselves to the extent that that is possible before accepting the security offered by the state where it is not.

I turn now to how our government is addressing issues of inequality. To the extent that we can, with the small cake which is the New Zealand economy and tax base, we are striving to even up life chances. Our direction is clear. My only regret is that we cannot do more and faster. I am very aware of how thinly stretched many household budgets are. Raising the minimum wage substantially and bringing in fair labour legislation are among the ways in which we aim to make a difference.

We start with the premise that a secure and affordable home is the bedrock on which a decent life is founded. In a secure and affordable home are the conditions for better health, and certainly for children a chance to enable one's potential through education to be realised. It is very difficult to do your homework when you are sharing your home with two or three other families. We have abandoned the destructive 1990s policy of charging market rents to all state tenants—a policy, I believe, which carries a very heavy responsibility for having cast tens of thousands of New Zealand families into poverty. That and the benefit cuts of 1991 taken together marginalised a significant minority of New Zealanders.

In 1998 that marginalisation was extended to superannuitants, who also had their standard of living slashed. The effect of lowering superannuation to the level decreed by the 1998 cuts would have been to throw between one-third and half of all superannuitants below the poverty line. That is obviously unacceptable. From 1 April last year the level of New Zealand Superannuation was restored to that agreed in the 1993 Superannuation Accord. That restored level is estimated to be sufficient to enable superannuitants to live in dignity and participate in society.

From 1 December last year the state house rentals became income-related again. The average decrease in rents granted was over $33 a week. For many it was substantially higher. And those households now have a chance to feed and clothe themselves and heat their homes in winter without falling into debt.

We also moved back to an allocation system for state housing based on housing need. In the market-rents era, allocation was based simply on ability to pay. Surely there could be no greater perversion than that of the state housing ideal set out by Michael Joseph Savage and John A. Lee. Now the challenge is to see that state tenants are accommodated in appropriate housing. In the high-rent, low-maintenance era of state housing, too many were in homes which were too small, and too damp and cold.

In a new healthy-housing programme launched in Auckland last month, we are moving to extend and/or modify almost 1,000 state houses in Onehunga, Ōtara and Māngere, where there has been particular concern about both overcrowded housing and its health consequences, such as higher levels of infectious diseases like meningitis. Indeed part of the programme involves co-operation between the public health and housing authorities. It is seeing Housing New Zealand tenancy officers trained to spot signs of serious illness like meningitis when they are visiting homes, and then encouraging people to seek urgent medical advice. I know of one case in Auckland where on the very day that a tenancy officer had that training, she visited her neighbour's house where a baby was exhibiting all the signs of meningitis which she had learned about that day. She urged her neighbour to take the baby to hospital. The verdict was that the baby would have almost certainly died if she had not taken that action.

Equality of opportunity through education is a top priority for the government. Our policies for schools are redistributive. When bulk-funding was abolished and the full budget for it was reallocated, the reallocation was weighted to lower decile schools.

On that same principle, a working party has been looking in recent months at how to introduce equity funding concepts into early childhood education funding to address the education disadvantage for small children which can spring from low income, rural isolation and non-English-speaking homes.

One of the most debated issues at international gatherings I attended last year was the digital divide opened up by unequal access to the new communications and information technologies. If no steps are taken to equalise access, then that divide will become a great gulf limiting the potential and opportunity of less advantaged communities. We have a number of initiatives under way to get the new technologies into lower decile schools. Many of those schools are also making their own moves. I was personally inspired by a recent visit to Waikohu College at Te Karaka outside Gisborne. There a cyber academy—they call it the 'cyberwaka'—has been set up to enable sixth- and seventh-form students to study for a CISCO computing qualification while still at school. That qualification will enable them to be work-ready in an area of skill shortage when they leave school.

In February, our government signed a digital opportunity protocol with leading information and communications technology companies to pilot a range of new initiatives for computer-based learning in low-decile schools.

High levels of education are obviously critical in every respect to New Zealand. We live in an age where information is power. Without education, the ability to access and comprehend information and to participate effectively in society is limited and job prospects are poor. Education has both intrinsic and material benefits. For society as a whole, high levels of education tend to equate with more progressive, tolerant, outward-looking communities. They also tend to equate with higher standards of living.

If we are serious about greater economic and social equality, then empowerment through education is critical for less advantaged communities. But, as well, lifting education participation and achievement is critical for the future of New Zealand as a whole. If we want higher standards of living for New Zealanders, we have to address the causes of our national decline. The big inequality staring at us is the inequality which has developed between us and other First World nations. The path our country has been on not only deepened inequality internally, but also did nothing to arrest our decline in living-standards ratings relative to the rest of the world.

It is no time for complacency. I am aware of a range of positive statistics about the New Zealand economy. It's good that unemployment at 5.6 per cent is at its lowest since June 1988. It's good that the economy has been growing, and exporting has been booming, and that tourism is doing well. It's good that people are feeling more confident, both as consumers and as business investors. And it's good that the current account deficit is coming down.

But unfortunately our economy remains far too dependent on good luck rather than on good management and foresight. We have had the good luck of good weather. We have had the good luck of high commodity prices, and we have benefited from an excessively competitive dollar. But the nation doesn't strike that trifecta very often.

What our government is acutely conscious of is the race for better living standards internationally. We have to lift our game as a whole society so that we are better able to address the inequality of access to opportunities at home.

The extent to which New Zealand has been slipping behind other nations is of great concern, and our government is determined to do something about it. That has led us to give a great deal of thought as to what the role of the state should be in the twenty-first century. Certainly, in my political lifetime, political leadership on economic issues has ranged from the totally heavy-handed under the Economic Stabilisation Act to the totally hands-off in the neo-liberal years to 1999. There has to be another way. The other way in the twenty-first century is to see government very active in leading, facilitating, co-ordinating, brokering and funding, and providing when necessary.

We need a vision for the kind of country we can be. The vision the government is aiming at sees New Zealanders as innovators to the world, turning great ideas into great ventures. To achieve that we need to lift our educational achievement, drive up our expenditure on science, research and development, and provide the means to commercialise the discoveries of our talented people where those discoveries have commercial potential. You will hear us talk a good deal about incubators attached to our universities, and seed capital for fledging businesses with good ideas. These moves are all part of how we drag the New Zealand economy up market. It's not something that can be done by a government alone. It needs buy-in from the community, and at the individual level it needs people being prepared to go that extra mile in education and skills training and in business investment.

Our government is taking an active interest in supporting and co-ordinating the development of industries with good potential. Wood processing is one example. Many years ago a lot of forestry planting was done in New Zealand, but no planning followed the planting. We are now facing a wall of wood ready for harvesting. Much of it is in regions which have known high unemployment for more than twenty-five years. If nothing is done, that wall of wood will be harvested, trucked to the ports, and exported with only minimal benefit accruing to New Zealand. Over three years from 2000 to 2003 the wood supply will increase by 50 per cent across the country. Between 2000 and 2010 it will quadruple on the East Coast of the North Island. Our challenge now is to attract more investment into the processing infrastructure and to create both more job opportunities and a better price for the end product when it leaves New Zealand. We are actively involved in persuading investors that an adequate skills base and communications infrastructure is here for an enlarged wood-processing industry to prosper.

I return back to the initial point about equality. Right now we do as much as we can in social policy with a shrunken tax base and an economy which has underperformed in the long term. But, to really deliver in the way in which people attracted to lecture series like this would like to see government deliver, we are going to have to grow the cake a great deal. That means doing whatever we can to provide access to opportunity through education, and intelligent government backing for business growth, science and research. The aim is to endow New Zealand with a different kind of economy which is not dependent on good luck, but is driven by the bright ideas and talents of its people.

I am very confident that in the transition to a new economy we will see a great deal more employment created. I do not believe unemployment should be seen as bottoming out at 5.6 per cent. That still leaves over 100,000 New Zealanders out of work. That is a level we would have thought intolerable 20 years ago. So we still have a long way to go.

I believe that we have it within ourselves and within the capacity of our country to make the changes which will transform our economy and enable us to deliver more opportunity to our people. The overall goal is to build a fairer, better, more secure society. There is no particular merit in having a strong economy for its own sake. A strong economy is needed for what it can deliver for our citizens. It enables us to deliver opportunity and security to all our communities. A strong economy is essential to achieving equality in New Zealand.

Seminar on Social Policy

Wellington
1 July 2001

*Sir Tony Atkinson was a leading British economist and warden
of Nuffield College, Oxford University, whose work in the field of
inequality and poverty studies was groundbreaking. He visited
New Zealand in 2001 and gave a series of seminars on trends in
social policy in Europe and the United Kingdom. In her speech at
one of these events, Helen spoke about the history of social policy
in New Zealand and her views on the way forward.*

———

It is refreshing to have Sir Tony Atkinson in New Zealand as a social
policy commentator. So often high-profile social commentators tour as
guests of the business round table, preaching a dreary gospel with which
we became all too familiar, over the many years of neo-liberalism's reign
in New Zealand. In those years the original vision of the New Zealand
welfare state was barely visible at all, as the struggling beneficiaries of
it were written off as hopeless bludgers who should go and get a job, or
get well, or grow younger.

I became politically aware when Norman Kirk was Leader of the
Labour Party and articulated quite a different set of values from that. He

spoke of the welfare state not as something which limited or restricted people, but as something which liberated people and set them free to reach their potential. Decades earlier, Walter Nash had spoken of the first charge on the state as being the needs of the young, the old, the sick, the unemployed and the widowed. Our government today is working towards rebuilding a New Zealand which is kinder and fairer in a twenty-first-century setting.

Social democracy has always been about trying to find a balance between market and society. Too much market and the social consequences are dire, as we know from our own recent national experience. On the other hand, an excess of caring without the prosperity to fund it also leads to ruin. That is why Sir Tony Atkinson's message about the importance of integration of economic and social goals and policies is so critical.

As a minister in the second term of the Fourth Labour Government, I could see very well that its economic and social policies were poorly aligned. For example, as fast as I, as Minister of Housing, could build new state houses in Auckland, people were crowding into the city from other parts of New Zealand, where corporatisation had wiped away jobs, and the rapid removal of subsidies on agriculture had ravished provincial economies. I am not suggesting that inefficient state companies and farm subsidies should have remained in situ, but rather that restructuring does need to be accompanied by measures which redeploy and upskill displaced workforces, and which facilitate the emergence of new industries in the place of the old. Only now is attention being given to that kind of support.

What has often struck me about neo-liberalism is how fundamentally anarchic it is. Neo-liberals relish the withering of the state, except in its coercive powers, which become so necessary to constrain the human wreckage which falls through the cracks of society as a result of their policies.

In the social democratic paradigm, however, the role of the state is critical. But it is not the role of the welfare state pioneers of New Zealand and Sweden in the 1930s, nor for those in Britain in the late 1940s. That era predates sweeping globalisation and the rapid mobility of labour and capital across borders. A nation back in those days was more like a cocoon: economies and societies were heavily regulated, and populations were largely accepting of that.

Those days have gone. Today's social democrats operate in an environment where it is critical to maintain the confidence of business for the nation's economic health, and critical to carve out the nation's competitive niche in the international economy.

At the same time, the nation's social health must be safeguarded—and, in New Zealand's case, it cries out for considerable improvement. The new role for the state becomes one of leadership, facilitation, co-ordination, brokering and in the social policy area of funding and provision. There is also a role—showing through in the work of Industry New Zealand and other initiatives—for active government to support economic development.

The state can define the values which are important in the nation's development. We also need to be not only innovative and enterprising to sustain economic prosperity in the twenty-first century, but also collaborative, compassionate and inclusive. Those values are not in conflict and, if taken together, can advance the economic and social health of the country substantially.

The challenge which lay before our new government was how to build support for a shared vision in New Zealand incorporating that broad range of values. Government changed hands in New Zealand at the last election precisely because people were looking for a better balance in our national life and for a broader shared vision. The direction we were going in was doomed—ever lower taxes, ever fewer public services, ever more crumbling infrastructure, ever less regulation, resulting, in the end, not in nirvana but in a state of misery for all but the most affluent, who could live behind the high walls they built.

We said we couldn't change the world overnight but we would like to make a good start. The compass had to be reset in a direction more in keeping with traditional New Zealand values of fairness, security and opportunity. We spent most of the first year in government addressing some of the most immediate concerns: lifting the level of superannuation; restoring income-related rentals for state houses; improving the student-loan system; abolishing bulk funding, a system which was so divisive for education; providing extra funding for elective surgery; raising minimum wage levels; repealing the Employment Contracts Act; reinstating ACC as a social insurance scheme; and raising the top tax rate to help pay for the essential social and economic infrastructure. We defied the conventional wisdom that parties couldn't win an election if they said they would raise taxes.

In the first nine months after the election, the government's focus was very much on the delivery up front of those core commitments. Apart from strongly believing that they were the right policies to be implementing, there was another very important reason for carrying them through. One of the legacies of neo-liberalism in New Zealand was the rise in the level of cynicism about the political process. Few people felt that they had ever voted for the policies which formed the dominant paradigm in New Zealand in the 1980s and 1990s. And, indeed, generally they had not voted for them. Eventually, if the act of voting consistently fails to deliver what the popular will wants, indifference to the whole process results and participation declines. Yet participation in society and its processes is itself central to the social democratic vision. Cynicism is very destructive of social democracy.

There is an old saying that without hope the people perish. Our job was to bring hope that things could be different, and, while acknowledging that substantial change would take time, to show that there were things which could be done immediately and which would make the change of direction clear, restoring hope in the political process.

While the change of direction was widely applauded and the government was given full marks for keeping its word, there was a reaction to our programme. It came in the decline in business confidence and in apprehension in that sector that the policy pendulum would keep swinging left to the extreme discomfort of business. That was never our intention. The government was very clearly focused on resetting the compass at a different point, and then in carrying on in a linear direction from there. We believed that it was possible to develop a broadly shared vision around that direction about the future of New Zealand, and to avoid polarisation around extreme viewpoints. To achieve that our style had to be inclusive too, and not set out to marginalise, except at the very extreme, those who had a different perspective but who also wanted a better future for New Zealand.

The style of politics the government has been engaged in has a very clear link to the goal of enhancing participation in society's processes. The style has seen us engage in a series of conversations with different sectors of society. The origins of those conversations vary. There are those in which we have been engaged for a very long time, for example with the labour unions. That relationship goes back to the formation of the Labour Party in 1916, and policy dialogue there is ongoing. There have also been relationships with many NGOs built up over the years. Then there is the central local government forum, which was foreshadowed before the last election and which has been successful in producing a shared vision for the future of local government.

There is a great deal of contact with Māoridom, and a real desire on the government's part to develop a partnership model where we support initiatives which come up from the community itself, rather than forcing community initiatives into preordained programmes. Traditionally the approach of government has been to say: 'have we got a great programme for you'. The strategies which emerge from the community's experiences, however, have a better chance of working. This is a new way of thinking, and it has not been fully operationalised, but it is the concept the government is endeavouring to follow in its interaction with Māoridom, and it has implications for interaction with the broader NGO sector.

An innovation in the second half of our first eighteen months in government was to find a way to engage business in conversation about the future, and to do so in a way which linked ideas about economic and social progress. The business-to-government forums enabled the dialogue to be established, although a number of other factors have also helped improve the relationship.

First, there was a realisation within business that the doom and gloom talk had become a self-fulfilling prophecy, and that if confidence was talked down investment and spending dropped and nobody benefited.

Second, despite the pessimism, the economy was recovering. Competitive exchange rates fuelled exporting, further aided by good farm seasons and good commodity prices. Unemployment is at its lowest level in thirteen years. New Zealand has just had its first current account quarterly surplus in seven years. The economy continues to grow modestly while other major trading partners face considerable difficulty.

Third, directional changes in areas like accident compensation and industrial law did not result in the worst fears of the business community being realised. For accident compensation, employers are actually paying less overall with the return to the social insurance model than they were before. With the Employment Relations Act, the emphasis on relationship building, good faith and mediation has been very productive. Indeed, I was talking only two days ago to someone on the employers' side of a dispute who had been engaged in mediation. The mediation had not as yet achieved an outcome, but he was very positive about the process.

Fourth, the credibility of the old hard-line voice of business has suffered because of its destructiveness, culminating in the underhand brain drain publicity designed to embarrass the government. Other organisations, like the New Zealand Business Council for Sustainable Development, have gained traction with their advocacy of the triple bottom line approach to business and the economy which says that economic, social and environmental considerations need to be balanced.

So where to from here? In the past eighteen months, new concepts have become established in the national debate about our future. The concept of the knowledge society conveys an inclusive vision of what New Zealand can be. The government has talked of pursuing a strategy of economic transformation, which to succeed must be augmented and go hand in hand with a social transformation strategy. The vision we have for New Zealand is not only for the nation to be more prosperous per se, but for that prosperity to be linked with fairness, and with more opportunity and security. We won't improve overall living standards if a significant proportion of New Zealanders is left behind with poor levels of education and low health status, and is badly housed or only occasionally employed.

So, alongside our economic agenda runs a substantial social agenda. Well-housed, healthy families, for example, are more likely to be able to take advantage of educational and employment opportunities. Superannuitants able to live in dignity can make an enormous contribution to the well-being of society, as can others who are not in paid work but who are supported to live in dignity.

We are now building on the early moves in superannuation, housing and health. Having restored the level of superannuation to one able to sustain people so they can participate in society, the planning has moved on to how to sustain in the long term a universal, adequate level of superannuation. The government has developed the concept of saving now to save superannuation for the future. Legislation is before parliament to provide for the long-term financing of superannuation as the number of New Zealanders in older age groups rises. The legislation will pass and, I believe, become part of the fabric of social security provision for the long term.

In housing policy, the government's first step was to bring back income-related rents for state houses. Now the government is looking at how to link together health and housing initiatives. There has been a very good initiative begun in Auckland suburbs with a high rate of meningococcal meningitis, an illness which thrives in conditions of overcrowded housing. A programme is under way in key suburbs such as Onehunga, Māngere and Ōtara to move families from poor-quality and overcrowded housing into better accommodation. Houses are being modified with improvements like insulation, which is critical to keeping a house warm and healthy.

The public health system is involved in the programme, and works with tenancy officers. Tenancy officers are given instruction on how to recognise illness which might be going undetected, with a particular focus on identifying meningococcal meningitis. There is a recent example of an Ōtara tenancy officer spotting a case of meningitis. The very day she had been on a course as part of the healthy-housing programme she was in a home where the baby showed signs of meningitis. She persuaded the family that a doctor should see the baby and it was soon in hospital with a case of meningitis diagnosed. Doctors told the tenancy worker that if she had turned up two hours later it would probably have been too late for the child.

It is a simple thing to have those who are in contact with the community, in a regular way like a tenancy officer, able to know enough to realise that something might be badly wrong. I thought it was a wonderful and heart-warming story.

The health system is a critical part of welfare state provision. Labour never supported the Americanisation of the New Zealand health system which began in 1991. Commercial boards were appointed to run the system and the community voice was removed from health decision-making. Our vision always was to move back to a collaborative system, with community involvement in decision-making, to set clear health status goals to improve the population's health overall, to stress equity of access and to enable New Zealanders to live the full course of their natural lives as healthy as possible. That vision was based on the WHO's 'Health for All by the Year 2000'. As Minister of Health in 1990, I thought we had a reasonable chance of getting somewhere near that goal. But the year 2000 has now come and gone, without New Zealand making enough progress towards it. The WHO's approach to primary healthcare, however, remains highly relevant. Primary healthcare cannot be fully effective in the absence of access to education, decent housing, adequate income, employment and a healthy environment, nor without peace and stability.

In the recent past in New Zealand, the conditions for effective primary healthcare were compromised, as the cost of public housing rose beyond the means of low-income households, as unemployment at the beginning of the 1990s rose to double figures in percentage terms, and as beneficiary and superannuitants' incomes were cut. The Employment Contract Act era saw little upward movement of incomes for the low paid and low skilled, and there was little opportunity to upskill. Those were the years of cutbacks to essential social services, when teachers doubled up their responsibilities as social workers, and when poverty became more widespread, taking its toll especially on children. One particular effect was an increase of dental disease. Until 1991, the number of caries in a child's teeth had declined very significantly nationwide to on average one at the age of twelve. The growth of poverty in the 1990s saw the rise of caries in children's teeth. There is also a very direct link between the rise of poverty and the spread of the infectious diseases like meningococcal meningitis.

Health outcomes cannot be changed by health policy alone. We needed to make a concerted attack on those areas where the pre-conditions for effective primary healthcare had been compromised. That reinforced the need for policies like raising the level of superannuation so that it was adequate to maintain older people in good health and dignity, having an enlightened public housing policy with rents which were fair and affordable, raising the minimum wage, and changing the Employment Contracts Act so that workers have a more level playing field on which to bargain. All these policies reinforce a health policy aimed at reducing health inequity. To improve health status, socio-economic issues must be addressed on a wide front.

The first year of the government's term saw important health legislation setting up the district health boards. Their job is to work holistically to improve the health status of their communities, to work collaboratively with stakeholders and communities, and to provide effective services. There has also been a great deal of heath strategy development. The New Zealand Health Strategy has been released, along with the primary care strategy. A Māori health strategy is out for consultation. There are new goals and objectives being set for Pacific people's health. A sexual and reproductive health strategy is planned for release in August. The New Zealand Disabilities Strategy has been developed in full consultation with the disability sector and is now being implemented.

In the government's first Budget, we concentrated initially on reducing waiting times for elective surgery. A very big commitment was also made to mental health. Over the next year and coming years, we are signalling that a major focus will be on primary healthcare. The proposals we have for primary health organisations envisage much more community participation in the planning and co-ordination of services at the primary care level, with the primary health organisations providing a mechanism for funding primary care services. Primary health organisations will need to have credible community input and participation.

The government is also looking at the access to primary healthcare. How could we fund primary care better? We are one of the few OECD countries where people pay significant fees for primary medical care. The public purse pays less than 40 per cent of the total cost of GP consultations over the whole country each year. Most adults pay the full cost of their consultation, and even those entitled to a subsidy are paying over a half to two-thirds of the cost on average. Costs such as these create barriers to timely access and eventually create more demand for hospital services, putting more pressure on secondary services. That is counterproductive. The challenge now is how to improve the funding. Improvements will need to be phased in, and they will be expensive, but it is clear that primary healthcare has to be the focus of much of the new spending on health in the coming years.

In Māori health, there are exciting developments underway. The government is keen to support Māori primary healthcare provision and co-ordination. There are already substantial networks of Māori health planners, strategists and providers. Many are very sophisticated. They deserve to be supported and partnered.

The role of education in the transformation of the economy and the society is obvious. The government's education policies have a strong equity focus. For the first time, for example, equity funding is being introduced into early childhood education funding. More funding is being put into the Pacific Island early childhood education sector, which has been under resourced. Its early childhood initiatives have found it hard to get registered and thereby qualify for the subsidies that are available. There is increased support for the low-decile schools. The bulk funding reallocation has been very much weighted to those schools, as are the digital opportunity programmes underway at present.

In tertiary education, achieving greater equity of access has been a major concern. That is why we have made student loans more affordable and endeavoured to freeze fees. Also of great interest to the government is improving the quality of tertiary education. You will be hearing quite a lot more in the course of the next year as to how we can stop the destructive competition which drives low-quality rather than high-quality provision.

The government has made skills training a high priority. Industry training is now much better funded, and the new apprenticeship initiatives are popular.

In the twenty-first century our economy needs more educated and skilled people, and more activity along the spectrum of science, research, development, innovation and new ideas for products and services. To develop that spectrum the government is funding centres of excellence in tertiary institutions, has increased funding for science and research, and improved tax treatment of research and development to encourage investment in it by the private sector.

Business incubators are being linked to tertiary institutions to support the commercialisation of research in New Zealand. In a move which complements these policies, the government is co-hosting with Auckland University the Knowledge Wave Conference, which is looking at how New Zealand can become an advanced knowledge society. The Science and Innovation Advisory Council is working on a national innovation strategy and an action plan to implement it.

Our vision for New Zealand also includes the building of a distinct identity around what is unique about us: Māoridom, the substantial Pacific component to our population, and several generations of Pākehā who have made this country their home and who look on the world with eyes quite different from those of the Old World from which our forebears came. We also have many new communities which are contributing to a very diverse society.

I have emphasised today the importance of linking progressive economic and social policy to build a fairer, more prosperous society. Each three-year term in government provides an opportunity to take the steps towards that overall vision. New Zealand can't go from misery to nirvana in one term of office, but over time we know we can build a better society.

Sir Arnold Nordmeyer Memorial Lecture

University of Otago School of Medicine, Wellington
7 August 2001

Sir Arnold Nordmeyer was a Labour MP who, among other things, served as Minister of Health from 1941 to 1947 and was Leader of the Opposition from 1963 to 1965. During his time as Health Minister, he was responsible for introducing state subsidies on doctor's visits. After his retirement from politics in 1969, he was appointed a Knight Commander of the Order of St Michael and St George 'for public services' in the 1975 Queen's Birthday Honours. The Sir Arnold Nordmeyer Memorial Lecture is hosted each year by the University of Otago medical school.

Thank you for the invitation to give this year's Nordmeyer Lecture. Sir Arnold Nordmeyer's contribution to public life was distinguished. He entered parliament in 1935 with the Labour landslide of that year as MP for Ōamaru. He played an active role in the development of the First Labour Government's social security policy, before himself becoming Minister of Health for six years in 1941. He then served as Minister of

Industries and Commerce, and in Sir Walter Nash's government from 1957 to 1960 as Minister of Finance.

In 1963 Arnold Nordmeyer became the sixth Leader of the New Zealand Labour Party and its first New Zealand-born leader. He served for only two years as Leader before being displaced by Norman Kirk. He retired from parliament in 1969, but remained in public life as a member of the Wellington Hospital Board in the early 1970s and chaired the Council of this Clinical School when it was established in 1974. It is a wonderful tribute to Sir Arnold to have this annual address dedicated to him and, from this evening, the Large Lecture Theatre will also bear his name.

In my address this evening I will talk about the health and social security legacy of Sir Arnold and his colleagues, and about how that legacy was undermined by both economic insecurity and by neo-liberal policies which created significant poverty and inequity in New Zealand.

It has fallen to this Labour-led government to address health inequities in the context of addressing broader socio-economic inequity, while also endeavouring to build a stronger base to the economy so that it can fund better health and other essential services for the long term.

The first Labour Government came to power as the Great Depression was ending, with an active programme for economic and social justice. Central to its programme was social security, of which health policy was a key part. That government achieved a great deal in health policy, ensuring free public hospital care and access to a wide range of health benefits. Unlike its counterpart in Britain in the 1940s, however, it did not persist with its efforts to ensure free primary medical care. Peter Fraser and Walter Nash overruled Arnold Nordmeyer in refusing to prevent doctors charging a fee over and above the state payment for seeing a patient. That had long-term repercussions for the affordability of primary medical care in New Zealand.

Over time, the state failed to increase its expenditure on the General Medical Services Benefit in line with increases in doctors' charges. The benefit came to constitute a smaller and smaller part of the total price of a consultation. In 1991 the last government removed the universal nature of the benefit and replaced it with means-tested payments through the mechanism of the Community Services Card. Reforming this unsatisfactory system is one of the key health-policy issues our government is working on now.

In other respects too we find ourselves dealing with health issues similar in nature to those confronted by our forebears elected in the 1930s. The Great Depression impoverished many New Zealanders. Poverty and unemployment make for poor health. The First Labour Government tackled both on a broad front. It successfully promoted full employment, educational opportunity and social security. Throughout its fourteen years in office and for long after, New Zealanders experienced more social security than they had ever known, with beneficial effects for health status.

Economic security, however, proved elusive. The early fifties were relatively good years, with export revenues fuelled by the wool-prices boom which accompanied the Korean War. Korea has exceptionally cold winters, and the United Nations soldiers, including New Zealanders, needed all the woollen clothes they could get.

The good times were not to last. On the day that Mr Nordmeyer became the Minister of Finance in 1957, Treasury reported to him that export prices had fallen heavily while imports were running well ahead of the previous year. Mr Nordmeyer's first Budget set out to deal decisively with the balance of payments crisis, and was labelled the 'black Budget' for its pains. Economic upsets, often caused by our dependence on commodity exports and the vagaries of their trade, were to recur again.

In 1967 the economy was hit hard by the downturn in wool prices. In the early seventies, Britain entered the European Economic Community and could no longer import the same quantities of our farm produce. In 1974 the price of oil rose sharply, putting huge pressure on our ability to pay our way. Rapid deregulation between 1984 and 1987 produced an economic bubble, which burst in late 1987 after the crash of stocks on Wall Street. Since then, as before, ours has been a stop-go economy as we have ridden the commodity cycle and experienced its highs and lows. The Asian economic crisis of 1997/98 also left its mark.

The reaction to economic crisis in the 1980s brought the introduction of neo-liberal economic policies. In a short space of time New Zealand went from being one of the OECD's most protected and regulated economies to being one of the least.

Unfortunately, no adequate policies were put in place to support the redeployment and upskilling of displaced workforces, nor to facilitate the emergence of sunrise industries. It is only now that priority is being given to that. To add insult to injury, the 1990s saw far-reaching changes in social and labour market policy which removed the cushion they had provided against the effects of major economic dislocation. In those changes:

- The Employment Contracts Act 1991 limited the bargaining power of workers, leading to the creation of a secondary labour market of the less skilled and un-unionised, who saw little movement in their incomes in the 1990s.

- Public housing rentals were applied at market levels. The accommodation supplement did not make up the loss for low-income households in state houses, and many were impoverished.

- Social security benefits were cut significantly in 1991. The age of eligibility for New Zealand Superannuation rose rapidly in the 1990s, disrupting retirement plans for many, and superannuation itself was more harshly surcharged from 1991. In 1998 the last government made a decision to cut superannuation further, and that policy took effect in 1999.

- Unemployment reached double digits in percentage terms in the early 1990s.

These far-reaching changes radically reduced living standards for lower-income people and had an impact on health status. Many more New Zealanders were quite simply not only poorer, but also living in poverty. These were the years when the food banks became an essential social service, when teachers doubled their responsibilities as de facto social workers, and when the spread of poverty took its toll on health status, with especially noticeable effects on children. The increase in dental disease and the rising incidence of infectious diseases like meningococcal meningitis were signs of the problem.

Faced with the health fallout of far-reaching change like this, the health system cannot produce miracles. The system itself had also been subjected to massive change, which in Opposition we labelled as a process of Americanisation. Eventually more resources seemed to be devoured by a business model for worse health results. Over the years in Opposition, Labour planned a return to a collaborative health system with community participation built into decision-making again. The vision was for a system with clear health goals and a commitment to equity of access and to lifting health status. The vision was based on the WHO's strategy of health for all by the year 2000. Unfortunately, the year 2000 came and went, without New Zealand having made great strides in earlier years towards the goal, but nonetheless the WHO's approach to primary healthcare remains highly relevant. That approach suggests that primary healthcare cannot be fully effective in the absence of access to good education, decent housing, adequate income, employment, a healthy environment and in the absence of peace and stability. In the New Zealand context, it is also important to add Treaty and cultural dimensions, acknowledging the importance of all peoples in New Zealand being able to stand tall in our society.

This approach enables us to see healthcare and policy in its broader context. My own background and continuing interest in health issues leads me to look at policy and progress overall from a health perspective. I believe that if we are addressing the sources of socio-economic inequity generally, then we will have an impact on health inequities. As well, I believe there are important interventions which the health system itself can make.

The government has taken a number of steps to address the broader economic and social inequities. It is true that resources are constrained, but we prefer to focus on what we can do, rather than on what we can't. We have endeavoured to lift living standards for low-income earners through a variety of means and to increase the resources for education and healthcare initiatives in low-income communities. For example, minimum wage levels have had two annual adjustments in the past nineteen months and have been significantly improved, especially for young people. The Employment Relations Act has replaced the Employment Contracts Act in order to give a more level playing field for wage bargaining and also to encourage better relationships between workers and employers.

The level of New Zealand Superannuation was raised in April 2000 to restore older people's living standards. We reversed the cuts announced in 1998, which if they had been allowed to have their full impact would have seen from a third to half of older citizens fall under the poverty line. By bringing the Superannuation level back up to what was agreed in the 1993 Accord, and previously, as adequate to enable older people to live in dignity, we hope to see positive health impacts. We are now focused on the longer-term plan to secure superannuation. Our view is that if we save now as a nation, we can save New Zealand Superannuation for the future and prevent elder poverty. I expect the legislation setting up the new fund for superannuation to go through parliament in the coming months.

Income-related rentals for state houses were reintroduced from 1 December 1999, with an average decrease across tenants of around $33 per week. That figure is far higher in high priced housing markets like the one I represent in the central suburbs of Auckland. In the 1990s state tenants in my electorate often told me that they could not afford to continue to live in traditional state house suburbs like Mt Roskill and Sandringham.

The move back to income-related rentals has given more discretionary income to lower income households, taking the pressure off paying the essential bills for electricity, food costs, clothing and healthcare. The latest analysis from New Zealand Council of Christian Social Services on food bank usage states that already in the first three months of this year there were fewer state house tenant households among their clients, and there was a decrease in the proportion of applicants for food parcels paying more than 50 per cent of their income on housing costs.

We have also been mindful of the need to join up housing and health policy. A programme is under way in Ōtara, Māngere and Onehunga to relieve overcrowding in state houses, and to upgrade state houses so that they are warmer and better to live in. Another component of the programme has housing tenancy workers going on a short course organised by public health officials, to help them identify signs of serious illness like meningococcal meningitis. There is a heart-warming story about the day Ōtara tenancy workers took this course. One tenancy worker later went to visit her neighbour and noticed that the neighbour's baby had symptoms very much like what she had been briefed on earlier that day. She urged that the baby get medical attention. The report I had was that if they had not got medical attention within two hours the baby may well not have survived, or had its health status very severely compromised. It is interesting how what can look like small initiatives, such as the housing tenancy workers being better linked into public health strategies, can have a very significant health impact.

In education policy, the government has also had a strong equity focus.

We are mindful that adequate, effective education is a precondition for effective primary healthcare. In early childhood education we have introduced equity funding for the first time. We have been targeting the participation rates for Māori and Pacific Island children in early childhood education to endeavour to bring those rates up. There have also been scholarships established for Māori and Pacific people to train, both in early childhood education and in teaching generally.

In schools, the abolition of bulk funding freed up a substantial amount of funding for reallocation to schools. The reallocation formula is weighted to low decile schools. There have been a number of initiatives to improve the responsiveness of the school system to Māori and Pacific people, along with initiatives to ensure that digital opportunity is available in low-decile neighbourhoods.

At the tertiary level our equity focus has seen us reducing the costs of study, by improving the loan system and freezing tertiary fees.

At 5.4 per cent, unemployment is at its lowest level in thirteen years, and can go lower. Our overall economic strategy has at its end point the creation of a more prosperous society which is inclusive, healthier and lifts living standards.

Many initiatives have been undertaken in health policy in the last nineteen months. The year 2000 saw the passage of new legislation setting up the district health board framework. The boards are charged with working holistically to improve the health status of their communities, to work collaboratively with stakeholders, and to provide effective services. While we expect the boards to be business-like in the way they operate, they are not primarily businesses. Rather we see them as public services, aiming to do the best they possibly can with the resources available.

The theme of reducing inequalities runs through the New Zealand Health Strategy we released last year. Other strategies are emerging, or have emerged. We have had the primary healthcare strategy in February, the strategy for palliative care, and I understand the Māori health strategy is out for consultation. Goals and objectives are being set for a Pacific peoples' health strategy, and the sexual and reproductive health strategy is planned for release in August.

The New Zealand Disabilities Strategy has tremendous support from the disabilities sector, and was developed in close collaboration with that sector.

In our first Budget we sought to take the pressure off waiting times for elective surgery, and provided more funding aimed at securing about 27,000 extra operations. The aim of funding levels this year is to maintain waiting times at that new lower level. We have not funded hospitals to make further reductions because funding pressures and needs are also present elsewhere.

We have made a huge commitment over a four-year period from 2000 to implement the Mental Health Commission's blueprint for services. I am optimistic that at the end of the four years we will see the mental health service in better shape than we have ever seen it before in New Zealand.

Over the coming year, as the health minister has signalled, the focus needs to be on developments around the primary healthcare strategy. The strategy generally has been well received. It proposes establishing primary health organisations and through them to bring much more community participation to the planning and co-ordination of primary services.

New Zealand is one of the few OECD countries where people are paying significant fees for primary medical care. This is the long-term consequence of the First Labour Government's unfinished business in healthcare. Over time, New Zealand just did not budget enough to maintain effective universal primary medical care subsidies, and eventually their universal character was dropped. The public purse now pays less than 40 per cent of the cost of GP consultations across the whole country. The majority of adults pay full cost, and even those entitled to subsidies are paying over half to two-thirds of the cost of the average consultation fee. That creates barriers to timely access, and eventually creates more demand for hospital services than there need be.

The big challenge is how to improve the funding. Improvements are likely to have to be phased in. They will be expensive. Needless to say, with our ambition to improve services in health, as elsewhere, you would not expect personal income tax cuts to be a priority for our government.

A big change from the time of Nordmeyer's involvement in health policy is the recognition that mainstream services do not meet the needs of all groups in the population well. These days, the government is very keen to support the development of Māori primary healthcare provision and co-ordination. I know from my round of community visits that networks of Māori health planners, strategists and providers are well established and many are exceptionally sophisticated and well organised. We all know that Māori have significantly lower health status than other

New Zealanders. Relevant population-based primary healthcare together with employment, housing and education initiatives can change that. The government sees itself as a partner with Māori organisations working for change in those areas.

What we are endeavouring to encourage from the bureaucracy, across sectors, is an approach to communities which, rather than saying 'Have we got a great programme for you', asks 'What strategies do you have for the development of services for your community, and what role can your community-based organisations play in delivering those services?' My strong belief is that we can enable people to make the choices which support better health. As Minister of Health I launched ten New Zealand health goals. Now there are thirteen in the New Zealand Health Strategy.

Reducing tobacco consumption is a top priority in those goals. We believe that a combination of good smoke-free legislation, significant taxation levels, a health promotion approach and other initiatives will make a big difference to smoking rates. New Zealand has made more progress in reducing smoking over the years than have many other countries. In the Social Report 2001 released recently there are figures, based on 1999 comparisons, showing that New Zealand men have the second-lowest smoking prevalence rates in the world. I am afraid my own gender only comes in at thirteenth lowest for women. Smoking poses a very high threat to the health status of Māoridom.

Two days ago I launched a new campaign to reduce Māori smoking rates. This campaign is designed by Māori for Māori. Entitled 'It's About Whānau', it appeals to the strong Māori sense of family in urging smoking cessation. The messages are clear: stop smoking so you will see your mokopuna grow up, or because you want to be there for your children. I believe these messages will have a big impact.

An early evaluation of recent initiatives to provide nicotine replacement therapy through the Quitline has been done. The evaluation after three months showed that 44 per cent of those surveyed who had rung the Quitline since the nicotine-replacement therapy was available through it are—to use the official phrase—'currently quit'. That compared with 20 per cent of those who had rung Quitline prior to the availability of the nicotine-replacement therapy being 'currently quit'. Nineteen per cent of those surveyed who were on the patches and gum programme had been 'completely quit' for the three months. A survey of those who had used Quitline before the nicotine replacement therapy was available found that only 7 per cent were 'completely quit' after six months.

These results look encouraging. Certainly one of the big changes in the approach to smoke-free policy since I was Minister of Health has been the new emphasis on cessation, in contrast with the prevention focus of the 1980s and 1990s. Prevention remains very important, but obviously cessation has a big role to play too. The Quitline nicotine-replacement therapy programme appears to be reaching lower socio-economic groups. Only 25 per cent of those accessing patches and/or gum were in full-time paid employment or were self-employed, compared to 45 per cent of the population which falls into those categories. That is an encouraging result.

Immunisation is another priority area for action. Extra resources were made available for immunisation for the 2000–01 financial year. A catch-up campaign is underway to prevent measles, and its two cousins, mumps and rubella. I understand that the health minister has committed to the development of a national register for immunisation. Work is ongoing on procuring a meningococcal meningitis vaccine. It will be expensive.

With population-based approaches across areas like immunisation, tobacco, better nutrition, early detection of cancers and alcohol abuse, we can make a real difference in enabling people to make choices for better health. That is certainly a very high priority for me.

Our government knows that there are significant health inequities. We know who is most disadvantaged by those inequities. We know that the health system can play an important role in tackling them. The health system, however, cannot reduce health inequities on its own. Housing policy, education policy, employment policy and economic policy all must be synchronised with health policy to reduce health inequities.

Last week I spent three days at the Knowledge Wave Conference in Auckland where more than 400 New Zealanders gathered to discuss how to modernise New Zealand's economy and improve our economic security and living standards. Social inclusion was also a strong theme. In the twenty-first century, catching the knowledge wave can aim to achieve for the economy what the guaranteed dairy price and high tariffs tried to secure in Arnold Nordmeyer's time. The objective is to find the means to fund the decent society for all New Zealanders. The government of which Sir Arnold was part found solutions which worked in their time. Our job is to find a new balance appropriate to the twenty-first century which secures health and other services of quality and provides long-term economic and social security.

New Century, New Economy: Developing in the globalising world

**Asia-Pacific Economic Cooperation (APEC) Chief Executives'
Forum, Shanghai, China
19 October 2001**

*Helen was travelling when the 11 September 2001 terrorist
attacks occurred in the United States, and Acting Prime Minister
Jim Anderton issued a ministerial statement to parliament in her
absence, saying, 'New Zealand will stand with all other democratic
countries to do whatever is necessary to prevent and remove threats
to peace and the devastating scourge of terrorism.' In October that
same year, in the wake of the attacks, Helen gave the following
speech while in China for a series of political and economic meetings
between APEC's 21 member states.*

———

Thank you for the invitation to participate in this APEC CEO forum. It
is good to see so many of you here. Indeed it was critical that the APEC
Summit and this CEO forum proceed. Our presence here signals our

determination not to be intimidated by terrorists, but rather to get on with the work of economic development and international co-operation in all its many forms, including trade. I hope that at the APEC Leaders' Summit this weekend we will make a strong commitment to collective action against terrorism. The terrorist attacks struck not against one nation, but against humanity. We are all in this together.

Our security, including our economic security, is interlinked. This year in Shanghai we must assert that trade and economic prosperity are also major forces for stability and confidence-building. We know that the successful launch of a new World Trade Organization (WTO) round will underpin confidence in the world economy and help stimulate growth.

This morning's session looked at the double edge of globalisation, at striking a balance between efficiency and equity. Let me tell you how we in New Zealand are seeking to achieve that balance. For New Zealand, globalisation is a given. Our history, our culture and our ongoing prosperity are about taking the opportunities globalisation offers us and applying them for our common good. We need markets offshore to sell our goods and services, we need capital from offshore to invest in our future, and we are involved continually in a dialogue of ideas at these and other forums in every walk of life with the rest of the world.

As a small and geographically isolated country with a well-educated population, New Zealand stands to benefit more than many from the new ideas and new technologies, especially in communications, which drive the globalisation process. Now, by riding the knowledge wave, we aim to speed up the transformation already under way in our economy, from what was largely a commodity-dominated export trade to a more sophisticated trade in goods and services. That transformation is critical as we aim to maintain and build on our First World living standards for all our people. Our government puts a high priority on social inclusion and participation, and on ensuring that the rising tide really does lift all boats.

Now, at the beginning of the twenty-first century, New Zealand is taking a new approach to economic development. It is an approach based on growing our levels of talent, innovation and specialisation. It is an approach which has worked well in other countries, and it is being adapted to our circumstances and opportunities.

Our vision is to see New Zealand back in the top half of the OECD economic indicators, as we already are on most social indicators. Our aim is to lever off a talented population with many great ideas in order to build an economy driven by talent, innovation and entrepreneurial skills.

We see the New Zealand of the future as an export-oriented economy with more globally oriented companies operating from a New Zealand base and developing strong clusters around them. We see New Zealand developing as a top place in the world to do business because:

- we have a highly educated and skilled workforce

- we have sophisticated infrastructure and are highly interconnected

- we have strong commitments to government, business and community partnerships

- we are a secure and stable place to live in and invest in, in every sense

- we have a fantastic physical environment for recreation and leisure

- we are culturally dynamic

- and we are a socially inclusive and tolerant society.

New Zealand is now in the process of creating conditions in which the highest levels of innovation can flourish and in which New Zealand has the capacity to create new knowledge and apply it to new and existing industries.

To achieve our goals, [the] government is working closely with business and other stakeholders. Our attention is on the longer-term changes needed for New Zealand to maximise its opportunities. Our government's first 22 months in office have seen significant progress made in putting in place the building blocks for the innovative economy. We are co-ordinating policies relating to innovation, talent and skills, investment and business growth, excellence in education, and science, research and development.

I would like to share with you some of the initiatives we are undertaking to transform our economy. They include:

- Placing huge emphasis on education. We have paid considerable attention to increasing participation in our early childhood education, which is already high by international standards. Our school sector is focusing on improving our rates of literacy and numeracy and fostering IT infrastructure and skills. Our fast IT rollout is being made possible through strong partnerships between government, business and schools. We are currently in the throes of a fundamental overhaul of the structure and funding of tertiary education to improve both its quality and its capacity for specialisation. We have put considerable emphasis on the emergence and fostering of centres of excellence for research at the tertiary level. There is significantly more investment in industry training.

- Taking a fresh approach to innovation with increased public funding for science and research, and providing more favourable tax treatment for research and development. We are emphasising the need to commercialise the new knowledge we generate. That has led to the development for the first time in New Zealand of business incubators, attached generally to research-based institutions. The government has also established a fund to provide seed and start-up capital, to be deployed in partnership with the private sector. Our new Science and Innovation Advisory Council has developed a draft New Zealand Innovation Strategy designed to position New Zealanders as innovators to the world.

- Taking a new approach to foreign direct investment so that we target sectors in which we can achieve global competitiveness. We aim to attract greenfield investment as magnets for cluster development around our areas of expertise and advantage.

- Emphasising skills in our immigration programme. Immigration policy has been changed to give priority to recruiting the talent needed to drive our innovative economy. We are currently working on the development of a talent visa to enable our businesses to tap even faster into the global specialist talent they need to grow and develop.

- Developing world-leading e-commerce and e-government strategies. We are developing ambitious targets for rolling out our broadband capacity. The telecommunications platform must enable all our businesses and homes to be rapidly connected.

In the twenty-first century we see the government's role as being a catalyst for the innovative economy. We will provide strategic leadership. We will facilitate, co-ordinate, broker and partner, and we will fund where appropriate. We are moving to identify areas of our economy in which world-class competitiveness is a real possibility where it is not already a reality. We will also provide leadership to ensure the growth we encourage is sustainable.

Four sectors stand out as warranting strategic targeting. They are biotechnology, information and communications technology (ICT), creative industries, and environmental technologies. They have high potential for growth and require further investment and capability building.

Other sectors have been identified for tactical targeting which builds on current capabilities and industry structures to achieve investment in chosen 'sweet spots' or attractive niches. This approach relies on the deliberate application of marketing and/or deal brokering, and may include specific grants and incentives. Sectors identified for tactical targeting include education, tourism, food processing, wine, leisure marine and professional services.

A central component of the innovative New Zealand strategy is to build a network nation. We are currently developing policies to tap into our networks of expatriate New Zealanders. The idea is to ensure that these networks are closely connected with our country to create a virtual New Zealand. We want to facilitate interaction between local talent and global talent centres, and articulate the value proposition of investing in, living in, working in and associating with the new New Zealand.

Many of your companies have long-established linkages with New Zealand. Many of you have visited. For those who have not, let me spell out again some of our many attractive features.

- We are a stable investment location with a strong record going back many years. We are an attractive proposition for those who seek security, high quality and a robust legal framework.

- We have world-class clusters of companies and supporting infrastructure developing fast in biotechnology and IT, leisure marine, wood processing and other areas.

- We are an easy and competitive place in which to do business. We have an efficient, market-oriented economy, a stable and secure business environment, and we are determinedly corruption-free. By First World standards our taxes are low.

- We are well connected with the world because of our sophisticated communications access.

- Finally, we are a superb place in which to live and work. Our clean and uncluttered environment makes our lifestyle proposition one of the best in the world.

Given this new course we are charting, it is not surprising that New Zealand is in the vanguard of APEC members which recognise the importance of international trade and facilitation. For a small economy like ours a key priority is increasing the size of the market for our goods. Comprehensive open trade agreements, like our recently negotiated economic partnership with Singapore, and that being discussed with Hong Kong, are important vehicles. We are keen to pursue other bilateral agreements.

A high priority for us is a bilateral trade agreement between New Zealand and the United States. We believe both sides would win. It would also make good sense for the United States to negotiate a high-quality agreement with New Zealand and our CER partner Australia together. Our two combined markets would be of greater value to the United States. From a strategic trade point of view, we would all benefit from an agreement which spanned the Pacific and showed the way for other APEC economies, as we have advocated by linking New Zealand, Australia, Chile and Singapore in one agreement with the United States.

A key political message which APEC must deliver this weekend is the importance of launching a new WTO round. We can invigorate that process through our willingness to act at the bilateral, regional and sub-regional levels. New Zealand itself is not interested in low-quality trade agreements. We advocate comprehensive, 'WTO-plus' agreements. They need to advance, not impede, both multilateralism and APEC's progress towards its goal of free and open trade and investment throughout the region.

I value very much the contact which APEC makes possible in the region. Equally I value contact with business in New Zealand and internationally, including through this forum. APEC offers excellent models for co-operation between government and business. All of us appreciate the value that has been added by APEC's Business Advisory Council (ABAC), of which a number of you are members.

New Zealand sees value in a similarly inclusive approach by APEC towards organised labour. Through informed and constructive input by labour representatives into the APEC agenda our work on human resource development and capacity building would surely be enhanced. Exclusion ignites the fear that globalisation is one-sided in its effects, and the sense of grievance which that creates has acted to harm international meetings from Seattle to Genoa. Our government in New Zealand practises inclusion at home and will advocate it internationally.

I would also like to see APEC raise the profile of its work on sustainable development. The organisation already does useful work through a number of its working groups. With the World Summit on Sustainable Development being held next year, APEC economies have the opportunity to make a major contribution by participating in the preparations and follow-up work.

The voice of business will be important too. In New Zealand I believe the Business Council on Sustainable Development will play a key role in the development of our national sustainable development strategy.

Many of you will be in the forefront of similar work in your own countries. I urge you all to give it priority so that when world leaders meet in Johannesburg next September we know that the corporate sector is engaged in the process. Making our economies both innovative and sustainable needs government, business and community buy-in.

In conclusion, can I say that, while terrorism has cast its shadow over us all in recent weeks, it has also seen us redouble our determination to work together as an international community. Our world faces challenges which no nation can meet on its own. Global prosperity and stability, and environmental sustainability, can only be achieved by working together. The message to the terrorists must be that their actions are leading us to work even more closely together rather than tearing us apart. This new impetus for multilateralism will drive a new WTO round, as it will drive many other global dialogues and initiatives. That makes me very positive about the future of APEC and of my own nation, and about the partnerships we can build at all levels to secure our common future.

Labour's Second Term

Parliament, Wellington
28 August 2002

The 2002 general election in New Zealand was held on 27 July,
resulting in a second term for Labour (in coalition with the
Progressive Party and backed by United Future) and for Helen
as Prime Minister. In this speech to parliament, she outlined
the Labour Government's goals and touched on world events,
such as terrorism and climate change, that continue to impact
politics today.

Ours is a diverse parliament. There are people here from many, many backgrounds of all kinds. This House is the richer and the more representative for that. It is indeed a far cry from the parliament I was elected to in 1981. I recall that there were about 92 members. The number of women had just doubled from four to eight. The commentators all said, 'What's happening to New Zealand politics? The women are taking over.' It actually took us quite a lot more years to take over, but we are starting to make our mark. There were four Māori MPs representing the Māori electorates, two from general electorates, and the ethnic diversity came from Eddie Isbey, who was Jewish, and Fred Gerbic, who was born of Croatian parents. We have a very different parliament today.

On 27 July the people spoke. New Zealanders were not looking for any radical change in direction, and there will be no radical change in direction. In government, the Labour Party has set out to be steady, reliable, predictable and progressive. We do not like surprises, nor does the public. To the best of our ability we set out what we intend to do in government, and we endeavour to stick to it.

Over the 21 years that I have been in this House, so much of politics has been a roller-coaster ride, with the public not knowing what to expect next. It is very unsettling. When I was elected in 1981, it was what was to become the last term of the Muldoon government. The economy was in difficulty, the sad state of the government's finances reflected that, and society was very polarised, for all kinds of reasons. Indeed, in the run-up to that campaign, society split and families split over the divisiveness of the Springbok tour.

Then the Fourth Labour Government came to power. It made a lot of change—some good, but some very difficult for its core constituency to swallow. That, together with the fall-out from the Wall Street crash, which was enduring in the late 1980s, saw us voted out in a landslide in 1990.

The decade of the nineties was the National Party's era. The tone though was set with the 'mother of all Budgets' in 1991, and that harsh image stuck. At the end of the decade people voted decisively for a change of direction, and, I believe, for much more balanced policies. Our government, elected in 1999, set out to find that balance by promoting a growing higher-value economy that could fund good public services and could offer fairness, opportunity and security to all our people, not just a privileged few.

We also set out to safeguard the environment, to promote the arts and culture, sport and recreation—all critical to the quality of life in our country. We sought to reinforce New Zealand's role in the world as a good international citizen, and as a nation that would speak up for disarmament, for human rights, for development and for the environment. We set out to modernise and develop New Zealand's defence forces and equipment, and to make them relevant to our own needs and the role New Zealand was playing internationally.

We embarked on major problems of capacity building with Māoridom and Pacific peoples in New Zealand, and we are seeing very exciting results from those programmes. We articulated from the outset a vision for a New Zealand that is tolerant, inclusive and welcoming of all those who live here, irrespective of ethnicity, religious belief, sexual orientation or any other factor.

In December 1999 we set out those ideals and goals in the Speech from the Throne. In the two years and seven months that followed, we followed through on that agenda, and come the election campaign we were able to report a lot of progress and that we had delivered in full on every pledge we made to the people of New Zealand in that campaign. We went into this last election with unemployment at its lowest level in fourteen years, at 5.1 per cent. That represents hope and opportunity for many more people. We were able to report a growing economy, even after the terrible shock of 11 September, and an economy growing faster than many of its First World counterparts. We were able to report that tertiary education was much more affordable because the unfairness of the student loans scheme had been tackled, and we were able to report so much improvement right through the education sector.

We were able to say that the health system had been funded to provide many, many more treatments, and that it had clear goals and direction. We were able to say that state housing was offering fair rents to its tenants again, helping many low-income households, and across all our state house households the average reduction in rent, when income-related rents came in, was more than $30 a week.

We lifted the living standards of superannuitants. We were able to say that under this government, by the end of 2002, superannuitants were $12 a week better off than they would have been under the previous government's policies, and married superannuitants were more than $20 a week better off. That was a contribution to seeing that our oldest citizens could live in dignity. We also could report a positive downward trend in crime rates, with burglaries at their lowest level in 20 years, and overall crime at its lowest rate in thirteen years.

So it was against that background that the Speech from the Throne for this week, for the beginning of this parliament, was prepared. The programme outlined builds on the platform established in the first term, and it is a very ambitious programme. The vision, as set out in the Speech from the Throne, reflects the vision of the growth and innovation framework—that vision being to see our country as a great place in which to live, learn and do business. It sees us as a birthplace of world-changing people and ideas, which we are. This country is a place where people will invest in the future, and a land where diversity is valued and reflected in our national identity. We want it, and we will fix it.

We see the role of government as critical in providing the leadership and the practical policies and programmes that will drive the ongoing rebuilding of this country. We know that years of indifference and 'hands-off' have let New Zealand down. We will work in partnership, as we have been doing, with everyone who shares the vision of New Zealand moving ahead. I expect this government, again, to work very closely with the business community, unions, local government, Māori, Pacific peoples, ethnic communities, our voluntary organisations and our communities to get this country moving. It is a partnership approach, and it is the way of government in the twenty-first century. We could never rule effectively by decree and by fiat. More than ever, modern governments must govern by consent. In a multi-member parliament where a government does not have a majority it is very important to build majorities around issues in this House, as we will do, and outside the House to build the working relationships that will make things happen.

The Speech from the Throne identifies continued economic growth as the key task for the government. We have clear objectives, we set them out in the growth and innovation framework in February, and we have a comprehensive agenda that flows from that. In this term again we will seek to further raise participation and achievement levels in education and skills training.

We will seek again to boost further public and private spending on science, and research and development. We will continue to implement well-targeted programmes to develop and grow new and existing businesses and exports. We will promote innovation right across the economy. We will back the strategies for the new high-value sectors, like biotechnology, and information and communications technology in the creative industries. We will prioritise improving our infrastructure of roading and public transport and of telecommunications, especially through the rollout of broadband being supervised by my colleague the Hon. Paul Swain.

Our goal is to see New Zealand back in the top half of the OECD over time. We know—and this distinguishes us from the Opposition—that our nation is capable of that. We also know that achieving it means a nationwide effort. It means lifting aspirations at every level, from the individual child in school, to whole communities and enterprises, as well as to government. We in government are prepared to play our part in that.

Economic growth—why is it important? Simply because it provides the means for our society to enjoy a higher standard of living and a better quality of life. However, I want to stress two particularly important things about economic growth for this Labour Progressive Coalition government. The first is that growth must be sustainable, and the second is that its benefits must be spread across the whole society—that is, the rising tide must lift every boat. It must not redistribute just to the top end. There has to be something in it for the ordinary person, the ordinary family in the community.

Sustainable development is currently the focus of the major World Summit in South Africa, with 65,000 delegates attending, and I will go to hold up my hand as one at the end of the week. In the lead-up to the summit a number of key New Zealand documents are being released. At the beginning of this month the Parliamentary Commissioner for the Environment released his report on sustainable development for New Zealand. It is called 'Creating our Future', and I commend it to members to read. This week, too, the government statistician will be releasing New Zealand's first-ever set of sustainable development indicators. Because they are the first, they are experimental in nature and will be open for consultation and for review.

Today, the Minister for the Environment and I are releasing two more documents. The first is the New Zealand report to the United Nations on the progress we have made on the items listed in Agenda 21, which came from the Rio Earth Summit in 1992. The country is required to make a report ten years down the track, and that is available as of now on the web.

Secondly, we are publishing a document setting out the government's approach to sustainable development, using the broad approach embodied in Agenda 21. The message that this government will be taking to the World Summit is that economic growth must be environmentally sustainable and it must be socially beneficial. There can be no long-term benefit to our country, or any other, from growth based on low environmental standards that degrades our natural heritage, or growth that fails to lift the quantity and quality of life for all our people.

Here in New Zealand we have, of course, made a lot of progress on safeguarding the environment. The Resource Management Act is playing a very big role, as are strategies now for waste management, water quality, biodiversity, fisheries conservation, renewable energy, sustainable land use and many more besides. Our government has also placed under permanent protection the remaining indigenous forest in public hands that was not previously protected. But there is so much more to do, and we will be inviting public comment on the New Zealand strategy for sustainable development that must be built.

As a good international citizen New Zealand will be ratifying the Kyoto Protocol on climate change, and we will meet the commitments entered into under that protocol. New Zealand as a primary producing nation has an enormous interest in getting a more stable world climate. That means we have to put our money where our mouth is, and I am proud that our country can put its hand up alongside those many other developed countries that are prepared to take the first step and give leadership. There is no point in exhorting China, India and everyone else to do something if we are not prepared to take the steps ourselves. We can, and we will.

The World Summit needs to come to grips with the many environmental problems the planet faces. Those problems are not only climate change problems, they are very basic problems, like a lack of clean water for the world's growing populations, incredible air pollution—and we read now of that large brown cloud that is stretching across China and over much of Asia, affecting air quality for people—the depletion of the world's fisheries and forestry, the loss of biodiversity and so much else besides. These are huge international issues, and New Zealand's voice must be heard on them.

On the social side of sustainable development, the government is setting out to improve well-being, health status and social services to reduce inequalities in the community and to build a society that respects and values diversity. Improving healthcare is the key focus in the health portfolio this term. We have primary healthcare organisations forming, and this year, through them, we can expect another 300,000 New Zealanders to get access to more affordable primary healthcare. We will, of course, be continuing the action to bring down hospital waiting-times for more people. The mental health strategy is in full stride, and the health goals are attracting a lot of positive attention and action from our health providers and communities.

For older people the key new initiative in this term will be the legislation that enables the beginning of the phasing out of asset testing on residential and private hospital care. New Zealand superannuation, of course, is absolutely safeguarded by this government at decent levels, and the Superannuation Fund locks it in for the future. We will also have a focus this term on family income levels, going to annual reviews of family support and family tax credit rates and thresholds that have not been adjusted for quite some time. New initiatives will be taken, under the Hon. Steve Maharey's supervision, to support more people moving from social security into paid work.

We will also be very proactive in tackling the crime rate. It has come down, but we all want to do better. The government has a crime-reduction strategy. It aims to tackle the root causes of crime through early intervention, and we are paying a great deal of attention with new policies, new programmes, to curb youth offending. The whole community is appalled at the sight of a thirteen-year-old being convicted of manslaughter. It is not good that younger and younger people are committing more adult crimes. We need better answers. Community safety is a top priority, but while we know we can lock up the worst offenders for longer, we need to do a lot more as a community to stop the next generation of hardened criminals emerging.

From 1999 when we took office, our government set out to extend opportunity and security across the community. We began building firm partnerships with Māoridom, and building its capacity for economic and social development. There is now an incredible amount of very positive activity in Māoridom around so many programmes. The unemployment rate was down 28 per cent from the time we took office. There are something like 300 new Māori businesses in New Zealand. Māori health and social service organisations are delivering, and delivering well, to so many people. There is a tremendous amount of leadership being shown in Māori education. I commend the rangatira of Tūwharetoa, Tumu te Heuheu, who has worked with the Hon. Parekura Horomia and with Trevor Mallard to develop iwi strategies for education throughout the country. We see iwi accepting responsibility, wanting to do more to see that their children can have the advantage of a good education. We look forward to more progress on Treaty settlements. We look forward to the final decision on the fisheries allocation—a long time coming—and we look forward to the Māori Television Service going to air.

I also want to emphasise the importance for us of the partnerships with Pacific peoples. Again, unemployment rates are down, around 25 per cent from the time this government came to office, and there are many good strategies and programmes in place for Pacific people's education, health and social services. New Zealand has many other ethnic communities, rapidly growing in size, and that creates new challenges of nation building and community building. I want to say that in the atmosphere of an election campaign those communities can feel very vulnerable because they are targeted, and to those who have come as refugees that sort of persecution is particularly unpleasant and worrying. I want to say that this government will protect the rights of all New Zealanders, and we will lead from the front in advocating a country that is tolerant, decent and inclusive.

The reality is that this country has skills shortages. The reality is that young Kiwis like to travel and see the world. As fast as other countries try to poach our talented young people we have to poach those of others back, and that is why we will continue to accept migrants who can help drive our development as a nation. We will certainly continue to accept our obligations internationally to resettle refugees.

I would like to see new initiatives develop in this next term that will work on linking our communities better together. I was particularly struck late last year by a visit I received from a group of citizens, which included Dr Choudhary and Dr Jim Veitch of Victoria University, who were interested in seeing whether the government was generally supportive of what they call an inter-faith dialogue. They wanted to reach out to each other across the Christian, Islamic, Hindu, Jewish and other faiths and build better understanding between them, and I think there is scope for such initiatives. I do not think they all need be driven by government; they can come from our churches and many religious faiths, from our non-governmental organisations and from our community organisations. I believe that Asia 2000 does a very good job of raising awareness about Asian heritage, culture and issues, and more such initiatives would be very, very welcome.

Opening Address to the Eighth ICFTU World Women's Conference

Melbourne, Australia
18 February 2003

The International Confederation of Free Trade Unions (ICFTU) was an international trade union federation that existed from 1949 until 2006, when it merged with the World Confederation of Labour to form the International Trade Union Confederation (ITUC). The ITUC continues to hold World Women's Conferences in order to provide a forum for women who are trade unionists to discuss issues such as gender equality and pay equity.

––––––

Thank you for the invitation to address the opening session of your conference today. First, let me acknowledge the significance of this conference. More than 300 women unionists from more than 90 countries are meeting here in Melbourne to develop strategies to advance the position of women and the work of unions.

As a woman, as the Leader of the New Zealand Labour Party, and as Prime Minister of New Zealand, I welcome the convening of the conference in this part of the world. Perhaps one day you might also consider meeting in New Zealand.

The ICFTU is a huge international organisation, with more than 231 affiliated union centres in 150 countries, representing a total membership of 158 million union members. By any standard, that is a major organisation. And it is to the ICFTU that the world's organised workers look for a lead on the issues affecting them their families, their communities and their countries.

Similarly, the world's women workers look to the ICFTU's women's leadership to give voice to their specific concerns and represent their interests. The issues concerning and affecting the world's working people range across and beyond national borders. They demand a transnational response and action, and that is what the ICFTU can provide.

I have prioritised attendance at this conference for a number of reasons. First, the political party I lead, the New Zealand Labour Party, was established primarily by trade unions in 1916 to give working people a political organisation to complement their industrial organisations. To this day, unions continue to affiliate to our party, and we continue a positive relationship with the union movement in general.

Second, I am a woman leader of a social democratic party which leads a government. That combination of factors is hard to find anywhere else in the world at this time. So I come to offer you my personal encouragement.

Third, the issues the conference will discuss are important to me and my government. We share your concern about the need to globalise equality and justice, to build inclusive societies, to fight all forms of discrimination, and to work for a more peaceful world. In my speech today I will talk about how our government tackles some of these issues.

Fourth, I wish to affirm the critical role which unions play in bringing about economic, social and political change. Unions are an essential part of democratic societies. Those governments which repress unions are generally authoritarian in nature and resistant to allowing any opposition voices to be heard. In this sense, free unionism and democratisation go hand in hand.

My country is one of the world's oldest democracies, and in 1893 was the first nation in the world where women gained the right to vote. We are one of a tiny number of nations which was able to maintain democratic government throughout the entire twentieth century. As early as the 1890s, New Zealand had progressive labour legislation, with an Industrial Conciliation and Arbitration Act passed in 1894. The First Labour Government came to power in 1935 and ruled for fourteen years, creating a strong base for workers' rights and for social and economic security.

But the twentieth century in New Zealand also saw many difficult years for unions and for the living standards of working people. Armed police were called out to suppress a strike in 1912, and a worker was killed. The depressions of the 1920s and 1930s were tough. In 1951 there was an extended lockout of waterfront workers, and the state assumed extraordinary powers to stop the locked-out workers publicising their cause.

The next four decades saw little significant change in the industrial relations framework, and unions largely got on with their business. But then the new right struck. Just as Mrs Thatcher's Conservative government had set out to constrain unions in Britain, so did her soulmates in New Zealand. New labour legislation was passed in 1991 which impacted severely on collective organisation and bargaining and on the right to strike. Union density fell from 35 per cent of the workforce in 1991 to 17 per cent by 1999.

Labour market deregulation did not occur in isolation. It was part of a radical right menu of change which also slashed welfare spending and public housing subsidies, leaving the poorest New Zealanders an estimated 20 to 25 per cent off worse off. In 1991, the unemployment rate rose to double figures, and a significant level of poverty reappeared for the first time since the Great Depression of the 1930s. The public health system was rearranged on a commercial model and the costs of gaining tertiary education rose steeply. The overall effect was a sharp increase in inequality.

What happened in New Zealand in the 1990s was very hard on ordinary working people. It followed on from the tumultuous years of economic deregulation and restructuring in the 1980s. The public became cynical about and distrustful of the whole political process, and especially resentful of the Westminster-style electoral system which gave single party governments tremendous power, even if elected with a low vote on a split poll. A referendum to change to proportional representation was carried in 1993, and the introduction of the new voting system has had profound effects on the political system.

My party was elected to government in 1999 as voters in New Zealand turned against neo-liberal policies and voted for parties which could bring about change. We emphasised the values of fairness, opportunity and security; and also in our multi-ethnic society the importance of tolerance, respect and inclusion across all cultures, ethnicities and beliefs. We have a strong commitment to partnership with Māori, New Zealand's indigenous people.

What we have been able to do in government reinforces my belief in the power of the democratic process to bring about positive change to benefit working people and their families. We rejected the neo-liberal agenda of carrying on deregulating, privatising and slashing taxes. Rather, we increased taxes on top earners to give room for sorely needed social spending across health, education, housing, pensions and essential services. We stopped the newly implemented private provision of workers' accident compensation and restored the public social insurance scheme with its strong no-fault basis. We moved to regulate the labour market to the extent necessary to create a more level playing field between employers and employees.

Overall, the change in workplace-related legislation has been substantial. The 1991 labour law was replaced with new law promoting collective bargaining and organisation and good faith in the employment relationship. A strong mediation service is central to the success of the new law. We also strengthened health and safety laws, and the provisions of the accident compensation scheme. Minimum wages are being regularly adjusted, and there have been dramatic rises in the youth minimum wage.

Last year the government established a paid parental leave scheme through legislation. Previously workers had had rights only to unpaid parental leave, and few had had the bargaining strength to negotiate paid leave in their employment agreements. The new scheme gives parents an entitlement to twelve weeks of paid leave after the birth of their child at a maximum payment equivalent to more than 50 per cent of the average weekly wage. The scheme is financed out of general taxation. We have promoted it as a social justice measure, recognising the financial pressures which a new baby and time off work place on families. Over time we believe employers will also appreciate the value of having parents return to work having benefited from time out with their baby.

Our government was re-elected in July last year, and has again prioritised improvements to workplace law. New legislation on holidays is being introduced, and we are grappling with how to safeguard agreed employment conditions when companies change hands. The paid parental leave scheme will be extended, and we are promoting a better balance between work and life outside working hours. A new position for an Equal Employment Opportunities Commissioner has been established in the Human Rights Commission, to give advice and leadership on EEO and promote best practice.

The social and labour policy changes we have introduced have been accompanied by a new direction in economic policy. There is a sense of urgency in New Zealand about restoring living standards relative to those of other OECD countries. New Zealand's place on the economic rankings slipped from third place in 1950 to around twentieth on GDP per capita by 1999. The impact of that on working people was exacerbated by the growing inequality which characterised New Zealand in the 1980s and 1990s.

In today's global economy, relative economic decline leads to an exodus of skilled people to other countries offering more opportunity. New Zealand has suffered a brain drain off and on for years.

Our task in government has been to play a leadership and strategic role in steering the economy, and to use the state's ability to facilitate, co-ordinate, broker and fund to promote the development of a stronger economy.

We promote a shared vision and consensus about our country's economic goals. We promote innovation, enterprise and participation, and we emphasise the importance of the social dividend which economic growth makes possible. We promote the concept of sustainability across economic, social and environmental policy. We know the importance of maintaining business confidence and of promoting partnerships for growth which are inclusive of industry, unions, regions and communities. In our quest to build a sustainable higher-value economy capable of paying a higher social dividend, we have prioritised policies and spending on education and skills training, science, research and development, the acceleration of business and regional growth, and developing sector strategies to lift whole industries.

What we have achieved is a social democratic government which not only has considerable social and environmental achievements to its credit, but also is regarded as a sound economic manager.

New Zealand is currently one of the OECD's star performers, with annual average growth coming in at 3.9 per cent. Unemployment is at a fifteen-year low of 4.9 per cent—lower than that of either the United States or Australia, and significantly lower than that of the Euro area.

For now, the brain drain has been turned into a brain gain, with strong inward net migration. More New Zealanders are coming home to live and many fewer are leaving. Consumer confidence is solid and business confidence has held up relatively well given the uncertain international climate.

As a government we set out to create a fair and just society with opportunity and security for all our people. In a fast-changing and complex world, we have to work hard to maintain and improve the living standards of our people. The pace of globalisation throws up new risks, but also new opportunities for countries like New Zealand. We used to suffer the tyranny of distance, but modern communications have largely overcome that. Now our relative isolation seems like a bonus in today's insecure world.

This week more than most, the world's attention is focused on a single critical issue: Will there be a war over Iraq? The Security Council held what has been called its most extraordinary meeting ever, and some six million people took to the streets to demonstrate their opposition to a war. The past seventeen months since September 11, 2001 have been, to my mind, the most destabilising period the world has known since World War Two. At the end of that catastrophe, the United Nations was founded, on the ashes of the old League of Nations, to promote international order, human rights and development.

Since then we have lived through some difficult periods, as the Cold War settled in, as East and West battled on the Korean Peninsula, during the Cuban Missile Crisis, and through the heightened awareness of the possibility of nuclear war in the 1980s. But nothing really prepared us for the shock of September 11, when low-technology, suicidal hijackers launched unprecedented attacks on the world's only superpower.

The international community is now transfixed by the problem of terrorism—and rightly so. Terrorists have struck again since, with particularly deadly results in Bali and in Mombassa, Kenya. Much military might has been devoted to tracking down the perpetrators, but that can only be part of the answer.

I believe that our security is now imperilled not because of any inevitable clash of civilisations—a theory I utterly reject—but rather because huge gaps have been allowed to develop between regions and nations, leading to bitterness, frustration, envy and hate. It has not helped that crises like that affecting Israel and Palestine have been left to fester for so long, and have created a climate for extremism in the Middle East directed at the West, which is held responsible for the stalemate.

A series of remarkable international summits over the past two-and-a-half years have endeavoured to address some of the fundamental problems. The Millennium Goals of the United Nations, the Monterrey International Conference on Financing Development, the Food and Agriculture Organization's Food Summit, the New Partnership for Africa's Development supported by the G8 and the World Summit on Sustainable Development have all set objectives for reducing poverty and hunger and increasing access to the basics of life like water and energy. There is a huge agenda to base international action on.

But the crisis over Iraq is now so serious and so polarising that it could jeopardise progress on that broadly based international agenda to promote development and greater understanding between peoples and regions.

The New Zealand Government has sought to uphold the principles of multilateralism, the international rule of law and the authority of the Security Council throughout this crisis. We do not support unilateral action against Iraq, whether it is taken by one country or a number of countries. We place considerable weight on the inspection and disarmament process which has been established. We have a strong preference for a diplomatic solution to the crisis. We recognise that the Security Council can authorise the use of force as a last resort to uphold its resolutions. We do not believe such authorisation would be justified while the weapons inspectors are still engaged usefully in their work, and we support them continuing that work. It is clear from their reports to the Security Council on Friday that they believe they should carry on.

At the same time, we urge Iraq to comply immediately and in full with all the United Nations requirements to prevent the catastrophe which war would bring to its people. Iraq should not mistake the strong desire which governments like New Zealand's have for a diplomatic outcome for tolerance of their failure to answer the questions about their weapons programmes which they have refused to answer for many years.

Should there be war in Iraq, my government fears for the widespread resentment that would provoke in the Middle East against Western nations, for the likely stimulus terrorist organisations would gain from that resentment, and for the high human costs a war would have. All diplomatic means to contain Iraq have to be preferable to that.

My government's support for a strong rules-based international order also extends to the areas of the environment, disarmament and trade. We have ratified the Kyoto Protocol on climate change, believing it is important to be part of the solution to the major international problem of global warming, and we urge all nations to ratify and meet their commitments under the protocol.

We work hard with like-minded countries on nuclear and other forms of disarmament of weapons of mass destruction. The problem of nuclear weapons did not disappear with the end of the Cold War, but rather has re-emerged in new forms. Proliferation of nuclear weapons among nations which do not accept the disciplines of the nuclear non-proliferation treaty is one problem. Another is the potential of proliferation to non-state actors in the form of transnational terrorist organisations. The potential proliferation of chemical and biological weapons technology to such groups is also a concern.

Economic globalisation is an area crying out for fair rules to be applied to it. Many believe globalisation has developed in an unbalanced way to meet the demands of First World corporate agendas. The interests of developing countries and the protection of labour rights and the environment are perceived to take second place. In developed countries where sufficient care has not been taken in becoming a signatory to the General Agreement on Trade in Services (GATS), national policy options can be severely limited in areas like culture which are critical to national identity. For example, in my country we are unable to legislate for local content quotas on radio and television as no reservation was entered to GATS at an earlier stage.

Now discussion is under way at the WTO negotiations on services. Nations which value, for example, their unique public services like health and education, will need to take care to ensure they are not adversely affected by a broad-brush approach to opening up service sectors.

I take the view that globalisation is a long-standing and ongoing process and that the key challenge is to put rules around it. As national borders around economies fall, we need to ensure that the result is an increase in opportunity overall, not an increase in human misery. Current world trade rules do discriminate against developing countries, and even against New Zealand with its large primary sectors, and these rules need to be changed. We are working hard to achieve that through the Doha Round of negotiations.

Our government has been prepared to raise labour and environmental issues in the context of trade negotiations. We have backed the call for a labour forum associated with APEC, and we have included union representation in the New Zealand delegation at WTO at Doha, and also will at Cancun. We look forward to the report of the International Labour Organization (ILO) on the social dimensions of globalisation, which is due next year.

Notwithstanding the size and influence of the ICFTU, delegates at this conference will be well aware of the challenges that confront modern unionism. In countries like mine, union organisation has found it hard to penetrate the growing ranks of technology workers, and marginalised groups like migrants and young workers which feature disproportionately in the secondary labour market are also hard to reach.

This conference will debate concrete and innovative strategies to make trade unions relevant to working women today. That is timely. Representation and strength require organisation well above what all but the most highly placed employees and managers can achieve. And without collective worker organisation there is an inherent inequality in the employment relationship.

The conference will also highlight the need to enhance the role of women in trade unions. Achieving that requires unions to be responsive to women's needs and concerns and to help to create strong women leaders in the movement at every level. A strong female membership base is needed too.

In my country, women have been able to conquer most of the commanding heights in society. We currently have our second woman Governor-General and our second woman Prime Minister. About 30 per cent of our cabinet and parliament are female. The head of the largest private-sector company is female, as is the Chief Justice. Women have occupied positions at the top of professional organisations in the law, medicine and accounting. Many women have headed local and regional government organisations. The generation of women which first came to the top was that of the post-war baby boomers who benefited from access to educational opportunities in a benign social environment. In a small society social change can spread quickly. Once some heads broke through the glass ceiling, the way was clear for others to follow.

Women's representation at the top of governmental, economic and social structures is a matter of social justice. Unions must be a positive force in promoting gender equality, in your own ranks, in the workforce and in the society at large. Unions also have a vital role in promoting a fair and just society.

I wish you well at this conference as you debate what is needed to strengthen women's participation in unions and to build a world which protects and promotes the rights of women to equality and justice.

Statement to Parliament on Iraq

Parliament, Wellington
19 March 2003

In the lead-up to the invasion of Iraq, Western nations were divided over whether the United States, under President George W. Bush, should invade the country. The Bush administration made its case for invasion to the UN Security Council, claiming to want to remove alleged weapons of mass destruction and unseat Saddam Hussein, but nations such as France, Germany and New Zealand argued for further diplomacy and weapons inspections first. Despite the fact that no real evidence of weapons of mass destruction was ever obtained by UN inspectors, and without the full backing of the UN Security Council, a United States-led coalition including the UK, Australia and Poland eventually invaded Iraq on 20 March 2003, the day after Helen made the following speech. The invasion lasted until 1 May 2003.

―――

The government deeply regrets the breakdown of the diplomatic process over the Iraq crisis. The New Zealand Government, like most governments, has been a strong supporter of that process running its course. Like most countries, our strong preference was for the disarmament of Iraq to occur peacefully through a strong and intrusive weapons inspection process. Such a process was re-established by Resolution 1441, which was passed on 8 November by unanimous resolution of the UN Security Council.

New Zealand strongly backed that process, sending thirteen military personnel to the UN weapons inspection team. The head of the team, Dr Hans Blix, has singled out the New Zealand contribution for special recognition in his reports to the UN Security Council.

The inspections recommenced at the end of November. Iraq proceeded to co-operate on process but not on substance. When Dr Blix reported to the Security Council at the end of January he expressed his concern at the lack of substantive co-operation. Thereafter, Dr Blix and Mr El Baradei returned to Baghdad to impress on it that only full compliance with the UN's requirements that it disarm and be seen to disarm would prevent the serious consequences warned of in Resolution 1441. It is a matter of record that Iraq then moved to accommodate more of the weapons inspectors' requests.

New Zealand was among many nations which have called on Iraq to comply immediately and in full with all requests made of it by the Security Council and the weapons inspectors. We have consistently said that only through full compliance could Iraq avert the catastrophe which war would bring to its people.

When Dr Blix and Mr El Baradei reported to the Security Council on 14 February, they were able to be more optimistic. The inspectors were getting more co-operation and had found no evidence of weapons of mass destruction. Nonetheless, Iraq had still to answer serious questions about weapons of mass destruction which had remained unanswered since 1998 when the previous inspectors left.

On 18 February, the New Zealand Government took the opportunity afforded by the open debate at the Security Council to state its view on the conduct of the crisis. We recognised the Security Council's ability to authorise force as a last resort to uphold resolutions, but we also said that we did not believe that such a decision would be justified at that time.

We said that we placed considerable weight on the inspection and disarmament process, and that as long as the inspectors' reports suggested that their work was useful in pursuing the Security Council's objectives it should continue.

We reiterated that we could not support military action against Iraq without a mandate from the Security Council.

The following week, the resolution promoted by Britain, the United States and Spain was tabled at the Security Council. It called on the Security Council to determine that Iraq had failed to take its final opportunity to disarm as set out in Resolution 1441 and to remain seized of the matter. Intense lobbying for support for the resolution ensued, focused on the six elected members who were undecided.

On 7 March, Dr Blix and Mr El Baradei again formally reported to the Security Council. Their reports were read as supporting a continuation of the inspection process. The Security Council debate which followed showed no change in position among its members.

A second open debate was held in the Security Council, in which New Zealand participated. Our government again urged that the diplomatic process which had gained traction be allowed to run its course, and that Iraq move rapidly to comply with all requirements made of it.

In the course of last week, genuine efforts were made by many people to see if the gulf between those who wanted to resort to force now and those who wanted more time for inspections could be bridged. I personally spoke with both the Canadian Prime Minister and the Chilean President to express our government's support for their efforts.

I regret that a solution could not be found. I believe that agreement could have been reached on benchmarks, but in the end there could not be agreement on the timeframe or on what should happen in the event of benchmarks for compliance not being reached within the timeframe.

The leaders of the United States, Britain, Spain and Portugal met in the Azores on Sunday and made it clear that unless Iraq capitulated immediately, force would be used, and that the United Nations Security Council had only one day left to decide whether it would authorise the use of force. The Security Council met yesterday, but no authorisation of force was forthcoming. The resolution which had been foreshadowed was not voted on.

Today President Bush has issued a final ultimatum to Iraq. He has given Saddam Hussein and his sons 48 hours to leave the country. If they do not leave, the United States and its supporters will embark on military action at a time of their choosing, which is expected to be soon.

At this eleventh hour, the New Zealand Government urges Iraq to seize this last opportunity to avert the catastrophe of war. The departure of Sadam Hussein and his sons now would give fresh opportunities to resolve the crisis.

It is important to emphasise at this time, when there has been great division over how to handle the Iraqi crisis, that there is overwhelming support for the disarmament of Iraq. That is an objective we share with the United States and its supporters, and with those who share our views on how to proceed. The difference of opinion and approach arises over the means and the timetable for meeting the objective, not the objective itself.

It is equally important to emphasise our strong sense of shared values with all Western democracies, and to note our concern at the strain this division over Iraq has placed on long-standing friendships and alliances between Western democracies. Our government is determined that this difference of opinion, substantial as it is, will not damage long-standing friendships which we value.

We fully understand the frustration, impatience and outrage felt by the United States, Britain and Australia at Iraq's slowness to comply and resistance to complying with UN resolutions. I do believe that Iraq would strain the patience and tolerance of a saint. But, notwithstanding that, our government did not believe that the diplomatic process, backed by inspections, and leading to disarmament, had run its course by yesterday.

New Zealand's position on this crisis has at all times been based on its strong support for multilateralism and the rule of law, and for upholding the authority of the Security Council. It is a principled position, it has integrity and we believe it is understood by our friends. It is a matter of profound regret to us that some of our closest friends have chosen to stand outside the Security Council at this point.

A new and dangerous precedent is being set. It may be possible to justify one's friends taking such action, but where then is our moral authority when other nations use the precedent which is being set?

These are troubled times for the United Nations. It has worked hard, and the Security Council has worked hard to address the issue. In the end consensus could not be reached. For the majority of nations on the council, the threshold for the use of force had not been reached. Our government supports and endorses that judgment.

The Hikoi of Hope:
Five years on

Christchurch Cathedral, Christchurch
4 March 2004

In 1998, as part of The Hikoi of Hope organised by the Anglican Church in New Zealand, nearly 30,000 people marched from Stewart Island and Cape Reinga to parliament to call on the government to do more to help those in poverty. Just over five years later on 27 January 2004, National Party Leader Don Brash delivered his infamous Ōrewa Speech, in which he argued against what he termed the 'special privileges' of Māori in New Zealand. The speech provoked a huge public backlash for what many, including the Anglican Church, saw as its racist sentiments, and set the scene for Helen's speech below.

It's a little over five years since the Anglican Church led the Hikoi of Hope to parliament. And it's just five days since the Anglican Church spoke out again on another significant issue of social concern. Tonight I want to speak on what links the two initiatives, and to address both the progress which has been made since the Hikoi of Hope and the direction we need to take together as a nation to build a common future.

The Anglican Church is not a political movement. It is a religious community with a strong spiritual and ethical foundation. It is based in communities throughout the land. It is able to perceive what the concerns of communities might be, and to reflect on how they might be represented and addressed. The church took a leadership role in articulating community concerns through the hikoi in the late 1990s. And, by its statement last Sunday, it has shown that it will not stand quietly by now when it perceives that destructive forces have been unleashed on New Zealand society.

For me, the Hikoi of Hope had enormous symbolism which transcended even its advocacy of the core planks of a decent life for all New Zealanders. That symbolism lay in the sense of social solidarity which it engendered. Here were close to 30,000 New Zealanders, drawn from across our communities and drawn together in a common cause. That was especially powerful because it came after years of division and growing inequity.

Since the Great Depression, New Zealand had known very little unemployment. Then it began to climb in the mid-1970s, and it accelerated in the 1980s and into the 1990s. Lives and communities were shattered as a consequence of far-reaching economic and social policy change. Benefit cuts, market rentals for state housing and the Employment Contracts Act had a particularly adverse effect.

We New Zealanders had always prided ourselves on having a country where everyone got a fair go and where everyone had the opportunity to succeed. That self-image was shattered as the queues grew at the food banks and real and absolute poverty was being experienced by our poorest citizens.

It was these concerns which were brought to the front steps of parliament by the Hikoi of Hope, and it was these concerns which I was determined Labour would address if we were given the privilege of forming a government in 1999. What I knew was that the path ahead wouldn't be easy. A lot of damage had been done to the fabric of New Zealand society and to social provision over a long period of time. But the longer the job of rebuilding was delayed, the more difficult the task would have become.

And so, in December 1999 we started on a journey of rebuilding opportunity and security and that sense of a fair go which most New Zealanders value so highly. We've made a lot of progress and a lot of changes, but none of what is happening now can be taken for granted.

What New Zealanders are enjoying today through more enlightened economic and social policy and increased social investment is the direct result of having a centre-left government. The same old agendas are still running on the other side of politics. Tax cuts for the rich will always be matched by spending cuts affecting everybody else. The sense of security and stability which our government, with the support of our parliamentary allies, has established would be quickly shattered by a change of government.

Take for example the living standards of older New Zealanders. One of our Labour-led government's first moves was to restore the level of New Zealand Superannuation. We reversed National's cuts to superannuation, which would have seen at least a third of older New Zealanders living below the poverty line. Yesterday the National Party indicated that it saw the age for receiving New Zealand Superannuation rising in 2020. That's only sixteen years away. The message to every New Zealander under 50 years of age today is that National would not guarantee them New Zealand Superannuation on the present terms and conditions. That is destabilising, and it threatens the security around New Zealand Superannuation which our government has built up with the New Zealand Superannuation Fund. There is only one message that the under–fifties can take from yesterday's announcement, and that is that only a Labour-led government is guaranteeing their retirement income.

It does not take a great leap of imagination to conclude that the tax cuts for the rich which will inevitably form part of National's election policy would be funded by the demolition of the New Zealand Superannuation Fund set up by Labour to guarantee retirement income into the future.

One of the key planks of the Hikoi of Hope was the call for income and benefit levels which lift people out of poverty. That linked to the calls for the creation of real jobs and for affordable housing.

Our government has been active across all these areas and has new initiatives coming as well. When we abandoned the failed policies of the 1990s, one of the first to go was 'work for the dole'. We believed that there were real jobs needing to be done in the economy, and that our priority must be to equip people with the skills and wherewithal to do them. That seemed a lot more appropriate than having armies of caseworkers trying to find make-work for the unemployed.

And so it's proved to be. Unemployment fell steadily from the time we were elected to a sixteen-year low of 4.4 per cent late last year. Compared to when the Hikoi of Hope came to parliament in late 1998, there are over 200,000 more New Zealanders working now. That is spectacular progress, and it's been felt across our communities. The annual average unemployment figures in December 1999 were 16.6 per cent for Māori and 13.6 per cent for Pacific peoples. By December 2003, they stood at 10.2 per cent for Māori and 7.7 per cent for Pacific peoples.

But are we satisfied to leave progress there?

Of course not.

Those unemployment rates are far higher than those for the general population. So, in the interests of everyone having a fair go and the chance to succeed, we have to try harder to spread the fruits of economic growth into every community.

What's more, each one of us has a stake in making that happen.

The Māori and Pacific communities are growing fast. Do we as a nation want those communities to be embittered by and burdened with the marginalisation which comes from high levels of unemployment, crime and underachievement? Do the rest of us want to pay and pay for the consequences of failure? Or do we want to build a strong nation which values all its peoples and finds ways to move us all ahead?

I strongly believe that our future lies together, not in being driven apart. That means finding ways to lift everybody's life chances across and within our communities, and not standing by and letting some fall behind.

Let's not forget what the legacy of the 1980s and 1990s was. Some communities saw lack of work affect three generations. Some children never saw mum or dad or grandma or granddad go to work. In such communities, crime, drugs, alcohol and ill health can take their toll.

The road back to independence can be long and slow. Rebuilding a work ethic is critical, and it is now happening. As a government we put enormous priority on supporting people into independence and creating opportunities to acquire skills. There is now a high demand for labour in the economy: a net 50 per cent of companies are reporting difficulty in hiring skilled labour, and a net 27 per cent are reporting unskilled labour shortages.

I believe our Jobs Jolt initiatives, which aim to get more beneficiaries into work, are well timed. Frankly, unless there is some compelling family, health or other reason, there is no sense in enabling people to move to areas where there is no work when there are other areas with plenty. The opportunity is there to get more people into real jobs. In these circumstances, suggestion of a return to 'work for the dole' is just plain stupid!

It's clear that modern economies are going to require ever higher skill levels, and that the more skilled people are the greater their chances of lifelong employment and independence will be. That's why our government has invested greatly in skills training, and in building new pathways for young people in particular into jobs in industry. Well over 6,000 young people have now signed up for the new Modern Apprenticeships, the flagship programme for our work-based trade and technical training programmes. In total we are aiming to have 150,000 industry trainees in place in 2005, and to build towards a total of a quarter of a million within two to three years thereafter.

It's initiatives like these which stand to guarantee New Zealanders good standards of living in the years ahead, but meantime we've also been active in lifting low incomes.

When the Hikoi of Hope came to parliament, the minimum wage was $7 an hour, and it was stuck at that level for three years from 1997 to 1999. We've lifted the minimum wage every year we've been in government, and it now stands at $9 an hour for adults. That means that an adult on the minimum wage and working 40 hours a week is paid $80 more a week than when people marched in the Hikoi of Hope.

The increases in the minimum wage have been particularly spectacular for young people. Back in 1998 the youth minimum wage stood at 60 per cent of the adult wage at $4.20 an hour, and applied to sixteen- to nineteen-year-olds. In March 2001 the age for the adult minimum wage was lowered from 20 years of age to eighteen, and the youth minimum increased to 70 per cent of the adult minimum. Then, in March 2002, the youth minimum wage for sixteen- and seventeen-year-olds increased from 70 per cent of the adult minimum to 80 per cent. Today the youth minimum stands at $7.20 an hour—over 70 per cent more than in 1998 for sixteen- and seventeen-year-olds.

Our government has also taken other steps to improve conditions for working people. In 2002, paid parental leave was introduced for a period of twelve weeks. The maximum payment stands at $334.75 a week and is adjusted by the rise in average weekly earnings each year. By late last year more than 14,000 people had accessed the scheme. The idea is to make it financially easier for working people to take leave to be with a new baby. It is a very important social justice and labour market measure, and of greatest benefit to lower-income families. Extensions to the scheme are due to be announced shortly.

Legislation has also been passed to give workers a right to a minimum four weeks' annual holiday from 2007. This, too, is of greatest assistance to the lower-paid and least-skilled workers, who have the least bargaining power. Australians have had a minimum four weeks' holiday for three decades. It's time our working people enjoyed the same. Only the continuation of a centre-left government guarantees that extra week's holiday. Does anyone really think it would survive under a right-wing government determined to tip the balance away from working people and their families?

The same can be said of decent industrial relations legislation. One of the key pillars of the social division and marginalisation of the 1990s was the Employment Contracts Act, which was heavily weighted towards employers' interests. Our government set out to strike a better balance with the Employment Relations Act. We've succeeded, with more support for collective bargaining, with good faith made central to the bargaining process, and with improved mediation services and procedures to help resolve disputes. It can surely be no accident that the numbers of industrial stoppages are falling, with almost 30 per cent fewer stoppages in the past year than there were in the last year of the Employment Contracts Act.

But on top of all these measures, we know there's more to do.

We've held back from significant upward adjustments to family incomes until we knew we could sustain the spending required. After several years of economic growth and careful budget management, we believe the time has come to do more. This year's Budget will deliver a further growth dividend to low- and modest-income families.

We aim to ensure that families with dependent children are always better off when in work, while also improving the circumstances of families with children whose parents are not currently in the workforce.

We will be addressing some of the most critical barriers to employment, such as access to affordable childcare and accommodation costs. In last year's Budget we increased the childcare subsidy from a maximum of 37 hours a week to 50 hours, making paid employment for parents more accessible and worthwhile. That and raising the threshold for Family Support were important steps in a longer-term plan of substantial improvement in assistance to families.

Big changes have also been made and more are planned to make housing more affordable for low-income people. We reintroduced income-related rents for state housing in 2000 and have ensured that low-income tenants pay no more than 25 per cent of their income in rent. We estimate that on average state house tenants are saving $1,800 per year as a result of the return to income-related rents. By doing that, we are helping those families get out of the poverty created for them by the policies of the 1990s. Around 90 per cent of tenants in Housing New Zealand's 64,000 households now have directly subsidised rents.

We also brought back a needs-based allocation system for state housing. In the bad old days of market rents, the houses went to those who could pay the high rents. Since then, turnover in state houses has decreased significantly. That contributes to greater stability for families and for communities.

Another legacy of the 1990s was National's sale of 13,000 state houses. We have been rebuilding the stock. To meet the demand for state housing in areas of high need, nearly 4,000 homes have been added to the state house stock since December 1999. That included buying 1,600 Auckland City Council homes—mainly pensioner units—which were to be put on the market by a privatising council. Nothing gave me more pleasure in the last four years than seeing the relief and smiles on the faces of those Auckland pensioners when they heard we had saved their homes.

We are also keen to work with local government and third-sector housing providers to get more affordable housing. Last year we allocated $63 million to a four-year programme of social housing programmes for that purpose.

We've taken a new initiative to bring home ownership within the reach of low- and modest-income earners by launching the pilot Mortgage Insurance Scheme in partnership with Kiwibank.

This year's Budget will see improvements to the Accommodation Supplement to help make mortgages and private rentals more affordable. And consultation will begin soon on a new Housing Strategy for New Zealand, setting out the steps to be taken to ensure that all New Zealanders have access to affordable, sustainable, quality housing appropriate to their needs.

The Hikoi of Hope called for a health system which was affordable, trustworthy and accessible to all. One of our first steps was to abolish the entirely appointed and business-oriented health boards across New Zealand, and replace them with boards with a majority of elected members. They are charged with the responsibility of being responsive to and meeting their communities' health needs.

We set goals of having all those referred for a specialist assessment in the public health system seen within six months, and then all those referred on for treatment seen within six months. By late last year 83 per cent of patients newly referred for specialist assessment were being seen within the six-month time frame, and of those meeting the criteria for treatment, 90 per cent were being treated within the six-month target time.

But we need to do more yet. Health is one of many areas where one's work is never done. I am particularly keen to see new initiatives to bring down waiting times in areas like orthopaedics, where progress hasn't been as fast as we would like.

One area of especially fast progress has been in primary healthcare. Already more than half the population is enrolled in primary health organisations (PHOs), and more than a million have access to low-cost primary care through their PHO. Last October, all six- to seventeen-year-olds enrolled in PHOs were added to the low-cost scheme. From 1 July this year, all those aged 65 and over enrolled in PHOs will also have access to low-cost care, and will pay only $3 for their prescription charges. These initiatives represent the greatest increase in access to primary care since the 1938 Social Security Act of the First Labour Government.

In addition, there have been big investments in mental health services, the new vaccine against the deadly meningococcal-B virus is being rolled out, the age range for the breast-screening programme has been widened to encompass all women aged 45 to 70 years [and] there are solid initiatives in many other areas of public health, including in targeting smoking levels.

We are also facing the reality that some of our communities have worse health than others. For example, Māori smoking rates are very high and Māori life expectancy is much lower than that of the general population. Research released only yesterday suggests that even high-income Māori have a significantly higher death rate than high-income Pākehā. Diabetes and its related health problems feature more prominently in Māori and Pacific peoples' communities.

It's important to our government that we endeavour to meet the health needs of all our communities, whoever or whatever they are. That may mean spending more in some and doing things differently to even up the odds. To dismiss such initiatives as unfair and discriminatory, as the National Party has done, is quite extraordinary. What is unfair and discriminatory is to see especially bad health and do nothing about it.

The final plank of the Hikoi of Hope called for accessible education. That means action at all levels, from early childhood education through to tertiary. We are steadily increasing the numbers of children in early childhood education, and there will be more initiatives in this year's Budget. In the compulsory sector, we've increased spending per student significantly and targeted more resources into lower-decile schools. Since 2001, we've created more than 2,000 new teaching positions. This year alone, there are an extra 774 more positions in our schools than were required for roll growth.

It's in the tertiary sector that rising costs were being felt most by families in the 1990s. In response, we froze the fees for three years, and from this year have introduced capped maximum fees to make sure they stay affordable. We stopped interest accruing on student loans while students were studying—a significant saving over the years of borrowing. We've introduced new Step Up scholarships for students from low-income families studying in the health and animal sciences. We expect to bring more students into the student allowance net to improve affordability.

As much as we can do we will do to improve access and affordability, because we believe in the inherent value of education and the difference it makes to life chances. As well we also need to be mindful of funding improvements in the quality of tertiary education.

Where to from here?

I believe that our government over these past four-and-a-half years has responded comprehensively to the call of the Hikoi of Hope for action. I don't pretend that the job is done, but I know that it is well underway, and that our will to continue on the journey is strong.

But we can only continue down that path with public support.

If New Zealanders want the growing opportunity, security and fairness which this Labour-led government has brought, then they will need to vote for it. The alternative is a return to the policies of division and despair of the 1990s, which caused so much heartache across our communities. Those forces of division have reared their head again in the wake of the now infamous Ōrewa speech. That is what moved the Anglican and Catholic bishops to speak out five days ago. I believe they spoke out because of that same sense of social solidarity which led to the launch of the Hikoi of Hope. I also believe that New Zealanders yearn for a nation which has a unity of purpose, which celebrates its successes and its strengths, and gives fellow citizens across our communities a fair go.

Perceptions have been fostered by right-wing parties that some New Zealanders, namely Māori, are better off than others. That's hard to sustain when one looks at the levels of unemployment, poor health, low educational attainment and poor housing in Māoridom. What the National Party now seems to resent is that Labour in government is trying to address those very serious problems in the national interest, as indeed it did in the past, albeit with less generosity and success.

This Opposition attack is a new and disturbing development. What it shatters is an informal consensus which has operated across governments of both kinds for many years about how to deal with disparities between communities. From the earliest days of the old Department of Māori Affairs, there were programmes designed to promote more equality of opportunity for Māori. In the late twentieth and early twenty-first centuries, Māori providers have been funded to ensure that nationwide strategies to lift educational achievement, health standards and many other indicators can also be effective for Māoridom.

Now it appears that all these positive initiatives are being questioned, and that that informal consensus has been shattered.

That does not call for a U-turn by Labour and there will not be one. What we will do is address the concerns and questions which the current debate has seen genuine people raising. It would be both irresponsible and insensitive not to be listening to that. We believe in fairness and equality of opportunity for all New Zealanders. What we will do is go back through all our policies to assure ourselves that they do indeed promote those values and are responsive to the needs of all our communities.

Where I believe perceptions of unfairness can arise is where policies move from a population focus to an individual benefit. For example, education spending targeted into low-decile schools, which in many communities have a significant proportion of Māori students, serves to lift performance across whole communities. Spending targeted into individual scholarships available only to members of specified groups can be seen to be unfair and should be re-examined.

If there is to be any good come from the gross and unpleasant Ōrewa speech, it may be that we can get the facts out on the table and encourage an informed debate about the kind of society we want—for I am very clear about the kind of New Zealand I want to develop. I don't want to return to the unfairness and the nastiness and the division of the 1990s. I do want to keep on addressing the key planks of the Hikoi of Hope and making life better for ordinary people across all New Zealand's communities. But our government can't achieve that if New Zealand's indigenous people are left behind as a marginalised community, permanently worse off than everyone else.

I strongly believe that our future lies together.

I know that people around the world have looked at New Zealand as an example of a country which has endeavoured to recognise the status of indigenous people and build an inclusive society. Many at home and abroad have seen the renewed focus on the Treaty of Waitangi as a strength and an asset, not as a liability. These past few weeks, offshore observers, like many of us at home, have wondered why New Zealand is suddenly turning itself inside out.

My commitment to New Zealanders is clear. I believe that one of the fundamental duties of leadership is to bring people together, not to drive them apart. We are a nation of many peoples, and we must respect and value them all. Our nation is likely to become more, not less, diverse.

I came into politics to work for a more just society. I know that to achieve that we also have to build a stronger economy. It is to these ends that I have devoted a political career which has stretched over more than 30 years, including more than 22 in parliament. I am not going to stand by and see a cynical and manipulative Opposition set out to destroy what our government together with New Zealanders has been busy repairing for four-and-a-half years. Nor do I believe a return to the bad old days of the 1990s is what New Zealanders want. Hikois of Hope would become annual and increasingly hopeless events if the forces behind the policies of the 1990s were let loose again.

We live in a democracy and the choices are clear: we can go forward together, or we can rip ourselves apart. We have recent experiences of both paths. The decision about which to take will be in New Zealanders' hands next year.

I know where I stand.

I know where my government stands.

A debate about the future of New Zealand has been launched.

I say: bring it on.

EEO Trust Work and Life Awards: Prime Minister's address

Auckland
2 September 2004

The Equal Employment Opportunity Trust (EEO) was set up in 1991 to address employment practices to foster equal rights in New Zealand workplaces, and in 2016 rebranded as Diversity Works NZ. In its current iteration, Diversity Works NZ's focus is on raising awareness about diversity and inclusion. The first EEO Trust Work and Life Awards were held in 1998, and honoured businesses that created healthy and happy workplaces for their staff.

Thank you for inviting me once again to present the EEO Trust's annual Work and Life Awards. First, I would like to acknowledge the continuing work of the EEO Trust. The trust has defined itself as a centre of excellence ever since its inception in 1991, and I commend its leadership on EEO issues over these past thirteen years.

Those who have entered tonight's awards understand well the business and workplace benefits of work–life balance. You also appreciate that your staff are your greatest assets. That's why you have looked outside the square and looked for new ways to improve recruitment and retention rates, reduce absenteeism, promote employee satisfaction and loyalty and improve productivity.

It's good to see that initiatives which were once the domain of only very committed and progressive workplaces are now becoming more standard practice. The principles and practice of work–life balance are becoming more deeply embedded in the culture of many more workplaces. I thank all those who entered tonight's awards for the leadership they have given on these issues.

Many countries like New Zealand are striving to achieve better work–life balance. In the past, the focus was on how to support women balancing work and family responsibilities. Governments tended to respond with initiatives of direct benefit to families, and employers were encouraged to respond with family-friendly policies. Over time, however, the complexity of the issues which put pressure on work–life balance have become better understood, and responses to them have become more sophisticated. Now, work–life balance is more likely to be understood within a broader decent work agenda, and it is more widely appreciated that productive economies depend on skilled, healthy and productive workplaces.

As well, developed countries face new population challenges, including declining fertility, an ageing workforce and the changing nature of families. These challenges require new responses too.

The need for healthy and productive workplaces must now translate into a broader interest in the health and well-being of all employees. There is, for example, more awareness of the importance of work–life balance for men, who have been more likely to put in excessive hours in their paid work. The EEO Trust survey of fathers in New Zealand last year showed that around 80 per cent of the fathers surveyed would like to spend more time with their families.

In New Zealand, the economic imperatives for work–life balance are growing. As our population ages, the challenge is to maximise the full potential of the workforce. The global pinch of skill shortages means that our workplaces need to be more innovative and more responsive to what matters to staff—if they are to recruit and retain them.

In meeting our workforce needs, the first place to look is to our own people. We do have a lower rate of participation by women, for example, than do top-performing Scandinavian economies. The nature and quality of our workplaces and working conditions does have a bearing on whether those who are presently under-represented will come forward to share their talents.

It's clear to me that generating higher growth and productivity will also be linked to removing the barriers to participation in the paid workforce. The government's big investments in paid parental leave, quality early childhood education, and the improvements to working family incomes are part of the answer. But so are initiatives in the workplace of the kind tonight's award winners have implemented.

For many of the organisations entering this year's awards, a culture which encourages work–life balance has become a natural expression of their organisational values. That culture has become integral to what the business is.

As well, the commitment of individual managers and employees is critical in making work–life balance policies part of a culture of best practice in the workplace. But those committed leaders need to be well supported. Small and medium-sized organisations, for example, can find it hard to develop the systems which are needed to support a productive and health workforce. The work of the EEO Trust and the leadership demonstrated by this year's award entrants are very important and the government also has a leadership role to play.

I spoke at last year's function about the Work–Life Balance Project the government had established. Research undertaken for the project suggests that people get caught up in the day-to-day business of living and that life can get out of balance without one being aware that that is happening. Often only a crisis or major event in one's life forces a re-evaluation.

The researchers spoke with people about the impact of imbalance on their lives. While participants tended to focus more on the impacts outside the workplace, the impact at work—such as through the deterioration of relationships, increased mistakes, lower quality of work and decreased job satisfaction—also came through strongly.

The issues raised in this research, and in the more than 700 other public contributions to the Work–Life Balance Project, identified key concerns for New Zealanders. Employees raised issues ranging from the intensity of work, to long hours and precarious work arrangements, adequacy of income and carer responsibilities.

Issues raised by employers suggest that the size of their organisation has a bearing on their ability to develop initiatives for work–life balance, with smaller employers finding it more difficult and expensive. The work–life balance arrangements described by employers and self-employed people suggested that they frequently operated within tight margins and found it difficult to take time off.

Community and voluntary sector concerns centred on the difficulty of attracting and keeping volunteer staff. It is notable that a number of community organisations went to some lengths to provide conditions supporting work–life balance as they did not have the resources to compensate staff with higher wages.

Officials are now considering what practical measures might assist people in balancing their businesses and working lives. They will look at which aspects of the problems or gaps in policies relate most appropriately to government, or to firms, families, communities and individuals.

Last year when I attended the EEO Trust Awards, the government had just set up a task force on pay and employment equity in the public sector. It has since reported, identifying factors which impact on achieving pay and employment equity, including women's position in the workforce, the undervaluing of jobs women do, and how work is organised.

The task force recommended a five-year plan of action to address those factors in the public sector. A dedicated unit in the Labour Department has been set up to work on implementation, with a steering group drawn from across the public sector overseeing the work of the unit and providing leadership for the action plan.

The government has also decided to extend the duration of paid parental leave. It moves from the twelve weeks introduced in 2002 to thirteen weeks in December this year, and to the International Labour Organization (ILO) standard of fourteen weeks by December 2005. We are also extending access to the scheme so that employees who have worked for the same employer for six months or more will also qualify for paid parental leave. Last year 16,000 women accessed the scheme, and feedback has been very positive. We are examining how the scheme might be extended to the self-employed as well.

The Working for Families package in the Budget is also positive for low- and modest-income working families with children. Apart from the increases in family income and accommodation supplement, there are specific initiatives supporting families needing their children cared for while parents work. From October, the rate of the Out of School Care and Recreation (OSCAR) subsidy for school-age children will come into line with the childcare subsidy rate for preschool children, and both rates will increase by 10 per cent. Both rates are scheduled to increase by a further 10 per cent from 3 October 2005. Then, from 1 April 2005, new funding into early childhood education will make it more affordable for families overall. And, from 1 July 2007, three- and four-year-old children will be able to receive 20 hours' free education in community-based services.

In conclusion, let me thank the EEO Trust once again for its leadership on work–life balance issues, and thank all entrants to the awards for their commitment to making workplaces healthier, happier places. To the winners, congratulations on setting new benchmarks for best practice, and showing others how to get the best results.

The New Zealand Labour Party Congress: Prime Minister's address

Wellington Town Hall, Wellington
2 April 2005

The year 2005 was an election year, with the general election held on 17 September. In November the previous year, the Labour Government had passed The Foreshore and Seabed Act 2004, and that same month had also commenced negotiations for a free trade agreement with China. Labour would ultimately win the election and enter its third and final term with Helen at the helm.

––––––

It's with enormous pride that I stand to address this election-year congress of the New Zealand Labour Party. I'm proud to see the party I've been a member of for 34 years do so well. I'm proud to lead a strong team inside and outside parliament. I'm proud to see our party attract so many outstanding new candidates—that bodes well for the future. But, most of all, I'm proud to see the progress our country is making under our Labour-led government.

I'm proud to see the solid economic growth, averaging over 3.7 per cent a year under Labour and among the fastest growing in the OECD. I'm proud to see New Zealand leading the developed world with the lowest unemployment rate at 3.6 per cent. I'm proud to see the investments we've made in health, in education, in housing, in services and security for older New Zealanders and families, and in infrastructure. And I'm proud to see the gains New Zealand is making felt in households across the land.

Along with the pride comes humility, and a strong sense of the enormous honour the people of New Zealand have done us by voting us into government. We must not let them down. No party has a right to govern this country. There is no natural party of government. There are parties of opportunity and there are parties of privilege. Our historic mission is to see that the parties of opportunity working for all the people are able to govern. Elections in New Zealand are an open contest, and they are keenly fought. In a democracy, the people choose—and it is an honour and a privilege to be chosen.

This election year, we will again go out and put our case—and we will take nothing for granted. Complacency is among the most perilous diseases in politics, and its twin sister is arrogance. No matter how good our record is, we can never rest on our laurels and think we've done enough for our country, because there will always be more to do. More opportunity to open up. More security to guarantee. More fairness to secure.

So, we can't stand still—neither as a party, nor New Zealand as a nation. We need to apply a restless energy to identifying the new issues, rising to the new challenges, and finding answers to them which resonate with our core values and beliefs.

This election will be about who has the best policies for the future, not for the past. It will be about looking forward, not backwards. It will be about building on the platform of steady achievement we've carefully built these past five years and four months. And it will be about inspiring all of us as New Zealanders to set our sights even higher, knowing that our country has the potential to do even better, and understanding even more than we did five years ago what New Zealand can achieve.

When we ran for office in 1999, we said we couldn't perform miracles overnight, but that over time we would make a difference for the better. We knew that trust in politicians and the political process was at a low ebb, and that New Zealanders were sick of being let down. We promised only what we knew we could deliver, so that we could maintain people's trust and confidence.

Each step of the way, we've set out our longer-term objectives, direction and vision, and sought a mandate for our policies. It's important to me that when New Zealanders vote for a Labour-led government, they know that they are electing people with credible policies who will deliver on their promises. That's been a hallmark of our Labour-led governments—and what a contrast it's been with the broken promises of those who preceded us in government, and who keep hoping that New Zealanders' memories are short enough to vote them back again.

Five years and four months ago, when we took office, our task was huge. New Zealand had undergone fifteen years of topsy-turvy change, but few felt better off and most felt worse off. Unemployment stood at 6.8 per cent, with economic settings making it unlikely that it could fall below 6 per cent. The government of the day maintained its faith in deregulation, privatisation and cutting back on government and public services—despite the obvious failure of its economic and social policies to deliver for New Zealanders.

Our job has been to change the direction, and to invest for growth and opportunity and for better public services and more security. Our reward has been to see the stronger economy, the falling unemployment, the better-funded health and education, the falling crime rates and the growing confidence in New Zealand's future.

Now our challenge is to build on that platform of achievement, so that New Zealand continues to go forward with confidence, not backwards.

This election New Zealanders will look at who has the best policies for the future, and who has the best track record, the best team and the best leadership to take New Zealand ahead. They will look at who can deliver for New Zealand. I have no doubt that the best policies, the best team, the best track record and the strongest leadership are to be found in the New Zealand Labour Party.

The best policies have not only seen New Zealand as a whole go ahead, but have delivered real gains to New Zealanders across the board.

Two-hundred and sixty-four thousand more jobs in the economy means higher incomes and more opportunity and security for our families.

Health spending per year is now $2.6 billion more than in 1999. That means cheaper doctor's fees for many, and more people getting the treatment they need and getting it faster.

Education spending is now $2.25 billion a year more than in 1999. That means more small children getting a good start in life in early childhood education, more teachers, bigger operating budgets and new technology in our schools and more people than ever before in education and training.

Income-related rents in state houses mean superannuitants and low-income families in them can afford their homes.

An extra 1,080 people in the police force have helped bring down the crime rate to its lowest level in 23 years and helped solve more crime.

Restoring the level of New Zealand Superannuation has lifted standards of living for older citizens. Establishing the New Zealand Superannuation Fund has secured New Zealand Superannuation for future generations.

And now the Working For Families policy is putting real money into the pockets of low- and modest-income families with children. This coming week, most families receiving Family Support will receive another $25 a week for their first child, and $15 a week for each other child. Within two years' time, under Working for Families, our government will have reduced child poverty by 30 per cent, to lower than the average rate in the European Union. That is something I'm very proud of.

And let me acknowledge here the fact that we could not have achieved any of this without the support of other parties in parliament. Jim Anderton and the Progressives as a coalition partner have been very reliable allies, and have brought real enthusiasm to reinvigorating our regions and tackling serious social issues like youth suicide. Peter Dunne and United Future as our confidence and supply partner have provided the stability which is enabling our current government to become the longest-serving one in New Zealand's MMP history, an event we marked this week. Jeanette Fitzsimons, Rod Donald and the Greens have also provided us with crucial support in many areas fundamental to Labour's vision, from employment relations to transport policies to social security policies to climate change and much more. And I also record our thanks to New Zealand First for its support on the Foreshore and Seabed Act, and to those members of National and Act who cast aside narrow party politics to support human rights legislation like the Civil Union Act.

So where does our Labour-led government go from here?

We seek to carry on as we have begun, opening up opportunity, encouraging innovation and creativity, building security and promoting

New Zealand, our people, our products and services and our country's achievements and qualities to the world. We know this country still has untapped potential. But we also know there's optimism and a high level of confidence about what we can achieve working together. Only a bad government and a return to the failed policies of the past can hold New Zealand back now—and who would risk that?

From the beginning, our government has laid long-term plans for building New Zealand's future. We haven't sought short-term fixes—they don't address the real issues. Others would have squandered the operating surplus, preferring tax cuts to investments in the basics and in the future. Our government already has $5.75 billion invested in the New Zealand Superannuation Fund, guaranteeing New Zealand Superannuation can be paid to future generations.

We've got a huge forward programme over the next four years of $18.9 billion into land transport, spread across public transport, roading and alternatives to roading. We've kept building up health and education and police spending year on year—and there's still unmet need. Our plans see Working for Families continuing to roll out over the next two years, to be fully operational at $1.1 billion a year. We've kept funding more apprentices and industry trainees every year and have more ambitious targets for the future. From 1 July this year, we begin the phase-out of asset testing on older people in continuing care, starting at around $103 million a year and rising to $345 million by 2020. This addresses a fundamental issue of discrimination for our older people at a pace New Zealand can afford. Every year we've kept building up the funding for economic development initiatives, to back growth and innovation in our industries and businesses. These budgets are now running at $150 million a year—and they'll keep growing.

But as well we must focus on the next generation of issues.

Our economy has grown fast—helped by more and more people coming into the workforce. Now we are running short of workers, particularly of those with skills. Our active labour-market policies are more important than ever. With 100,000 fewer working-age adults on benefits, we've already been spectacularly successful in getting people back to work, but we can do better yet.

Through our drive for better value for money in tertiary education and training, we can channel even more money into the education and skills training which leads more people to real jobs and better jobs.

Through our better-targeted immigration system, we will get migrants with more skills to help fill the gaps in our workforce. And with extended paid parental leave, longer holidays and more affordable early childhood education and childcare, we can give real choice to women with children as to whether they work or not. Work–life balance and having enough time for family is fundamental to the New Zealand way of life.

An economy short of workers must also work to raise its productivity. This is now a major focus for us in government, and we will work with leaders in industry, both employers and unions, to bring about the changes which will boost productivity, profitability and living standards. Our investments in skills and innovation, and the policies we develop to encourage more business investment, and safe, healthy and collaborative workplaces are all-important—both in their own right, and in encouraging companies to prioritise these areas to boost productivity.

More New Zealanders working, in better jobs, with more skills and higher incomes means more New Zealanders with a strong stake in our society. Having a strong stake means having a sense of ownership and being able to realise one's aspirations for the future. Labour's message to New Zealanders is, 'We want you to be able to get ahead, and to be able to build a secure future for your family and for your retirement.'

We are developing new policies to encourage New Zealanders to build up their assets through saving—saving for a better retirement income, saving for a first home and saving to ease the costs of tertiary education for children. Given the opportunity to save, we believe New Zealanders will plant that firm stake in the future which gives each of us greater control over our own destiny and that of our families.

Creating opportunity and security for New Zealanders means opening doors beyond New Zealand as well. Our government has developed a huge trade agenda to secure more openings for New Zealand exports, whether they be traditional commodities, processed and manufactured goods, or services like education.

Our vision sees New Zealand as a prosperous, sophisticated global trader succeeding because of the quality of our exports and our smart marketing and branding.

At home, through our innovation initiatives, we seek to inspire New Zealanders to develop that X-factor about their businesses which will enable them to succeed in the global market. And what a buzz there was at the Better by Design conference in Auckland this week as people learned more about the power of design to transform the quality of everything we produce and market. Top-quality products and services are what we seek to take out to the world.

Through the Doha Round of the WTO, through all the trade agreements we are negotiating, we are determined to bring more opportunity for New Zealand businesses and workers. Many of our new trade initiatives are focused on Asia. The FTA with Singapore is in place; one takes effect with Thailand in July; and we are negotiating with China and ASEAN, and about to begin with Malaysia.

But it's not only in trade that Asia looms large on our agenda. Good relations with the nations of Asia are critical to New Zealand's future prosperity and security, and we will work as hard as we can to secure both.

It hasn't gone without notice that New Zealand attracts a lot of high-profile international visitors these days. That's because we are actively engaged in many issues and with many regions, both advancing our interests and being part of addressing issues affecting the international community. Whether it's delivering aid for tsunami-stricken nations or peace-building in Afghanistan and East Timor, whether it's working for global solutions on climate change, trade, nuclear disarmament or terrorism, New Zealand is to be found doing far more than just pulling its weight. That makes me proud to be a New Zealander too.

We've got big challenges to meet at home and abroad in the coming years. We are building a strong, inclusive nation with our many ethnicities, faiths, beliefs and orientations, and we must find strength in our diversity. For New Zealand to succeed, we must draw on all the talents, and see no one excluded because of who they are or what they believe.

We need to protect and promote what is unique and special about us as a nation, from Māoritanga to our unique sense of community, values and lifestyle. Where there is division and conflict between us, we need to find fair and just solutions which strike a balance in the interests of all.

Many New Zealanders of my generation and older generations have found issues dating back to the signing of the Treaty difficult to comprehend and hard to resolve. The processes established to achieve resolution and fairness aren't always understood, but in the international context New Zealand's efforts to seek truth and reconciliation stand second to none.

On the historical claims, the time has come to seek finality. Our policy will set a date by which all those claims must be lodged so that we can proceed to settle with those who wish to settle within a reasonable timeframe.

Much of Māoridom, like most of the rest of us, looks forward to the potential of the future, and it is easier to move on as the past is addressed. The Hui Taumata last month demonstrated beyond doubt that there is an energy and vitality in Māoridom that makes its future development unstoppable—and that is good for New Zealand.

Our pride in our nationhood can only soar higher as we see all our communities—Pākehā, Māori, Pasifika and many others from around the world—succeeding, contributing and participating in a nation which for many of us has been and still is 'God's own'.

I go into this election full of optimism—not only about our prospects, but about New Zealand's prospects. Have we got everything right? No, not always, but we've given it our best shot and we learn from our mistakes. Is New Zealand a better place because of our efforts? I believe it is, but I can see much more that needs to be done.

As we move ahead, my eye will be on keeping the balance between growth and development—and our unique environment and quality of life.

Nature cannot defend itself against humankind. If we want clean air and water, healthy cities and the values of our natural heritage preserved, we humans will have to make the accommodation—or that heritage will not be there for future generations.

Our drive for higher living standards for all must also be consistent with our people's desire to balance family, work and community responsibilities. In the end, we work to live—and not the other way round.

I spoke earlier of the danger of complacency. We woke yesterday morning to see very gratifying poll results. The challenge before every candidate and organiser in this hall today is to turn that poll into a strong election result. Because there is only one poll that counts—and it's on a date yet to be determined.

Our opponents are desperate—and it shows. They'll attack anyone and anything to get a headline, regardless of the damage they do to critical institutions like the New Zealand Police.

We stand for something better: for a higher purpose, for long-term and sustained progress, for opportunity not privilege, for inclusion not marginalisation, for security and not fear in old age and adversity.

We stand for what will secure our standards of living, prosperity and security for the future, and we are not afraid of meeting new challenges head on.

We will continue to offer the stable, sensible, reasonable, consistent, predictable government with strong leadership and a clear vision for the future which has served New Zealand well since 1999 and will, I hope, for many years to come.

Labour's Third Term

Parliament, Wellington
6 November 2005

In September 2005 Labour was elected to a third term in government, in coalition with the Progressive Party and with confidence and supply support from New Zealand First and United Future. Helen delivered this speech to parliament at the start of what would prove her final term as Prime Minister of New Zealand.

———

I regard it as a great honour to be elected to this House, and I regard it as a very special honour to lead and form a government. This is the ninth time I have been elected to this House and spoken in the Address in Reply debate, and it is the third time I have had the privilege of being sworn in as Prime Minister. I thank the many hundreds of thousands of New Zealanders who cast their vote for the Labour Party to go back into government. Indeed, not far short of a million New Zealanders voted for this party to lead the government again.

I also record my thanks to the other parties in this parliament who were prepared to negotiate working relationships with Labour. I set out after this election to negotiate arrangements that would be stable and durable—as they will be. I thank New Zealand First and United Future for the confidence and supply arrangement, and I thank the Green Party for the abstention and working relationship that we have with it. We worked hard over the course of a month to put those arrangements in place, and now it falls to us to provide the leadership and the good government that will take New Zealand further ahead. I said from the time of election night that Labour did want to reach out across the parliament to a range of small parties and to be as inclusive as possible in arrangements for government. We have shown our willingness to share power and work collaboratively in the MMP environment, and that, I believe, is what New Zealanders want from our electoral system.

Ever since the infamous Ōrewa speech, our opponents set out to gain power by dividing Kiwis against each other. Our route to power has been very different. Where others preach exclusion we preach inclusion, and we do see it as our historic duty to play a role in bringing New Zealanders together—not driving them apart and splitting our society down the middle. We also see it as the historic duty of the Labour movement to see that every New Zealander gets a fair go and has opportunity and security, and that as our country grows and develops every single Kiwi has a chance to share the fruits of that progress. We are dedicating our third term in government, as we dedicated the first two, to our work to strengthen our economy and to make sure that the fruits of that go to every household in the land—as they do.

We also dedicate ourselves to building a strong and confident nation. We are proud of the cohesion in our society relative to that of many others. We are proud of the achievers New Zealand has in every field. We are proud of the unique cultures and heritage of our county, proud of the natural environment, and proud of the role our country plays in world affairs. There is no doubt that there will be challenges ahead in this term in government. Of course, New Zealand has had six years, first with a government of Labour and the Alliance, then of Labour and the Progressives, and now of Labour and the Progressives again, where there have been good growth rates and a fantastic fall in unemployment rates. We are proud of that. We are proud of being able to reinvest back into our public services and infrastructure, into areas like the arts and sport and the environment, into policing, into the justice, defence and security areas and into getting better representation of New Zealand offshore.

But we know that we can never stand still in government. As fast as our country grows and develops, and as fast as we lift the level of skill and innovation our country has, there are other nations that are striving to catch up with us, and others are keeping that critical margin ahead of us in the living-standards stakes. It will take very smart thinking and very smart strategies to stay positioned as an affluent nation in today's global economy. And we have to stay positioned as affluent; there are no prizes for failure. As we look around the world, we see China and India emerging as mega-economies. Each of them produces four million university graduates a year—each of them as many graduates as our total population. We see them competing not just for the low-wage, low-skill jobs but for the high-tech, high-skill, high-value work as well. So we have a race on to keep our position as an affluent nation, and we cannot afford to waste the talent of a single New Zealander. We say that the New Zealand way in the twenty-first century has to be to mobilise all the skills, the talent, the ideas and the passion of every New Zealander, so that our country can succeed. I believe New Zealanders want to accept that challenge. Our role in government is to provide the leadership and the inspiration to lift our people's aspirations, so we can succeed in this century.

I do see the immediate challenge before us as being to help facilitate the economy to move into a better balance between its export and its domestic sectors. Monetary policy, obviously, is tightening in order to head off domestic inflation, and the effect of the higher interest rates and the higher currency exchange rate has undoubtedly hurt our export sectors. In managing through this period we believe it is very important for the government to continue to run a conservative fiscal policy, so that we do not put pressure on monetary policy. I want to say this: there is no doubt in my mind that the National Party's reckless tax cuts policy could only have led to very severe monetary policy or to radical cuts in public spending. It is with great appreciation that I record that enough New Zealanders were aware of that not to give National the chance to wreck the economy and public services as well.

As a government we have always looked far beyond any short-term fix that might have presented itself in economic issues to the medium and the longer-term strategies. As in the past six years, our emphasis will be on improving the foundations for long-term and sustainable growth. That means lifting our skills levels. It means lifting our savings levels. It means lifting productivity. It means lifting our capacity for innovation. It means lifting the capacity to export, and to produce goods and services of a higher value. It means modernising our infrastructure. We cannot ask New Zealanders to work any harder. Already our people are working many more hours every year than workers in other comparable countries, and record numbers of us are working as well—the participation rate is extremely high. So our future to prosperity is about working smarter.

Of course that will require commitment from the workforce and from business, but it is also helped by the government's willingness to invest and to adjust policy settings so that we enable a continual move of our economy upmarket to occur. That is why, in our election programme, we set new targets for skills training. That is why we are moving more of our science and research spending into the longer-term funding arrangements. That is why we are reviewing corporate taxation to see what practical signals we can give to lift productivity. That is why we will do more to back the commercialisation of innovation. That is why creating opportunities for our exporters is central to our economic policy. We will be designating 2007 as export year, and New Zealand Trade and Enterprise will be expected to increase its focus on exporting.

We know, though, that the big export gains for New Zealand will be made in the breakthroughs we get in trade negotiations. We know our primary sectors would be huge winners from success in the World Trade Organization's Doha Round, and those negotiations are, and must remain, our top trade priority. As well, of course, we will continue to follow bilateral and regional free-trade agreements such as those we are currently negotiating with China, Malaysia and all of ASEAN. Our belief is that New Zealand will succeed as an open trading economy, and that we must be smart, creative, entrepreneurial and innovative as well. We have policies aimed at positioning New Zealand with a competitive edge in the global economy. That is the route to prosperity.

I believe what distinguishes governments of the centre-left from those of the right is our determination to see the benefits from a growing economy reach households across the country. Our government's policies have been exceptionally job-rich, with more than 270,000 more people in work than there were when we came into government in 1999. That has boosted household income. We have been able to invest heavily in public and social services. We have built up health and education. We have built up support for families and superannuitants, and we have built up the capacity of our police force.

But we have new goals and targets to meet in a third term. Before Christmas we will have passed legislation for two critical parts of Labour Party policy. The first is the extended tax relief for our families—in total, around 77 per cent of our families with dependent children will qualify for that. We can say that this is the biggest investment in families made by any government for many decades, and it will have a dramatic effect on child poverty. It still excites me to know that the effect of Working for Families will be to drop child poverty rates in this country down to the level of those in the Netherlands, which we all look up to as being an advanced social democracy that delivers for its people. It is a proud day for us to be able to achieve that. Labour has said that the top priority for tax relief right now is our hard-working families. They do face the costs associated with raising children, and I think the well-being of the next generation is a vital concern to every New Zealander.

The second key initiative that will be legislated for before Christmas is getting rid of the interest on student loans—getting rid of it. This is a very big investment in our young people and in our country. It gives a hand up to those graduates who are prepared to put their skills at the service of New Zealand. It gives fresh hope to young Kiwis who would otherwise have been saddled with very high debt. It means they can plan ahead with confidence, and it means that they will stay in New Zealand. That is good for our country.

I want to refer to the boost coming for superannuation on 1 April, because superannuitants are also going to get a greater share in the growing economy. The annual adjustment for superannuation next year will be set at 66 per cent of the net average ordinary-time weekly wage rather than 65 per cent, and I acknowledge that this was part of the arrangements entered into for confidence and supply with New Zealand First. As well, there will be many superannuitants who will benefit from the improved rates rebate scheme that is due for introduction next year.

We also have very ambitious new policies right across education, health and social development. In education, particularly in terms of the priority being given to the early years, from July 2007 we will see three- and four-year-old children in our licensed teacher-led early childhood centres being funded for 20 hours of free education a week. That will be an enormous help to our families. Over the next three years we will be implementing a 1:15 ratio in the new entrant classes in our schools. At the other end of the school system, the goal is to see all our young people move on from school into some form of further education, training or work. We have many new initiatives coming on stream for youth transitions and, of course, the many thousands of new places for apprenticeships as well.

Health ranks with education as a top priority for us, and is right at the top of the public's list of what it expects a government to deliver. We do deliver, with many thousands more treatments at our public hospitals, with more affordable primary care, and with huge investments in mental health as well. We have new targets to meet for orthopaedic surgery and for cataract surgery, we have the rollout of lower doctors' fees coming across all age groups of our community, and we have many new initiatives for child health as well. Among them are more funding for the Well Child checks of the kind done by Plunket, the free child health check before a child starts school in order to pick up any problems that might impact on the child's ability to learn, and, very important, the hearing check for newborn children. New Zealand has been picking up deafness in children far too late because we have not had a systematic programme of testing, and that is about to change. We also have very big improvements planned for child and young persons' dental services.

As well, at the other end of the age scale, there are the many challenges in the aged-care sector. There will need to be more funding. The staff there are lowly paid, the numbers in care have been growing rapidly, and the truth is that when unemployment is low it is very hard for the aged-care sector to hang on to good staff. All of us have an interest in knowing that our older citizens in care are well looked after.

Looking to the future, the KiwiSaver scheme has benefits for the whole economy in helping to boost our savings rate. It has benefits for future generations saving for their first home, and it has benefits for future generations who can supplement their income in retirement. What we know is that generations of Kiwi families got their first home with government support in the past. That all stopped when National sold the mortgage portfolio of Housing New Zealand in 1991, and the homeownership rates dropped off. Now it falls to Labour to put back in place schemes that will help people to get their first homes. We will do that through KiwiSaver, through the mortgage insurance underwrites, and through the new equity-sharing initiative to be developed this term. As well, of course, our policy of fair income-related rents, which the National Party has always totally opposed, will continue.

We have made huge changes in the social assistance area, to focus the system on getting people off a benefit and into work. Our very low unemployment rate is a product of both high economic growth and very proactive labour market policies, and we have to keep being proactive. We still have pockets of higher unemployment in some communities than others. For example, Māori unemployment, while half what it was, is still two-and-a-half times the national rate. When one looks very closely into those figures, one can see that about two-thirds of Māori on the unemployment benefit actually have no formal educational qualifications at all, as opposed to about half the other New Zealanders on the unemployment benefit. We also find that, with the exception of Auckland, among four of the big northern regions for employment statistics, for Māori unemployed whose first job choice is labouring, the number of vacancies is vastly fewer than the numbers looking for that kind of unskilled work. So that tells us that critical to lowering Māori unemployment further will be lifting skills levels. And that is not just for the young people coming through school and transitioning into a first job; it is for the people out there who would like to work but who did not get the opportunity to get the skills, the literacy, the numeracy or the information technology skills at an earlier stage in their lives.

I want to say that I am very optimistic about Māori development. I was at the Hui Taumata; I saw the huge momentum that Māori development has. I want to commit our government again to working with Māoridom not only to resolve historical grievances—which we must do—but also to see that Māoridom, too, benefits from our country's growth and development.

This Labour-led government puts enormous emphasis on social solidarity and on building a strong nation in which everyone has an opportunity and a stake. In any nation where communities experience long-term marginalisation, disadvantage or discrimination, the social breakdown that results can be traumatic for the whole society, not just for the marginalised group. Over the past two-and-a-half weeks we have watched with the rest of the world as parts of France have been set alight, just as in decades past we saw the riots in deprived areas of the United States and Britain. In New Zealand we worry about the gang warfare in some of our suburbs, and about how to get the young people caught up in that on to a better path ahead. Offshore, we see minority communities generating home-grown terrorism that involves second-generation community members. The ripples of bombings offshore reach all the way to our families and cause heartbreak here.

I think the challenge for us in New Zealand is to keep building in our small country the tolerance and mutual respect for each other that allow diverse peoples to live alongside each other in peace. Trying to enforce a monoculture that does not allow for diversity of culture, heritage and belief would be a disaster for this country. Trying to force everyone into some kind of mythical mainstream would blow up in our face. In our nation-building in New Zealand the unifying concept has to be love for our country, whoever we are and whatever our backgrounds. I know that proud Kiwis can be people of any religion, any faith or belief, any ethnic or cultural background and any gender or orientation. The New Zealand way has to be to build unity and diversity, to avoid the marginalisation of communities, to practise inclusion in the national interest and to encourage all of those who want to be part of the building of New Zealand.

I illustrate that point with a practical example. Last week the Hon. Marian Hobbs and I were privileged to be at the second award of the Sonja Davies peace prize. This year that award went to an association of young Muslim women in Auckland. Their project was to work on how they can contribute to better understanding and religious tolerance and better community relationships in our country. It was really inspiring to hear the CVs of the young women who came forward to get that prize. They were academic high-flyers—absolute standouts in any crowd. I believe that our hopes for our future rest on encouraging young people like that to make investments in the relationships that have to bind each of us to each other in our country. I believe that our common future will be reinforced by seeing that fairness, opportunity and security are the common experience of every community that chooses to make its home in New Zealand.

It is well known that I see the arts and culture and heritage as central to the building of New Zealand identity. I have always believed that through New Zealand's creative people we express the essence and soul of what it is to be a New Zealander, and we express our perspectives. Through our creative people we define ourselves to the world as a uniquely creative nation. I believe our filmmakers, writers, poets and visual and performing artists do us proud, alongside those of anywhere in the world. So do our sportspeople, whose many achievements keep New Zealand in the world headlines probably far more than for any other small country.

We may be small, but we are never insignificant. I know that in world affairs New Zealand's voice is respected because it is reasoned, constructive, principled and independent. I am proud of that. I am one who sees New Zealand's nuclear-free stand as an asset, not a liability. Nothing on earth would cause me to want to change that. I also believe that our refusal to participate in the war in Iraq because it lacked multilateral sanction from the UN Security Council laid down very important and principled markers for our country, and I would make the same decision again any day.

Doing the right thing is not always easy. It is not easy to meet our Kyoto Protocol commitments, it is not easy to implement our trade agenda, and it is not easy to wrestle with the great pressures put on our oceans from damaging fishing practices. But wrestle with such pressures we must, as a concerned nation. Nor does our reputation as a peace-maker, and as a tolerant and an inclusive country, insulate us from the pressures of terrorism. Our people are affected when attacks occur on others, and we cannot and will not be a weak link in the chain. Over the past four years since September 11 we have strengthened our border security and our intelligence and policing capacity for counterterrorism, and we have passed new legislation to implement international conventions on terrorism. Like all nations, we are striving to get the balance right between individual rights and freedoms on the one hand and the right of the community to be protected on the other, and it is not always an easy balance to strike.

I go into this third term as Prime Minister full of optimism for New Zealand and our government. Of course there are challenges—there will always be challenges—but I believe we are well positioned to meet them. I do expect to see—as we have seen today—a somewhat embittered and angry Opposition in the House, as it contemplates three more years in Opposition, which is very hard for those who once saw themselves as the natural party of government. My message to them is that there is no natural party of government. My message is that being in government is a privilege bestowed on those who keep faith with the public, and whose policies and values are consistent with where most New Zealanders want to be. I say that our government will work inclusively and collaboratively with everyone who shares our vision for a strong, proud, confident New Zealand, growing and developing and enabling all our people to share in the progress. That is the New Zealand way, and that is what we are dedicated to.

Address at the Tangi of Te Arikinui Dame Te Atairangikaahu

Tūrangawaewae Marae, Ngāruawahia
18 August 2006

Dame Te Atairangikaahu was the Māori Queen from 1931 until her death in August 2006, making her the longest-reigning of any Māori monarch. In the New Year Honours in 1970, she became the first Māori woman appointed Dame Commander of the Order of the British Empire 'for outstanding services to the Māori people'. In 1987, she also became the first person appointed to the Order of New Zealand. She was buried in an unmarked grave on Taupiri Mountain, along with her tūpuna.

———

E te whānau pani, āku mihi aroha kia koutou,
Koutou o Waikato Tainui, tēnā koutou katoa.
E ngā iwi o te motu, ngā karangatanga maha, tēnā koutou, tēnā
*   koutou, tēnā koutou katoa.*

To the bereaved family, to Waikato Tainui, our aroha and sympathy are with you at this time.

We know of Te Arikinui's great struggle, particularly these last few months. We know of Te Arikinui's determination to be here for the great celebration of the fortieth anniversary of her late father's passing, and her own coronation. We know that only a few short weeks ago, Te Arikinui's seventy-fifth birthday was celebrated here. To be present for those events, while so ill, took great courage.

But courage was characteristic of Te Arikinui's life. Born in the depths of the Great Depression in 1931 in Huntly, educated in the very different environment of Diocesan School for Girls, as a relatively young woman Te Arikinui was chosen to lead the Kīngitanga and to fill the big shoes left by her father, King Korokī. As a child of the Waikato I remember that transition.

Over the past 40 years, Te Arikinui has been a source of continuity, a link to the past, but also the creator of a new future. Wherever there was opportunity for development for Māoridom, Dame Te Ata was to be found: with the Māori Women's Welfare League, with the Kōhanga Reo and the kura kaupapa, with the kapa haka, backing the sports teams, supporting the growth of Māori business.

Dame Te Ata's influence was felt throughout the land. Here at home in Waikato Tainui, she stood with her people as they moved to conclude the first major Treaty settlement with the Crown. That took courage—to go where no iwi had gone before; to set the benchmarks against which others would settle; to forge settlements which were durable. But it happened first here, with this remarkable leader's support.

Te Arikinui knew the importance of reconciliation. She knew too of the role her office could play in bringing us together. Māori and Pākehā beat a path to her door. She was a force for unity in our country, and we are the stronger for it.

For New Zealand, Te Arikinui performed outstanding representational duties here at home, welcoming guests from far away, including royalty, heads of state and governments and many other dignitaries. And she travelled widely to represent us. She forged strong friendships throughout the Pacific, and the tears of the Pacific nations flow here this week too.

Dame Te Ata brought us together in life, as she now brings us together at her death.

We all stand here knowing that one who has always been there for all of us will no longer be there: not at poukai, not at the annual conference of the Māori Women's Welfare League next month, not at her koroneihana anniversary in June, not at the annual celebration of Tahupotiki Wiremu Ratana's birth in January, not at the innumerable cultural festivals, sports events and business awards.

Her presence will be greatly missed for her smile, her warmth, her dignity and her wisdom.

Te Arikinui, you are about to make your last great journey down the river of your forebears, past every bend where the taniwha lies, to the sacred mountain of Taupiri. There you will lie with those of your whānau who have gone before. You go with our love, our respect and our admiration.

Our nation is the beneficiary of your work. May the leaders who follow you adopt your mantle and share the vision you have had for your people and our country.

Haere, haere, haere,
No reira, rau rangatira,
Tēnā koutou katoa.

Prime Minister's Tribute to Te Arikinui Dame Te Atairangikaahu

Parliament, Wellington
22 August 2006

Just over a week after the death of the Māori Queen Dame Te Atairangikaahu, Helen delivered the following official tribute, noting the monarch's contributions to Māoridom and to Aotearoa as a whole.

———

Madam Speaker, over the past week, many fine tributes have been paid to the late Te Arikinui Dame Te Atairangikaahu. Dame Te Ata passed away eight days ago, only a few short weeks after the celebrations for her fortieth anniversary as Māori Queen and then of her seventy-fifth birthday.

Dame Te Ata was a humble and unassuming woman who, over 40 years as Te Arikinui, made her presence felt in innumerable ways. She has been a source of continuity and a force for stability throughout that time. She represented links to the past and to the origins of Kīngitanga, but she was also one of the creators of a new future for Māoridom.

She was patron of the Māori Women's Welfare League, and in turn the league was an important support system for her throughout New Zealand. Similarly, she was a strong supporter of the revival of te reo Māori and all initiatives associated with that, from the establishment of Kōhanga Reo and kura kaupapa to Māori Television.

In the world of arts and culture, she gave strong backing to kapa haka across New Zealand, but could also be seen at the local arts festival in Huntly—and occasionally at opera and ballet in Auckland's Aotea Centre.

She was a lover of sport and a promoter of physical activity for young people, through rugby league, through the waka competitions on the Waikato, and could often be found at other major sporting events.

Wherever anything held opportunity for Māoridom, Dame Te Ata could be found.

It is significant that it was in Dame Te Ata's own rohe, Waikato Tainui, that the first major Treaty settlement with the Crown in modern times was made. This took courage. To be first is to lead, and in this case to set benchmarks for others which would be carefully scrutinised. Not all were supportive, but Waikato Tainui's settlement with Dame Te Ata's backing paved the way for a new era for Māoridom.

This was consistent with Dame Te Ata's quest for reconciliation between Māori and Pākehā. She saw us as two peoples in one nation. She wanted New Zealand to work for all of us. She knew that righting the wrongs of the past would help us build a better future, as it has. Dame Te Ata was a force for unity in diversity in our country, and I believe we are the stronger for it.

In recent days I have highlighted the extraordinary representational job Dame Te Ata did for New Zealand. At home she was a gracious host to many dignitaries—royalty, heads of state, heads of government, ministers, diplomats and other dignitaries. She travelled widely, to Europe, Asia, the Americas and particularly to the Pacific, where she built strong links. Our Pacific neighbours were well represented in the ceremonies of recent days in recognition of the time Dame Te Ata had invested in relationships in the Pacific.

Over the past week, countless thousands of people have flowed to Tūrangawaewae [Marae] to pay their respects. The tears have flowed for Te Ata and the whānau pani. Waikato Tainui have been outstanding hosts to so many. Organisation of a tangi on this scale for one so widely revered is a massive undertaking, and it has been undertaken with great skill and enormous dignity.

More broadly, this last week's events have drawn us together as a nation. Respect for Dame Te Ata flowed across our communities. Dame Te Ata brought us together at the time of her passing as she did throughout her life.

As a young person growing up in the Waikato in 1966, I recall the vivid images of King Korokī's passing, and of that last journey up the sacred mountain of Taupiri. Yesterday it was Dame Te Ata's turn to be carried up Taupiri to journey there one last time. The image which will forever stay with me is that hillside erupting spontaneously with song, chanting and haka as her casket moved towards it.

Dame Te Ata will be greatly missed for her friendship to all, her dignity and her wise counsel for so many.

To the new king, Te Arikinui Tūheitia Paki, we wish you well as you shoulder the responsibilities of leadership of the Kīngitanga. The new king brings the qualities to the job of his mother before him: dignity, warmth, a willingness to listen. Like Dame Te Ata, he too will become a force to be reckoned with in Māoridom—and a force for unity in New Zealand as a whole.

Speech at Women's Organisations Function

Wellington
12 September 2006

Equality and women's rights are issues that Helen has always championed. The following speech was given at an event that brought together leaders from a range of women's organisations around the country.

_____

Welcome everyone and thank you for joining us tonight. Next week we will celebrate Suffrage Day and 113 years since women in New Zealand won the right to vote. That milestone—the fact that New Zealand was the first country in the world where women were able to vote in national elections—is a great source of pride for our country.

New Zealand has often led the world in social reform and in protecting the rights of women. Women's suffrage was part of a series of progressive measures adopted by the Liberal government in the 1890s, along with land reform and industrial arbitration and conciliation. During the second great wave of social reform in the term of the First Labour Government, New Zealand had its first woman MP, Elizabeth McCombs, MP for

Lyttelton. That government introduced many changes which benefited women. Since then, successive New Zealand governments have legislated to remove the legal barriers which women faced, and to promote policies and programmes which support equality.

Our government has continued to promote policies which support the advancement of women in all fields. We are now implementing the Action Plan for New Zealand Women, the five-year whole-of-government plan which aims to improve outcomes for women. The plan focuses on three areas: improving the economic independence of women, achieving greater work–life balance for women and their families, and improving the health and well-being of women.

Examples of initiatives under the plan include:

- The introduction of paid parental leave, and then the extension of cover to fourteen weeks by the end of last year and to self-employed people from 1 July this year.

- Significant improvements to childcare and early childhood education, including 20 hours per week of free early childhood education, which will be available for all three- and four-year-olds at teacher-led early childhood education services from July next year. Already there have been significant funding increases for childcare and out-of-school care.

- The Taskforce for Action on Violence Within Families, which is leading efforts to address New Zealand's totally unacceptable level of family violence.

We are also addressing the issue of pay equity, starting with the state sector. Over the past year, ten public service departments have undertaken full pay and employment equity reviews, and they are now developing plans to address any inequities they identified. This is the start of a process which will extend to the whole of the public service and to the public health and education sectors. It aims to ensure that equal pay for equal work is true in reality as well as in law.

New Zealand has a comprehensive set of laws designed to protect human rights and ensure that every person has full equality before the law. This is acknowledged in our recent report to the United Nations on meeting our obligations under the Convention for the Elimination of [All] Forms of Discrimination Against Women, or CEDAW. For some years New Zealand had two reservations to full implementation of CEDAW—one in relation to paid parental leave, which our government has now addressed, and one in relation to removing the remaining restrictions on a full combat role for women in our armed forces. This latter issue is the subject of a Member's Bill in the name of Labour MP for Waitakere Lynne Pillay. It has been drawn in the ballot for Members' Bills, and parliament will shortly have the opportunity to debate it.

I mention these issues because they illustrate that New Zealand is now virtually in full compliance, without reservation, with CEDAW. While there are still inequalities in the status of women in New Zealand, what needs to change now are primarily attitudes rather than laws. For example, while we have strong laws against violence, we are still a long way from eliminating the family violence which blights too many women's lives. We will continue to look for effective government interventions, along with the gains which can come through education and through partnerships between government and non-government organisations.

In this room tonight are leaders of organisations which represent women in many areas. We want, and need, to work closely with you to change the attitudes which now represent the greatest remaining barriers to women realising their full potential.

My message tonight is simple: we need your help to build a future where nobody is inhibited in reaching their potential because of their gender. We greatly value the contribution each of you makes individually and collectively to achieving that goal, and as a government we want to continue to work very closely with you in future.

Next Tuesday, Suffrage Day, let's not just celebrate the achievement of our grandparents and great-grandparents in gaining for women the right to vote; let's also celebrate the prospect of fully realising their vision of a nation which fully harnesses the strength and talent of all its citizens.

Investing in Social Success

Wellington
3 April 2007

Helen gave this speech as the opening statement at the Social Policy,
Research and Evaluation Conference. She had addressed the same
conference just over two years previously, so this was an opportunity
for her to reflect and report on progress made by her government on
social issues, and to talk about the critical next steps.

———

It's a pleasure for me to be giving this opening address at this 2007 Social Policy, Research and Evaluation Conference. This is the largest social policy conference held in all of Australasia. Gathered here is a wide cross section of those who develop, understand, implement and evaluate social policy. You come from the government and non-government sectors, and from academia.

What happens at this conference matters. It offers an unparalleled opportunity for everyone with an interest in social policy to hear informed speakers, participate in debate and reflect on the key opportunities and challenges we have before us in social policy.

In preparing for this speech today I went back to my address to the previous conference in November 2004. At that time, I set out the rationale for the government's social policy programme, and the steps which we had taken away from the legacy of the 1990s with its high unemployment, surge in poverty and sense of social exclusion. I was able to report on five years of social investment which had made a big difference to New Zealanders' lives.

Now, more than two years later, I can report on more initiatives and new investments in social success—which happens to be the theme of this conference. What our Labour-led government has effected over the past seven and a quarter years is a major paradigm shift in social, economic and other policy. The era of neo-liberalism had left us as a divided society where many had little hope of success. Our aim has been to give all New Zealanders a stake in society, and to ensure that the benefits of economic growth can be more widely shared.

This conference addresses the global context in which we are designing our social policy. In that global context all First World societies face considerable challenges. We need smart strategies to maintain and improve our living standards, and to do so in our open, competitive economies. Our challenge in New Zealand is to build a sustainable economy based on innovation and quality in a world where high-volume, low-quality goods and services will always undercut us on price.

Sustainability is a term most commonly applied to the need for sound environmental policies. But it is a concept I believe we need to apply across economic, social and cultural policies too. Building a sustainable economy, society, environment and national identity requires smart and active government working with key stakeholders. It doesn't happen by accident nor as a result of market forces.

I believe the four pillars of sustainability are mutually reinforcing. We cannot build a strong economy on a society where too many are left to fail and where we plunder the natural environment for short-term gain. Conversely, we cannot build a strong society on an economy which fails to generate the wealth required to fund opportunity and security for our people, protect our environment and develop our culture. The investments we make in social success will continually reinforce our nation's ability to build a strong economy and deliver the non-material benefits of a sustainable environment and high sense of self-esteem and pride.

I believe that the investments our government is making across education and skills, health and housing, and support for families young and old and workers have been a stimulus to ongoing economic transformation. The high-value, innovative economy we seek to build needs an educated and skilled, healthy, well-housed and secure society with the confidence to grasp opportunity and take risks.

Since I last addressed this conference there has been a lot more investing in social success—and a lot more positive results. There's no doubt our policies have been job rich. Under Labour, unemployment has more than halved and generally sits at or near the lowest level in the OECD. More than a third of a million more New Zealanders are at work today than there were in 1999. The drop in unemployment has come across all communities—Pākehā, Māori, Pasifika people and members of emerging ethnic communities all grasp the opportunity to work. The Ministry of Social Development's proactive case-management approach has helped move many people from [the] benefit to work, and we are now moving to make those services available to people on all categories of benefit.

The past seven years have seen the number of working-age beneficiaries drop by over 28 per cent—or by close to 115,000 people. We believe that with the right support the numbers can drop even further. Working for Families has played an important part in reducing the numbers of people living on benefits, as well as lifting family living standards. Since it was introduced, we have seen a downward trend in the numbers of domestic purposes beneficiaries. That's not only because of the increased family tax credits, but also because of the increased support for early childhood education.

What working parents with young children seek is quality affordable early childhood education and care services—and those services are also fundamental to giving our children the best possible start in life. The policy we are implementing to enable three- and four-year-old children to have access to 20 hours' free early childhood education in teacher-led services ranks as one of the most significant extensions to the education system since the introduction of free secondary education in the 1930s. There is widespread approval of the goal, and we are optimistic about the uptake by providers as they become more familiar with how the policy will operate. There is no credibility in the opposition attack on the policy, which simultaneously seeks to oppose it in general and demand that more money be thrown at it!

Working for Families and the huge boost to early childhood services are about lifting family living standards and expanding opportunity through education. Working for Families is now available to around three-quarters of all families, and is reducing our child poverty levels to below the OECD average. The stories of delight and relief so many families are telling about the difference these policies are making for them are heart-warming. Our families overwhelmingly want to do the very best they can for their children. Substantial tax credits for families with children have been our government's top priority for tax relief.

I see our policies for investing in social success as being steadily cumulative over time. Critical moves were made after 1999 to change the existing paradigm and to build a new platform for social policy based on expanding opportunity and security which complemented policies for economic growth and development. There has been a family-friendly focus across our policies—from education, health, housing and family services to savings and industrial relations.

Having built the platform early on in our time in government, we have kept constructing and expanding the house which sits on it. So, since I addressed the last Social Policy Research and Evaluation Conference, paid parental leave has been expanded, from the original twelve weeks to fourteen, enabling parents to take more time off work to be with and bond with new babies. The four weeks' statutory minimum annual holiday has taken effect, giving workers more time to refresh and giving our working parents more scope to spend time during school holidays with their children. I do believe the most important gift we can give our children is our time.

In housing policy, we have worked on new initiatives to support first-home ownership, recognising the difficulties many people have in saving for a deposit. The mortgage insurance scheme, promoted as Welcome Home Loans through Housing New Zealand, supports modest-income earners into their first home. We are developing a shared equity scheme with the same objective, whereby the state will take an equity share to support the home purchase in the first instance. As well, on the supply side, we are undertaking a major residential development through Housing New Zealand in West Auckland at Hobsonville. Of the 3,000 sections available, 15 per cent will be for public housing and another 15 per cent will be for modest-income first-home owners. The benefit of this kind of development is that it creates more balanced communities across socio-economic groups.

One of the greatest social policy innovations in this term of government and into the future is the introduction of the KiwiSaver scheme, beginning on 1 July this year. Its objectives are simple: to boost our nation's rate of savings, and through those savings also to enable people to aspire to home ownership and a more secure retirement. Home ownership and a secure retirement are both central to the Kiwi dream. By making savings as easy as possible through enrolment in KiwiSaver when one signs onto a new job, we can support New Zealanders reaching their dreams.

This move also complements the savings the government is banking on behalf of New Zealanders in the New Zealand Superannuation Fund, which has been designed to make our universal retirement income sustainable for the future. Stop-go retirement polices have been utterly destabilising to New Zealanders in the past. The Superannuation Fund our government has built is critical to assuring New Zealanders that they will have a secure and reliable income in retirement. But building secure and reliable futures for New Zealanders lies at the heart of all our policies.

Having ensured that hundreds of thousands more New Zealanders are in work, we have also endeavoured to underpin incomes and to support the education and upskilling which leads to more sustainable work and helps build our economic capacity. On the income side, the minimum wage has this week risen by 9.8 per cent. The adult minimum, now on $11.25 an hour, is on track to reach $12.00 an hour next year, as was signalled when we came into government for a third term in October 2005.

The improved collective bargaining arrangements under the Employment Relations Act have also given workers a better chance to negotiate fair pay and conditions, and to claim their share of our growing economy. Amendments in recent years have given greater protection to vulnerable workers and enabled bargaining fees to be negotiated.

The numbers of workers in industry training have more than doubled in the last seven years, delivering the prospect of better pay from higher skills.

And the interest-free student loan policy has been implemented this term to keep the cost of tertiary education down and thus enable young people to move ahead to build their homes and careers after graduation without the encumbrance of an unfair loans scheme.

In health policy, this year brings the last phase of the rollout of more affordable primary healthcare, so that people can seek health advice early. There can be no more sound investment than that. In health, a stitch in time truly does save nine later.

As well, this term there are new initiatives for hearing checks for all newborn babies to pick up any disability as soon as possible, more Well Child visits, expanded school dental services, and preschool checks to pick up health issues which could impact on a child's ability to learn.

In my view, our government has been and continues to be innovative in social policy. Social policy can't stand still. It must continually respond to new issues, and as we make improvements we see the scope for more to be done.

Some of the issues we are tackling are difficult and intractable, and have long defied solution. But that's not an excuse for inaction. Dealing with a number of these issues effectively requires cross-agency collaboration—often a challenge in itself. It also requires close collaboration between government and our NGO partners, without whom effective delivery of many programmes in the social sector would be impossible. This is undoubtedly true of the efforts we are jointly making to reduce family violence, where NGOs play a huge role.

This year a major community campaign will begin to reinforce the unacceptability of family violence and change attitudes towards it. And we are giving high priority to the SKIP programme, which supports positive parenting and the use of alternatives to physical discipline.

The government sees the changes to Section 59 in the Crimes Act as an important contribution to the overall campaign to make our homes safer for children. We are encouraged by the strong support for the Bill before parliament by so many respected organisations with proud records of working for children. We are appalled by the misrepresentation of the Bill by its opponents. The facts are clear: everyday parents have nothing to fear from the Bill. The Bill simply gives children the same protection from assault under the law as adults have. It removes a statutory defence in our law against the charge of assault on a child. That defence has seen those who have violently assaulted their children walk free from court. That is wrong, and that is why the law should change.

We are also addressing New Zealand's high rate of imprisonment and of recidivism. Britain has a prison crisis with around 140 inmates per 100,000 population. We can hardly be surprised that our system is creaking at the seams with a ratio of 180 per 100,000. Too many low-risk offenders are ending up in jail, sentencing is inconsistent across New Zealand, and too little is done to address the causes of offending and to rehabilitate prisoners. More community sentences, along with more drug and alcohol and special treatment units in prisons, and more employment opportunities for prisoners are being implemented, and are expected to get better results.

The paradigm shift we have effected in social policy is about building a fair and sustainable society. It runs parallel to proactive economic policies—and the two are interactive. These are policies for our times. Our growth and development as a nation requires us to invest in social success, but I also believe that social success is an end in itself.

Our added challenge is to achieve that success in our increasingly diverse society. The recent census told the story of the strength of the Māori, Pasifika and emerging sizeable ethnic communities. This means that a commitment to social cohesion and inclusion across ethnicity, culture and faith is more important than ever before. And so is completing our own unique reconciliation process through the settlement of historical claims by Māori against the Crown. If we understand and reconcile with our past, we can better plan for our future together.

Campaign for Action on Family Violence Launch

Michael Fowler Centre, Wellington
4 September 2007

The 'It's Not OK' campaign, an initiative of the Taskforce for Action on Violence Within Families, is a community-driven campaign that aims to change how New Zealanders think about and respond to family violence. In 2006, the year before the launch of the campaign, nationwide concern about family violence reached fever pitch when three-month-old twins Cris and Cru Kahui died at Auckland's Starship Children's Hospital after being admitted with serious head injuries; a coroner's report released in 2012 concluded that the injuries had been inflicted when the infants were in the sole care of their father.

———

Today we are launching the Campaign for Action on Family Violence, a four-year campaign led by the Families Commission and the Ministry of Social Development. Over many years, efforts to end family violence have been supported and promoted by many people—social workers, doctors, nurses, teachers, community agencies and everyday Kiwis who care. What we are launching today is the next step in our joint efforts. And it must be seen as an important one.

This campaign has been in development for some time now, and flows from the work of the Taskforce for Action on Violence Within Families established in 2005. Recent events involving deaths of small children are a reminder of the continued urgency of our work, and they weigh heavily on the minds of us all. We are left shocked and appalled when we read about acts of senseless violence perpetrated against defenceless children.

No New Zealander—whether a parent, a police officer, a paediatrician or a Prime Minister—should have to say that such violent acts are not OK. But that is exactly what we now have to do. The campaign we launch today has a simple message: family violence is not OK. It is not OK at any level, from verbal abuse to violent assault.

In most cases, someone beyond the immediate family knows that violence is occurring. Yet too often a veil of silence lies over what is happening, putting vulnerable lives at risk. Despite the progress made in moving family violence away from old perceptions that it was a private matter, there is more work to do to ensure that it is widely understood to be a community issue. And that means for all our communities, not just some of them. That is why this campaign is so important. We need to eliminate any remaining acceptance of violence which exists in New Zealand.

The simple message at the heart of this campaign is a reminder that none of us should ignore signs of family violence. We all have a responsibility to speak out against it. We must make it clear that it is not OK to hit your spouse or partner, it's not OK to verbally or physically abuse your children or an older family member, and it's not OK to take the life of anyone, let alone someone you are meant to care for.

But that is just the first step. Standing up and saying that family violence is not OK must be seen as a call for further action. We must accept that as New Zealanders we have a collective responsibility to end family violence in our country. That means taking every possible and reasonable step we can to prevent and address specific cases of violence. Those who commit violence should not be protected by friends, family or neighbours. That is not loyalty. It is harbouring criminality. It is wrong. And doing so guarantees that violence persists.

We also need to challenge those in our families and communities who are violent towards their family members to seek help, to recognise that it is OK to admit that what they are doing is wrong, to recognise that it is hurting their family, their community and themselves, and to recognise that it is possible to make the change to non-violence.

At a community level, local leadership is crucial. The health and education sectors and non-governmental organisations and religious organisations all have a role to play. Government cannot do the job on its own, but we do accept the responsibility to lead and to co-ordinate. That's why two years ago we established the Taskforce for Action on Violence Within Families. Its work led to this campaign. I thank all those senior representatives from government and non-governmental organisations who have driven this work.

Since the establishment of the task force much has happened. Four new family violence courts have been established, family violence co-ordinator positions have been created within the police, and there is better information and access to legal aid for victims of family violence.

Across government, we are making a big effort to combat family violence. The Vulnerable Families initiative launched in the wake of the Kahui tragedy last year has already been involved with 79 families and over 200 children. An additional $9 million over four years was made available to the non-government organisations who support people who are affected by family violence. Last month, Health Minister Pete Hodgson launched the Health Family Violence Intervention Programme, which is focusing on providing practical advice and tools to the thousands of health professionals who come into daily contact with the impact of family violence.

The seven iwi of Te Tai Tokerau have been funded to develop the Amokura project, a comprehensive community-change initiative which seeks to establish safe and secure whānau which are violence free.

Funding of $8.6 million has been invested in providing 45 full-time equivalent advocates nationwide to support children who witness violence in their homes. A professional infrastructure and a training package for the advocates has been developed.

Our work to reduce tolerance of family violence has already begun to pay off, with a significant increase in notifications to Child, Youth and Family. The biggest driver of this increase has been more collaboration between the Police and women's refuges after police have attended a family violence incident. This collaboration has enabled families to be connected with support and crisis services in their communities, and is a welcome sign that we are working well together across government and with the community sector.

Parliament has also taken an important step in the work against family violence by giving overwhelming support to the amendment to Section 59 of the Crimes Act earlier this year. The law as it stood had allowed too many people who had acted violently against their children to walk away without punishment. The so-called 'reasonable force' defence had allowed that to happen. We now have better law, and that too sends strong signals about the unacceptability of family violence.

My government is determined to speak out against and act out against family violence. It is a stain on our country's reputation. We all want our country to be a great place to grow up in and a great place to raise a family in, and for most of us it is. But that isn't good enough. Too many women and too many people experience regular violence and abuse from their partners. Too many children have their self-esteem eroded by bullying. Too many older New Zealanders have their vulnerability taken advantage of by their caregivers or relatives. And too many people—on average fourteen women, six men and ten children every year—are dying because of family violence. One death is one too many.

None of that is OK.

Working together, we can get that message across. That's what this campaign is about: providing the tools, the information and the encouragement for all of us to play our part in ending family violence. Starting on Sunday a series of powerful television advertisements will promote the 'It's Not OK' message. The ads will be shown following my speech. In addition, an 0800 Family Violence Information Line will be available from next week to provide self-help information and connect people with services when appropriate.

The campaign website will become a valuable tool for community organisations and members of the public who want to play their part in ending family violence. A Community Action Toolkit will be made available and will provide practical advice about how to organise community action against family violence. The Community Action Fund is already providing financial support for community-led activities, recognising that local communities know what works best for them.

As the campaign progresses, an evaluation programme will let us know what is working well, what needs to be adjusted, and what additional efforts we might undertake. We know we need to get this right, and we want to make sure the campaign is as effective as it can be.

We can already be certain of one thing. We would not be here today without the commitment of the people in this room and the people around New Zealand who are working to address and prevent family violence. And we can be certain that this campaign will succeed only with their continued dedication.

Thank you all for your support of this campaign and for your ongoing commitment to making New Zealand a better place, and a safer place, for all our families across our communities.

Opening Address to the Māori Women's Welfare League Conference

Copthorne Hotel, Paihia
21 September 2007

Te Rōpū Wāhine Māori Toko i te Ora, the Maori Women's Welfare League, is a national organisation (with branches also in Australia) that is focused on improving the position of Māori, particularly women and children, in the fields of health, welfare and education. Formed in Wellington in 1951, it was the first national Māori organisation. Dame Whina Cooper, who would many years later while in her seventies lead the 1975 Māori Land March from Te Hapua to Wellington, was the league's first president.

Thank you for the opportunity to open this conference. Greetings to past presidents of the league, and to you all gathered here today. Just a few weeks ago, I had the honour to be present at the first anniversary celebrations of the coronation of King Tūheitia. We look forward to his continuing reign, while we also remember the legacy of his mother, the late Dame Te Atairangikaahu.

Te Arikinui was a firm supporter of the league, and a tireless advocate for Māori women and for Māori development. She is sorely missed, but I know you will continue her work and that you will have the support of the new king.

It is good to be back in Te Tai Tokerau. Just a few weeks ago I was here with members of the Labour Māori Caucus. We had a hectic two days travelling between Whangarei and Kaikohe and being updated on progress, particularly in health and education. I found the Ngati Hine Health Hauora Whanui in Kawakawa was bigger than ever and doing many things to improve the health of whānau in the area. We also visited Kamo High and Northland College, where we met talented rangatahi and teachers, and we met with a cluster of Kōhanga Reo leaders, parents and children too. We finished our visit with a hui focusing on policies and initiatives, and how to improve on how we support Māori development. We got lots of constructive feedback—and a lot to follow up on when we returned to the Beehive!

What struck me then, as in a similar visit to Tairāwhiti a few weeks earlier, was the sense of optimism for the future. What I experienced on those visits is happening around the country in Māoridom and in the broader community alike. There is nothing less than a renaissance of Māori art, language, education, business and culture, which is having a pronounced impact on how we see ourselves as New Zealanders.

We see it in the success of Māori language week and in the increasing use of te reo by Pākehā as well as Māori, especially our rangatahi. Morning Report on Radio New Zealand is leading the way in the mainstream media.

We see the renaissance in the increasing economic power of iwi, in the rising employment levels, and in the improving incomes of Māori families due to sustained economic growth and government initiatives like Working for Families.

We see it in Māori leadership, be it in the inspiring courage of VC [Victoria Cross] winner Willie Apiata, in Māori business success, or in Māori stepping forward to own problems, such as whānau violence, which impact on our communities.

We see it in Māori tourism ventures, such as the $10 million expansion of Rotorua's Māori Arts and Crafts Centre, and in the increasing recognition that Māori culture is a central factor in making Aotearoa truly unique.

And we see it everywhere in art, in music, in film and television, and in the face we present to the world.

I want to speak a little about this new world of potential today, because I believe that many of the things which the league has worked so hard for over the past 55 years are beginning to bear fruit. There are still many challenges, but the prospects for Māori development and whānau are better now than at any other time in the lifetime of the league.

Māori are taking up every opportunity available to move ahead. Our Labour-led government has worked alongside Māoridom to enable and encourage Māori development. Nearly a decade of strong economic growth has created hundreds of thousands more jobs in New Zealand and has helped to reduce unemployment to the lowest level in 27 years. There are now over 35,000 fewer Māori on the unemployment benefit than there were in December 1999—a drop of more than 80 per cent. That's 35,000 people and their whānau with more income, more hope and more opportunities.

And those whānau are among the up to 360,000 families which are able to benefit from the Working for Families family tax credits—that's three in every four families in New Zealand. Working for Families has made a major dent in child poverty by lifting the incomes of families, but it is just one of many policies we have implemented for whānau.

It's a long list, but here are a few examples.

- Paid parental leave, introduced by the Labour-led government in 2002, has recently been extended to fourteen weeks. It's important for parents to have time at home with a new baby.

- There's the big investment in 20 hours' free early childhood education for three- and four-year-olds, which began on 1 July this year and I understand that we will be seeing more participating in the scheme by the end of the year.

- Cheaper doctor visits are now available to everyone after the final rollout of the Primary Healthcare Strategy earlier this year. The costs of going to the doctor and prescriptions are now far cheaper—and, for small children, government pays enough for them to be seen for free.

- Now there are the new before-school health checks for all children. That's to make sure we identify any health issues which might hold back their education.

- In another new initiative, newborn babies are now being screened for hearing loss, so that those born with serious hearing problems can get the support they need for the best possible start in life. And from 1 January 2008 all babies will get free immunisation against pneumococcal meningitis.

- In education we have just launched Ka Hikitia—Managing for Success: The Draft Māori Education Strategy. Ka Hikitia is a far-reaching draft five-year strategy aiming at changes in the education sector to ensure equality of opportunity. The strategy was launched for public consultation on 16 August 2007 and consultation on the draft ends on 31 October. It's relevant to everyone interested in education and the success of the future generations of Māori, and I invite the league to provide feedback. Ka Hikitia will be implemented from next year.

On the broader front, there is a lot of traction in the Treaty settlement process. In May this year, a significant agreement in principle to settle Waikato Tainui claims to the Waikato River was released. In the last three months, the minister has signed agreements in principle with two more groups. More agreements are in the wings, and we expect to be announcing those over the coming months. More groups than ever are beginning negotiations. Iwi in Tūranganui-a-Kiwa [Poverty Bay] signed Terms of Negotiation with the Crown earlier this year. Other groups, like those in the northern South Island, are expected to do so shortly. Major groups like Tūhoe are in the process of appointing mandated negotiators. Others are approaching the government wanting to enter direct negotiations.

All this demonstrates that there is a strong desire on the part of iwi and hapū to get on with the settlement. Through settlements we can rebuild relationships which will stand the test of time. A strong relationship between the Crown and Māori is to the ultimate advantage of both Treaty partners. We need to have strong, honest relationships because we only have one waka, and we are all in it together.

And, while we have much to celebrate, we also have challenges to face. We are making significant inroads in areas like employment, educational achievement and health status, but there is always more to be done. One of those challenges, which has been in the headlines a lot, is ending the scourge of family violence that has such terrible impacts on too many New Zealand families. Earlier this month I launched the Campaign for Action on Family Violence, a four-year campaign led by the Families Commission and the Ministry of Social Development. Over many years, efforts to end family violence have been supported and promoted by many people and organisations—the league for one, plus social workers, doctors, nurses, teachers, community agencies and everyday Kiwis who care.

Despite the progress made in moving family violence away from old perceptions that it was a private matter, there is more work to do to ensure that every community in New Zealand understands that they have a role to play in reducing it. That means all our communities, not just some of them—and I'm pleased to say that Māori communities are certainly taking up the challenge.

The seven iwi of Te Tai Tokerau, for instance, have been funded to develop the Amokura project, a comprehensive community change initiative which seeks to establish safe and secure whānau that are violence-free. Amokura is a good example of a community-based project using local people and local initiatives. Government's role is to provide the support and funding to help local people get on with the job. We also have a role in helping to change attitudes towards family violence through the powerful advertising campaign which has just started.

The simple message at the heart of this campaign is a reminder that none of us should ignore signs of family violence. We all have a responsibility to speak out against it. We must make it clear that it is not OK to hit your spouse or partner, it's not OK to verbally or physically abuse your children or an older family member, and it's not OK to take the life of anyone, let alone someone you are meant to care for.

The Māori Women's Welfare League has a long, strong and proud commitment to helping whānau do their best for their tamariki. You advocate for a better deal for Māori women, whānau and communities. You provide practical advice and support through your programmes, such as your parenting programme Whānau Toko i Te Ora.

The league is one of a handful of distinctly New Zealand institutions which has proved its worth over many decades, and is as strong and as relevant today as it was when it began.

Please be encouraged to keep on with your work, and please do not stop talking to the government and bringing your unique perspective to the debate about the most important issues facing Aotearoa.

The league's views are respected, because they reflect what is in your hearts, and they are always motivated by a strong and genuine desire for the betterment of the Māori women and communities you represent.

Nāu te rourou, nāku te rourou, ka ora te iwi!

Social Democracy Under the Southern Cross: New Zealand in the twenty-first century

Southampton, England, United Kingdom
2 October 2007

Helen was invited to give the following address at the University of Southampton as part of a lecture series organised by the Centre for Imperial and Post-Colonial Studies. The centre had been established the previous year, with the aim of stimulating the study of empire and decolonisation and exploring the legacy of imperial power. It was interested in the development of social policy in New Zealand.

———

Thank you for the opportunity to speak to you today on the topic of 'Social Democracy Under the Southern Cross: New Zealand in the twenty-first century'. I would like to express my appreciation of the University of Southampton's academic interest in New Zealand, and its organisation of this lecture series on the new New Zealand.

It's perhaps ironic that this forum has been initiated by the School of Humanities' Centre for Imperial and Post-Colonial Studies—the very term 'the new New Zealand' implies that we have well and truly cut those imperial apron strings, and that we are well beyond the post-colonial period too. Only last week, on 26 September, New Zealand marked the centenary of long-forgotten Dominion Day—the day on which we formally ceased being a colony of Britain and became a dominion within the British Empire. Little in effect changed that day. New Zealand had been self-governing to all intents and purposes for more than half a century. Our first parliament was elected in 1854. Solid constitutional change came later when we ratified the Statute of Westminster in 1947, making it abundantly clear in law that we had full competence over our own affairs.

Social democracy under the Southern Cross has a long history in New Zealand. The New Zealand Labour Party is New Zealand's oldest political party, celebrating its ninetieth birthday last year. Labour was first elected in 1935 and governed for fourteen years. We have been in government for 34 of the 72 years since 1935, and the Labour government which I lead is New Zealand's fifth.

Historically Labour has been the party guaranteeing fairness, security and opportunity. It was built on the legacy of the Liberal government of the 1890s and early 1900s. That government introduced women's suffrage—making New Zealand the first country in the world to do so—industrial conciliation and arbitration, the first publicly provided workers' housing in the world, and the old-age pension.

Coming in to power at the end of the Great Depression, Labour in the 1930s legislated for a comprehensive welfare state covering social security, healthcare, public housing and education. Our mandate to this day has been to run a strong enough economy to provide good public and social services.

The New Zealand paradigm built by earlier Labour governments came under tremendous strain from the 1970s on, when the country's economy faltered badly. The entry of Britain to the European Economic Community (EEC) took away guaranteed access to this market, on which we were over reliant, and exposed our old-style protected economy with its overwhelmingly primary commodity exports as inadequate to maintain high living standards.

New Zealand went through painful years in the 1980s and 1990s, as neo-liberal policies were applied first to the economy and then to social policy. We went from being the most protected and regulated Western economy to arguably being the least. In 1991, unemployment rose to over 10 per cent, the labour market was deregulated, social security benefits were cut, market rents were applied to public housing and user charges were applied to public hospital services. The cost of tertiary education to students rose steadily in the 1990s. Hands-off was the name of the game in the economy.

By the time my government was elected in 1999, voters were desperate for change.

The first three-year term of our government was spent resetting the compass for New Zealand's direction, so that the fairness, opportunity and security New Zealanders traditionally valued could take pride of place again. The second term built on that work, while our third term has seen a lot of work done around sustainability in its widest sense. The result of eight years' work in office has been the reassertion of social democratic policies, with which I believe New Zealanders are fundamentally more at ease than those of the neo-liberal variety of the late 1980s and 1990s.

The benefits of these policies are also very obvious. New Zealand is close to its longest run of economic growth since World War Two, with the economy 28.3 per cent larger in the year to June 2007 than it was when Labour was elected in December 1999. Average New Zealand economic growth under Labour has been 3.4 per cent per annum, which compares well over the same period with growth in Australia of 3.2 per cent, the United States of 2.5 per cent, the United Kingdom of 2.7 per cent, the OECD of 2.5 per cent, the Euro area of 2.0 per cent and Japan of 1.7 per cent.

Our unemployment has halved, and now sits at around the lowest levels reached in the OECD. Latest figures put the rate at 3.6 per cent, and that has been achieved at the bottom of the business cycle. Our major family tax credit package, called Working For Families, has dropped our child poverty rate to below the European Union average. We are investing heavily in education at all levels, particularly in early childhood education to boost participation and quality, and in tertiary where affordability had become a significant issue in the 1990s.

On 1 July this year, we made all three- and four-year-olds eligible for 20 hours' free early childhood education in teacher-led centres. This is an important step not only in improving the uptake of early childhood education especially among Māori and Pacific communities but also in making it more affordable for working families.

Our tertiary students and graduates now enjoy interest-free conditions on their student loans, provided they stay in New Zealand. The numbers in skills training in industry have doubled, and we have a particular focus on school-to-work transitions through trade and vocational training.

We have increased the minimum wage eight times in eight years to ensure that all workers can benefit from the growing economy.

Health has absorbed rapidly growing funding, as we move to achieve shorter waiting times for elective surgery, support the care needs of our older citizens and provide more affordable primary care for all New Zealanders. The cost of seeing a doctor and getting prescription drugs has fallen dramatically.

In housing, having re-established a fair rents policy for the public stock and increased the number of homes in it, we have turned our attention to the vexed issue of housing affordability. We have already implemented a mortgage guarantee scheme for those who can afford repayments but struggle to save a deposit, and we will be piloting a shared equity scheme next year. We are now planning a Housing Affordability Bill which will give local councils the power to require developers to provide affordable housing. The government is practising what it preaches in this respect by requiring 30 per cent affordable housing in a large subdivision of 3,000 sections it is undertaking in Auckland. As well, the new KiwiSaver savings scheme has spin-offs for aspiring home owners.

New Zealanders traditionally have had low rates of savings, other than in home ownership. We do have a universal pension scheme, paid at age 65 at a rate of no less than two-thirds of the net average ordinary-time wage for a couple, and pro rata for a single person. This rate enables our older citizens to live in dignity and participate in society.

New Zealand Superannuation, as our pension is called, is now underpinned by a dedicated fund, invested in each year from the government's sizable operational surpluses. It will be drawn from at the height of the demographic bulge, when post-war baby boomers reach retirement, to cushion the fiscal impact of pensions on the reduced proportion of taxpayers in the population. The philosophy is for government to save now to save universal pensions for the future. Private savings over and above the universal scheme, however, certainly boost living standards in retirement, and we have designed new schemes to encourage them. In the first place, employer-subsidised superannuation has been reintroduced for the core public service with good take up rates.

But the major innovation has been the KiwiSaver scheme, which was introduced in July this year. Under this scheme, all employees signing on to a new job are automatically enrolled in a quality-assured savings scheme, which requires them to save 4 per cent of their income. While they will have a short period in which to opt out, the expectation is that making the mechanics of saving simple will lead to good take-up rates. For those who stay in the scheme, employers will be required to contribute to their KiwiSaver accounts, and in four years' time will be matching the 4 per cent employee contribution.

Every new account will be kick-started with $1,000 from government. Savings will be locked in until retirement, but may be drawn on for a first-home deposit. In the latter case, the government will contribute another $1,000 per year for up to five years of savings to help with the deposit. After five years in the scheme a couple where each earns half the average couple's income would have a $35,000 deposit for a home. If they continue saving towards retirement, they will at age 65 have doubled the value of their universal pension.

Delivery on social policy which provides opportunity and security is fundamental to a social democratic programme. In our government's agenda, delivery for families young and old is one of our three top priorities. An aspect of the new New Zealand is our innovation in social policy.

But we need a strong economy to do that well. Good social policy is resource intensive. So another of our top-three priorities is achieving economic transformation by building a qualitatively different economy which produces goods and services the world will pay a premium for.

Those who knew the old Kiwi economy would hardly recognise it today. Tourism competes with the dairy industry as the top export-dollar earner. The turnover in the screen-production industry in recent years has almost equalled that of forestry and of horticulture. International education, the technology sectors, the marine industry and niche manufacturing are all important second-tier export earners. In wine, New Zealand competes well at the premium end of the market. We launched kiwifruit to the world as an exotic fruit and set the standard for quality and branding, commanding a premium price.

Meantime, our mega dairy co-operative is the world's largest seller of internationally traded dairy products, and along with our meat industry has made considerable strides in lifting the value of what it exports—in dairy's case, by focusing on the development and branding of functional foods.

New Zealand has been unusual as a developed economy in having such a large primary-sector base. But that base itself is being transformed beyond recognition, as it must be to thrive in the twenty-first century.

Our relatively small land mass and First World living standards combined mean that our commodities will find it increasingly hard to compete on volume and price in a more open agricultural trading system. The low-cost, high-volume producers stand to be the big winners from a successful World Trade Organization (WTO) round. So we have to be more strategic, innovative, smart and skilled in how we take our primary industries and indeed our whole economy forward.

Our time in government since 1999 has been marked by a strong focus on education and skills, science, research and development, exporting, and on the enabling technology and creative sectors which help lift the value and profile of our industries and of New Zealand as a whole. The hands-off days have gone as our government engages with a wide range of stakeholders to strengthen the economy.

Current priorities are heavy investment in the transport infrastructure, far-reaching telecommunications changes to get faster, cheaper broadband services, getting more effective commercialisation of our innovations, improving the business tax regime to encourage more investment, working with major sectors like food and beverage and tourism on higher-value strategies and lowering the barriers to our trade through bilateral and regional agreements—and through the WTO's Doha Round, if it can be revived.

As I said earlier, we have been working hard to ensure that New Zealand is more sustainable in the widest sense, including economically and socially. But central to the ability of all nations to make economic and social progress in the twenty-first century is achieving environmental sustainability, particularly to meet the challenge of climate change. My government has for many years accepted the importance of this issue and the need to contribute to solutions.

New Zealand is neither an economic giant nor a global superpower. It is a small nation with a proud history of being a responsible international citizen which acts on its values. We ratified the Kyoto Protocol, even though it poses major challenges to us. Of our top four trading partners, two—the European Union and Japan—have ratified, and two—Australia and the United States—have not.

But we do believe in being part of the solution to global problems.

As a major primary producer, we have much to lose from unstable and extreme climatic conditions. We are also a nation with a very long coastline along which many communities dwell. Our neighbours on the small South Pacific atolls are in an even more dire situation. Our problem in meeting our Kyoto commitments is that around half our greenhouse gas emissions come from our agricultural sectors. There are neither quick nor easy solutions to lowering these emissions—although we will be world leaders in the research into how that might be achieved.

As well, the combination of a high exchange rate and low commodity prices have led to land being deforested for the more profitable pastoral agricultural uses, which both diminishes our forest sinks and increases methane emissions. This has resulted in New Zealand facing a liability in the first Kyoto commitment period. We will take responsibility for that, but we are also taking action to enable us to reduce emissions further in the future.

In economic terms, sustainability can be a key competitive advantage for New Zealand. In today's global marketplace, consumers are increasingly concerned about ethical and environmental issues, and the carbon footprint of products and services is becoming an issue. To protect our markets and our nation's reputation, we need to act pre-emptively. Important sectors of the economy—notably tourism, the wine industry and agriculture—are already developing long-term strategies based on achieving sustainability. New Zealand Winegrowers, for example, have set the goal of having 100 per cent of their industry operating under independently audited sustainability schemes by 2012. Grove Mill winery in Marlborough reported a 100 per cent rise in sales to the UK supermarket giant Sainsbury's after becoming the world's first CarboNZero certified winery.

The tourism industry contributes close to 9 per cent of GDP and just under one in every five export dollars we earn. Sustainability is at the heart of the Tourism Strategy 2015 which the sector is finalising this year.

But, while all these initiatives are encouraging, as a government we recognise that we need a comprehensive set of climate change policies ranging across policies for forestry and agriculture, and the energy and transport sectors. Nearly two weeks ago I had the pleasure of launching one of the results of the work we have been doing on that: our Emissions Trading Scheme. This scheme will be comprehensive in that it will cover all sectors of the economy and all greenhouse gases. Putting a price on emissions through the scheme will, over time, change investment and consumption patterns so that we develop an economy and lifestyle with lower emissions.

But we have also recognised that, for the scheme to be sustainable, it must be designed to be fair both between sectors and to consumers. That is why we have decided to phase the entry of sectors into the scheme and have also committed to providing low- and modest-income families with assistance to adjust to the higher electricity costs which arise from putting a price on carbon.

We believe that taking action is not only the right thing to do; it is the smart thing to do.

New Zealand has an enviable reputation as a country with a clean and green environment, high-achieving and honest people, an inclusive community and a commitment to peace and justice. But we are also an economy a long way away from most of our markets. So our international reputation and positioning is priceless. Failure to protect our reputation for being clean and green would pose a considerable economic risk to New Zealand. That is why I have set out the challenge to our nation to become the first truly sustainable nation on earth—and to dare to aspire to be carbon neutral. To that end we have set some medium- and long-term objectives and targets.

- By 2025 our target is to have 90 per cent of electricity generated from renewable sources.

- By 2040 our target is to reduce by half per capita emissions from transport.

- We aim to be one of the first countries to introduce electric vehicles widely.

- And by 2020 we aim to achieve a net increase in forest area of 250,000 hectares.

Achieving those targets will move us significantly towards our vision of New Zealand becoming carbon neutral. With this programme, our electricity sector could reasonably be seen as carbon neutral by 2025, the rest of our stationary energy sector by 2030, and our transport sector by 2040.

In a fast-changing world, environmental issues have leaped to the top of the global agenda, along with trade and terrorism. The big challenges nations large and small face defy national solutions and demand multilateral action. New Zealand is a firm multilateralist—as small countries must be. We depend on a stable, rules-based international environment. We don't have hard power, only soft.

Our changing world has seen us increase our focus on our immediate neighbourhood and broader region. New Zealand's web of foreign relationships and connections is unrecognisable from that of 60 years ago. In the South Pacific, we have worked on an ambitious regional plan focused on growth, development and sustainability. The Pacific's small economies run the risk of even greater marginalisation and dependency in a globalised world.

And in the twenty-first century fragile states can become havens for criminals, through money laundering and the drugs trade—and even unwittingly assist financial flows to terrorist organisations. Good governance, economic and social stability and environmental sustainability are increasingly the focus of Western development partnerships in the region. The past four years have seen us playing a significant role maintaining law and order in the Solomon Islands, which has become our biggest development partner. Over the past seventeen months, we have had troops and police in East Timor again, after the serious breakdown of law and order there. Last November we had to respond to chaos in Tonga following serious rioting by securing the airport to ensure links with the outside world and providing policing support.

These episodes, and the fourth coup d'état in Fiji in the past nineteen years which occurred last December, remind us that democratic institutions are dependent for their stability on democratic values and the rule of law, and can be easily shaken where those have not firmly taken root.

The new New Zealand is also heavily engaged in East Timor. As a long-standing ASEAN (Association of Southeast Asian Nations) dialogue and development partner, we took the further step of acceding to ASEAN's

Treaty of Amity and Co-operation in 2005. That was the key to securing a seat at the new East Asia Summit as a founder participant.

East Asia has been the main focus of our bilateral negotiations for free trade agreements (FTAs). We have now concluded FTAs with Singapore and Thailand, and have a Trans-Pacific FTA with Singapore, Brunei and Chile. We are currently negotiating FTAs with China, Malaysia and all of ASEAN. New Zealand has reasonable prospects of being the first developed country to conclude an FTA with China. Given that we are an overwhelmingly open economy, and that our major exports face significant tariff barriers in China, we see this as a highly desirable outcome.

Overall we are seeing our relations with East Asia grow and develop at a fast rate. Asia overall accounts for 40 per cent of our trade. It is a source of tourists and migrants. Our universities and cities have many linkages with Asia. Increasingly we feel at home there.

There is a further new dimension to our outreach to the region, and that is through interfaith and intercivilisation dialogue. In May this year, we hosted both the world's first regional symposium on the UN's Alliance of Civilizations initiative, and the third regional interfaith dialogue, bringing together multi-faith delegations from South East Asia, Australia, New Zealand and the South Pacific. As so many conflicts in the region and worldwide relate to tensions between faith communities, so a solution to those conflicts may lie in seeking to increase understanding between faiths. And overall we all have reason to be concerned about the extent of polarisation between the Western and Islamic worlds. New Zealand can be seen as a relatively honest broker in this respect, with our even-handed policy on Israel and Palestine, and our non-participation in the war in Iraq.

At home too we are emerging as an increasingly multi-ethnic, multi-faith society which, by world standards, lives harmoniously. The new New Zealand's population is 14.6 per cent Māori, 6.9 per cent Pacific peoples and 9.2 per cent Asian. Peoples of European descent now number under 70 per cent.

Modern New Zealand and our world today are light years away from that earlier era which saw New Zealand function as a dominion in the British Empire and an offshore farm for Britain itself. Today we have a sophisticated economy, a multicultural society and a great deal of confidence in the part we can play in the wider region in which we live. We maintain close contact with those who form part of our wider community of values in Europe and North America, and we engage fully and willingly in international efforts to make our world more sustainable, more peaceful, fair and just. The creative sector of our society is flowering across all art and cultural genre, and playing a big role in both reflecting and defining New Zealand's unique identity.

Our high level of social cohesion and inclusion, and our international good citizenship was recognised in May this year with the release of the Global Peace Index, compiled with the support of the Economist Intelligence Unit. New Zealand's ranking was second only to that of Norway, and reflects our social democratic government's strong commitment to peace and security at home and in our relations with other countries. The index rated levels of peace for over 120 nations across 24 indicators, ranging from a nation's level of military expenditure to its relations with neighbouring countries and its level of respect for human rights. Its report commented that 'New Zealand's lofty position in the Global Peace Index partly reflects its lack of internal and external conflicts and its very good relations with neighbouring countries'. It pointed out that New Zealand's stable political scene and its measure of domestic safety and security all contributed to our high ranking. This to me is a vote of confidence in social democracy in the new New Zealand.

It gives me considerable pride to address you tonight as Prime Minister of our small but remarkable country.

Partnerships for Development: Prime Minister's address to Waitangi Day breakfast

Kāretu Marae, Bay of Islands
6 February 2008

On Waitangi Day in 2008, in the interests of, in her own words, a 'programme which contains dignity', Prime Minister Helen Clark opted not to attend official events at Te Tii Marae in Waitangi. Instead, she hosted a breakfast meeting, saying, 'The atmosphere is such that if I don't go there probably won't be incidents, and if I did there would be.' In October the year before, armed police had conducted raids on an alleged paramilitary training camp in a small Māori community near Ruatoki; the raids sparked protests and drew criticism from both the Māori Party and the Green Party.

―――

Distinguished guests, ladies and gentlemen. I acknowledge all those present who come to Waitangi every year. You come because of the significance of this beautiful place as the birthplace of our nation. Here, 168 years ago, the signing of the Treaty symbolised the beginning of a partnership. But as we all know, the early promise of that partnership was not fulfilled. And Waitangi the place has often been associated with discord and disharmony.

But we can't build a nation on those attributes.

So there have been genuine efforts to deal with the colonial legacy, and those efforts began to gain traction in the latter part of the twentieth century. Many people in this room today have played a big part in that. And we are now seeing the positive outcomes, not only in major Treaty settlements, but also in what is flowing from them: the economic development which is seeing iwi emerge as major players in their region's economies, the social development, and the evident pride and confidence of Māoridom in moving forward.

I spent Thursday and Friday morning of last week with Waikato Tainui, who negotiated the first of the modern Treaty settlements with the Crown. Their $170-million settlement has become close to a half-billion-dollar asset base. There are ambitious plans for growing the portfolio. Waikato Tainui today are seen as core partners through the region. Their support and assistance on issues and initiatives is widely sought. Indeed it is hard to imagine much happening without their involvement.

The bedding-in of that 1995 settlement has made it possible to take the next step: towards settlement of the Waikato River Claim. The settlement of that claim is now well advanced, and involves an exciting model of co-management to ensure the restoration of the good health of the river. At the Rakaumangamanga School in Huntly, they told me that they are now encouraging their students to consider studies in environmental science so that they can work on these initiatives in the future.

The Waikato River Claim is one of a number of significant settlements being progressed as we speak. Yesterday, the progress of a settlement of another kind was marked in Wellington with the signing of Heads of Agreement between the Crown and Ngāti Porou. The agreement provides that for those areas where, prior to passage of the Foreshore and Seabed Act, it is established that Ngāti Porou would have had a claim for customary title there will be a permission right instrument giving Ngāti Porou the right to approve or withhold approval for resource consents where the activity proposed would have a significant adverse effect on the relationship of hapū with the environment. There will also be an extended fisheries mechanism giving the power to make bylaws under customary fishing regulations, and an extended environmental covenant bringing Ngāti Porou into the statutory planning process of the Gisborne District Council. These and other covenants and accords will be enshrined in legislation.

The Heads of Agreement are the outcome of three-and-a-quarter years of negotiation.

Other iwi are also in negotiation with the Crown or in various stages of exploring the possibilities. Engagement with Māori must be and is very much part of the core business of government these days, with a particular focus on matters relating to the environment and natural resource issues, from climate change and water allocation and management to sustainability in fisheries, coastal management, marine reserves and management of our interests in the great oceans. Progress in all these areas cannot be advanced without engagement with Māoridom.

Now let us cast our minds back just 30 years ago to a very different New Zealand when none of this was envisaged. On 25 May, 30 years ago, Ngāti Whātua were evicted from their land at Bastion Point. So much has changed since then for the better.

Today, the Māori asset base in the primary industries alone is worth around $16.5 billion—up 83 per cent in six years. Māori are in businesses and occupations across the board. Promotion of te reo is strong, through education and the mass media. And note this year the launch of Māori Television's second channel, funded by government to broadcast exclusively in te reo between 7.30 and 10.30 every night.

As we [near] the end of the first decade of the twenty-first century:

- ninety per cent of Māori children beginning school have been in early childhood education

- greater numbers of rangatahi are emerging from the education system with qualifications—but this is still an area where our whole nation needs to lift its sights

- Māori unemployment has more than halved in the past eight years

- Māori life expectancy is up.

All this is positive—not perfect, but positive.

Going forward, I hope we can all continue to focus on potential and opportunity, not on deficits and negative stereotypes.

I really do believe Māoridom is on a roll. That is not only good for New Zealand—it is essential for New Zealand. Supporting partnerships for our nation's development and cohesion is the spirit which should guide us on Waitangi Day.

Valedictory Speech to Parliament

Parliament, Wellington
8 April 2009

The 2008 general election, held on 8 November, spelled the end of Helen's time as Prime Minister of New Zealand and drew to a close the nine-year term of the Fifth Labour Government. Helen was replaced as Prime Minister by National Party Leader John Key. On election night, after the results were declared, Helen announced she would step down as Leader of the Labour Party. Afterwards she told the media, 'If I couldn't lead the party to victory then it was time to go.' Just a few months later, over 12,000 people participated in an online poll hosted by The New Zealand Herald *that named Helen 'Greatest Living New Zealander'. On 19 April, Helen stepped into her new role as Administrator of the United Nations Development Programme (UNDP)—breaking yet another glass ceiling, as she became the first woman to lead the organisation.*

———

E te Kiingi Tūheitia, te Ariki Tumu, e ngā iwi o te motu, e rau rangatira ma, tēnā koutou, tēnā koutou, tēnā koutou katoa.

This speech is my last in this parliament, and that is something I view with a mix of emotions. Being a member of the New Zealand Parliament has been a big part of my adult life, and my involvement in New Zealand politics more broadly long predates my election as MP for Mt Albert in 1981.

In 1968, fresh from Epsom Girls' Grammar School, I enrolled at Auckland University, to study History, English, German and, yes—as an after-thought—Political Studies. What a year that was for students around the world, with unrest spreading across the campuses of many a country as the post-war baby boomer generation came of age. Here in New Zealand, those of us who were politically minded were not short of causes to get involved in. Opposition to the Vietnam War, apartheid sport, nuclear testing in the Pacific—all these issues sent fault lines through New Zealand politics, some ideological, some generational. The great strength of Norman Kirk as Labour Leader was that he reached across the generations to speak for us as young people on these issues and in articulating an independent foreign policy.

In my childhood and teenage years, a television set was not a feature of every home. That meant that politicians were rather remote figures whose voices were only occasionally to be heard on one of the handful of government-owned radio stations—this was before Radio Hauraki broke the monopoly by broadcasting from a boat in the Hauraki Gulf—or were read about in the then rather dry columns of the print media.

I remember Sir Ronald Algie MP coming to prize-givings at my secondary school. I recall being barked at by Sir Leslie Munro in the Te Pahu Hall when, as a student, I had the temerity to ask him a question about the wisdom of deploying New Zealand troops in Vietnam. But other exposure to politicians was non-existent in my earlier life. In recent years, when children have asked me whether I wanted to be Prime Minister when I was a child, I could only reply that I couldn't have imagined that happening, as the politicians of my childhood and youth were almost invariably rather elderly gentlemen.

Those perceptions changed for me during my student days, and upon joining the Labour Party as I did in 1971. There was a new generation coming into parliament for Labour, beginning with the election of Jonathan Hunt in 1966. Outside parliament there was the extraordinary energy of Jim Anderton in Labour's Auckland local body campaigns, and later as party president. As well there was the growing stature of Norman

Kirk as Leader of the Labour Party and Leader of the Opposition. I was proud to be a mere foot soldier in the campaign which saw him lead Labour into government in 1972.

But the Third Labour Government suffered greatly from Norman Kirk's untimely death and major economic shocks, leading to its defeat after only three years. And so it was back to the politics of Opposition for nine years, in the course of which I myself entered parliament as the MP for Mt Albert.

As many are well aware, I grew up on a farm in the western Waikato and did not prima facie have a background of the kind associated with Labour leaders of the past. But my wider family, like many, had a range of political allegiances. Politics was definitely of great interest to us, and not something just to be engaged in via a vote on election day. My parents were perhaps initially surprised at the direction my politics took, but within a relatively short period of time they extended their strong personal support for me to strong political support. That continues to this day, with my father who is 87 being present in the gallery, and my mother, who is not well enough to travel, being able, I hope, to watch proceedings on television today along with my sister Jenefer, who is caring for her. Words cannot adequately express my gratitude to Mum and Dad for their lifelong love and support of me.

My first general election campaign as a Labour candidate was in 1975 in Piako, one of National's safest seats, held by the gentleman Jack Luxton, and later by his son John. What a great learning experience that was for me, moving through the small towns of the east and south Waikato, drawing support in particular from workers and their families associated with the Kaimai Tunnel project, the dairy and timber factories and the Arapuni hydro village. I well remember a campaign visit in support of me by Sir Basil Arthur, Minister of Transport, where superstition dictated that as a woman I could not accompany him into the Kaimai Tunnel. The highlight of the campaign was the late Bill Rowling putting Putāruru on his whistle-stop tour of the Waikato. The hall we hired was filled to overflowing for the morning tea held in his honour.

My advice to young people starting out in politics is to be prepared to run first for their party in electorates which are highly unlikely to be won, but where one will learn a lot and have more to offer when a winnable seat comes along. Success is seldom instant in politics, and, where it does come quickly, it can equally quickly fizzle out.

The parliament I entered in 1981 was far less diverse than that we see today. That year the number of women elected to parliament doubled from four to eight, and there were only six Māori MPs. The main forms of recreation were the billiards room in what is now the Grand Hall, the Bellamy's bar, and the card schools in members' offices.

To say that this was an alien environment for a 31-year-old woman, fresh from a university teaching position, would be an understatement. It was hard going, as frankly a lot of my political career has been, but it was character forming, and gave me the experience and confidence to go all the way in the system, and, importantly, to be part of changing it for the better.

But saying that parliament was hard going and an alien environment brings one to the issue of motivation—of what exactly it was which attracted me to this life. What brought me here was idealism, values, a sense of community and of internationalism, a desire to make a contribution to public life and overwhelmingly a sense of gratitude for the opportunities New Zealand has offered me and which I believe should be the birthright of every New Zealander.

I have always been proud of New Zealand's egalitarian traditions. Deep in our nation's roots is the ethos that Jack is as good as his master—and these days that Jill is as good as her mistress. Many of our forebears came to this land to escape the class-bound nature of Britain, where their place in the economic and social order was largely prescribed from birth. I deeply detest social distinction and snobbery, and in that lies my strong aversion to titular honours. To me they relate to another era, from which our nation has largely, but obviously still not completely, freed itself.

Entering parliament was for me a way of translating ideals into positive action—hard as that can sometimes be. There have been many issues over my 41 years of political activity when I've perhaps been ahead of public opinion at the time. Yet, so often, today's avant-garde become tomorrow's status quo. Such thoughts cross my mind when I see a cross section of New Zealand families celebrate their children's civil union or a government delegation from Vietnam welcomed as friends and regional partners, when once to support relations with their country was thought to be beyond the mainstream.

My first six years as an MP saw me focused on three main areas of activity. First there was my electorate work in Mt Albert. How grateful I will always be to the wonderful people of those central Auckland suburbs for the opportunities and support they gave me to grow and develop as a politician and leader over 27 years.

Mt Albert was formed as a new electorate in 1946. It faced a by-election the following year, when the long-serving Arthur Richards, the former Member for Roskill, retired. Warren Freer was then elected at the age of 26 and served for 34 years, rising to the number-three position in Labour's parliamentary hierarchy and becoming a senior minister. It is certainly my hope that Mt Albert will support and nurture Labour successors to Warren and me who have the capacity to rise to the very top of New Zealand politics and serve their electorate and our country with distinction.

The bread-and-butter constituency work Mt Albert is interfacing with government agencies and departments on matters like housing, social welfare and immigration, and supporting the endeavours of our fine local schools, sports clubs and communities. The communities which make up Mt Albert are strong and diverse, making it a very rewarding electorate in which to live and work. I will miss it a lot over the next four years—but home is where the heart is, and my heart will always be in Kingsland where Peter and I have spent our 27 years of married life.

Second, there was the work here in parliament—for me, mainly focused around various permutations of what is now the Foreign Affairs and Defence Select Committee, of which I became Chair from 1984 to 1987. The nuclear-free legislation was a highlight of that period, as were the major reports our committee produced on disarmament and on New Zealand's relationship with China.

Third, there was the broader work within the Labour Party, where I had been a New Zealand executive member since 1978. There was the excitement of the 1984 campaign, and the trauma of the economic shock and adjustments which followed the election. Victory in 1987 disguised the fact that in our heartland seats held by ministers, the Labour vote slumped, as the Fourth Labour Government had delivered economic policies to which our traditional supporters could not relate and which had not been foreshadowed.

That experience and the subsequent massive 1990 defeat left a lasting impression on me—along with a determination for the future to be transparent about election policy, to deliver on it, and to keep faith with the loyal, long-term Labour supporters who sustain our movement through good years and bad. There are always fair-weather friends in politics—one knows who one's true friends are when they are still standing with you in the aftermath of defeat, when the phone (and now the texts) have otherwise gone rather quiet.

My time as a minister from 1987 to 1990 was very rewarding and enabled me to engage with communities across New Zealand. As Minister of Conservation, I returned to the extraordinary places I had last visited on South Island family holidays in the 1950s and sixties. I was able to strike the occasional blow for the environment by rejecting obtrusive development projects, like the Monowai Mine on the Coromandel and the Nukuhau Marina proposed for Lake Taupō.

Public housing and health were passionate interests of mine and so much was achieved, from the acquisition of many more state houses to passage of the pioneering smoke-free legislation, and of the innocently named Nurses Amendment Act which freed midwives to practise autonomously.

As Minister of Labour in 1990 I took the Employment Equity Act through parliament, only to see it gone by Christmas that same year. In the face of a retailer revolt, I also promoted the legislation for seven-day shop trading. While that was not welcomed by retail workers, the introduction was softened by my writing what amounted to an advanced industrial agreement into a schedule of the Act. Alas, that didn't long survive the 1990 election either.

The nine years in Opposition in the 1990s were tough years, as we in Labour worked to restore our electoral credibility. There was the shock treatment of the new National government's health, superannuation, welfare and industrial policies, and unemployment rose above 10 per cent in 1991. The electorate clearly wasn't happy in 1993, but still saw Labour as having a lot of baggage from the 1990s.

This 'plague on both your houses' sentiment was then expressed in the resounding vote for a change to the electoral system in 1992, and the binding referendum on MMP in 1993. The New Zealand electoral system has never been the same since. The two-party system crumbled as the first MMP election approached, with MPs leaving both major parties to sit elsewhere in the House.

I became Leader of the Opposition at the very point that the old electoral order began to crumble, and smaller parties had a chance of finding a niche in the political spectrum. Labour lost support to the Alliance and to New Zealand First in particular. The nadir came with a Colmar Brunton poll in the mid-1990s which put Labour on 14 per cent and me on 2 per cent as preferred Prime Minister. It doesn't get much worse than that—and looking back on it now I am only surprised that concerned delegations of colleagues didn't beat a path to my door more often.

Against that background, success in the 1996 election was impossible, but nonetheless it marked a turning point for me and for Labour. The coalition government stitched together was not a marriage made in heaven, and eventually dissolved. Meanwhile, Labour and the Alliance were able to effect a rapprochement and to campaign as a ready-made coalition in 1999.

The rest is history. The year 1999 delivered a Labour–Alliance minority coalition government with support on confidence and supply from the Green Party. Our government then and in subsequent terms embarked on a programme of change across the economic, social, environmental and cultural spheres, which over time has made a substantial difference for the better to many New Zealanders' lives. Fairness, opportunity and security were our core values, and they were applied across the board.

We took a long-term approach to investment—in the Superannuation Fund, in KiwiSaver, in early childhood education, in skills training, in research and development, in primary healthcare, in public transport and much else besides.

Workers' rights were enhanced through the Employment Relations Act, paid parental leave and a fourth week's annual holiday.

The economy experienced its longest run of continuous growth since World War Two, and unemployment remained low for years. These successes gave us the capacity to make significant investments in families, services and infrastructure. The rising tide did lift every boat, transforming the circumstances of Māori, Pākehā, Pasifika, Asian and all other communities.

In our last term in particular, comprehensive sustainability policies were put in place to put New Zealand on the front foot in combating climate change. I strongly believe that it is important for our country's international credibility that we are seen to take these issues seriously and be prepared to act.

Over nine years we made substantial acquisitions for the conservation estate, with the jewels in the crown being the transfer of Molesworth Station to the Department of Conservation and the purchase of the pastoral lease of the spectacular St James Station.

It was my pleasure to lead our work on arts and culture—to encourage the development of New Zealand talent, audience enjoyment, economic opportunity and the promotion of our unique New Zealand identity and perspectives.

The heritage part of my portfolio was also immensely satisfying. I look back on years of significant projects from the Tomb of the Unknown Warrior to the new 'born digital' official encyclopaedia Te Ara to volumes of oral and other histories of World War Two and the Vietnam War, and to the major regional museum and gallery projects for which the government become a substantial funding partner.

There's also been the ongoing process of reconciling with our past, of recognising injustice and addressing it. New Zealanders are now very familiar with the settlement of historic grievances going back to the time of colonisation and the signing of the Treaty of Waitangi. These settlements must be completed so that we can move forward together as a nation. As one who grew up on a farm on raupatu land in the Waikato, where our family's presence felt like it had been for ever, I cannot even begin to imagine the scale of loss felt by Waikato Tainui from the mid-nineteenth century, but I hope that I and my government have played our part in putting things right. The presence of Kingi Tūheitia and his delegation here today means a great deal to me, as did the friendship of the late Te Arikinui Dame Te Atairangikaahu over many years.

As well in my time as Prime Minister, there was the apology to New Zealand's early Chinese settlers and their descendants for the unique and severe discrimination they suffered for many decades, and the apology to Samoa for the injustices perpetrated by the New Zealand colonial administration. And just last year I issued on behalf of the government and people of New Zealand an apology to Vietnam veterans and their families for the manner in which their loyal service to New Zealand was not recognised as it should have been and for the inadequate support extended to them and their families.

Reconciliation, respect, inclusion, human rights—these were important themes for me as a Prime Minister with a deep belief in equality.

Māoridom in recent decades has undergone a profound renaissance and stands very tall today as New Zealand's first people, as substantial economic stakeholders and as contributing so much which is fundamental to New Zealand's unique national identity. Our government was a willing partner in that renaissance.

Our substantial Pasifika populations have also made their presence felt from the professions to the factories, from the movie screens to the sports fields and beyond, to become a quintessential part of the fabric of New Zealand society.

I have enjoyed my involvement with New Zealand's many emerging ethnic communities, whose cultures, heritage, languages and faiths add so much to the richness of our nation. The Civil Union Act enabling rainbow couples to express their love for each other by cementing their relationship in law, the Property Relationships Act applying the principles of fair division of property on the dissolution of a de facto relationship, and our work guided by the New Zealand Disability Strategy were all important to me.

There is so much about New Zealand which is special and marks us out as a unique and gifted nation.

We have evolved distinctive reconciliation and constitutional processes. Our institutions from our parliament and executive government system under MMP to our Supreme Court have evolved a long way from our colonial heritage. It is inevitable that our constitutional status as a monarchy will also change—it's a question not of if, but when.

My government sought to reflect our nation's unique personality in New Zealand's international relations. For us, New Zealand needed to stand for peace, justice, reconciliation and sustainability. Our refusal to participate in the war in Iraq was a decision based on principle—involvement would have ripped our country apart for no good purpose. I take pride in the high regard in which New Zealand is held internationally, and the work our government did in the Pacific and East Asia, in rebuilding the relationship with the United States, in broadening relations with Europe, in engaging strategically with Latin America and in deploying peace-keepers around the globe.

That high regard for our nation and our constructive way of working internationally was the background against which I went forward as a candidate for the position of Administrator of the United Nations Development Programme. I regard my selection as a huge honour for me and for New Zealand and I will seek to carry out my duties there in a way which reflects well on our country.

I have no regrets about leaving parliament at this time. I have had an incredible career here and have been given enormous opportunities. But it is time to go and for others in my party to take forward the cause we believe in and I will always believe in.

The election result of course was disappointing after so many years of hard work and a sense of achievement in so many areas. But we live in a democracy and the people's will must be accepted and respected—as it is by me.

A long and rewarding political career is not a solo act. I stand here knowing that I have been supported by so many people for so long because they believed in me and in the values I represented. My parents gave me the best start in life any child could have—a secure and loving home, and support for my education at every stage. My three sisters, my brothers-in-law, and my nieces and nephews, aunts, uncles and cousins in our large extended family have been very supportive of Peter and me over our many years in the public eye. Peter himself has been a staunch supporter of my aspirations and career—no matter how unpleasant and difficult things got in political life from time to time. There have been immensely more high points than low points.

For ten consecutive elections I have received solid support from the Mt Albert electorate, and I thank all those who have voted and worked for me there over 27 years. Special thanks are due to the Mt Albert Labour Electorate Committee, which has worked hard to make our electorate one of the best organised in New Zealand, and to my hardworking electorate office staff led by my long-time friend and supporter Joan Caulfield.

My political career has been based on the values and principles of the New Zealand Labour Party, and I thank all those at all levels and in all regions across New Zealand for their constant support. Here in parliament I have been privileged to work with remarkable colleagues, from my deputy leader for many years, Dr Michael Cullen, to those who made up our cabinet and caucus. I have made many friends in politics, and I know those friendships will be lifelong. The texts will keep coming—and maybe even some tweets.

Other political parties played an indispensable role in the success of the Labour-led government over our nine years in office. I worked particularly closely with the Honourable Jim Anderton, and was pleased to see a friendship formed in the 1970s which had been put under great strain in the 1980s and 1990s resume in the twenty-first century. Jeanette Fitzsimons and the Green Party worked closely with me and Labour for many years, because we shared common approaches in many areas.

While there was less commonality, nonetheless honourable relationships which guaranteed confidence and supply were established with Honourable Peter Dunne and United Future, and Right Honourable Winston Peters and New Zealand First. A relationship based on considerable common interest was also possible with the Māori Party during the last parliamentary term. Honourable Tariana Turia and I go back a long way, and I acknowledge in particular her generous comments in parliament last week.

My contact with the National Party and ACT has not been significant given the significance of the philosophical differences between us, but I do wish on this occasion to acknowledge the leaders of both parties, John Key and Rodney Hide, for their courtesy in recent times, and also the courtesy of numerous other members, going back to the time of Marilyn Waring and Katherine O'Regan, Paul East and Simon Upton. I've also enjoyed Jim Bolger's company post-politics. I have very much valued the ongoing wise counsel and advice of Geoffrey Palmer, and the support and insights provided by Mike Moore on moving into the international system.

As Prime Minister I was supported by the broader public service in general and by those departments and agencies for which I had direct responsibility. In particular Mark Prebble and then Maarten Wevers as heads of the Department of Prime Minister and Cabinet, and Marie Shroff, Diane Morcom and Rebecca Kitteridge as Cabinet Secretaries, and their staff all worked hard to ensure that Labour as a democratically elected government could implement its policies.

Martin Matthews, Jane Kominik and all at the Ministry for Culture and Heritage helped me to give arts, culture and heritage a higher profile than ever before in our country. The Department of Internal Affairs supported me in my role as Minister of Ministerial Services and as host of countless international delegations at head of state and government level.

I enjoyed my work with the Security Intelligence Service and the government Communications Security Bureau led variously by Richard Woods, Warren Tucker and Bruce Ferguson. I placed trust in them and their staff as they did in me, and I believe that their work is in the interests of New Zealand.

I also owe a great deal to the Ministry of Foreign Affairs and Trade, which supported me and my ministers on so many complex issues, and me personally through many summits and bilateral visits.

It was also a privilege to be involved in many ways with the New

Zealand Defence Force and to see its work on- and offshore. I will always remember the amazing visits to Kabul, Bamyan and Basra, and the Sinai, East Timor and the Solomon Islands to see New Zealand military personnel at work.

Close personal support for me as Prime Minister came from my private office and the talented teams led by Heather Simpson and Alec McLean, and to this day comes from my parliamentary staff, Jacque Bernstein and Dinah Okeby, as it has always come from generations of personal secretaries, researchers, press secretaries, messengers, diary secretaries, typists and receptionists in the past.

Personal protection came from the Diplomatic Protection Squad (DPS) of the New Zealand Police who stayed very close to me for the whole nine years. To DPS and the New Zealand Police across our country, thank you for your support. You are New Zealand's unsung heroes and deserve much greater recognition for what you do to protect us all.

Over the 22 years since I first became a Minister of the Crown, I have been not just driven but fully looked after and supported by the government drivers in the VIP service of the Department of Internal Affairs. I have come to know many well, and they are my friends. As a former Prime Minister, I am privileged to continue using their service, so today marks not an end, but an interlude. As General McArthur once famously said, 'I will return.'

It is 27 years to the month since I made my maiden speech in this chamber at the tender age of 32. I said then that 'My greatest wish is that at the end of my time in this House, I shall have contributed towards making New Zealand a better place than it is today for its people to live in.' I leave knowing that I have fulfilled my wish and that I played a part in making New Zealand a better place. It has been a privilege to be a member of this House for 27 years and Prime Minister for nine years. I wish my successor Phil Goff and the Labour team all the best for the next election, and I wish New Zealanders well for what are undoubtedly challenging times ahead.

Commemorating ANZAC Day

New York, United States of America
25 April 2009

ANZAC Day, on 25 April, marks the day that New Zealand and Australian troops (among others) landed on the Gallipoli Peninsula in 1915. Each year, events are held by Kiwis and Australians the world over to remember those who have been killed in war, and to honour returned servicewomen and servicemen. Helen gave the following speech at the commemorative service held at ANZAC Garden at the Rockefeller Center on ANZAC Day 2009.

———

E ki ana ngā tūpuna,
Ko ngā mea nui,
Te whakapono, te tūmanako
Me te aroha.

Your Excellencies, distinguished representatives of the United Nations and the Diplomatic and Consular Corps, ladies and gentlemen. We gather here today to pay tribute to those who have served our countries in times of war, to those who gave their lives, to those who were wounded—and to those who returned home, many carrying with them for life the trauma of what they had experienced.

ANZAC Day commemorates the landings of Australian, British, French, Indian and New Zealand forces on the Gallipoli Peninsula 94 years ago. It is also the day on which we honour the courage of all New Zealand and Australian servicemen and women deployed overseas since that time.

Yesterday, here and throughout New Zealand and Australia, at Gallipoli and in other places around the world, New Zealanders and Australians gathered to commemorate ANZAC Day. Today we stand in awe at the courage of our forebears at Gallipoli, on the Somme, at Passchendaele and in Palestine; before that in South Africa, and for Australia in Sudan, in World War Two in Europe, the Middle East and the Pacific, in Malaya, in Vietnam and in many other deployments since that time.

It matters not on a day like this what our opinions were on one deployment or another. Today we recognise courage, endeavour, mateship, service and sacrifice, and we honour all who answered their nation's call to serve.

Like many here I have traced for myself the footsteps of forebears caught up in these epic events. This January in frozen Flanders I contemplated how our people could possibly have endured those dreadful winters, and the courage it took to advance against entrenched positions over relatively low-lying ground. The Ypres Salient is truly a sacred place for all nations who fought there. I recall the small cemetery at Marcoing in the north of France where one of my great-uncles is buried, and then going to the site on the Hindenburg Line nearby, where he was killed.

Gallipoli, however, has a special place in New Zealand and Australian hearts as our first engagement in World War One, as a military disaster which touched families and communities throughout our lands, and for the generosity of spirit long shown by Turkey towards the ANZACs, their families and their descendants. In acknowledging our own citizens today, we also pay our respect to the soldiers of Turkey who fought so bravely for their country.

It is humbling indeed to view the small beach at ANZAC Cove; to contemplate the landing, the assault on the cliff face beyond, and the ascent—all under fire; and to reflect on what it was like to dig in on the ridge with the opposing front line only a few metres away. We reflect then on the deadly stalemate, with both sides vulnerable to sniper fire, the heat of summer, and the disease and illness our people suffered.

Two particular attempts to break out are of special significance to New Zealanders. There was the extraordinary capture of Chunuk Bair on 8 August 1915—the most forward point reached in the entire campaign. The ridge there was held for two days, but with no back-up and supplies the few survivors retreated. Colonel Malone, and 90 per cent of the men of the Wellington Infantry Battalion he led, perished in the battle.

Less than two weeks later, New Zealanders made their last attempt to break through Turkish lines at Hill 60. When we view it today, there is no hill—only a gentle rise. Another of my great-uncles wrote from Hill 60 on 21 August that, 'There are stray bullets flying everywhere and one stands a chance of "stopping one" at any time. Our sergeant was standing in our trench yesterday and he got one in the right breast.' He wrote further, 'The big guns from land and sea make an awful row and this is accompanied always with machine guns and rifle fire. We can hear the shells screaming overhead and shrapnel bursting all day long.'

Uncle Frank died seven days later.

Every family whose loved ones went away has these stories—devastating human stories. In commemorating ANZAC Day as our national day of remembrance, we ensure that we never forget the loss of life, the tremendous suffering, the grief of the families at home, the children and young people who grew up without fathers, brothers, and uncles, the many widowed and the impact of so many fallen on our communities and nations.

It is often said that our people went away as colonial soldiers in the service of the empire, and that those who returned came home as New Zealanders and Australians. The heavy price our peoples paid left a legacy which helps define our independent nations today and built deep bonds between New Zealanders and Australians.

Today, in the Solomon Islands and Timor Leste, our people serve alongside each other. In Afghanistan we have both deployed substantial numbers of personnel. Many others serve elsewhere in a range of capacities—for New Zealand, as peace-keepers. None of these twenty-first century deployments is without risk, and personnel from our nations have suffered fatalities and serious injury this century. Today we remember them and their families too, and all those serving offshore at this time, as we remember all those who have served since our nation's first deployed personnel overseas.

ANZAC Day is a day for reflection and remembrance. It is also a day for committing ourselves to working for a world where differences between nations can be resolved without resort to war. In this way we can best honour and pay tribute to the fallen and to those who have served.

Women and Power

HuffPost
11 June 2010

*In April 2009, Helen retired from parliament to become the
Administrator of the United Nations Development Programme
(UNDP). She was the first woman to lead the organisation and,
for many, it is in her career post-politics that Helen's status as an
unofficial spokesperson and role model for gender equality has
become firmly established. In this, a blog post published on the
website* HuffPost *(formerly* The Huffington Post*), she discusses the
importance of gender equality in an international context.*

————

As Prime Minister of my country for nine years and the first woman
to lead the United Nations Development Programme (UNDP), I
believe that achieving gender equality is not only morally right but also
catalytic to development as a whole, creating political, economic and
social opportunities for women which benefit individuals, communities,
countries and the world.

This strong belief underpins my contribution at the Women Deliver
event in Washington, DC, during a discussion on women and power
with an impressive panel of powerful women, including the creator of

The Huffington Post, Arianna Huffington, former Chilean Prime Minister Michelle Bachelet, actress Ashley Judd and Valerie Jarrett, Senior Advisor and Assistant to Barack Obama for Intergovernmental Affairs and Public Engagement.

Women Deliver was launched in 2007, and works globally to focus attention on fulfilling what is called Millennium Development Goal 5. This goal calls for a reduction in maternal mortality and universal access to reproductive health globally.

There are eight Millennium Development Goals (MDGs). They are the most broadly supported, comprehensive and specific development goals on which the international community has ever agreed. These eight time-bound goals aim at tackling poverty in its many dimensions. There are goals and targets on income poverty, hunger, access to education, maternal and child health, deadly diseases, inadequate shelter, gender inequality, environmental degradation and the Global Partnership for Development.

The MDGs were adopted by world leaders in 2000 when they signed the Millennium Declaration, with a target date of 2015. As one of the world leaders who travelled to New York that year to sign the Millennium Declaration, I am personally committed to their achievement. If they are achieved, world poverty would be cut by half, tens of millions of lives would be saved and billions more people will have the opportunity to benefit from access to schooling, health services and clean water and sanitation.

Investing in women and girls will be critical for achieving the goals. Development progress is lagging where the needs and status of women and girls are given low priority. Women's reproductive health needs remain hugely under-served. More than half a million women die every year— or one woman every minute—from complications related to pregnancy and childbirth. Moreover, 25 years into the HIV/AIDS epidemic, gender inequality and unequal power relationships expose women to great risk. While about half of all people living with HIV/AIDS globally are female, in Sub-Saharan Africa approximately 60 per cent are female, and in some areas girls are two to four-and-a-half times more likely than boys to become infected.

Achieving real progress on maternal health requires a broad approach towards empowering women, and a greater investment in achieving gender equality. Ensuring political and economic empowerment is crucial to speeding up development progress and improving women's lives.

As a former head of government, I know that getting to the top of the ladder in politics is possible, but I also know how difficult it can be for women to do so. With women currently comprising only 18 per cent of the world's legislators, we are far from parity. At the current rate of progress, it would take another 40 years to reach gender parity in the world's national legislatures. I applaud initiatives like legislative quotas, civic education drives and voter registration campaigns, which seek to boost the numbers of women legislators. These programmes can and should be replicated.

On the economic front, women are joining the workforce in increasing numbers, but almost two-thirds of women in the developing world work in vulnerable jobs where they are either self-employed or work as unpaid family workers. Despite this, there are strong examples of programmes which countries and the international development community can help implement to provide economic opportunities for women.

On my recent visit to Mali, I visited a women's co-operative which picks and processes high-quality mangoes for the global market. Analysis supported by UNDP suggests that Mali could lift its export of mangoes from 2,915 tonnes in 2005 to 200,000 tonnes. Already, with UNDP's support, exports had risen to 12,676 tonnes by 2008. The women in the co-operative, their families and communities and their country are all better off.

The knowledge and expertise is available to significantly improve the lives of women the world over. What we need now is the global will to make a difference. My message today in Washington is that, with support from developed and developing countries alike, we can achieve the MDGs, substantially improving the lives of millions of people. But we can only fully succeed if we commit to a focus on women's empowerment.

This is also the strong message which UNDP and I are conveying to world leaders as they prepare to come to New York this September to review progress on the MDGs.

I am inspired by the many examples of substantial progress for women I hear of every day. My dream is to see the progress which is being made broadened, so that all of the world's women can experience the benefits of greater economic, social and personal security in their own lives.

The UN and New Zealand: Peter Fraser's legacy

Wellington
12 August 2010

Peter Fraser served as Prime Minister of New Zealand from 1940 until 1949. Along with Michael Joseph Savage, he was involved in the formation of the Labour Party in 1916, and went on to become a major figure in the party's history. Notably, he signed the founding charter of the United Nations, personally leading the New Zealand mission to the UN founding meeting in San Francisco in 1945. Each year, the Labour Party hosts the Sir Peter Fraser Memorial Lecture in his honour.

It is a great pleasure for me to be addressing you here in Wellington on 'The UN and New Zealand: Peter Fraser's legacy'. Peter Fraser was one of my illustrious predecessors as Labour Prime Minister and an international statesman. He passed away in the year of my birth, and I grew up in a New Zealand which owed a great a deal to his dedication to public life.

As the title of this address implies, however, Peter Fraser's influence was felt far beyond the shores of our small country.

In my current role as head of the UN's Development Programme, Peter Fraser's contributions to multilateralism and the founding of the UN and his commitment to fostering international co-operation on issues of global concern resonate especially strongly with me. In San Francisco in 1945, Peter Fraser himself led the New Zealand delegation to the UN's founding conference. There, a mere 50 nations—far short of today's total of 192 member states—gathered to produce the UN's Charter. So many of the nation states which exist today were still colonies at that time.

During the two months of deliberations in San Francisco, Peter Fraser argued strongly against granting the great powers a veto at the Security Council. While there were limits to what he could achieve, he pressed hard for the rights of smaller nations to be expressed through the General Assembly, and he contributed to the establishment of the Trusteeship Council, which was tasked with supervising the administration of trust territories.

The world has changed in countless ways since 1945. Today's technology, geopolitics, environment, societies and economies are in many respects unrecognisable from those of a few decades ago. So is the United Nations, which in the last 65 years has spawned myriad organisations, including the multi-billion-dollar-per-annum programme which I now lead.

The Trusteeship Council itself, which Peter Fraser worked to establish, suspended its operations in 1994, when Palau, the then last-remaining UN trust territory, changed its status. But many of the challenges the world faced after World War Two, especially by the poorest and most vulnerable people and countries, unfortunately endure to this day. Take the very topical example of the human tragedy unfolding in the eastern Sahel today, where many millions of people have exhausted their food supply and their assets. Niger has been particularly badly affected.

Overcoming such challenges is at the heart of the mission not only of UNDP, but of the whole UN development system. One can't help thinking that those visionaries like Peter Fraser who gathered in San Francisco would have envisaged overcoming such abject poverty long before now.

At the beginning of this century, Heads of State and government, including me, representing New Zealand, gathered in New York at the United Nations to make another commitment to addressing development challenges. There we signed the landmark Millennium Declaration, which enshrined the Millennium Development Goals (MDGs). These eight goals provided a blueprint for creating better lives for billions of people by 2015.

It is for good reason that the UN Intellectual History Project credits the MDGs with being one of the great ideas to emanate from the United Nations system. They are the most broadly supported, comprehensive and specific poverty-reduction targets the world has ever established. They address extreme poverty and hunger, access to education and health services and to clean water and sanitation, gender equality, environmental degradation, and the deadly diseases of HIV/AIDS, malaria and tuberculosis. Important also, they call for greater global partnerships for development.

The MDGs have since inspired a decade of concerted efforts to lift the living standards of hundreds of millions of people across the globe. In that time, many impressive advances have been made towards the MDGs. Despite a series of recent crises, about which I shall say more shortly, the developing world as a whole remains on track to achieve the MDG poverty reduction target by 2015.

Significant advances have been made in getting children into primary school in many of the poorest countries, including in Sub-Saharan Africa.

The world is now on track to meet or even exceed the MDG drinking water target by 2015.

Between 2003 and 2008, the number of people in low- and middle-income countries receiving antiretroviral therapy increased tenfold from 400,000 to four million. But HIV remains a devastating problem, and the rate of new infections continues to outstrip the expansion of treatment.

Deaths of children under five have been reduced from 12.5 million in 1990 to 8.8 million in 2008—a huge achievement. Yet, the number of deaths is still far too high, especially when one considers that most of them are preventable or the conditions which caused them were treatable. As well, the rate of reduction of child mortality would need to speed up to meet the 2015 goal.

The same is true of a number of other goals. For example, preliminary new data does show signs of progress in reducing maternal deaths, but the rate of reduction is still far short of what is required to meet the MDG target of cutting the maternal mortality rate by three quarters between 1990 and 2015.

On top of the pre-existing challenges of underdevelopment, the multiple crises the world has experienced in very recent years haven't made achieving the MDGs any easier.

The food and fuel crises, catastrophic natural disasters and the global recession have all taken their toll. Newly updated estimates from the World Bank suggest that the economic crisis will leave an additional 64 million people in extreme poverty by the end of 2010, relative to projections before the crisis.

In some parts of the world, the number of people who are undernourished has continued to grow, and slow progress in reducing hunger prevalence had stalled even before the global economic crisis hit. Last year, for the first time in history, more than a billion people were estimated to have suffered from chronic hunger—around 130 million more than before the combined impact of the food, fuel and economic crises.

In San Francisco, Peter Fraser had helped ensure that the issue of promoting full employment was reflected in the section of the UN Charter dealing with international economic and social co-operation. This too has reverberations today. In addition to reducing the proportion of people living in poverty and suffering from hunger, MDG 1 includes a target calling for the achievement of full and productive employment and decent work for all, including women and young people. Yet the global recession has had a devastating impact on jobs, with the numbers of unemployed worldwide estimated to have increased from around 178 million in 2007 to over 211 million last year. An additional 3.6 per cent of the world's workers were at risk of falling into poverty between 2008 and 2009, reversing many years of steady progress on pushing people above the poverty line.

The Global Jobs Pact, developed by the International Labour Organization (ILO), calls for jobs to be put at the very centre of responses to the economic crisis. It has received support from the G20 and the G8, as well as from the entire UN system. UNDP has been directed by its Executive Board to work with the ILO to operationalise the Pact in programmes in developing countries.

While the challenges facing developing countries are great, this is not a time for despair in the UN or anywhere else. Through collective endeavour, as Peter Fraser and the UN's other founding fathers believed, the international community can build a better world.

Right now we see developing country economies leading the return to global growth. In our part of the world, we are most aware of trends in China, but it should also be noted that Sub-Saharan Africa is projected by the International Monetary Fund (IMF) to be the second fastest growing region in the world this year and next. Africa with its young, dynamic and aspirational populations is very much part of the solution to the world's problems.

The self-evident truth is that our world does possess the knowledge, the technology and a wide menu of possible solutions to a multitude of development challenges. We know how to provide skilled attendance at birth, carry out successful vaccination campaigns for children, enrol girls in school, increase crop yields and combat the spread of HIV. Adding to this knowledge, and in preparing for the MDG Plus Ten Review Summit at the UN in New York this September, UNDP recently completed an International Assessment of what it will take to reach the MDGs by 2015. We have identified common and underlying MDG success factors, and the constraints which exist in making progress.

We have presented eight priority areas for action to accelerate MDG progress. They include supporting country-led development, fostering inclusive economic growth, improving opportunities for women and girls, targeting investments in health, education and energy access, scaling up social protection programmes, enabling effective domestic resource mobilisation and allocation and urging donors to honour the official development assistance (ODA) commitments they have made.

An action-oriented outcome to the September MDG Summit will be very important in generating momentum to reach the 2015 targets.

Helping the poorest and most vulnerable is especially vital now. In my position I see countries and communities reeling from the effects of crises they played no part in causing—including climate change.

The risks of social and political instability will increase in coming decades, if climate change provokes large population transfers and growing tensions over the allocation of essential natural resources like water.

The lack of a new climate agreement does not help development. Nor does the stalemate on the WTO trade round. Commitments to ODA need to be complemented by what is called, in the trade, broader policy coherence. That includes fair trade rules—something New Zealand itself would appreciate on agriculture—and climate justice.

While personally I am always an optimist, the question which must at least be asked is whether we as human beings currently have the collective capacity and will to deal effectively with these and other challenges.

So often we see our increasingly multi-polar world struggling to come to terms with what it will take to address the complex issues it confronts, in the face of divergent ideologies, disjointed institutions and plentiful rivalries.

In tackling problems without borders, far too often we see national concerns prevent agreement on taking the action required by the world as a whole. More than ever the world needs the strong and effective United Nations which Peter Fraser and his colleagues worked so hard to create.

At its best, an effective multilateral architecture can defuse tension, overcome challenges and promote social and economic progress. But such an architecture needs to be backed by the strong will of political leaders and member states, and it needs to be based on governance structures which promote inclusive, legitimate and effective agreements.

The case for a renewed and strengthened multilateral system which reflects the realities of and responds to the challenges of the twenty-first century—a system which supports the delivery of improved living standards for the poorest and most vulnerable people and nations—has never been stronger.

The structure of the UN Security Council itself urgently needs updating to be relevant to today's geopolitics. If one began on the task of designing the Council today, there would not be agreement on the current structure.

Perhaps such reform would be easier had Peter Fraser got his way in convincing the great powers not to insist on a veto at the Council.

The world also needs to update the global economic governance system which was established at the end of World War Two.

Without other formal multilateral mechanisms able to respond comprehensively and decisively to the economic crisis, the G20—previously meeting at finance minister level—began to convene as a leaders' summit. Its April 2009 meeting in London led by Right Honourable Gordon Brown took decisive action to limit the impact of the global recession.

Now, post-crisis, the G20 leaders continue to meet, and have designated their summit as their premier forum for economic co-operation. Yet, when countries representing more than 80 per cent of the world's economy decide on a course of action, that inevitably has impacts on those not present—made up of close to 170 nations, including New Zealand. Ways have to be found to link the G20 into the formal multilateral system, so that broader perspectives can be brought to the table.

The UN with its universal membership, broad mandate and unique convening power can certainly play a role in ensuring that the G20 is well informed about the range of views and perspectives of member states. As well, within its funds, programmes, specialised agencies and departments, the UN has huge expertise which is relevant to and can contribute to the G20's deliberations.

When the UN was established, the Economic and Social Council (ECOSOC) was given a mandate for the overall co-ordination of UN system activities in economic, social and related areas. Despite several reforms aiming at strengthening its role, however, ECOSOC has not developed in the way the UN's founders originally envisaged. Perhaps now is the time to consider again proposals which have been put forward in the past to strengthen ECOSOC. It should be noted that its recent session in New York was particularly substantive, with quality forums and presentations, and high level participation.

Meanwhile, out on the front lines of development, one of the UN's greatest strengths is its country-level presence and capacity. It is hard at work every day assisting countries to reduce poverty and promote inclusive and sustainable development.

To go forward and not backwards on the MDGs, the world needs strong global leadership for development, and it needs to support the UN's comprehensive development work. As a small country, New Zealand is obviously not a large player in development co-operation. But for UNDP, and for all the other voluntarily-funded UN organisations, all contributions count. New Zealand has been among the top 20 donors to UNDP over the last ten years.

Bilateral resources for development can have a bigger impact when they are joined with those of other donors and centred on a common strategy. This is often especially true for small countries like New Zealand which lack a development presence on the ground in all countries—but it is also increasingly true even for larger donors which are reducing the number of countries where their bilateral aid is directed.

The development field is a competitive one. Development contributions these days are being made on a large scale not only by the traditional donors, but from across the South, civil society and the mega-philanthropic funds, and increasingly through the private sector too.

The UN, however, with its universal membership, its perceived neutrality, and the idealism which characterised the writing of its Charter, has a special role to play in providing global leadership for development.

Indeed, the world looks to the UN in times of crisis to rally the international effort—as in Haiti earlier this year. Within a few days of that devastating earthquake, and while the humanitarian relief effort got underway, UNDP itself had a job creation programme running in Port-au-Prince to begin clearing away rubble and inject spending power into local communities. That work continues to this day, providing short-term jobs to Haitians clearing sites for safe resettlement, repairing surface water drainage, and improving road access to and through affected areas.

Despite all the UN's inherent flaws and limitations from its establishment, which may have been evident even in San Francisco, the UN remains an essential presence in overcoming today's challenges. Its role in convening nations, contributing bold ideas of global significance, and generating collective international will and commitment to act for development, peace, the environment and human rights is indispensable to promoting a more peaceful, just and secure world. If the UN had not been invented—if those like Peter Fraser gathered in San Francisco had not succeeded in their mission—we would undoubtedly be hard at work trying to create it today.

Perhaps its shape and contours would be different. Perhaps its peace and security, its development, and its human rights pillars and work would not look quite the same. But a body of nations united and co-operating to tackle the world's most intractable problems—problems which ultimately affect us all—would still be needed.

That such a body does exist and has for the past 65 years is part of the enduring legacy of Peter Fraser—a truly great New Zealander.

Inclusion and Equality: Why women's leadership matters

Cardiff, Wales, United Kingdom
11 April 2012

The National Assembly for Wales, formed in 1999, is the democratically elected body that represents the interests of the country and its people, makes laws for Wales and holds the Welsh Government to account. In March 2010, the assembly reopened the Pierhead, a listed historic building in Cardiff Bay, and marked the occasion with the Pierhead Sessions, a series of lectures bringing together international speakers to discuss politics and culture. Helen gave the following speech two years later, as part of the Pierhead's ongoing programme of lectures by key public figures.

————

My thanks go to the National Assembly for Wales for inviting me to speak in this Pierhead Session series of lectures. It is a pleasure to be back in Wales, which I first visited in 1976, and returned to twice as New Zealand Prime Minister. The 2007 visit is seared in my memory as the occasion when New Zealand lost the quarter-final of the Rugby World Cup to France. I know I will find empathy in Wales for that!

I was happy to be in Cardiff a year ago for the Commonwealth Local Government Conference, and to talk there about the work UNDP does to build better governance at the sub-national level. The theme of this year's Pierhead Session—'Sex Matters: Women and their impacts on politics and society'—is of great importance to me professionally and personally. Promoting gender equality and women's active political, economic and social participation is central to my work now as Administrator of the United Nations Development Programme (UNDP).

On a personal level, I count myself very fortunate to have been a member of the post-war baby boom generation in New Zealand, where, as a girl, educational opportunities were wide open to me, and, as a woman, I was able to pursue a career of my choice and meet my professional aspirations. As Prime Minister of my country for nine years, Leader of the Opposition for six years before that, Leader of the New Zealand Labour Party for fifteen years, and as a Member of Parliament for 27-and-a-half years, I am well acquainted with the challenges women face when entering the hitherto male-dominated field of politics.

My remarks tonight on 'Inclusion and Equality: Why women's leadership matters' will focus primarily on women's participation in leadership, decision-making, elected office, public administration and peace-building, in all of which there is still a considerable way to go globally in advancing gender equality.

My starting point is that it is a basic human right for women to enjoy full legal equality and equality of opportunity, and for a girl born today in any country to have the same life prospects as any boy. All our societies are the poorer if they fail to tap the full potential of half their population, and do not remove the obstacles which so often prevent women from rising to leadership positions in political systems and elsewhere.

I do believe that having a critical mass of women in leadership and decision-making positions is positive for human development in all countries—whether developed or developing, and whether countries are living in peace, recovering from conflict or in the process of a democratic transition.

At the outset, I wish to commend the people and the National Assembly for Wales for the prominent role women have assumed in leadership here. It is commendable that, since Welsh devolution, the proportion of

Assembly Members who are women has never dropped below 40 per cent, and indeed once reached a high of 51 per cent. The National Assembly has encouraged these trends by adopting family-friendly policies in its scheduling of committee meetings and plenary sessions, thus translating gender equality principles into policies which help realise it. There is much to learn from Wales' inclusive and dynamic democracy.

My remarks tonight seek to highlight the transformative role of women's political leadership and participation, and some of the successes we see around the world, while also acknowledging the remaining challenges.

Gender equality: a human right

Achieving gender equality is a top priority for the United Nations. It is enshrined as a fundamental human right in Article 1 of the UN Charter, which states that one of the purposes of the UN lies in 'promoting and encouraging respect for human rights and for fundamental freedoms for all without distinction as to race, sex, language or religion'.

A number of UN instruments, conventions and decisions reinforce that commitment, including:

- The Convention on the Elimination of All Forms of Discrimination against Women (CEDAW, 1979), which stresses the equality of men and women across human rights and fundamental freedoms in the political, economic, social, cultural, civil or any other field. On political and public life, it notes that state parties should take measures to ensure that women, on equal terms with men, have the right to hold public office and perform all public functions at all levels of government.

- The Beijing Declaration and Platform for Action, adopted by governments at the 1995 Fourth World Conference on Women, also affirms gender equality as a human right and commits governments to enhancing women's rights.

- The UN Millennium Declaration of 2000 promotes equal rights and opportunities for women and men. Millennium Development Goal 3 set specific targets for gender equality.

- In 2010, the UN created UN Women, the United Nations
  entity for gender equality and the empowerment of women.

Promoting gender equality, however, runs across the mandates of UN organisations as a whole. At UNDP we pursue gender equality across our work on poverty reduction, democratic governance, environmental sustainability, crisis prevention and recovery, and combating the spread of HIV. We see advancing gender equality as not only an end in itself, but also as catalytic in development. The investments made in women and girls are great multipliers of development progress. Failing to make those investments, and failing to boost the status of women and girls, thwarts the potential not only of individuals, but also of families, communities and nations.

As well, fair representation and participation of women in governance is one of the preconditions for achieving genuine democracy. There can be no real democracy if half the population is excluded from participation and power. Athenian democracy, where only some men had voice, will not do in the twenty-first century.

So where are we today?

The first woman who was not a monarch to become a national leader was the Prime Minister of Sri Lanka, Sirimavo Bandaranaike, in 1960. A total of three women were national leaders in the 1960s, six in the 1970s, and seven in the 1980s. The total number of women who have reached these positions has risen only slowly since, with New Zealand supplying two. Today, there are only eight women heads of state, representing slightly more than 5 per cent of the total. This seems extraordinary in the second decade of the twenty-first century.

The global average of women holding parliamentary seats remains under 20 per cent, which is well below the 30 per cent target set in the 1995 Beijing Platform for Action and in the MDGs. At the current rate of progress, that target will not be reached globally before 2025, and long beyond that in many countries. That is too long for women and the world to wait.

There are currently only 41 women heads of parliament. Only 16 per cent of ministers are women, and most often they are allocated portfolios like those for social welfare, women and children. In a country I have recently visited, the one woman minister had exactly those responsibilities.

The proportions of women in national legislatures in the world's regions range from roughly 22 per cent in the Americas and Europe—with the 42 per cent in Nordic countries pushing the average figures up—to 20.2 per cent in sub-Saharan Africa, 17.9 per cent in Asia, 14.9 per cent in the Pacific, and 10.7 per cent in the Arab States. Five countries—all in the Gulf and the Pacific—have no women parliamentarians at all.

Women as decision-makers

When women are 'out of sight, out of mind', meeting their needs does not get prioritised. Conversely, when there is a critical mass of women decision-makers, the issues which previously went unaddressed can become priorities.

Rwanda is the nation with the highest proportion of women parliamentarians in the world—currently at 56 per cent. It is no surprise therefore that its parliament drafted a far-reaching law to combat gender-based violence. It was passed in 2006 with cross-party support brokered by the Forum of Rwandan Women Parliamentarians, which also involved men in the work to craft the new law.

In 2002, at a time when Costa Rica's numbers of women in parliament exceeded 30 per cent, a law on the protection of adolescent mothers was passed to provide those young women with free health services and education.

In Tanzania in 2004, four years after the constitution was amended to state that women had to hold no less than 20 per cent of the seats in parliament, an amendment to the Land Act granted equal rights and access to land, loans and credit for women.

In Spain, with women MPs also over the 30 per cent mark, a 2007 law mandated affirmative action measures for employment and working conditions.

In 2007, when Nepal's share of women in the interim legislative assembly was at nearly 20 per cent, the finance ministry adopted gender-responsive budgeting for all government expenditure. For the 2008 elections, quotas helped ensure that a third of the members elected to the Constituent Assembly were women.

It is not only at the national level that women's leadership is driving change of benefit to women. This is also happening at the local level.

In India, for example, women-led councils approved 60 per cent more drinking-water projects than did those led by men. This matters hugely for women and girls, who bear the brunt of water collection, often on foot over long distances, in many countries to this day.

It is to be hoped that, as many more women take their rightful place in the ranks of decision-makers, more such issues will come to the top of political, legislative and budgetary priorities. Indeed, a number of areas of great risk for women need far more attention, for example:

- The rate of decline in maternal mortality globally is well below what is needed to achieve the MDG 5 target of a 75 per cent reduction between 1990 and 2015. Far more priority needs to be given to ensuring that women are well nourished and have access to sexual, reproductive and maternity services. MDG 5 also targets universal access to sexual and reproductive health, yet high levels of unmet need for services exist in many countries.

- More than 25 years into the HIV/AIDS epidemic, women's inequality and lack of power in relationships both puts them at greater risk of exposure to HIV and increases their burdens of care. In Southern Africa, girls are two to four-and-a-half times more likely than boys to become infected.

- In every country of the world, women are subjected to gender-based violence, and in many the levels are chronic. These issues need to be addressed in the law, and through police, prosecutor and judicial training to ensure that the law is upheld.

Personally, I take great pride in having led a government in New Zealand which did look at policy through a gender lens, and implemented many policies of significant benefit to women. Examples include enshrining in law the right to paid parental leave, and to a statutory minimum entitlement for all to a fourth week of annual holidays. Twenty hours' free early childhood care and education and interest-free loans for tertiary students were also of particular benefit to women.

Crisis and post-crisis contexts

With more than one-fifth of the world's population estimated to be living in states which are considered fragile, women's participation and leadership in building peace and the foundations for development is especially critical. No state in this fragile category is on course to achieve all of the Millennium Development Goals.

While crisis increases the economic and social burdens on both women and men, the specific social obligations and responsibilities placed on women impose a greater burden on them. Added to that is the horror of sexual- and gender-based violence and exploitation which afflicts women in so many nations during and after conflicts.

The impact of armed conflict on women has received increased global attention since 2000, when the UN Security Council adopted its landmark Resolution 1325 on Women, Peace and Security. It called for special measures to protect women and girls from gender-based violence, and for consideration to be given to the special needs of women and girls during repatriation, resettlement and post-conflict reconstruction. The resolution also affirmed that, for peace and security to be sustained, women must be empowered, their voices must be heard and they must be included as active participants in conflict prevention, management and resolution.

Subsequent resolutions have further recognised the key role women can play in peace-building and recovery. The UN Secretary-General noted in his 2010 'Report on Women's Participation in Peace-building' that 'ensuring women's participation in peace-building is not only a matter of women's and girls' rights. Women are crucial partners in shoring up three pillars of lasting peace: economic recovery, social cohesion and political legitimacy.'

There are many good examples of the role women have played and are playing in building and consolidating peace. For example, in Guatemala, Burundi and Bosnia, women's peace organisations and coalitions played a significant part in helping to bring about peace. Following the horrific genocide of the 1990s in Rwanda, women emerged as central arbiters of peace and reconciliation. In Liberia, women pushed for the disarmament of the fighting factions before the signing of a peace accord, thereby making an important contribution towards the peaceful resolution of years of conflict.

UNDP has placed a strong emphasis on conflict prevention, using both formal and informal peace and mediation processes and establishing and strengthening national and local systems and mechanisms. Within this, UNDP has supported women's groups and voices to contribute to inclusive and peaceful conflict resolution. In Timor Leste, for example, UNDP helped increase women's participation in informal peace processes and mediation. In Fiji, UNDP supported women to play a role in the first broadly based dialogue between state officials, members of the military council and non-governmental organisations to be held since the current military-led government took power.

Yet research, including that done by UNDP, confirms that women are still under-represented at peace tables, donor conferences and in decision-making, planning and budgeting in post-crisis settings. Financing for gender equality in post-conflict recovery and reconstruction is rarely a priority. This needs to change.

There can be no real and lasting peace without ensuring that women's voices and perspectives are well represented. Women bring the everyday issues of concern to communities to peace discussions, calling for more representative governance following conflict, improved access to livelihoods and economic opportunities, and increased access to justice through strengthened rule of law, especially for survivors of sexual and gender-based violence.

An inspiring example of women's leadership in the aftermath of conflict is that of Liberia's President Ellen Johnson Sirleaf, the first and only elected female African head of state. In her inaugural address in 2006, the President recognised the key role Liberian women had played in achieving peace and pledged 'to give Liberian women prominence in all affairs of our country'. She proceeded to nominate women as two of the five members of the Supreme Court, and to appoint many women to her cabinet, including her first Minister of Finance and Ministers of Agriculture, Commerce, Foreign Affairs, Gender and Development, Justice, and Youth and Sports.

During President Johnson Sirleaf's first term, a specialised rape court was set up to expedite the processing of rape cases. This was vital. The high rates of sexual violence experienced by women during the Liberian civil war meant that there were a great many cases to investigate and prosecute. There were also changes to the general law on gender-based violence, including domestic violence and rape. Penalties were increased for these offences to demonstrate their gravity.

Public administration

Advancing women in the ranks of public administration is also important as a gender-equality goal, and because gender balance in public administration ensures that a wider range of perspectives is brought to bear on policy-making and service delivery. While public administrations are sometimes among the most important employers of women, in many countries they perpetuate rather than challenge gender bias. The largest numbers of women continue to be found at the lower levels of public service structures, where they have the least influence.

To date there have been no mechanisms for tracking the numbers and progress of women globally in leadership positions in public administrations. To fill that gap and inform policy-making, UNDP has undertaken the first global stocktaking of women in public administrations, particularly in leadership positions. It examines a range of strategies to increase the number of women in public administration, such as targets and quotas, and capacity-building and advocacy to discern which strategies are yielding the best results.

Democratic transitions and women

Over the past fifteen months, uprisings and change in a number of the Arab States have dominated international news bulletins. Women have been actively involved in these events, as protest leaders and participants, and in spreading the word through conventional and new social media. It is to be hoped that, as new systems of governance are built, women too will benefit as equals. A joint publication of the UN, including UNDP, and the Arab League in 2010 reported that women constituted only 10 per cent of the total of parliamentarians in the region—the lowest rate in the world. The unemployment rate for Arab women last year was double that for Arab men. The economic participation of Arab women remains the lowest of women anywhere in the world, at 26.3 per cent, and it is concentrated in the informal sector. In some countries, illiteracy levels remain high for women, along with maternal mortality rates.

Democratic transitions where women are fully involved can provide new opportunities to address such gender inequities. Yet, to date, women are not making the breakthroughs in the region which might have been hoped for. In Tunisia, work was done to promote women's participation in the elections and have electoral processes which enabled fair competition. The adoption of an electoral law which mandated the alternation of men and women on political party lists was seen as an early victory. Nevertheless, the proportion of women in the new Constituent Assembly is similar to pre-revolution levels at 24 per cent. While that is higher than the global average, it maintains Tunisia below the 30 per cent target for women's representation in the national legislature. At the time of the Tunisian election, women held under 10 per cent of decision-making positions in the political parties, and only one party was led by a woman. Only three of the 44 cabinet posts are currently held by women.

The elections in Egypt resulted in only nine women being elected. With the addition of two women appointed to the 508-seat assembly, they constitute just 2 per cent of the membership.

Now women's and other civil society organisations in states in transition in the region are advocating for the anchoring of women's rights in the constitutions and laws to be written. To be effective, advocates and experts need to have meaningful input into the decision-making and drafting processes. UN agencies with expertise on gender equality, including UNDP and UN Women, are available to give support to these processes. It is our hope that both women and men will see lasting benefits from the democratic transitions.

Some next steps in promoting gender equality in decision-making

The quickest way to lift women's representation in parliaments is through the use of quotas. Their implementation can be highly controversial. Legislation for quotas in the parliaments of India and Papua New Guinea has been stuck in political processes for a number of years, and the debate over the bills has been rancorous. Another way forward is to adopt proportional representation systems, which do put pressure on political parties to choose women candidates for winnable positions.

The hardest electoral systems for women to penetrate are those based on single-member constituencies. There, the stereotypical image of an MP is that of a man, and often of a man with a wife who helps in the constituency and runs the home. While these stereotypes are breaking down in many places, the process has not been fast.

Where electoral systems are based on national or regional party lists, however, or on multi-member constituencies with, say, the single transferable-vote procedure, the circumstances are more conducive to the entry of women—not least because parties are less appealing to women voters if they exclude them from party lists and multi-member constituencies. The gender inequity of that is just too blatant.

Of the 59 countries which held elections in 2011 for lower or single houses of parliament, seventeen had legislated for electoral quotas for women, nine had used quotas within political parties, and 33 did not employ any special measures. Women won 27.4 per cent of the places in those parliaments which had legislated for quotas, and only 15.7 per cent of the places in countries without any form of quota.

In emerging democracies, gender quotas can play a critical role in electing more representative parliaments. A 2011 review of 23 countries with a history of conflict reveals that where the rejuvenation of their political systems included introducing gender quotas for election, women held one-third of the parliamentary seats. Of the eleven other countries emerging from conflict which had not implemented quotas, women held only 16 per cent of the seats.

Rwanda provides a compelling example of a society where the empowerment of women as decision-makers has played a key role in its transformation. As mentioned earlier, quotas helped place Rwanda in the first place in the world for the proportion of its parliamentarians who are women. A 30 per cent quota for women MPs was established in the country's 2003 constitution. Rwandan women now hold 56 per cent of seats in their parliament's lower chamber. In addition, 32 per cent of ministerial positions are held by women. Women parliamentarians in Rwanda led efforts in the transitional parliament set up after the 1994 genocide to amend discriminatory statutes, such as the old laws on nationality and citizenship, which were not gender equitable.

Next door in Burundi, the introduction of quotas, along with support by UNDP and the broader UN to encourage women to register and vote, and the provision of skills training for those interested in running for office, played a role in lifting women's representation. A 30 per cent quota for national elections was exceeded, as women took 34 per cent of the parliamentary seats in 2010. Burundi also has the highest proportion of women senators in Africa at 46 per cent. UNDP, with UN and civil society partners, is continuing support for the women who have been elected.

Beyond quotas, it also helps for women to have fair access to public and private sources of electoral finance in their campaigns. As well, electoral commissions need to be vigilant in their oversight of electoral finance laws to reduce bribery and corruption before and during campaigns.

Campaign violence can be another obstacle to women's full political participation. Security for women candidates and voters is needed to encourage full engagement.

Political parties are generally the gatekeepers to political representation. Women within parties worldwide tend to be highly represented at the grassroots levels and in supporting roles, but under-represented in higher-level positions. Women comprise 40 to 50 per cent of the membership of political parties globally, but only around 10 per cent of the leadership positions. Yet if women do not lead political parties, they will be unlikely ever to lead governments.

Acknowledging that political parties play the crucial roles in determining who is selected for winnable positions at elections, UNDP has been working to advise them on how they can make a difference for the better for women's representation. Together with the National Democratic Institute of the USA, we recently launched a guidebook called *Empowering Women for Stronger Political Parties*. It is the first of its kind in compiling a range of measures which have been taken by political parties to boost women's participation throughout the electoral cycle, including skills training for and mentoring of women candidates, ensuring women's visibility in campaigns and making sure that electoral monitoring, security provisions and voter information are gender-sensitive.

Even when women are more fairly represented in decision-making, progress on gender equality on all fronts is not guaranteed. The engagement of men is also essential in creating a culture of inclusion and equality. There needs to be general acknowledgment that women in decision-making are an asset to whole societies.

As well, women's organisations are vital advocates for and independent agents of change everywhere in the world. It is especially important to affirm their role in the aftermath of crisis, peace-building and democratic transitions.

Investment in women's well-being, potential, empowerment, participation and leadership across the board is needed. Educated, healthy and empowered women drive development faster. Women with equal rights as basic as being able to own and inherit land and property, access credit and open bank accounts can play an even greater role in the development of their societies.

The general point is relevant to developed countries too. The gap between New Zealand's GDP per capita and that of Scandinavian countries owes a great deal to the lower level of labour force participation of women in New Zealand. That was one of the reasons why my government pursued work–life balance policies, like implementing the extra week of annual holidays and a right to paid parental leave. The universal right to 20 hours' free early childhood education was established both because of its importance for children *and* because it made the option of paid work for both parents a realistic one.

Conclusion

A huge focus for me as a leader is to contribute to building a more equitable and sustainable world. Gender equality at every level must feature in that world.

Truly equitable and sustainable development requires the weaving together of its economic, social and environmental strands through 'triple win' approaches and policies. Gender equality and women's empowerment must always be fully integrated in these approaches.

At the global and national levels, our world faces complex and interlinked challenges. They demand policy-making which positions economic growth, poverty reduction, social development, equity and environmental sustainability as interconnected objectives which are best pursued together. Policies and initiatives which empower women must be part of that fabric.

A key part of making sure that they are is having women much better represented in leadership and decision-making than they are today. Countries which are serious about equitable and sustainable development will make sure that they make that happen.

The benefits of women's participation and leadership are well established. As the post-2015 development goals are defined, and as new and more sustainable democracies are being built, higher levels of women's representation should be aimed for.

Here in Wales, you are reaping the benefits of involving men and women as equals in your growth and development. In many other places, the story of women's full empowerment is still to be written. Women's full participation and leadership are prerequisites for sustainable development. If we are to build sustainable routes out of poverty, women must be full beneficiaries of and contributors to their country's progress. The time for talking about what to do next is over. It is time for action and it is time for change for women.

Our World in 2050: More equitable and sustainable—or less?

San Francisco, United States of America
7 November 2012

The World Affairs Councils of America are a non-partisan network of councils that aim to promote cross-sector discussion on matters of global importance. In November 2012, World Affairs hosted a mini-series of talks called 'Spotlight on Development Challenges', in which Helen delivered the following speech to the World Affairs Council of Northern California. The other sessions in the mini-series were 'Asia's Challenge: Ensuring sustainable growth' by Rajat M. Nag, Managing Director General of the Asian Development Bank, and 'Defending Human Rights in Central Africa' by Abbé Benoît Kinalegu, head of the Catholic Church's Peace and Justice Commission in northern Congo.

———

I thank the World Affairs Council for inviting me to deliver this lecture as part of its ongoing mini-series 'Spotlight on Development Challenges'.

As Administrator of the United Nations Development Programme, I find the topic of this lecture series and the council's interest in what the world might look like in 2050 particularly relevant to our work to help address one of humanity's most pressing challenges: how to lift human development while staying within planetary boundaries.

It is timely to raise these issues, just months after the conclusion of the UN Conference on Sustainable Development Rio+20 and when UN member states are beginning discussions around the post-2015 development framework, which could guide development thinking and work for years to come.

The title of my lecture tonight is 'Our World in 2050: More equitable and sustainable—or less?' Let me begin by putting the year 2050 into perspective. It sounds far away. Yet, with half of the world's population today under the age of 30, and current global life expectancy at almost 70 years, we can expect that more than half of all people alive today will also be alive in 2050. It is not some theoretical year in a science fiction future.

This is not to say that if 2050 weren't on our horizon, the responsibilities towards future generations would be less compelling. In 1987, the Report of the World Commission on Environment and Development (the Brundtland Commission) defined sustainable development as 'meeting the needs of the present without compromising the ability of future generations to meet their own needs'.

That definition has guided the work of UNDP ever since. It reflects a fundamental tenet of justice: that no one should be denied the ability or opportunity to live lives they value because of their gender, ethnicity, religion or any other factor, including, in this case, the generation in which they happen to be born.

Recognising that our actions today impact on our world of tomorrow, acting accordingly is necessary for achieving the 'future we want'—the call emerging from Rio+20.

My lecture tonight will address three issues. First, I will examine global drivers of change which affect how the world may look in 2050. Second, I will argue that poverty, inequity and environmental sustainability are inter-linked global challenges and need to be tackled concurrently. Third, I will examine how countries and communities, guided by global norms and standards, are employing innovative approaches to address these challenges in integrated ways.

Global drivers of change and projections to 2050

So what are some of the trends and projections identified by researchers as critical in shaping the world of 2050? I will focus on three major drivers of change involving population dynamics, environmental constraints and geopolitical shifts.

1. Demographic pressures and urbanisation

According to UN estimates, the global population will reach 9.3 billion by 2050—some 2.3 billion more inhabitants on our planet than we have today. This demographic trend is expected to be associated with rapid urbanisation and ageing. Both are important considerations for development planning.

Urban areas are expected to absorb all this population growth. Currently more than half of the world's population live in urban areas, but that ratio is not consistent across all regions. It is expected to be reached in Asia by 2020, and in Africa in 2035. By 2050, therefore, the urban population is due almost to double, from 3.6 billion in 2011 to 6.3 billion, and to make up around 68 per cent of the total world population. Most of this urban growth will be concentrated in developing countries.

The World Health Organization projects that by 2050 the proportion of the world's population over 60 will double from the 11 per cent of 2000 to 22 per cent. In 2050, for the first time in history, the number of older persons (over 60 years) will exceed the number of the young (under fifteen years).

Both challenges and opportunities arise out of this projected rapid population growth, and related ageing and urbanisation. To name just some:

- Food supply will need to be adequate for this large population. That creates opportunities for the world's farmers and food processors, but there will need to be considerable adaptation to the more extreme and volatile climatic conditions which are already affecting food production.

- Pension and social security systems will need to be fine-tuned to be affordable for those populations which live much longer and work later in life.

- Healthcare systems will need to cater for the needs of significantly more older persons, and for the expected increase in non-communicable diseases. These diseases, often thought of as a problem of developed countries, are now posing significant challenges in developing countries too.

- Urban planning and urban governance systems will need to be updated to address dramatic increases in the demand for housing, electricity, water, health, education, transport, energy and other services.

- Triggers and consequences of social unrest—including poverty, violence and inequality—will need to be monitored and addressed.

- Developing countries could experience a significant demographic dividend from their dynamic youth populations, but only if there is significant investment in the potential of young people, and if jobs and opportunity creation become a specific and high priority of public policy.

While this list of challenges is long, it is also true that demographic trends are largely predictable and can be planned for at an early stage. They are also not as contested as the next area I will discuss, which relates to the environmental pressures on the planet.

2. Climate change, pressures on natural resources and disaster risks

Climate change is a major challenge to development today. The OECD estimates that carbon emissions will more than double from 1990 levels by 2050. That increasingly puts already hard-won development gains at risk, introducing more complexity to our work as development actors.

There is broad scientific agreement that without urgent action the world will move beyond what has been termed its 'planetary boundaries' for climate and on other dimensions. For climate, we are told that means 'irreversible and catastrophic change'. For biodiversity, it means the disappearance of species. For water, it can mean not only hardship, but also more conflict over access to a scares resource.

The Intergovernmental Panel on Climate Change has concluded that increases in extreme weather are already a discernible trend. The impact of that includes the depletion of natural resources, threatening food security and livelihoods, more frequent natural disasters from flooding to heat waves and droughts, and an increase in the incidence of natural resource-related conflicts both within and across borders.

Of particular concern to me is that the groups and individuals which are already disadvantaged face the harshest repercussions from environmental degradation. That is because the poor disproportionately rely on access to natural resources for their livelihoods. Women and girls in developing countries, who often bear the responsibility for collecting fuel and water, face extra burdens when these resources become scarcer and lie further away from home.

The growth of informal settlements in many countries, fuelled by urbanisation and migration, has led to the growth of unstable living environments. Vulnerable and marginalised communities are impacted more from natural disasters because of this. I saw the impact of this when visiting the neighbourhoods in Port-au-Prince, Haiti, which cling to deep ravines. They were destabilised by the January 2010 earthquake, and are threatened by landslides and/or flooding in extreme weather.

With the expected rapid expansion of urban communities by 2050, the challenges for cities will be even greater. The poor will continue to carry a double burden of exposure to environmental risks, both in their immediate home environment from air and water pollution and lack of sanitation, and from such long-term global trends as extreme weather hazards and rising sea levels.

Conflict over natural resources is also more likely to erupt where there is poor governance, with bad or inequitable management of land and other resources. This will be exacerbated by the environmental and demographic pressures the world will face in 2050.

3. Globalisation, shifts in geo-political dynamics and role of non-state actors

We live in an era of unprecedented globalisation and interdependence, where the impacts of policies, decisions and initiatives in one place can ripple across the globe. Most recently, the crisis generated in the markets of the north spread to all corners of the earth, affecting the poorest and most distant nations which experienced weaker demand and lower prices for their exports, higher volatility in capital flows and commodity prices, and lower remittances.

But this interdependence can also bring benefits in the form of new job opportunities and the spread of innovation and technologies which accelerate development. We see in Africa how information and communication technologies are bringing services like mobile banking to previously under-served populations—and there are countless other applications of these technologies too.

The rise of the major economies in the south, and ongoing political transformations in the Arab states region and elsewhere, are already impacting on traditional patterns of global economic and political governance, as well as on development co-operation frameworks.

The drivers of change in geopolitics include:

- the waves of democratisation—in Europe following the end of the Cold War, in Latin America following the era of the generals, in parts of South East Asia and in the Arab states region

- the emergence of mega economies in the South, with China, India and Brazil already among the world's ten largest economies

- South–South co-operation, through technical assistance, grants, loans, trade, investment and knowledge sharing, is growing fast.

Greater realisation that global public goods cannot be secured and protected by one nation alone, and that emerging threats and challenges require co-ordinated action, have led to new partnerships not only between countries, but also with non-state actors across the private sector, civil society and mega-philanthropic foundations. The role of the non-state actors in local, national, regional and global development and discourse can only grow.

From trends to projections

The demographic, environmental, economic and geopolitical trends I have described will have a direct impact on how poverty eradication and development are broadly addressed, and how the world of 2050 is shaped.

Whether that world will be more equitable and sustainable—or less—

depends on the policy choices made at the global, national, company and societal levels. At each level, decision-makers will need to be agile to address emerging challenges which we cannot foresee today, and to do so through new partnerships and innovation. Forty years ago the HIV/AIDS pandemic had yet to emerge. When it did, it had a serious impact on development in a number of countries, including through life expectancy falling, the rising costs of treatment impacting on health and development budgets, a loss of productivity, an increased burden on women and growth in the numbers of orphaned children without adequate support.

Trends and risks can be modeled to enable us to plan and to inform policy decisions. UNDP's 2011 global Human Development Report (HDR) on equity and sustainability produced a range of different scenarios for what our world could look like in 2050, based on how much progress was made on combating inequality and environmental risks.

Before I delve into these, let me define human development—the paradigm within which UNDP has consciously worked since the production of its first global Human Development Report in 1990. Human development is seen as enlarging people's choices and freedoms, and enabling them to live long and healthy lives, be educated, and have a decent standard of living. Using the Human Development Index (HDI), which encompasses health and education components alongside GDP, UNDP's annual Human Development Report ranks countries according to this composite measure, believing it to be a better measure of development than GDP alone.

The 2011 Human Development Report constructed three scenarios, modeling different trends in environmental degradation and inequality, and their consequence on human development over the next four decades.

The 'base case' scenario—and in this case the best-case scenario assumes limited changes in inequality and environmental threats and risks—anticipates that the global HDI could be 19 per cent higher by 2050 than it is today. That would represent a rate of progress in lifting human development similar to that achieved between 1990 and 2010.

On these projections, HDI would increase faster in developing countries, leading to ongoing convergence of development status. In Sub-Saharan Africa, the HDI would increase by 44 per cent—the biggest increase in any region of the world, and one which would propel much of the continent into what are now classified as medium or high levels of human development.

But the report also has a sobering central message: that this scenario is very unlikely to materialise, unless we take bold steps now to avert future environmental calamities, ensure no further environmental degradation and reduce deep inequalities within and among nations.

An 'environmental challenges' scenario was then constructed which takes into account, among other things, the impact of global warming on agricultural production, challenges related to water, sanitation and pollution, and growing inequality and its consequences, such as a higher probability of intrastate conflict. In this model, the increase in the global HDI was predicted to be eight percentage points lower than in the base case scenario, and twelve percentage points lower for Sub-Saharan Africa.

Under an even more adverse 'environmental disaster' scenario, which amplified the magnitude of the impacts modeled, the global HDI would be fifteen percentage points below the base case scenario in 2050. The most dramatic impact of that would be on Sub-Saharan Africa, which would fall 24 percentage points below the base case scenario, and on South Asia which would fall 22 percentage points below.

Overall, this worst-case scenario would see human development progress slow to a crawl, and actually regress in Sub-Saharan Africa and South Asia by 2050. There is surely a compelling need for action at every level to prevent this scenario materialising.

A renewed focus on inequality and sustainability

The key message emerging from our 2011 HDR and its projections is that to maintain and accelerate human development progress we must tackle inequality and sustainability together. The 1995 Human Development Report identified three essential elements of the human development paradigm: equality of opportunity for all people in society, sustainability of such opportunities from one generation to the next, and empowerment of people so that they participate in—and benefit from—development processes.

Last year's report on equity and sustainability demonstrated that these elements, beyond being conceptually important to the framework, were also important for getting development results. Indeed, this call for a renewed focus on sustainability and equity has also come from other scholars whose work demonstrates that poverty, inequity and environmental sustainability are inter-linked global challenges.

And global leaders agree. The Rio+20 outcome document concludes that sustainable development is the only viable path for development. It highlights how environmental protection and economic development are linked, and gives, for the first time at a global conference of this kind, equal emphasis to the social—or people-centered—dimension of sustainable development.

The 'Resilient People, Resilient Planet' report of the Secretary-General's High Level Global Sustainability panel, issued ahead of Rio+20, suggested that 'most economic decision-makers still regard sustainable development as extraneous to their core responsibilities'. Yet integrating the environmental and social dimensions can be vital to the success of economic decisions.

As we approach 2050, the more polluted and unequal our world becomes, the more governments will need to view environmental and social protection systems not as luxuries to be acquired when countries become wealthy, but as necessities, vital to sustain development and meet the needs of citizens. The costs of such mitigation then will be much higher if we don't take action now. This was a central message of Nicholas Stern's landmark report to the British government in 2006 on the need for urgent action on climate change.

This conclusion is increasingly compelling for developing countries with restless young populations, overstretched services, rapidly expanding cities and growing exposure to disaster risk. The challenges are especially daunting for small island countries faced with obliteration from rising sea levels, and for other poor countries also bearing the brunt of extreme climate events—including through the deadly droughts regularly affecting parts of Africa, and the catastrophic flooding in Pakistan and elsewhere.

But let me also talk a little more about the links between inequality and development. Debates around income inequality, especially as seen in the recent 'occupy' movements around the world, have often been framed as ideological and not relevant to development outcomes. Yet, in their 2009 book *The Spirit Level: Why greater equality makes societies stronger*, Richard Wilkinson and Kate Pickett demonstrated that more equal societies do better on most measures of human well-being, and that these benefits are accrued not only by the poorest, but also by all segments of society.

A major essay on 'Income Inequality and the Conditions of Chronic Poverty' in a recent UNDP publication describes the potential mechanisms involved, asserting that 'High and rising inequality also reduces the likelihood that economic and social policies fostering inclusive growth and human development will be delivered and implemented. For instance, richer groups may secure economically inefficient advantages such as regressive taxes or an allocation of public funds for their own interest rather than for that of the country.'

This concern has been raised by a range of leading thinkers, from Nobel Laureate Joseph Stiglitz to Robert Putnam, who postulate that more unequal societies, where levels of trust and social cohesion are low, are less likely to invest in public goods and infrastructure—such as conserving the environment, public health or improving education systems. Yet such investments are critical for the well-being of current and future generations.

When we think about sustaining development, we must take into account the stocks of our capital—economic, human, social and environmental—and how much of those stocks we are bequeathing our children. Rising inequality can have a negative impact on all of them. At times, this impact is highly visible—when rising inequality, for example, leads to violence and armed conflict with human, social, economic and environmental costs, and thus blight an entire society's development trajectory. At other times, the impact may be less visible, but rising inequality nonetheless may be leading to the rich and poor in a society living such separate lives that they cannot imagine a shared future worth working for together, and therefore cannot take the steps needed to achieve it.

As Nobel Laureate Joseph Stiglitz reminds us, 'growing inequality is the flip side of something else: shrinking opportunity'.

It is rather important that the post-2015 global development agenda which is now being debated should see promoting greater equality and environmental sustainability as linked goals. That is needed to sustain the development gains of the last 40 years, and to ensure that future generations will not be worse off than those of the present.

What are the policy choices and interventions that can ensure a more equitable and sustainable 2050?

Let me now look at some of the approaches that can, and have, been taken to tackle poverty, inequality and sustainability by a) building consensus on the future we want at the global level, b) making smart policy decisions at the country level, and c) finding innovative solutions at the local level.

Building consensus at the global level

A challenge which policy-makers face in promoting sustainable development is that electoral cycles and related political pressures lead to a shorter-term focus. That can mean that the priorities of the day are addressed in a piecemeal fashion, and that longer-term risks are inadequately addressed. This is where the UN, with its role in building consensus around norms and setting long-term global development goals and targets, can help chart a way forward.

The Millennium Development Goals (MDGs) were successful in focusing development efforts and mobilising diverse actors around a common cause over a long-term horizon of fifteen years. Governments performing well and keeping their countries on track to meet the goals are recognised at regularly held UN conferences, and those needing increased support from the international community are identified.

Rio+20 reiterated the need to accelerate progress to meet the MDGs by 2015, something UNDP is fully committed to supporting, and also agreed to craft 'Sustainable Development Goals'. In addition, it drew attention to the pressing need for universal access to modern and reliable energy services, at the same time as there is also a need to move away from the high level of dependence on fossil fuels.

Member states noted the UN Secretary-General Ban Ki-moon's Sustainable Energy for All initiative, which includes three targets for 2030: achieving universal access to modern energy services, doubling the share of renewables in the global energy mix, and doubling the rate of improvement in energy efficiency worldwide. Of the US$500 billion pledged through voluntary commitments at Rio+20, more than 60 per cent were dedicated to this initiative, indicating that global targets can encourage financial support to complement political commitment needed for change.

The UN Secretary-General also issued an ambitious challenge to achieve 'zero hunger' in his lifetime. Specifically, he called for a world in which everyone has access to sufficient levels of nutritious food all year round, there is no malnutrition in pregnancy and early childhood, all food systems are sustainable, smallholder farmers have the inputs and opportunities they need to double their productivity and income, and food losses stemming from waste, poor storage capacity and infrastructure are brought to an end.

Policy decisions at different levels can help meet these goals. For example, investments in sustainable agriculture have the potential to alleviate food insecurity and malnutrition, mitigate climate change, and protect the environment. As well, the United Nations Environment Programme estimates that these investments have the potential to create up to 50 million more jobs by 2050.

Building consensus around where we want our world to be in 2030, 2040 and 2050 is a necessary step. Concerted action by governments, NGO and civil society actors, the private sector, philanthropists and researchers could help us get there.

Action at the country level

To be successful, countries will need to adopt integrated policy-making and pursue objectives across the three strands of sustainable development—economic, environmental and social—simultaneously. That requires effective public administrations and governance systems, and broad buy-in from diverse stakeholders.

UNDP is committed to supporting countries to develop these capacities and plans for green and inclusive economies, which can achieve national development priorities while limiting future emissions and responding to the needs of vulnerable, poor and excluded groups and communities.

In our recently published report, 'Triple Wins for Sustainable Development', we show through case studies how integrated policies actually work in synergy and challenge the outdated thinking which views economic growth as antithetical to environmental protection. Some successful examples include:

- Brazil's Bolsa Verde (or Green Grant) programme, creating income transfers, targeted specifically for families in extreme poverty, which promote environmental conservation in areas where they live and work.

- Ethiopia's Productive Safety Net Programme, which to date has provided income and predictable food supply to more than eight million beneficiaries in 300 food-insecure districts. Those participating in the scheme work on environmental conservation, water management and terracing, building greater resilience to climate extremes for the future.

- India's Mahatma Gandhi National Rural Employment Guarantee Act, which has delivered a minimum of 100 days' work a year to eligible rural poor, with a quota for women's participation, on projects determined by village councils with a focus on environmental rehabilitation and water conservation. This scheme now benefits upwards of 46 million households.

Through South–South co-operation, developing countries can share such best practice and lessons learned, and UNDP will continue to be a strong partner in promoting this.

Innovation and partnership at the local level

Beyond what the international community and governments can do, the significance and relevance of global summits ultimately lie in their ability to connect with and influence what people are doing on the ground around the world to 'think globally while acting locally'.

Rio+20, with its huge engagement of sub-national governments, NGOs, communities and businesses, can be seen as promoting bottom-up leadership for sustainable development, based on pragmatic, multi-sectoral, issue-based coalitions. In the end, what will motivate governments to act is the knowledge that there is a groundswell for change.

Innovative initiatives at the local level, shown to be successful, can be scaled up. In my work, I encounter countless examples of successful community-based action. In Senegal recently, I met local women replanting and then protecting the mangrove forests, which, once re-established, nurture fish and shell fish stocks, thus generating new sources of incomes for their families.

The important role of philanthropic organisations in building partnerships for the future is also worth highlighting. Venture philanthropy can help spur innovation and solutions for addressing sustainability and equality, among other things, which can be adopted by local communities and then scaled up.

Conclusion

In my remarks tonight I have examined different global drivers of change—demographic, environmental, economic and geopolitical—and the policy choices needed to ensure the world is more equitable and sustainable in 2050.

Understanding trends and applying sophisticated modeling techniques can help us plan for the future. But ultimately political will and strong leadership at every level is needed to dedicate adequate human and financial resources to tackle the challenges identified, find innovative solutions and build strong partnerships.

I have highlighted successful examples of such action, from every corner of the globe. Speaking here in the Bay area—a global hub for technological innovation and social entrepreneurship, as well a community which respects the diversity of people and protects the environment—I am optimistic that the world can be more equal and sustainable in 2050.

I look to all of you to be part of the discussion on the post-2015 development framework, and to share your ideas, creativity and dedication to help shape the future we want.

Yes She Can: Women and leadership

Aotea Centre, Auckland
3 August 2013

TED is a non-profit organisation famous for short, interesting and clever talks no longer than eighteen minutes that cover a broad spectrum of topics. Every year all around the world, offshoot TEDx events are held. TEDxAuckland 2013 featured speakers from a wide range of fields, including professors, writers, musicians, filmmakers, politicians and activists—and, of course, Helen. A video of the following talk is available online at tedxauckland.com.

My topic today is 'Yes We Can: Women and leadership'. I guess in a way I can exemplify that. I want to talk a little bit about why it is important. I will draw from my own experience, and those of you who have been watching TV3 over the last couple of weeks might know a little bit more about that, and I want to end with a rallying cry for all of us to support women coming into leadership positions, whatever they are. Obviously my experience is mostly in political leadership, but I advocate for women in leadership right across every area of life.

So, do we need to ask the question: Is it important to have women in leadership? I think we do. You know, when you count up the number of elected women leaders around our world, at any one time I understand it has never exceeded 20. The United Nations has 193 member states—under 20 is a pretty small proportion of that.

Back in 2000 I went up to the UN Millennium Summit, and Mary Robinson, who had been President of Ireland and was the UN Human Rights Commissioner, decided to convene a meeting of all the women heads of government who were attending that big summit and the women heads of agency at the UN. I won't say we would have fitted in one telephone box, but we probably would have fitted in two. That wasn't good, but it is not immensely better today.

So, let's then look at the women who make it to parliament as decision-makers. Again, back around the time of that Millennium Summit, there was a goal set to have women as 30 per cent of the legislators in each country. It's not 50 per cent, but it is not a bad start, and it's where New Zealand got to in 1996—and we haven't moved a lot above it since—but we got there. We achieved the goal.

What is it today globally? On average, under 20 per cent. So I think we do have to ask the question: Is it important? And answer: Yes. Because in my experience, if you are out of sight you are out of mind. I think our decision-makers and our parliaments and all our representative bodies should look like the society we represent, not like some segment of society which doesn't then share the perspectives of a much broader cross section.

So who misses out because women aren't putting issues on the agenda at the top tables? Well, let's come back to those millennium development goals, which came out of the 2000 Millennium Summit. Another of those goals was MDG 5, which was to reduce the rate of maternal mortality—that is, women dying in pregnancy and childbirth—by three-quarters between 1990 and 2015. Has this been achieved? No.

What about another target in that goal—universal access to sexual and reproductive health services. Has that been achieved? No.

I go to a lot of countries around the world. It is not uncommon to go to countries and see that, when women are surveyed [on questions such as] 'Do you have access to family planning services and would you like them?' more than 30 per cent say, 'We would like to, but it is not there for us.' What does that do? It fundamentally disempowers women from making their own decisions about the number of children they wish to have, and how they wish to space them. And, of course, it's hard to stay healthy if you are having too many children in quick succession and you haven't been able to control those decisions.

So, in my view, if we have more women at these top tables in these legislatures, these things would start to become rather more important. I will give you an example of the kind of difference which having a lot of women in decision-making can make. It is an example drawn from India, where when you look at the councils led by women as against the councils led by guys, the ones led by women are 60 per cent more likely to prioritise clean and safe drinking water as a priority for their area— really emphasising something so basic, so important to health and to society. I really believe that it does make a difference.

Another example: a lot of people go hungry in our world today— around a billion. So food production is pretty important. You go to Sub-Saharan Africa where more than half the farmers are believed to be women. But, all the evidence suggests that the women farmers are not as productive as the male farmers. I am sure they work every bit as hard, but they are not as productive. Why is this? Well, firstly, in many cases they can't own the land, they can't inherit the land, they can't borrow money, they may not be able to open a bank account. Apparently they can't even get equal access to the advisory services which make you a more productive farmer. Add it all up, and you produce less, you are less productive. And yet, if you could shift that, if you could really put the emphasis on women's status and rights, which would enable the women to be as productive as the men, you could start some real inroads—not only into women's poverty by lifting incomes, but actually by lifting the production of food you could have fewer hungry people as well. So we need women putting these issues on the agendas from the top table.

Now, I said I would draw a little bit from my own experience. I think it probably does help on the journey to leadership to be born the first in the family and not have any brothers, but we tend not to have much control over that. But that was part of my story. I grew up in a home where there were no girls' jobs and boys' jobs—there were just jobs, and you mucked in and you did those jobs. I also had parents who really believed in me and backed me all the way. Everyone can be that parent and back their girl children as much as they back their boy children. I went through life with this background of believing that girls could do anything, going to university—not seeing so many top women staff in the university, I have to say. When I was a student they were a very, very rare breed as well.

But, moving on to the political scene, as a young person it did strike me as a little bit strange when I first stood for parliament in a seat that really could be won by my party that not everybody thought girls should or could do everything. And that you started to run into some barriers. Now, I think with taking women through into decision-making and leadership positions, there are personal factors and there are structural factors.

On the structural factors, political parties have to believe in women and they have to back them for selection where they can win. Then, in the campaign phase, parties need to back the women there too because we look around the world and we see women are less likely to have access to the money that funds campaigns, so that has got to be looked after. In quite a lot of places women need physical security while they are campaigning. It can be extremely dangerous to put yourself up for public office.

Then, another structural factor: when women are elected the organisation of the workplace needs to be conducive. Yes, you need the parliamentary crèche. Yes, you need the parliament organised so that the school holidays are when the breaks are. You need the working hours to be reasonable, and you need to keep supporting and encouraging the women who are there. And I think back over many long and difficult years in politics—the upside usually more than the downside, but there is a downside. To have a very strong network of people backing you and believing in you is absolutely indispensable.

So you take those hard yards, but it has to mean something. There has got to be a purpose to wanting these jobs. There were many purposes for me, many parts of the mission, but I like to think that as a woman leader and looking at many other women leaders—not all, but many, and many other women in elected positions—you try to bring a gender sensitive eye to policies. You try to look out for things that would really make a difference to women.

Back in the late 1980s I was a health minister. One of the things I got to do was to legislate through parliament for our midwives to practise autonomously. I really believed in that. I believed that the midwife was very, very capable, competent and professional and should be able to work with a women and her family right through the birthing process. Today in New Zealand this almost seems like ancient history, because almost everywhere the birth is conducted by the midwife. But it was a huge breakthrough going back more than 25 years, and one I'm proud of.

But then fast forward to Prime Minister. What are some of the things you can do that will make a difference? Well firstly, paid parental leave as a right. I think it is important and it shouldn't just be something that comes because you are a member of the strongest union that has been able to negotiate it. Some had it, but many didn't. And so to have that right for women and men to have time to bond with a small baby, a paid period of leave, I thought was important. I also thought it was important to provide for the 20 hours' free early childhood education, because again a woman is weighing up—will I go back to work, what choice will I make? And sometimes that choice can be very hard if the money you are making for working so hard barely pays the early childhood fees. So to have that support was very, very important.

Then there was the annual holiday allowance, which had been stuck at three weeks a year since 1972 or '73. That got extended out a week, again because when parents are working they need a bit of time to cover the school holidays and be with their families. That is really important, I am proud of that.

One other issue of this kind I want to mention, is those student loans. When I became Prime Minister they were extortionate. The calculation showed that many women would die still owing the money because the income they earned through life and the proportion they paid back just wasn't enough to actually pay the loan back. One of the best things I think we ever did was to get rid of the interest on the student loans, and it certainly helped the women go through life without owing a lot of money.

I want to mention one last issue that I saw through a gender-sensitive lens. It is an issue of war and peace. When I was a kid I was very close to my grandmother, and she lost her closest brother about a month before the end of World War One. He was in the New Zealand expeditionary force. They stormed the Hindenburg line, somewhere near Le Quesnoy, and he was killed. It was very devastating. When World War Two broke out my grandmother had two sons, one of whom was my father, who were pretty close to call-up age. And as the story went, she burst into tears and said, 'Are we born as women to bear sons who will be sent away and never come back?' And I never forgot that. For me, when the pressure went on around the invasion of Iraq I knew it wasn't right, and I would think there would hardly be a woman in New Zealand who agreed with that, and a lot of guys as well. Because if you are going to take that decision to send other people's kids away to fight, you better know it is pretty important, and if it is not right you should not take that decision. And I think that that is perhaps very much a women's way of looking at it, but it is one that is important to me.

So what I'm arguing for is: Yes we can. But when we get to these positions of leadership it has got to mean something. There has got to be a passion for it, there has got to be a mission. I also argue for looking after yourself while you do it. Positions of power and leadership come and go. I had a career that kind of went like that . . . like that . . . like that. Careers do. Now, it is important to come out of it still having your health. You have got to eat properly, you've got to sleep properly, you have got to exercise and you have got to stay close to your family and friends, because otherwise you come out of a very intense period of a career and leadership of some kind, and you might think you can flick back to where you and the family were a few years before. They will have moved on, and they will have moved on without you if you haven't kept them close. So I always argue for an approach to career and leadership which is a balanced one. Again, I think that women perhaps see those issues much more personally because no matter how much gender equity we think there is, isn't it somehow always women who take disproportionate responsibility for the care of the older and frail relatives, the relatives with disability, relatives with illness and children. And we do like to have that balance in our lives so we can look after that part of our lives as well.

So, reflecting on these things I say: Yes we can. I say it is important, because there are a lot of issues out there which are so important to women. In my job now I see the life-and-death issues which are so important to women. Where women are out of sight, out of mind, they are not at the top table, they are not driving the decisions. If they were there in the numbers that are warranted, I think our world would be a different and a better place. And I said I'd end with a rallying cry, and it is a rallying cry to support those women who are prepared to stand up and walk over burning coals to make a difference for other women and men and families. This matters to me and I hope it matters to you too.

Beyond the Millennium Development Goals: What could the next global development agenda look like?

The University of Auckland, Auckland
19 August 2013

*Robert (Bob) Chapman was the founding Professor of Political
Studies at the University of Auckland, and a noted political scientist
and historian. In 2000 Helen, a former student of Bob's, gave
the inaugural Chapman Memorial Lecture, noting that the series
was established in honour of both Bob and his wife, Noeline, and
'designed to recognise Bob's considerable academic achievements,
especially in the study of New Zealand politics and in bringing the
results of his academic study to the wider public.' Helen was invited
back in 2013, when she gave the following lecture.*

My thanks go to the Political Studies Department of Auckland University for inviting me once again to give the annual Chapman Lecture, in honour of the greatly respected former Professor of Political Studies Robert Chapman. Bob Chapman had a major influence on me and countless other students during his long career at this university. He was an astute observer of domestic politics and world affairs. He helped me to hone my ideas and beliefs into a coherent philosophy, which I could later apply to a political career, and now to my position at the UN Development Programme. I owe Bob Chapman a great deal for his interest in my intellectual development, and for instilling in me a drive for rigour and evidence-based approaches in my career at this university, in parliament and in government, and now at UNDP.

Such a seminal figure in our country's intellectual life fully merits the naming of an annual lecture series in his honour. I hope it can continue long beyond the contributions of those of us who knew Bob personally and who benefited from his sage advice.

I gave the foundation Chapman Lecture in November 2000. To me that seems like a lifetime ago. Those were very different times for me, for New Zealand and for our world. There is, however, a link in that lecture to my topic today. In it, I referred to the Millennium Summit of the United Nations, which I had attended as Prime Minister just two months before.

I remember the year 2000 as a time of hope—once the fears of a Y2K bug proved not to be justified! Indeed, hope was the spirit of the Millennium Declaration issued by world leaders at the United Nations that year. It was a clarion call for a more peaceful, prosperous and just world in the twenty-first century than that which the twentieth century had delivered. The declaration foreshadowed the Millennium Development Goals (MDGs) later launched by the UN Secretary-General, and specifically called for realising a number of development targets by 2015. They were:

- halving the proportion of the world's peoples living in extreme poverty, in hunger and unable to access safe drinking water

- for all children to complete their primary education

- substantial reductions in maternal and child mortality

- turning the tide on HIV/AIDS, malaria and other diseases, encouraging the pharmaceuticals industry to make essential drugs more accessible, and giving special support to HIV/AIDS orphans

- significantly improving the lives of slum dwellers by 2020

- promoting gender equality and women's empowerment

- making the benefits of new technologies available to all

- and developing strong partnerships with the private sector and civil society in pursuit of development and poverty eradication.

All these elements of the Millennium Declaration were further elaborated on in the MDGs. While the MDGs have been dismissed in some quarters for not being the product of a broad consultative process, the fact that leaders of 189 delegations at the summit—many of them heads of state and government, including me—agreed to a declaration containing key elements of what were to become the MDGs gave them weight.

Whatever the debate about the MDGs' origin, they certainly gained traction. A great many developing countries incorporated the targets into their national development plans, and have measured progress against them ever since. There have been a large number of national, regional and global reports produced on MDG progress over the past thirteen years, and there is a particular focus now on accelerating achievement of the goals and targets by the end of December 2015.

Concurrent with that effort, an international debate is well under way on what a global development agenda should look like beyond 2015. Should there be one at all? Should it apply to all countries? Should global targets be set? If so, what should they be? I will comment on some of these issues this evening.

Should there be a renewed global development agenda at all?

This question begs rather more fundamental questions, such as what is the point of multilateralism—in general and when applied to development in particular—and are there development objectives which are more likely to be achieved through global focus and effort than by each country acting alone?

The experience with the MDGs suggests that global priority-setting, backed by action, does generate results. For example, the global poverty-reduction target set in the MDGs has been met, most of the world's children now go to school, and the tide has been turned on HIV/AIDS and malaria. In the context of HIV/AIDS, tuberculosis, malaria, maternal mortality and under-five mortality, the decline by nearly 32 per cent in the burden from these MDG-related disorders between 1990 and 2010 is considered to be greater than pre-MDG trends would have produced. This suggests that the increased global attention these areas got from the MDGs, and the extra funding which followed, helped.

On reflection, the development progress stimulated by the MDGs should not surprise us. Overall, the evidence seems to suggest that norms and priorities established through international agreements and agendas can and do have an impact on the attitudes of societies, the laws and policies of countries, and ultimately on the well-being of people.

[American political scientist] Robert Putnam has argued that international agreements can 'change minds and move the undecided', especially where political leaders and opinion-formers champion them. The impact may not be immediate, but over time the UN's conventions, declarations and conference outcomes have shifted domestic and global debates, for example on gender equality and on women's sexual and reproductive health rights—although clearly there is still some way to go.

The mission of the United Nations itself rests on a foundation of universal values enshrined in a series of agreements, beginning with the UN Charter in 1945 and the Universal Declaration of Human Rights in 1948, and continuing to the Millennium Declaration in 2000 and beyond. These agreements provide an ethical framework for the work of the UN. The studies conducted by the UN Intellectual History Project concluded that they have inspired change in the way countries understand and approach development. That, in turn, has helped trigger long-term and under-the-radar change in public norms and values. That same intellectual history project rates the MDGs as among the UN's greatest ideas and initiatives.

The UN Charter took the unprecedented and, in 1945, extraordinary step of calling for global development action to increase standards of living in all parts of the world. The UN's founding members realised that a more peaceful world would not be possible without stable societies, more prosperous communities and universal respect for the human rights of all people, regardless of race, sex, language or religion—the list has expanded since that time. Ever since 1945, the UN has linked the three pillars of its mandate: peace and security, human rights and development.

That has helped to broaden the focus on development. Richard Jolly, one of the lead authors in the UN Intellectual History Project, argues that the UN's many agreements and conference outcomes have shifted the common understanding of development from a narrow economic concept to one which is broad, people-centred and multidisciplinary.

Pioneering UN conferences and agreements, particularly in the 1970s and 1990s, were successful in making human rights, conflict resolution, environmental sustainability, gender equality, and peace and peace-building integral to what UNDP considers today to be sustainable human development. Jolly notes, however, that rising debt and recession in the 1980s brought early thinking and co-operation along these lines to a halt. In those years the International Financial Institutions dominated the international development agenda with their focus on stabilisation and structural adjustment programmes.

The priorities of those programmes were lowering inflation and deficits and generating economic growth—not human development. It was said that some of the architects of structural adjustment went so far as to argue that making poor people's lives worse in the short term could be justified in the name of development. The result was what has been described as 'a lost decade for development' for sub-Saharan Africa and Latin America.

During this time the UN's development arm took on the role of constructive dissent. In 1985, UNICEF began promoting the need for 'adjustment with a human face'. In 1990 UNDP issued its first annual Human Development Report, crystalising earlier thinking and offering an alternative approach to the 'Washington Consensus' by putting people firmly at the centre of development. This approach, pioneered by Nobel Laureate Amatya Sen and his colleague Mahbub ul Haq, saw development as being about enlarging people's choices and strengthening human capabilities. In the human development paradigm, which owes so much to Sen and ul Haq, it is the extent to which people are healthy, educated and free which provides the yardstick for a nation's progress, expressing in effect the aphorism that 'man does not live by bread alone'.

A second round of global conferences and summits in the 1990s linked human development and social priorities to sustaining the environment, understanding population dynamics, ensuring food security and promoting gender equality. The UN Millennium Summit in 2000, where leaders from 189 countries adopted the Millennium Declaration and in effect set the Millennium Development Goals process in motion, was a natural outcome of all these discussions, and had a strong focus on human development.

In the follow-up to its major development summits and declarations, the UN has long adopted and promoted goals, for example, to provide universal access to sexual and reproductive health services, or to increase healthy life expectancy and eradicate illiteracy. The assessment made for the UN Intellectual History Project of the progress on the economic and social goals set by the UN from 1960 to 2000 suggests that most have been partially or largely achieved. For me, this makes the case for global agenda-setting for development.

The drive to achieve internationally agreed goals can also spur countries on to greater achievements. I know from my own experience in government how prized a high ranking in an international index was—and how a low ranking could motivate urgent action to address the problems it exposed. In a similar way, the MDGs have had a galvanising impact on many countries, as they put the spotlight on basic benchmarks of human development.

As well, the indicators linked to the MDG targets have incentivised countries to invest in better data against which progress can be more reliably measured. An expanded post-2015 development agenda could go further in stimulating both action and better information collection on huge issues like gender violence and unemployment. On both of these, many countries currently lack sufficient data on what is happening—perhaps because tackling them has not had the priority it deserves.

International agendas and goals also help build alliances for change—within and between governments and civil society especially. The MDGs brought together diverse development actors around a common cause. The measurability and focus of the Goals helped draw broad public attention to the development challenges of particularly the poorest countries.

After a period of stagnation in the 1990s, official development assistance (ODA) did rise sharply in real terms from 2000 onwards. Many attribute that rise in aid quantity and also in quality to the MDGs—in itself a major achievement. Now as ODA levels are dwindling, perhaps a renewed global development agenda could reignite enthusiasm for eradicating poverty once and for all, and for building a more sustainable world.

Moving beyond 2015: broader issues to address

There is no doubt in my mind that a renewed global development agenda is desirable, and that it would re-energise human and sustainable development. In renewing, though, there is no need to start from scratch. The next agenda should build on the MDGs' success, aim to complete their 'unfinished business', and reflect the profound global changes since 2000.

To do that, what has been learned from the MDG experience needs to be analysed. Having supported countries to pursue the MDGs over these past thirteen years, UNDP has come across both inspiring success stories and significant weaknesses. Both are relevant to designing a new agenda. But a lot has changed since 2000. The world has been exposed to numerous crises, from the global financial crisis to major natural disasters, and to profound conflict with regional and global spillover effects.

In 2000, there was nothing like the awareness which exists today of the threat of climate change. Now the predictions pour out on global warming not being on track to peak at two degrees Celsius above pre-industrial levels, but at three or four or even six degrees. Huge losses have been suffered from extreme weather events—drought, floods and storms. The stress of unsustainable global production and consumption patterns are reflected in high rates of deforestation, water scarcity, food waste and greenhouse gas emissions. Current development models have brought us to the brink of planetary boundaries.

Continuing business as usual risks not only irreversible damage to ecosystems, but also arresting human development. The poorest people on earth are bearing the brunt of climate change. It is not sensible to talk about poverty eradication and environmental sustainability as separate issues—they are closely linked, and a renewed global agenda needs to be premised on a strong vision for sustainable development.

A new agenda could also make the links between development and the rule of law, effective and responsive governance, and the importance of peace and citizen security.

The MDGs were silent on the devastation caused by violence and conflict, the importance of open, accountable and responsive governance, the need for inclusive growth and decent work, and the exclusion of persons with disabilities. Some countries have taken the initiative to add their own MDGs at national or local levels to help address such issues. Mongolia, Albania and Tonga, among others, for example, introduced national goals and targets aimed at good governance.

Should there be a universal agenda with local targets?

The MDGs were set as global benchmarks. Some developing countries had met most of the targets when they were launched, but some still haven't.

The Secretary-General's High Level Panel on Post-2015 [Development Agenda], co-chaired by the presidents of Indonesia and Liberia and the Prime Minister of the United Kingdom, has suggested that 'all goals in the future agenda be universal, representing the common aspirations of all countries; while almost all targets be set at national or local levels to account for different starting points and contexts'. In UNDP's experience, localising the targets and getting buy-in at all levels of government—national and sub-national—helps drive MDG achievement.

A universal global agenda could also help address an often-cited weakness of the MDGs. The imbalance between having mainly performance criteria for developing countries and aid-centric delivery criteria for donors. Correcting that will be critical for reaching consensus on a new development agenda.

In reality, the global sustainable development challenge requires all countries to act. A shift to more sustainable production and consumption patterns, for example, will require concerted action from the developed world to cut carbon emissions, but that does not mean that others need to do nothing. Even heroic action by advanced economies to reduce their carbon footprint is not enough to ward off catastrophic climate change. 'Common but differentiated responsibility' must remain a key principle for action on climate change.

Should there be a focus on tackling inequalities?

It is commonplace to observe that progress on the MDGs has been uneven across and within countries. By 2010 the world is estimated to have met the MDG target of halving the proportion of people living in extreme poverty. This achievement owes a lot to the exceptional progress made in just one very large country: China. Some countries, however, have seen little reduction in their extreme poverty rate. On another dimension, a country may be encouraged by national reports of fewer child deaths, even where the poorest of its people see no change.

Since the Millennium Declaration was signed, inequalities have increased in many places, even where economic growth and development progress have been rapid. The poorest 1.2 billion people in the world account for only 1 per cent of the total global consumption of goods and services, while the richest one billion consume 72 per cent. Already poor and excluded groups may face the added burden of discrimination—whether that is due to age, gender, ethnicity, indigenous status, disability, place of residence, HIV status, sexual or gender orientation or other factors. They typically have the least resources and remain the furthest behind.

The High Level Panel Report recommends that the next development agenda should aim to 'leave no one behind'. That could lead to formulating a global goal aimed at eradicating extreme poverty worldwide. An ambitious agenda might also seek to eradicate preventable deaths, chronic hunger and illiteracy. It should also target gender inequality—widely recognised as the single largest driver of inequality in today's world. More broadly, targets and indicators focused on excluded groups could be included across the agenda, ensuring that the world's progress is gauged by the status of its poorest people.

Increased access to technology and social media has better enabled people to highlight the extent of inequalities and demand change. These tools and better data can help to track progress of those once invisible in the tyranny of averages.

Enabling broad participation in the development of the new agenda

While the Millennium Declaration which foreshadowed the MDGs was agreed on by the UN's member states, there was not broad public outreach when either it or the MDGs were developed. These days there are much greater expectations that people's voices will be heard when global agendas are developed.

An expert review of what makes international agreements work, conducted by New York University and the UK Overseas Development Institute last year, concluded that 'multilateral agreements that bring a range of actors into the process to support the accord, including domestic actors like government officials and civil society groups, are more likely to be agreed and implemented'.

To increase the involvement of civil society in debate about the post-2015 development agenda, UNDP and sister UN organisations launched a global conversation through social media, other websites and face-to-face meetings. More than one million people from across all UN member states have shared their priorities to date.

When those member states move to negotiate the next agenda and Sustainable Development Goals, it is to be hoped that these many voices will be heeded.

What do people want from a future agenda? Where do their interests converge?

In addition to inviting broad public engagement, the UN Secretary-General sought the advice of world leaders and experts by convening a High Level Panel on Post-2015. The Panel issued its far-reaching Report last month.

This month, the business, academic and scientific communities have weighed in with joint reports and recommendations. There appears to be consensus emerging across this wide range of experts, leaders, citizens and groups from the public consultations, the SG's High Level Panel, and the Sustainable Development Solutions Network on a future agenda which tackles the unfinished business of the MDGs, a future agenda centred on sustainable development with the eradication of poverty at its core, a universal agenda which mobilises countries north and south, and a limited number of goals and targets which capture the key challenges for humanity in a compelling way.

At UNDP we are advising UN member states in the early stages of their negotiations to 'bank' areas where there is broad agreement. This would then open up space for negotiators to focus on the topics which are more challenging.

In the discussions to date, higher human development and ecosystem integrity are seen as compatible objectives. Green and inclusive economies and societies can deliver both—it's not a question of either/or. But achieving both requires integrated approaches, bringing together sectors and policy-makers often not accustomed to working together.

Coming to consensus in a multipolar world: tackling the hard issues

Among those hard issues is the place of peace and good governance in the new agenda. They were not specified in the MDGs, perhaps because of the difficulty of reaching agreement on how to reflect their importance. In the post-2015 consultations, however, there has been a groundswell of support among citizens for honest and effective governance to be recognised as a critical driver of development. This ranked third in the global My World survey on priorities.

The UN Secretary-General's High Level Panel describes 'personal security, access to justice, freedom from discrimination and persecution, and a voice in the decisions that affect their lives as development outcomes in their own right'. They suggest global goals with nationally adopted targets aimed at, for example, increasing public participation in political processes, guaranteeing public access to information and reducing the number of violent deaths. These concrete suggestions, backed by a mobilised citizenry, could help the negotiating member states overcome doubts and hesitations in this area.

Another bone of contention will be over what in the jargon is referred to as the 'means of implementation' of a transformative global agenda.

For sure, more and better-quality development assistance for poor countries would help—along with greater policy coherence in a range of areas, from trade to migration and tax avoidance. MDG 8 aimed to 'create a global partnership for development', and contained targets on trade reform, debt relief and access to new technologies and essential drugs, but progress across these areas has not been stellar.

A report from the UN development system to the Secretary-General on the post-2015 agenda suggested that countries could set out how—given their particular abilities, capacities and resources—they could each contribute to advancing the global goals, by specifying the partnerships and policy 'enablers' to which they would commit.

But a new global agenda also needs to take into account the partnership possibilities emerging from today's shifting geopolitics and geo-economics, and from the widening range of development actors—across the emerging economies, the private sector, the mega-philanthropic foundations and NGOs, and a vibrant civil society in developing countries. South–South co-operation will have a growing role to play—but as a complement to and not a substitute for traditional ODA.

Where to from here?

The process of reaching agreement on the future global development agenda still has some two years to run. This September, the UN General Assembly will hold a special event with world leaders looking at how to accelerate progress to meet the MDGs between now and the 2015 deadline. The event may also plot a roadmap for nations to decide—between now and 1 January 2016—on what the next development agenda, with goals therein, should look like.

By September next year, UN member states involved in the UN General Assembly Open Working Group on Sustainable Development Goals are due to issue their recommendations. UN member states will then—or before—begin negotiations on the renewed agenda, with a view to that being affirmed that at a high-level UN meeting in 2015.

Some concluding thoughts

Two things are important now: one, maintaining a high level of public interest in the outcome of the negotiations on post-2015 and Sustainable Development Goals, and two, accelerating achievement of the goals we have. The greater the success of the MDGs, the greater the credibility of the process of negotiating a new agenda will be.

A sobering reflection: whether or not the MDG targets are met, around one billion people will still be living in extreme poverty in 2015. Many still will not have clean drinking water or improved sanitation. Many will still be suffering from hunger, malnutrition, gender discrimination and more. Such suffering is inconsistent with the vision for dignity, equity, peace and prosperity of the Millennium Declaration.

The future global development agenda can be the next stage of implementing the vision of the Millennium Declaration. To rise to that challenge, the international community needs to agree on a reinvigorated and transformational global agenda.

Twenty years ago, could we have imagined that one billion more people would have been lifted out of extreme poverty by now, or that polio would be gone from all but three countries, or that four out of five of the world's children would be vaccinated, as is the case today? The world is demonstrably healthier, more educated and prosperous than ever before.

In the face of today's daunting global challenges, we cannot allow ourselves to be condemned by a collective failure to imagine a better world. Rather we should work for a world where poverty in all its dimensions is consigned to history, and where we pull back from the brink of environmental catastrophe to a new, sustainable global equilibrium. It is to be hoped that the outcome of the post-2015 debate rises to this challenge.

The Effect of the Global Financial Crisis on Women

Oslo, Norway
15 November 2013

In 2013, Norway celebrated the centenary of women's suffrage in the country with a series of events throughout the year. The final event, held in Oslo in November, was an international conference on 'Women, Power and Politics: The road to sustainable democracy', at which Helen gave the following keynote speech as part of a wider discussion on the effect of the global financial crisis on women. The conference's central focus was the importance of women's political rights in relation to matters of international peace, security and sustainable development.

————

Thank you for inviting me to contribute to this discussion on the effect of the global financial crisis on women. I look forward to engaging with State Secretary Hans Brattskar, Professor Radhika Balakrishnan, and with you all on this important topic. I trust that our moderator,

Gro Lindstad, Executive Director of the Forum for Women and Development, co-organisers of this conference, will steer us in the right direction.

At the outset, let me congratulate Norway on this centennial celebration of women's suffrage. The right to vote and choose one's parliamentary and subnational representatives is one of the most basic civil and political rights. In my country, New Zealand, we celebrated our centennial of women's suffrage in 1993, and take pride in being the first nation in the world to achieve this.

Article 1 of the United Nations Charter states that one of the purposes of the UN lies in 'promoting and encouraging respect for human rights and for fundamental freedoms for all without distinction as to race, sex, language or religion'. A number of UN instruments and conventions, including the Convention on the Elimination of Discrimination against Women (CEDAW), the Beijing Declaration and Platform for Action—which will have its twentieth anniversary in 2015—and the Millennium Declaration of 2000, all reinforce the global commitments made to women's empowerment and gender equality.

Norway is among those countries with high levels of gender equality and has, in ten of the last eleven reports, ranked first in the world on UNDP's Human Development Index (HDI). In the latest Human Development Report, it ranked first in the HDI, and fifth using the Gender Inequality Index.

Gender equality remains an elusive goal in many parts of the world. A new report from UNDP to be launched shortly, 'Humanity Divided: Confronting Inequality in Developing Countries', argues that while women have experienced significant progress in education, with most countries coming close to achieving gender parity in primary education and almost three-quarters of countries achieving gender parity in secondary school enrolment rates, women remain disproportionately represented in vulnerable employment and continue to earn significantly less than men. Furthermore, they remain grossly under-represented among political decision makers.

A number of structural factors, as well as social norms, are standing in the way of achieving gender equality in incomes, access to livelihoods and decision-making. This has implications for the way in which financial crises—and indeed other shocks—impact on women and girls. For example:

- pre-existing inequitable power relations between men and women, and boys and girls, are exacerbated in times of crisis

- times of crisis may lead to a shift in national priorities away from efforts to empower women and girls, resulting in progress towards gender equality stalling or even reversing

- and social spending may be cut, increasing the burden on women and girls as carers of elderly, frail and/or young family members—this may be one of the pressures leading to girls being pulled out of school.

My remarks today will touch on these concerns.

I will begin by discussing the economic and social impacts of the global financial crisis on women and girls, drawing on the available evidence. I will then provide examples of the types of policies and initiatives which could be implemented to mitigate such impacts. Finally, I will make the case that times of crisis—while challenging and painful—can offer opportunities to tackle structural barriers to women's equality.

The social and economic impact of the financial crisis on women

Let me turn to the main question for our discussion today: Have women been disproportionately impacted by the financial crisis? And, if yes, in which ways?

This is a challenging question to answer, because there is often not adequate gender-disaggregated data for quality analyses of the differential impacts on women and for evidence-based policy-making. Studies looking at the impact of the global crisis consistently make this point.

As well, women's circumstances vary greatly across countries and regions. The impact of a global crisis on women living in a very high human development country like Norway will be very different from that on women in least developed countries, and where, for example, remittances have dried up because of the impacts of the crisis on migrant workers in countries far away.

Differences may also be profound within the groupings of developed and developing countries, depending on a country's level of exposure to the crisis and the way in which it responded—this has been very much the case in Europe in recent years. And even within countries, developed and developing, certain groups of women may be harder hit, depending on their age, ethnicity, or socio-economic or immigration status—to name just a few factors.

While some impacts of the crisis may have been immediate, for example where women lost their jobs, others, such as the impact on nutrition for pregnant women and subsequent poorer developmental outcomes for their children, may not be evident for years to come.

With these caveats in mind, it is possible to assert that women will have suffered disproportionately from the crisis by extrapolating from the evidence available from study of previous crises, as well as from what we know about the recent one.

1. Economic impact: Labour market participation and access to credit

The International Labour Organization's Global Employment Trends for Women 2012 report finds that the conditions of women's engagement in the labour market worsened during the global crisis, and that gender gaps in indicators of unemployment and employment, which had been reducing between 2002 and 2007, began to grow again from 2008 in many regions.

In developed countries, evidence summarised by the IMF suggests that in the early years of the crisis, specifically from 2007 to 2009, fewer women than men in OECD countries lost their jobs, as male-dominated industries like construction were hit harder. Thereafter, however, as the male unemployment rate began to stabilise or fall, women continued to lose their jobs.

In a number of developing countries, the economic crisis did affect women disproportionately from the outset because they dominated employment in export-oriented industries. In Latin America, for example, sectors with a predominantly female workforce like textiles, apparel and tourism were hit harder. Evidence from Mexico suggests that women accounted for 71 per cent of all lay-offs there in 2008.

Women are often over-represented in the informal sector, so the data available on the impact on jobs is unlikely to reflect the full impact of the global crisis on them. In the Central African Republic, for example, the mining industry was hit hard by the crisis. While men represent the majority of workers in the industry, women are over-represented in the informal sector concentrated around the mines. It stands to reason that if the mines' paid workforce is earning less, there will be impacts on the informal female workforce.

For women who remained in the workforce, there is concern that the crisis has led to worsening conditions. For example, for self-employed women pre-existing barriers to accessing credit and financial services may have increased. Drawing on evidence from the Asian crisis, a report by the Levy Economic Institute of Bard College in New York suggests that policy responses should address the 'limitations women face in gaining access to credit and assets, as these are all the more exacerbated at times of crisis'.

2. Social impact: Health, education and unpaid care work

The full social impacts of the crisis are still being documented, but we can expect there to have been education- and health-related impacts in the short and long term, with younger girls particularly impacted.

A recent report by Plan International and ODI, 'Off the balance sheet: the impact of the economic crisis on girls and young women', reviews the evidence to date, and draws particular attention to the impact on this younger group. It notes that:

- Infant mortality rates for girls are particularly sensitive to drops in per capita GDP. It has been calculated that a one per cent decline in GDP per capita increases average infant mortality by 7.4 deaths per 1,000 live births for girls, whereas for boys the increase is much smaller at 1.5 deaths per 1,000 live births.

- For children under-five, the food crisis in 2010–11, which pushed 44 million people into poverty, had a greater negative impact on the weight gain of girls than of boys.

- During times of economic contraction, primary school completion rates often decline, with the decrease among girls being higher than that among boys (29 per cent versus 22 per cent).

- Girls and young women are often compelled to take up riskier employment to compensate for decreases in family income. This can involve sexual exploitation, and can increase young women's risk of contracting HIV.

- For pregnant adolescent girls, who are already vulnerable to poor health outcomes, cuts in health budgets are particularly worrisome if they lead to fewer antenatal check-ups and an increase in unattended home births, as in previous crises.

Similar concerns are raised by a recent UNAIDS (Joint United Nations Programme on HIV/AIDS) discussion paper which notes that, 'During times of economic crisis, global gender inequalities mean that women and girls, particularly in low-income countries, are more likely to be taken out of school, are the first to reduce the quantity or quality of food they eat or forgo essential medicines, and are more likely to sell sex in order to survive.'

It also notes that to compensate for shrinking wages and to remain competitive, women often need to work longer hours, at the same time as cuts in public spending in care-related sectors may have increased the burden of their work in the home.

Given that the evidence points to these disproportionate impacts of the crisis on women and girls, it should be possible to design and advocate for policies which could avoid or at least mitigate such impact, and could help remove some of the structural barriers to gender equality.

Building the resilience of women to economic crisis

In December 2009, UNDP issued a guidance note titled 'Turning the Global Financial and Economic Crisis into Opportunity for Poor Women and Men'. It outlined the threats posed by the economic and financial crisis to developing countries and how they could impact on advancing gender equality.

This note set out an action plan for 'Gender-Responsive Recovery at the Country Level'. It emphasised the need to identify the sectors and areas where the crisis has had the greatest impact on poor women and men, implement quick-win solutions while also promoting medium- and long-term policies to empower women, institutionalise gender-responsive budgeting and build capacities of stakeholders where needed.

To support countries in such efforts, UNDP works with governments to help mainstream gender considerations in national policies, strategies and budgets through a range of advisory services, advocacy work and capacity-building activities. For example:

- Through our Global Gender and Economic Policy Management Initiative, which addresses gender-related capacity constraints in economic planning processes, UNDP has trained policy-makers to use gender frameworks, analysis and applications in the design of economic development and poverty reduction policies. Such training programmes have been held across the Africa and Asia-Pacific regions.

- In Colombia, UNDP is supporting the Ministry of Labour to include gender analysis in Labour Observatories and in its main Labour Equity Programme.

- In Zimbabwe, UNDP supported the Ministry of Water Resources and Development to produce a gender-responsive water policy which includes strategies to reduce women's unpaid care work.

In times of crisis, social protection schemes are very important in shielding the most vulnerable from the worst effects, as they strengthen the resilience of individuals, families and communities. Studies suggest that, where social protection schemes were already in place when the financial crisis hit, they helped the poor cope better with its impact—for example, by enabling families to continue to pay for food, education, health and other costs. When gender considerations are integrated in their design, social protection systems can also ensure that women and girls are not disproportionately impacted by shocks.

For example, I have often highlighted India's Mahatma Gandhi National Rural Employment Guarantee Act, which guarantees a minimum of 100 days' work a year to eligible rural poor, sets a minimum quota for women's participation in the scheme, and prioritises work on environmental sustainability, including water and reforestation. This scheme can simultaneously empower women, provide jobs and incomes, and have a positive impact on the environment. Women also have 30 per cent representation guaranteed on the village councils, which determine the priorities for the work to be done.

In Bangladesh, UNDP has supported the Rural Employment Opportunities for Public Assets (REOPA) initiative for helping female-headed households. It provides two years' employment for destitute women and employment for casual labourers in six food-insecure districts during the lean period. In addition, the women undertake various training sessions on social and legal issues, gender equity, human rights, primary healthcare, nutrition and income generation. So far nearly 25,000 women have moved out of poverty through being employed in this scheme.

Working at the local level, UNDP's initiatives on women's economic empowerment have also helped sustain human development, even in highly adverse circumstances, by building the resilience of women to shocks. An important part of this work has been around supporting female entrepreneurship. This provides women with alternative livelihoods when formal employment options are unavailable. For example:

- In Benin, Burkina Faso, Democratic Republic of the Congo, Gambia, Mali, Senegal and Sierra Leone, UNDP provided financial and technical support to improve women's entrepreneurial, marketing and income-generating skills, through training and provision of improved seed. This enabled them to access decent work, increase their agricultural productivity and enhance their own and their families' livelihoods.

- In Georgia, vocational education courses provided through local implementing partners have contributed to economic empowerment of women from vulnerable communities. Around 60 per cent of the women graduates from the programme went on to become self-employed entrepreneurs.

- In FYR Macedonia, a programme on the economic empowerment of female victims of domestic violence is providing opportunities for self-employment and training for skills in demand in the job market.

- In response to the global crisis, in Serbia UNDP's Severance to Jobs project supported the self-employment of women who lost their jobs in 2009.

Recovering from crisis: an opportunity to expand women's leadership

As today's session comes under the overall title of 'The Road to Sustainable Democracy', it is useful to consider the role of women's leadership and involvement in recovery from crisis. In 2009, the Commission on the Status of Women held an expert panel discussion on gender perspectives on the financial crisis. There, experts warned that government policy responses must focus on the role of women as economic agents, in order to contribute to growth and recovery, and to enable women to participate fully in financial and economic decision-making processes.

Women must also have the opportunity to be political agents more broadly, so that they can help shape the transformation of their societies. It is unjust for women to have to shoulder a disproportionate share of the burden in times of crisis, yet not to have the opportunity to participate in redesigning the systems which made them vulnerable in the first place.

Based on data from the Inter-Parliamentary Union, the proportion of women in national legislatures in the world's regions ranges from roughly 24 per cent in the Americas and Europe, to 22 per cent in sub-Saharan Africa, 19 per cent in Asia and 16 per cent in the Pacific and in the Arab States. As Prime Minister of my country for nine years, Leader of the Opposition for six years before that, Leader of the New Zealand Labour Party for fifteen years and as a Member of Parliament for 27-and-a-half years, I am well acquainted with the challenges women face when entering the hitherto male-dominated field of politics, and with how decisions which impact on the lives of women have often been made without women at the table, particularly economic decisions. In my current position, I note how few women there often are at major international meetings—focused on economic and financial matters.

This needs to change. Perhaps there should be an explicit call from the international community to guarantee women seats at the table in economic and financial decision-making. This is not as far-fetched as it may at first seem. Security Council Resolution 1325 on Women, Peace and Security, and subsequent resolutions on the same topic were revolutionary in affirming that for peace and security to be sustained, women must be empowered, their voices must be heard and they must be included as active participants in conflict prevention, management and resolution. It called for women to have a seat at all relevant decision-making tables.

In Rwanda, for example, which experienced genocide, women now hold 64 per cent of seats in parliament, taking that seat at the table by breaking into the previously male-dominated space and thereby permanently transforming the political landscape.

Clearly it is possible to emerge from crisis with structures transformed and, with that, the opportunity for improvements in people's lives. We should apply this thinking to recovery from economic and other shocks—like major disasters—just as it is being applied to recovery from war and conflict.

Already, I am pleased to note, such concepts are being applied to how climate change is addressed. Last year, at the UN Climate Change Conference in Doha, COP18, a decision was taken to increase women's representation in climate negotiations, and to set 'a goal of gender balance in bodies established pursuant to the Convention and the Kyoto Protocol, in order to improve women's participation and inform more effective climate change policy that addresses the needs of women and men equally'.

UNDP will continue working with political parties, electoral commissions, parliaments, local assemblies and other national partners on measures to strengthen women's political participation in countries around the world, and advocate for women's leadership in the political, social, economic and environmental spheres.

Conclusion

In closing, I refer to a powerful quote from the Women's Major Group statement at the civil society conference on 'Advancing the Post-2015 Sustainable Development Agenda' in Bonn this March: 'We do not want to be mainstreamed into a polluted stream. We call for deep and structural changes to existing global systems of power, decision-making and resource sharing. This includes enacting policies that recognise and redistribute the unequal and unfair burdens of women and girls in sustaining societal well-being and economies, intensified in times of economic and ecological crises.'

The latest global crisis has more or less passed, despite its lingering impacts, which are serious for many, but it certainly will not be the last. Our world's problems are deeply interconnected. Countries and their citizens are exposed to economic crises emanating far away. The challenge is to support all countries to put in place systems to mitigate the impacts. Had such systems not been in place in those Western European nations where the crisis hit hard, even greater economic and social distress would have been suffered. The same applies to developing countries which had built effective social protection systems—the impact of the global crisis on the poorest there was reduced.

The consultations which took place on the post-2015 development agenda, globally, regionally and in 88 countries around the world, revealed that there is strong interest among the world's citizens in being part of the process of shaping a new development agenda.

This agenda must help build the resilience of women and men, girls and boys, and their communities to future challenges. Promoting gender equality and women's active political, economic and social participation is central to that. Gender inequality is unacceptable from a human rights perspective, and is also a significant impediment to development progress. Investments made in women and girls are great multipliers of development progress. Failing to make those investments and failing to boost the status of women and girls thwarts the potential not only of individuals but also of families, communities and nations.

At this centennial commemoration of women's suffrage, let us celebrate the progress made towards gender equality in Norway and elsewhere, but also acknowledge that much remains to be done. Times of crisis expose vulnerabilities and inequity, and threaten to reverse human development progress—but crises can also enable transformative change if managed well.

I hope that our discussion today will help identify some of these opportunities to expand women's empowerment.

The Things That Make for Peace

**New York, United States of America
19 September 2014**

The date of 21 September has been designated by the UN General Assembly as World Peace Day, also known as the International Day of Peace. First celebrated in 1982, World Peace Day is observed around the world and is devoted to strengthening the ideals of peace both within and between all nations and peoples. Helen gave the following keynote speech at the International Day of Peace Symposium held at the United Nations in New York in 2014.

———

Many thanks for inviting me to today's International Day of Peace Symposium on 'The Things That Make for Peace'. This year marks the thirtieth anniversary of the UN General Assembly's Declaration on the Right of Peoples to Peace. It is appropriate therefore that this year's theme for the International Day of Peace on 21 September is the 'Right of People to Peace'.

Today's symposium invites us to paint with a broad brush what the preconditions for peace are. Peace never exists in a vacuum—it struggles to exist where there are gross inequalities and extreme poverty, injustice, oppression and a poor distribution of power and resources locally, nationally and globally. In a world threatened by climate change, the stresses of water, energy and food scarcity could also provoke more conflict. In communities threatened by deforestation, indigenous communities often face serious violence and conflict.

We live in turbulent times—indeed it is hard to remember a time when more crises were simultaneously preoccupying the United Nations, its agencies and the broader international community. From Syria to Iraq, the Central African Republic, South Sudan, Gaza, Libya, Ukraine and more, civilians have been caught up in vicious conflicts this year, and human development has been rolled back.

Yesterday, I returned from visiting Lebanon, a very small country geographically with a population of under 4.5 million, which is now host to just under 1.2 million refugees. Per capita, it hosts far more refugees than any other country. There are huge concerns there over whether the country's stability can hold, with the Syria conflict continuing and spilling over into Lebanon itself in violent incidents and hostage-taking.

The issues around climate change and the issues of central importance to indigenous people will be the focus of the two major summits at the high-level week of the UN General Assembly in the coming days. Everything discussed there will have a bearing on whether our world is capable of constructing a peaceful, equitable and just future.

This goal must also be central to the post-2015 development agenda to be negotiated over the next year. To tackle the challenges to peace and human and sustainable development, it must be a transformational agenda which addresses the drivers of poverty and inequality, volatility and the fragility which leads to a breakdown of peace within countries.

UNDP works in more than 170 countries around the world. We see peace and stability as a prerequisite for human development. We see conflicts diverting scarce resources away from development and costing developing countries hundreds of billions of dollars a year. We see conflicts making it impossible for people to improve their lives. We see conflicts undermining social trust, the rule of law, and human rights, and giving licence to impunity. As homes and communities are destroyed, people become increasingly vulnerable to poverty, crime and exploitation. Women and girls bear the heaviest burden of such breakdowns of order.

We see how rising GDP per capita is no guarantee of peace. Many of the breakdowns of peace witnessed in recent years have been in countries classified as middle income. There too, the unequal distribution of power and resources, leading to economic, social and political exclusion, may tip over into outright conflict.

So, at UNDP we welcome the willingness shown by the UN General Assembly's Open Working Group on Sustainable Development Goals (SDGs) to tackle the drivers of conflict in a comprehensive way. Its recent report proposes a goal to promote peaceful and inclusive societies, provide access to justice for all, and to build effective, accountable and inclusive institutions at all levels. Among the targets it proposes to achieve those ends are promoting the rule of law and participatory and representative decision-making, tackling corruption, and promoting and enforcing laws against discrimination.

At UNDP, we see how building peace involves almost every aspect of development, including:

- fostering inclusive political settlements and conflict resolution

- establishing and strengthening citizen security

- addressing injustice and enabling people both to be heard and to seek redress under the law

- generating jobs and livelihoods

- and delivering services effectively and fairly.

In practical terms, this can mean a wide range of measures, including:

- helping people reintegrate back into their communities after a conflict—including by enabling them to access jobs, training and/or credit for micro-enterprises

- training and boosting the capacity of the police and courts

- helping to put in place institutions and democratic mechanisms, such as functioning parliaments, constitutions and human rights institutions

- and developing crime and violence observatories and early warning systems, especially around political transitions and elections when violence may be more likely.

We see many examples of countries turning a corner because they tackled hard issues which had previously contributed to conflict. For example, Kenya, which saw horrific violence after its 2007 elections pursued wide-ranging reviews and reforms of its constitution and institutions, including of its electoral arrangements. It followed a proactive and comprehensive conflict prevention and reconciliation approach, supported by UNDP and other international actors. It held credible and peaceful elections in 2013. In Ghana, once known for its military coups, nationally led efforts over many years, backed by international support, to promote dialogue across all sectors of society have paid off. Ghana has had more than 20 years of constitutional government, four peaceful elections and impressive human development gains.

In pursuing peace and development, the role played by women is crucial. In countries affected by conflict, women suffer enormously, yet, time and time again, women are the agents of change who make a durable peace possible. UN Security Council Resolution 1325 on Women, Peace and Security calls for the full and equal participation of women at every stage of peace-building. The role of Liberia's women in bringing about peace in a nation ripped apart by civil war was inspirational.

Elsewhere we see many examples of women's leading roles in preserving peace. Take Senegal, a country with democratic elections since independence, but where the polarisation around the 2012 elections raised concerns about potential outbreaks of violence. Women's organisations networked widely for peace, reaching out to youth, civil society and the political parties. They set the tone for calm and for the peaceful transition which followed the elections.

The future peace and stability of many societies also hangs on whether they are investing enough in opportunities for their youth and enabling them to play a meaningful role in shaping their future. Our world has its largest ever generation of adolescents and youth—standing at 1.8 billion. These young people have hopes and dreams, and with doors open to them will bring a demographic dividend to their nations. But unemployed and frustrated youth are a time bomb in any society. We neglect youth at our peril.

My comments today have focused on the creation of peace within societies. At the global and regional levels, some of the drivers of conflict are not dissimilar to those within countries. Conflict may arise over the allocation of natural resources—from water to fisheries, oil, gas or minerals. In a climate-, water- and energy-stressed world, we may see more such conflicts.

The United Nations was created as World War Two came to an end to promote peace and security, development and human rights. Conflicts between nations are now relatively few in number, but distressing wherever they occur for the citizens caught up in the middle of them. But whether the conflict is between nations or internal to nations, the UN must continue to be a voice for dialogue, understanding and tolerance between peoples of all faiths and creeds. And member states must see development and human rights as the foundations of lasting peace and stability.

2015: An Important Year for Gender and Development

New York, United States of America
20 January 2015

The Women's International Forum (WIF) was founded in 1975 by a group of diplomats' wives who, at that time excluded from the sessions on international politics, established the forum so they too could keep informed on international events. Today, the New York-based WIF has a membership of over 300 women and men and a self-declared mission 'to provide a forum for briefings and discussions on international affairs, in order to promote understanding and mutual appreciation among members of the diplomatic community, the United Nations Secretariat and the United Nations community at large'. Helen delivered the following speech to the forum at the UN Headquarters Building.

It is a pleasure to address the Women's International Forum. I thank the President of the Forum, Sahar Baassiri Salam, for her kind introduction, and the previous President, Nareumon Sinhaseni, for extending the original invitation to me.

We are at the beginning of a very important year for gender equality and women's empowerment. This year marks important milestones on two landmark global agendas on gender equality: the twentieth anniversary of the Beijing Declaration and Platform for Action, and the fifteenth anniversary of Security Council Resolution 1325 on Women, Peace and Security. The UN will review progress on implementing both agendas this year.

As well, in September the General Assembly is due to adopt a new sustainable development agenda, replacing the Millennium Development Goals (MDGs), which run their course at the end of this year. Gender equality and women's empowerment will be crucial to achieving this new agenda, as they were for making progress on the MDGs.

These are issues of great personal importance to me. I consider myself fortunate to have been born into the post-war baby boom generation in New Zealand, where the doors of education, healthcare and opportunity were wide open to me, and where, as a woman, I was able to pursue a career of my choice and meet my professional aspirations. That is not to say that the road was always easy. Having been the first woman elected as Prime Minister of my country, and before that the first to hold the position of Leader of the Opposition, I am very well acquainted with the challenges which women face when entering hitherto male-dominated domains. Making the path to leadership easier for other women across all sectors is a top priority for me.

I believe it is important for women who do reach the top despite the odds to help build an overall environment in which all women can thrive. For me in New Zealand, that meant leading a government which opened up choices for women through policies like free early childhood care and education for 20 hours each week giving mothers the opportunity to enter the paid workforce if they wished, entitlement to paid parental leave when babies were born, expanded annual leave and more financial support for tertiary education. On average, women earn less across their lifetimes than men do, which means that student debt can be particularly burdensome for women. My government tackled that by providing no-interest student loans for all students who stayed in New Zealand.

In my remarks today, I will comment further on why gender equality and women's empowerment matter, and highlight progress made and challenges remaining. I will share some examples of how UNDP integrates gender equality and women's empowerment into its work. I will conclude with a few reflections on the process now underway towards the new, post-2015 sustainable development agenda and the importance of prioritising gender in that agenda.

Gender equality matters in and of itself. It is a basic human right for women to enjoy full legal equality and equality of opportunity, and for girls born today, in any country, to have the same life prospects as their male counterparts. But, as Hillary Clinton and others have observed, gender equality is not only the right thing to do, it's also the smart thing to do. Basic arithmetic tells us that if all members of society are equally empowered to contribute, the sum of their efforts will be far greater than if whole groups, like women, do not enjoy equal opportunity.

As well, investments made in opportunities and services for women and girls are great multipliers of development progress. The benefits to child and maternal health—MDGs 4 and 5 respectively—are very clear. Children born to women with some formal education are more likely to survive to their fifth birthday, receive adequate nutrition and be immunised and enrolled in school. Access to sexual and reproductive health services enables women to plan their families and expand their opportunities, and it also helps reduce maternal and child mortality.

Access to midwives and/or other skilled birth attendants is crucial to ensuring that women can access sexual and reproductive health services. As Minister of Health in my country 25 years ago, I was responsible for the passage of new legislation providing for the independent and autonomous practice of midwifery. I strongly believe that empowered midwives play a critical role in improving maternal health.

The economic benefits for families and for whole nations of empowering women are clear too. Ensuring that women farmers have equal access to agricultural resources boosts women's incomes and status, and has a positive impact on a country's agricultural sectors and food security. According to a report by the UN's Food and Agriculture Organization, if women had the same access to productive resources as men, they could increase yields on their farms by 20 to 30 per cent. That could raise total agricultural output in developing countries by 2.5 to 4 per cent per annum, and could reduce the number of hungry people in the world by 12 to 17 per cent.

Women in many countries still have unequal access to credit and other financial services, such as savings, digital payment methods and insurance—all critical inputs to livelihoods. Women with equal rights as basic as being able to own and inherit land and property, access credit and open bank accounts can play an even greater role in the development of their societies.

UN member states have affirmed time and time again the importance of gender equality and their commitment to achieving it. Gender equality is affirmed across a number of UN instruments, conventions and decisions, including the Universal Declaration on Human Rights, the Convention on the Elimination of All Forms of Discrimination Against Women, the Beijing Declaration and Platform for Action, and the Millennium Declaration. These agreements provide the foundation for the support which the UN system provides to countries on achieving gender equality and empowering women.

So how is the world doing on its commitments to gender equality?

There has been progress in some important areas, but it is slow and uneven. On average around the world, gender parity in primary education has been achieved. Most children now enrol in primary schooling, although completion rates and the quality of education are not high across all countries.

While the rate of maternal mortality has dropped in the last two decades, approximately 800 women continue to die every day from preventable causes related to pregnancy and childbirth. It is one of the MDG targets on which the least progress has been made—a sad commentary on the priority which tackling these tragedies has had.

Sexual and gender-based violence sadly continues in every country of the world—developed and developing. It has been seen to reach horrific levels where there is war and conflict. Then, in these traumatised and destabilised societies, the war or conflict may not end for women when a peace settlement is reached, with the incidence of rape and other sexual and gender-based violence often remaining high.

More women than ever before are participating in the workforce, but generally women earn less than men. Women's earnings fell short of men's by 23 per cent from 2008 to 2009. This represented only a small improvement since 1995, when women's earnings were 26 per cent less than those of men. At this rate, according to the International Labour Organization, it would take 75 years to achieve equal pay for work of equal value.

Around half of all working women have jobs which lack security and benefits. Globally, more women than men have such jobs. The disparity is much larger in certain regions. For example, in North Africa 23 per cent more women have insecure jobs than do men, and in the Middle East and sub-Saharan Africa the difference is about 15 per cent. Following the global financial crisis of 2008, women suffered almost two-thirds of the total job losses—despite the fact that they comprised less than one-third of the actual labour force.

In rich and poor countries alike, women carry a disproportionate burden of unpaid care work: looking after children, caring for elderly, sick and disabled family members, obtaining and preparing food, and particularly among poorer, rural households collecting and carrying water and wood for fuel.

UNDP is very committed to supporting countries to advance gender equality and women's empowerment, and we do so in a number of ways. Gender equality is integral to our work on democratic governance, a key part of which is to support countries to ensure that women are included in political processes. We do this by partnering with constitutional commissions, governments, parliaments and civil society. In Tunisia, which adopted a ground-breaking constitutional provision last year on gender equality, UNDP assisted the Constitutional Assembly to engage civil society around a range of constitutional themes, including gender equality.

In Libya, UNDP has been working with partners across political parties who want to advance equal rights for women, and has supported them to articulate what they would like to see included in the new constitution. Issues like citizenship being able to be inherited equally from mothers and fathers, and the upholding of international conventions and human rights mechanisms protecting women's rights, are being raised by our Libyan partners. We have supported many other countries to legislate for and implement the international commitments on women's rights which they have made.

Addressing gender-based violence has been a particular feature of our work—we have supported more than 100 projects around the world in this area with total funding exceeding US$300 million. As well as supporting the drafting and adoption of laws on gender-based violence, we support their implementation by working closely with police officers, judges, court administrators and civil society. I received very positive feedback on this aspect of our work in Iraq from women's organisations when I visited there.

Another practical example: in Sierra Leone we have supported regular sittings of Saturday Courts, which managed to eliminate a backlog of cases on sexual and gender-based violence, ensuring more speedy delivery of justice for survivors.

As the fifteenth anniversary of Security Council Resolution 1325 on Women, Peace and Security is marked this year, UNDP, along with other UN agencies, is taking a fresh look at how we support women to participate fully in building peace and security, and in helping their countries recover from crises.

Around the world, UNDP has worked to promote women's participation in peace processes. For example, we have supported the networking of over 2,000 women community leaders across the Asia Pacific region who are actively engaged in mediation processes in their localities. We host an annual award celebration to recognise these women in partnership with N-Peace, a multi-country network of peace advocates in Asia which supports women's leadership for conflict prevention, resolution and peace-building.

While the proportion of women in national parliaments has grown, women still comprise only 21.9 per cent of the world's parliamentarians—a level well below parity. In some regions, the average is much lower, and some countries still have no elected women Members of Parliament. Time and again, we have seen how a critical mass of women decision-makers makes a difference in bringing forward issues which previously went unaddressed. In 2006, Rwanda passed a far-reaching law to combat gender-based violence—I am sure it is no coincidence that Rwanda had the highest proportion of women parliamentarians in the world at that time at 49 per cent. Today, the proportion of women parliamentarians is even higher at 63.8 per cent, and is still the highest in the world.

Making progress for women can be accelerated when women have that critical mass of seats at decision-making tables. Where women are out of sight, they are out of mind. In my own experience, those women participants also need to be determined to make a difference for women. At UNDP, we support women's leadership and participation, particularly in political institutions and public administration.

In El Salvador, UNDP supported the women's group in parliament to design a quota law which required a minimum of 30 per cent of seats to go to women. The law was subsequently adopted two years ago. We have worked on legislation for parliamentary quotas in a number of other countries too.

We also work in practical ways around the world to support women's economic empowerment, and to ensure that women can take advantage of programmes for micro-entrepreneurs. In The Gambia, for example, we supported co-operatives of women who harvest oysters and cockles. Through the co-operatives women learn about the sustainable management of these fisheries and have been able to boost their incomes. From Colombia to Former Yugoslav Republic of Macedonia, Egypt and beyond, I read of initiatives we are involved with to ensure that women have the skills and knowledge to lift their incomes.

The year 2015 is a big year for global development—and it must be a big year for gender equality, too. The current global development agenda—the MDGs—will come to an end, and it is hoped that at the General Assembly a new sustainable development agenda will be adopted in September.

The emerging post-2015 agenda can be bolder and transformational. There is broad agreement that it should be a universal agenda—applying to all countries. This recognises that development is not just something which happens somewhere else to other people. Developed countries have substantial development challenges too, as I know well from leading one for nine years. This new development agenda must be bold and transformational for women too.

Since late 2012, UNDP and the broader UN development system have reached out to the world's citizens for input into the post-2015 agenda, supporting large-scale consultations through 88 national dialogues, eleven major thematic consultations, including one on inequalities, and an ambitious social media platform.

The worldwide survey MY World has had an especially wide reach. So far more than seven million people, about half of whom are women, have participated by voting on their priorities for the new agenda. Over 2.2 million people put 'equality between men and women' in their top six priorities, alongside better education, healthcare, jobs, honest and responsive government, and affordable and nutritious food.

The Open Working Group on sustainable development goals (SDGs), consisting of 70 governments and drawing on technical inputs from the UN system and civil society, has proposed seventeen goals and 169 targets. The proposal builds on the legacy of the MDGs with goals on poverty and hunger eradication, health, education, gender equality and environment, but also broadens the scope with goals on infrastructure, energy, peaceful and inclusive societies, and reductions in inequalities. The agenda would be applicable to all countries, and aims to shift the world towards sustainable consumption and production.

The UN Secretary-General's recent Post-2015 Synthesis Report 'The Road to Dignity by 2030' welcomes the Open Working Group's proposal and provides an integrated set of six essential elements to help frame and reinforce the sustainable development agenda. These six elements are dignity, people, prosperity, planet, justice and partnership.

The post-2015 agenda is an enormous opportunity to finish the unfinished business of the MDGs and accelerate inclusive and sustainable development for all—girls and boys, women and men. Through our support to member states and their partners, UNDP is committed to doing its part to deliver on an ambitious agenda which will improve the lives of people everywhere.

Statement on International Women's Day 2015

New York, United States of America
8 March 2015

International Women's Day (IWD) falls on 8 March each year, a day for people around the world to celebrate the social, economic, cultural and political achievements of women. At the same time, IWD is a call to action: a reminder that work continues, and needs to continue, in promoting gender equality in all aspects around the globe. In recent years, IWD has become an occasion for public figures such as Helen to draw attention to the issues surrounding gender equality. In 2015 she released the following statement.

———

This week, the United Nations Commission on the Status of Women will commemorate the twentieth anniversary of the Beijing Declaration and Platform for Action, which remains the world's best blueprint for achieving gender equality and empowering women. The review of this visionary roadmap, adopted at the Fourth World Conference for Women in 1995, is an opportunity to celebrate the world's progress towards ensuring the rights and opportunities of women and girls, and also to renew and reinvigorate commitments to achieve gender equality.

One of the great achievements of the Beijing Platform for Action was the clear recognition that women's rights are human rights. Since that historic gathering in Beijing, when 17,000 participants and 30,000 activists gathered to voice and demonstrate their support for gender equality and women's empowerment, there has been increasing recognition that gender equality, in addition to being a human right, is also critical to making development progress. If women and girls are not able to fully realise their rights and aspirations in all spheres of life, development will be impeded.

Twenty years on, we can see both progress and challenges in the twelve areas of critical concern laid out in the Beijing Platform for Action. Gender parity in primary education has been achieved, but completion rates and the quality of education are not high across all countries. More women have been elected to public office—about 21 per cent of the world's parliamentarians are women, up from about 11 per cent in 1995—but we are still far from parity. More women than ever before are participating in the workforce, but women generally earn less than men and, in rich and poor countries alike, carry a disproportionate burden of unpaid care work which deprives them of time for valuable pursuits like earning money, gaining new skills and participating in public life. And, while more laws exist to protect women from violence, sexual and gender-based violence continue to occur on every continent and in every country, often reaching horrific levels where there is war and conflict.

Fortunately, there is encouraging momentum not only to renew the promises of Beijing, but to address issues which were not in the spotlight in 1995, such as the need to ensure women's participation in responding to climate change, building peace and security, and helping their countries recover from crises. These issues are central to UNDP's efforts to help partner countries build resilience to sustain development results. By promoting gender equality and empowering women as agents of change and leaders in the development processes which shape their lives, UNDP envisages a more inclusive, sustainable and resilient world.

Today is International Women's Day, which this year is devoted to the theme 'Empower Women, Empower Humanity—Picture It!' Join me in supporting this call to fulfill the promises made in Beijing 20 years ago, and to realise a world in which every woman and girl has the opportunity to fulfill her potential and enjoy equal rights and status.

Women and Social Inclusion: From Beijing to post-2015

Buenos Aires, Argentina
6 May 2015

The United Nations Development Programme (UNDP) together with UN Women and the Argentinian Government convened 'Women and Social Inclusion: From Beijing to post-2015', a global conference from 6–8 May 2015 that was part of a year-long series of events commemorating the twentieth anniversary of the Beijing Platform for Action, which recognised women's vital role in development. Helen gave the following address at the conference's opening session.

─────

It is a pleasure to speak at the opening of this international conference in Buenos Aires on women and social inclusion. I would like to thank the government of Argentina for generously agreeing to host the conference.

I am pleased to greet Her Excellency Alicia Kirchner, the Minister of Social Development of Argentina. I also greet my colleague, Phumzile

Mlambo-Ngcuka, Executive Director of UN Women, who is doing so much to advance gender equality and women's empowerment within the United Nations and in the world at large. I welcome Her Excellency Joyce Banda, former President of Malawi, and Her Excellency Aisha Buhari, who will soon be First Lady of Nigeria. We are honoured to have you both with us. Finally, I greet all Ministers, women leaders, civil society representatives, eminent academics and activists who are with us today.

This conference takes place in the twentieth anniversary year of the Beijing Declaration and Platform for Action. Our focus here is on 'Women and Social Inclusion: From Beijing to post-2015'.

Argentina is a very fitting setting for our conference, given the long-standing vibrancy of Argentina's women's movement and the country's commitment to elevating the voices of women. In 1991, four years before the adoption of the Beijing Platform for Action, Argentina adopted a gender quota law aimed at increasing the number of women in the national legislature. The law was mandatory across all political parties. Now women hold not far short of 40 per cent of seats in the Congress of the Argentine Nation. I understand that quota provisions are also widespread at the level of sub-national governments.

The Beijing Platform for Action remains as relevant today as it was when it was adopted at the Fourth World Conference on Women in 1995. In Beijing, women gathered from around the world and from all walks of life to commit to a bold agenda for gender equality and women's empowerment.

Now, 2015 presents new opportunities for setting a transformational agenda for women. Full gender equality and women's empowerment must be at the very heart of the new Sustainable Development Goals (SDGs). These are due to be adopted by world leaders at the United Nations Summit to adopt the post-2015 development agenda in New York in September. The new goals, which will succeed the Millennium Development Goals (MDGs), are expected to include a standalone gender equality goal, and to integrate gender equality across the other SDGs. The challenge then will be to go from goal setting to taking the actions which will bring real benefits to the lives of women and girls.

Over the next two days, this conference will review the progress made with and for women on social inclusion, and poverty eradication. It will look at the challenges still standing in the way of development which is fully inclusive of women and girls.

At least 50 per cent of the world's women are now in paid employment, an increase from 40 per cent since the 1990s. Gender parity in primary school enrolment has been achieved in much of the world, and more women than men are enrolled in tertiary education. In most of the world's regions, life expectancy for men and women has consistently risen, with women on average living longer than men.

Women's participation in the national parliaments of the world has also increased. In 1995, when the Beijing Platform of Action was adopted, women comprised 11.3 per cent of parliamentarians worldwide. Today, women make up 22.1 per cent of parliamentarians—twice as many, but still short of the 30 per cent target set in the MDGs.

Since 1991, when Argentina passed its gender quota law on women's parliamentary representation, eleven more countries in Latin America have done so. Today, among all regions of the world, the Latin America and Caribbean region has the highest proportion of women parliamentarians at 25.9 per cent of the total number.

Yet, despite progress at the global level in a number of areas on human development, more than 1.2 billion women and men around the world still live in extreme poverty. Despite the increased number of women in paid employment, women remain disproportionately represented in vulnerable employment. Globally, on average, women earn 24 per cent less than men. Overall, women are less likely than men to have access to decent work, assets and formal credit.

Women also suffer from what can be called 'time poverty'. In rich and poor countries alike, women carry a disproportionate burden of unpaid care work, which deprives them of the time needed for jobs and livelihoods, education and skills training and participating in public life.

Several countries in Latin America are developing and adopting multi-dimensional poverty measurements which integrate the concept of time poverty in order to identify it, recognise it as a problem and address it. The issue of women's unpaid care work will be addressed in the global Human Development Report to be launched later this year by UNDP, titled 'Rethinking Work for Human Development'.

Women's poverty and exclusion are often compounded by non-income issues, including lack of access to education and training, healthcare, and water and sanitation. Inequalities in access to reproductive healthcare are stark. Pregnant women in rural areas are much less likely than women in urban areas to receive the care from a skilled birth attendant which is so important for ensuring the health of women and newborns. This disparity in turn contributes to the differences seen in maternal mortality rates between rural and urban areas. Full sexual and reproductive health and rights are an essential part of the agenda for women's empowerment and social inclusion. Many women and girls also face multiple and intersecting forms of discrimination across age, ethnicity, indigenous status, disability and/or as migrants.

So how can growth and development be made more inclusive of women?

Determined action at all levels is needed to develop and implement laws and policies which integrate the empowerment of women with the drive for sustainable development. No country can reach its full potential without doing that. It is important that women can participate in the decisions which affect their lives, and that the barriers and discrimination which stand in the way of women are removed. UNDP is committed to these ends in its work for gender equality and women's empowerment.

In practice, this means supporting partner countries to apply a gender lens to all their policies to ensure that they are inclusive of women. For example, by recognising how much time unpaid care work consumes, policies to reduce it can be prioritised. Those could include bringing water and energy to villages, or in other settings ensuring affordable care and support for small children, older relatives and family members with disabilities.

Other measures can include:

- supporting law reform to give women equal access to land, credit and assets, guarantee equal pay for equal work and strengthen labour protections

- promoting jobs and livelihoods creation, skills training and entrepreneurship programmes which target women

- and ensuring that social protection meets women's needs across unemployment and health insurance—including during pregnancy and childbirth.

Sexual and gender-based violence must also be addressed as a significant barrier to women's empowerment. It denies the right of women and girls to be safe in their homes and communities, and it poses steep costs on societies—both directly and indirectly.

There are challenges to gender equality which have become more pressing since the adoption of the Beijing Platform for Action in 1995. Climate change is one example. While it affects all of us, it hits first and hardest the poorest and most vulnerable, including women and indigenous people. Responses to climate change must recognise this, and must ensure that both women and men at the community level can access and control the resources they need to adapt to and mitigate climate change. In the new global climate agreement due to be agreed in December, the central role of women in managing and protecting natural resources must be recognised, and investments aimed at adapting to and mitigating climate change must be of benefit to women too.

Today, an unprecedented number of people are living in communities and countries experiencing conflict and/or high levels of citizen insecurity. This is particularly harsh on women. Levels of sexual and gender-based violence and exploitation rise during conflicts, and often persist at high levels long afterwards. During the negotiation of peace settlements and during recovery processes, women's voices are still not well represented—despite the landmark UN Security Council Resolution 1325 of 31 October 2000, which urged member states to ensure increased representation of women at all levels of decision-making related to the prevention, management and resolution of conflict. Advancing gender equality is crucial for the economic recovery, social cohesion and political legitimacy which are required for lasting peace.

The complex and multi-dimensional challenges of empowering women and of driving inclusive and sustainable growth are reflected in the breadth of the agenda of this conference. The discussions before us are highly relevant to the post-2015 sustainable development agenda. This new global agenda has the potential to transform the lives of women and girls everywhere—surely that is the future we want.

Nurly Zhol:
New opportunities

Astana, Kazakhstan
21 May 2015

Nurly Zhol was a $9 billion economic stimulus plan for Kazakhstan announced in November 2014 by President Nursultan Nazarbayev. The following year, Helen was asked to address the Astana Economic Forum in a session on women's leadership and on opportunities that the plan might bring for businesswomen of the region.

—————

It is a pleasure to be here at this event on 'Nurly Zhol: New opportunities' for women. I thank Gulshara Abdykalikova, Secretary of State of the Republic of Kazakhstan, and the Women's Business Association for organising this session. I also acknowledge Tawakkol Karman, 2011 Nobel Peace Laureate.

The issue of women's leadership is very close to my heart. As the first woman elected as Prime Minister of my country, New Zealand, and, before that, the first to hold the position of Leader of the Opposition, I have long been committed to making the path to leadership accessible to other women as well. But my belief in the importance of women's leadership is not just personal. Gender equality is a matter of human rights. It is a matter of sustainable development. And it is a matter of common sense. If all members of society are equally empowered to contribute, the sum of their efforts will be far greater than if certain groups, like women, do not enjoy equal opportunity.

Here in Kazakhstan, as in countries throughout the world, gender equality is about creating equal opportunities for women and men, and about making it possible for all to reach their full potential and contribute meaningfully to society. Investing in women and girls is one of the best investments any country can make in its future.

This year, 2015, presents a once-in-a-generation opportunity to put women's empowerment at the centre of sustainable development. The Millennium Development Goals (MDGs) will run their course at the end of this year. In September, UN member states are expected to adopt a new set of Sustainable Development Goals. They are likely to include a standalone gender-equality goal, and to integrate gender equality across other goals.

In December, a new global climate agreement will be adopted at the United Nations Climate Change Conference COP21 in Paris. The challenge for both agendas is to go from goal setting to taking action which will bring real benefits to the lives of all—women and men, girls and boys.

Advancing gender equality and women's empowerment requires approaching development through a gender lens. If we do not specifically ask ourselves how women are affected by laws, policies and norms in their communities and countries—and how development plans may impact on women and men differently, we will hold back progress for women and for whole nations.

The challenges are clear. Today, women make up 22.1 per cent of the world's parliamentarians. That's twice as many as 20 years ago when the landmark Beijing Platform for Action was adopted, but it's still short of the 30 per cent target set by the UN Economic and Social Council in 1990. I am pleased to note that with women comprising 26.2 per cent women of its parliamentarians, Kazakhstan exceeds the world average. I commend Kazakhstan on this achievement, and encourage the country to build on it and lift the levels towards the target of 30 per cent, and beyond.

Women face many economic challenges. At least 50 per cent of the world's women are now in paid employment. That's an increase from 40 per cent in the 1990s. But women remain disproportionately represented in vulnerable employment. Globally, on average, women earn 24 per cent less than men. Overall, women are less likely than men to have access to decent work, assets and formal credit.

It is encouraging to see that women in Kazakhstan run 41 per cent of all active, registered small- and medium-sized enterprises. But women in the labour force here earn on average only 67 per cent of what men earn.

I am pleased to see that the new UNDP Country Programme Document for 2016–20, currently being finalised with the government of Kazakhstan, will focus on more targeted support to women entrepreneurs, and to women who are at risk of poverty and social exclusion. Specifically, UNDP will support the growth of small- and medium-sized enterprises in non-extractive sectors, including in green energy and utility services, sustainable agriculture, and eco-tourism. These are areas which can generate jobs and promote environmental sustainability and gender equality.

UNDP works to share knowledge and experience from other countries in this and other regions. We are engaged with Kazakhstan in developing a vibrant platform for South–South exchanges and co-operation, involving experts and practitioners from our global network.

Earlier this month, I participated in the global conference on Women and Social Inclusion which UNDP co-hosted with the government of Argentina and UN Women. Initiatives like those which the government of Kazakhstan and UNDP have agreed to, which promote jobs and entrepreneurship programmes targeting women, and at the same time promote the 'green' economy, generated great interest among participants at the conference.

It's also vital to support greater women's participation in all levels of decision-making, from national legislatures to local councils and public administrations. Ensuring that women have a seat at decision-making tables is not just a matter of fairness; it makes a positive difference in shining light on issues which previously went unaddressed and which matter to the lives of women.

In 2006 Rwanda passed a far-reaching law to combat gender-based violence. I am sure it was no coincidence that 49 per cent of its parliamentarians were women. That was the highest proportion in the world then. Today, women MPs comprise 63.8 per cent of the Rwandan legislature—and that's still the highest proportion in the world.

Progress for women will be accelerated when women have a critical mass of seats at decision-making tables. If more issues of importance to women are to rise to the top of political, legislative and budget priorities, more women must sit at the top tables. At UNDP, we support women's leadership and participation in many ways, including by promoting the inclusion of women in constitution-making bodies, national and local legislatures, and electoral authorities, and by supporting women standing for public and other office.

Finally, let me emphasise that women must be drivers of development—not just passive beneficiaries of plans designed by others. Those gathered here today have a wealth of experience in women's leadership and political participation. Women in Kazakhstan like women everywhere must be agents of change, contributing to and driving development. I look forward to a lively discussion today on how to advance gender equality and women's empowerment.

An Opportunity for Women's Equality

HuffPost
5 July 2015, updated 7 May 2016

In 2015 the UN's Millennium Development Goals (MDGs) came to an end, and were replaced by seventeen Sustainable Development Goals (SDGs) broadly covering social and development issues. In this blog post published on the website the HuffPost *(formerly* The Huffington Post*), Helen discusses the opportunity the SDGs present for the empowerment of women and for gender equality.*

––––––

The Fourth World Conference on Women held in Beijing in 1995 was a momentous gathering of women from around the world and from all walks of life. They committed to an agenda for full gender equality and women's empowerment. Their aspirations were enshrined in the Beijing Platform for Action which remains as relevant today as when it was adopted 20 years ago.

The Beijing Platform envisages a world where every woman and girl can exercise their freedoms and choices and realise all their rights, including the right to live free from violence, be educated, exercise their sexual and reproductive health and rights choices, participate in decision-making and earn equal pay for work of equal value.

Now, in 2015, there is a new opportunity to establish gender equality and the empowerment of women and girls, as both critical issues in their own right and as essential foundations for inclusive and sustainable development. In September, world leaders are expected to endorse an ambitious set of Sustainable Development Goals, including a gender equality goal. These goals must then be translated into concrete actions which will improve the lives of women and girls everywhere.

Progress on development, including on gender equality and women's and girls' empowerment, has undoubtedly been made at the global level over the past two decades, but it is far from even. The number of women in paid and wage employment has increased, as has life expectancy for both women and men. Gender parity in schooling is close to being achieved in primary education, although very few countries have achieved that target at all levels of education.

Women's participation in national legislatures has risen. In 1995, women comprised 11.3 per cent of parliamentarians worldwide; now women make up 22.1 per cent of the total. That's twice as many, but still short of the 30 per cent target set by the Millennium Development Goals (MDGs).

But 1.2 billion people are still living in extreme poverty, and women continue to be more likely than men to be among them. Despite the increased number of women in paid employment, women remain disproportionately represented in vulnerable employment, and globally on average earn 24 per cent less than men. Women are also less likely than men to have access to decent work, assets and formal credit.

How can this situation be changed?

Achieving gender equality requires determined action at all levels. It is important to focus not only on ensuring that women can participate in the decisions which affect their lives, but also on eliminating the discriminatory institutions, attitudes and practices which stand in the way of gender equality and women's and girls' empowerment.

In practice, this means supporting a range of measures including those which will give women equal access to land, credit and assets, guarantee equal pay for equal work and strengthened labour protections, create jobs, livelihoods, skills and entrepreneurship programs which are fully open to women, and establish social protection measures such as maternity benefits, unemployment and health insurance.

Another major barrier to women's empowerment is sexual and gender-based violence. It denies the right of women and girls to be safe in their homes and communities, and it also imposes steep costs on societies.

Other challenges to gender equality have become more pressing since the Beijing conference, including that of climate change. While it affects all of us, it hits first and hardest the poorest and most vulnerable. In the new global climate agreement due to be agreed in December, the central role of women in managing and protecting natural resources must be recognised, and investments aimed at adapting to and mitigating climate change must be of benefit to women too.

No country will reach its full potential without empowering women. It is important that women can participate in the decisions which affect their lives, and that the barriers and discrimination which stand in the way of women and girls are removed.

As the world comes together around the new global development agenda in September, we must seize the opportunity to have gender equality and women's and girls' empowerment feature prominently in that agenda, and aspire to be as bold as the women who met in Beijing 20 years ago.

Gender Equality and Women's Leadership

Tokyo, Japan
28 August 2015

In August 2015 the Japanese Government hosted the second World Assembly for Women (WAW! 2015), an 'international symposium towards achieving a society where women shine'. Helen, who had also participated in the first assembly, joined around a hundred world leaders in the speaker line-up.

———

It is a pleasure to be in Tokyo again to participate in the World Assembly for Women. I thank Prime Minister Abe and Foreign Minister Kishida for the invitation. I was honoured to participate in the inaugural World Assembly for Women last year.

It has been 20 years since the adoption of the landmark Beijing Declaration and Platform for Action at the Fourth World Conference for Women in China in 1995. It has also been 20 years since Japan established the Japan Women in Development Fund as a follow-up to the commitment Japan made in Beijing. I commend Japan for its leadership on promoting gender equality and the advancement of women.

Women's leadership is a topic which is dear to my heart. I was fortunate to have been born into a family which believed that girls could—and should—accomplish as much as boys. I was also lucky to be a member of the post-war baby boom generation in New Zealand, where, as a girl, equal educational opportunities were open to me. This gave me the freedom to make my own decisions. My fervent desire is for every woman and girl to be able to make their life choices for themselves.

Of course, the road for me was not always easy. Having been the first woman elected as Prime Minister of my country, and before that the first to hold the position of Leader of the Opposition, I am very well acquainted with the challenges which women face when entering hitherto male-dominated domains.

So, making the path to leadership easier for other women from all backgrounds across all sectors is a top priority for me. It's a matter both of equal rights and common sense. We face too many challenges in this world to think they can be solved without engaging the talents and participation of all people.

The recently issued 'Millennium Development Goal Report 2015' shows that women have gained ground in parliamentary representation in nearly 90 per cent of the 174 countries with data on this over the past 20 years. The average proportion of women in parliaments has nearly doubled during the same period. Nonetheless, only one in five members of national legislatures are women. There is a long way to go to reach gender parity in parliaments.

In 1893, my country, New Zealand, became the first in the world in which all women gained the right to vote in parliamentary elections. Earlier this century, women held simultaneously each of the country's top constitutional positions: Governor-General, Prime Minister, Speaker of the House of Representatives, Chief Justice, Attorney-General and Cabinet Secretary. A woman also headed the country's largest private corporation.

Around the world, laws which support women's rights are a necessary step for achieving gender equality, but they do not automatically translate into changes in practice. That is why UNDP works with countries and other UN agencies to support implementation of international, regional and national commitments on women's participation in decision-making and gender equality more broadly.

One way to accelerate the numbers of women in decision-making is to use temporary special measures, including gender quotas. UNDP has supported a number of countries to develop options in this area, and has an important guidebook on this. It looks at support for women at the candidate selection stage, in the campaign phase and once elected.

Throughout the world, women face many barriers to empowerment—both attitudinal and structural—which is why it is important to build overall environments in which all women can thrive. During my tenure as Prime Minister of New Zealand, I am proud that my government continued to expand choices for women, enacting an entitlement in law to paid parental leave, and increasing by 25 per cent the annual holiday entitlement set in law for all employees. We also provided a minimum of 20 hours a week of fully paid early childhood care and education to take pressure off household budgets and give women a more genuine choice as to whether to return to work or not. These are critical issues, and I applaud the government of Japan under Prime Minister Abe's leadership for moving decisively in these areas.

In rich and poor countries alike, women carry a disproportionate burden of unpaid care work: caring for young, elderly, sick and/or disabled family members; obtaining and preparing food; and particularly among poorer, rural households collecting and carrying water and wood for fuel, often over long distances.

My experiences in New Zealand and as leader of UNDP have given me a keen awareness of the many barriers to economic equality which women face—from lower average incomes and often a lack of equal access to assets and formal credit to the attitudes and practices which can hinder women acceding to certain positions like leading companies and countries. Some of the barriers are those erected by custom and culture; others are erected by law. If you can't inherit the family property, if you can't borrow money, if you can't hold title to land or rent property because you're a woman, this will hold you back. It will also hold back the development of your country.

I have broken many glass ceilings, so I know it can be done. But I also know that I didn't do it by myself. We all need support networks of women and men. The HeForShe campaign launched by the UN Secretary-General is important in this respect—it calls on men and boys to commit to gender equality too.

Empowering women in their homes and communities and achieving true gender equality also requires tackling gender-based violence. This is a problem around the world, and it reaches horrific levels where there is war and conflict. It impacts very adversely on the health and well-being of women and girls. It is a blight on society, and must be addressed everywhere. UNDP supports the drafting, adoption and implementation of laws to tackle gender-based violence, and works closely with parliamentarians, police officers, judges, court administrators and civil society to do so. Just one example: I received very positive feedback on this aspect of our work in Iraq from women's organisations when I visited there.

As the fifteenth anniversary of UN Security Council Resolution 1325 on Women, Peace and Security is marked this year, UNDP along with other UN agencies is taking a fresh look at how we can better support women to participate fully in building peace and security, and in helping their countries recover from crises. We promote women's participation in all aspects of peace processes, and have supported the networking of over 2,000 women community leaders across the Asia-Pacific region who are actively engaged in mediation processes in their own localities.

My experiences as an elected leader in my home country over many years, and now as Administrator of UNDP, have given me the evidence that equal rights and opportunities enable women to reach their full potential, make their own choices, and make substantial and lasting contributions to their communities and nations. Their contributions are essential for building inclusive, sustainable and resilient societies as the new global sustainable development agenda calls on us to do.

Statement on International Women's Day 2016

New York, United States of America
8 March 2016

The theme of International Women's Day (IWD) 2016 was 'Planet 50-50 by 2030: Step It Up for Gender Equality', asking governments to make national commitments to addressing the challenges holding women and girls back from reaching their full potential. It was in this spirit that Helen issued the following statement.

———

This International Women's Day the world stands well positioned to move forward on gender equality. The 2030 Agenda for Sustainable Development, adopted by the UN General Assembly last year, asserts that gender equality is not only a human right but also a necessary foundation for a peaceful and inclusive world. Gender equality is the sole focus of one of the seventeen Sustainable Development Goals (SDGs), and is also integrated in the other goals, reflecting the growing consensus that gender equality is not just a worthy goal in its own right, but also a driver of progress across all development goals.

By closing gender gaps in labour markets, education, health and other areas, we can reduce poverty and hunger, improve the nutrition and education of children, and drive inclusive growth. It's not a choice, but an imperative: failing to address gender inequalities and discrimination against women will make it impossible to achieve the Sustainable Development Goals.

This is why we must heed the theme of this year's International Women's Day, 'Planet 50-50 by 2030: Step it Up for Gender Equality'. Getting to Planet 50-50 requires realising the foundation of the 2030 Agenda for Sustainable Development, which is to leave no one behind. Women and girls must not be left behind when it comes to education, decent work, equitable wages and decision-making at all levels of government. They must not be left behind when it comes to legal rights and access to services—including to safe water and sanitation and to protection from gender-based violence.

Next week, the 60th Commission on the Status of Women will convene in New York. Its discussions will focus on women's empowerment and its link to sustainable development. With the 2030 Agenda for Sustainable Development, the roadmap for achieving gender equality and women's empowerment is clear.

Let's mark this International Women's Day by stepping up our commitment to make sustainable development a reality and leave no woman or girl behind.

Women: The key to a sustainable world

Oslo, Norway
8 March 2016

On International Women's Day 2016, Helen was in Norway, where she spoke on the topic of 'Women: The key to a sustainable world' at an event hosted by the United Nations Association of Norway and FOKUS. FOKUS, the Forum for Women and Development, is a Norwegian non-governmental organisation that works to promote women's empowerment, rights and access to resources through advocacy and international development co-operation.

———

My thanks go to the United Nations Association (UNA) of Norway, FOKUS: The Forum for Women and Development, and the Nobel Peace Center for hosting today's event on 'Women: The key to a sustainable world'. It is an honour to be speaking on this topic on International Women's Day here in Norway—this country is a long-standing champion of gender equality and women's empowerment.

Last year was a watershed year for global development, including on gender equality and women's empowerment. We celebrated the twentieth anniversary of the landmark Beijing Declaration and Platform for Action, with the Beijing+20 review taking stock of progress and challenges encountered on gender equality since the adoption of the Declaration in 1995. We also marked the fifteenth anniversary of UN Security Council Resolution 1325, on the occasion of which the Security Council adopted a new and a more ambitious resolution on Women, Peace and Security—Resolution 2242.

Norway has been a strong backer of the Beijing Platform and the wider women, peace and security agenda. This commitment is reflected in Norway's National Action Plan on Women, Peace and Security.

In 2015, UN member states also reached major new global agreements, which together set the broader context in which progress on gender equality and women's empowerment will take place. These include:

- the Sendai Agreement on Disaster Risk Reduction

- a positive and realistic new framework on financing for development, the Addis Ababa Action Agenda

- the new global climate change agreement reached in Paris

- and—a central focus of my keynote address here today—Agenda 2030 and the Sustainable Development Goals (SDGs).

It is worth noting that, as the Chair of the World Commission on Environment and Development, Gro Harlem Brundtland, the first woman to become Prime Minister of Norway, played a major role in putting sustainable development firmly on the global agenda. In many ways the thrust of the Brundtland Report of 1987 is echoed in the SDGs.

Agenda 2030 and the SDGs have the potential to make a real difference for gender equality and women's empowerment. Among the seventeen SDGs are goals seeking to eradicate poverty, reduce inequality significantly and promote peace, security, good governance and the rule of law. Gender equality is asserted as a fundamental human right, and as a driver of progress across all development goals. Reflecting this, it is both the sole focus of one of the goals—Goal 5—and is also integrated into the other goals.

The SDGs address important structural drivers of gender inequality. They include targets on eliminating gender-based violence, child marriage and female genital mutilation, and calls for equal rights to economic resources, including access to land and property, equal leadership opportunities and a more prominent role for women in peace- and state-building.

Many voices helped shape Agenda 2030. Norway played a key role in this process, including by hosting a global consultation on energy and actively participating in the Open Working Group of the General Assembly on the SDGs. Norway also co-facilitated the intergovernmental negotiations on the Addis Ababa Action Agenda on financing for development. Norway's high-level engagement continues with Prime Minister Solberg serving as Co-Chair of the UN Secretary-General's SDGs Advocacy Group, the aim of which is to build political will and generate momentum for SDG achievement. I understand that the SDG agenda enjoys wide support across the political spectrum in Norway, and that in a recent debate in the Storting, parliamentarians expressed solid support for the 2030 Agenda.

UNDP along with agencies across the UN Development Group contributed to shaping Agenda 2030 and the SDGs. By facilitating national, thematic and global consultations, as well as the MY World survey which has now engaged almost ten million people, we helped to ensure that the goals were informed by an unprecedented global conversation about a UN process. Women participated equally in the My World Survey, representing 50 per cent of respondents.

Of course, having had a say on the new global agenda, people are expecting to see results. Agendas are mere words on paper, unless concrete action is taken to implement them. We all have work to do to drive progress, including with and for women.

In today's development context, this must be done amid major global challenges—challenges which often have unique and specific impacts on women. For example, we are living through the most profound displacement crisis since World War Two. The Syria conflict has had major spillover impacts on the sub-region and beyond, including all the way to Norway. I understand that there were more than 30,000 unplanned arrivals of migrants from a range of countries here last year, many of whom were seeking asylum.

As women and girls comprise about half of any refugee, internally displaced or stateless population, it is imperative that their voices and needs inform decision-making on their conditions and/or the environment in which they find themselves, and that they are equal beneficiaries of initiatives designed to support displaced people. We must also recognise that in some settings for displaced people, women are particularly vulnerable to violence and to trafficking.

It should be noted that when women stay behind as male members of families migrate, they must then fend for their families alone, sometimes with limited access to services and livelihoods. This underscores the importance of empowering women economically, reinforcing their resilience when faced with such circumstances.

Economic and social shifts are creating new opportunities, but also new risks. Fast technological progress and deepening globalisation offer opportunities for some, but also profound challenges for others. Compounding these challenges is a less than robust global economy in which a number of major developed countries continue to record low growth, and a number of the emerging economies which held up global growth in recent years have now themselves slowed.

As UNDP's 2015 Human Development Report on the role of work for human development made clear, women continue to be disproportionately represented in the informal work sector. Within the formal labour market, they are concentrated in lower waged jobs. The higher-paying jobs of the technology and science sectors will remain out of reach for many women until they have greater access to training and education in these spheres.

Many countries are being affected by unprecedented natural disasters. Recurrent severe weather events in the Sahel and in the Horn of Africa, for example, are devastating people's lives. This year we see particularly severe drought impacts in Southern Africa and Central America too. With climate change, we can expect worsening weather for decades.

While climate change and natural disasters affect everyone, women and girls bear the heaviest burden because of structural issues, including unequal access to credit, land ownership and decision making. As generally the providers of food, water and fuel for families, changes in the climate and environment impact on women directly. Norway has been among those countries calling for the recognition of gender considerations in global climate agreements.

These challenges have implications for women's lives. Addressing them not only calls for targeted, gender-focused programmes, but also requires that all development efforts take the experiences, needs and contributions of women into account. With the integration of gender equality throughout the SDGs, the 2030 Agenda provides the international community with an ambitious roadmap to do just that. In particular, to make progress towards the targets of the new agenda, there is a need for:

- Getting more women into decision-making positions. Today, women comprise only 22.7 per cent of the world's parliamentarians—a level well below parity. In some regions, the average is much lower, and some countries still have no elected women Members of Parliament. A gender imbalance is also widespread in other forums for decision-making in many countries, from the executive branch of government to the judiciary, the private sector and beyond.

- Increasing the proportion of women in decision-making is not just a matter of equity—a critical mass of women decision-makers also makes a difference in bringing forward issues which previously went unaddressed. Norway has been a leader in advancing gender parity in both the public and private sectors, with women now holding close to 40 per cent of seats in parliament, and, as of last year, 41 per cent of the seats on boards of public limited companies.

- Investing in women and girls as active agents of change. Investments in gender equality and women's empowerment not only improve the lives of individual women, but also bring multiple dividends to families and societies. Norway's emphasis on education for girls in its development assistance programme represents an important contribution in this regard.

- Closing gender gaps in labour markets, education, health and other areas reduces poverty and hunger, improves the nutrition and education of children, and drives economic growth and agricultural production. A recent report by McKinsey Global Institute concluded that as much as $28 trillion, or 26 per cent, could be added to global annual GDP in 2025 if women participated in the labor force at the same rate as men.

- Removing structural barriers to women's economic empowerment. Women with equal rights as basic as being able to own and inherit land and property, access credit and open bank accounts can play an even greater role in the development of their societies. The same is true of ensuring women's access to decent work and equal pay. While at least 50 per cent of the world's women are now in paid employment—an increase from 40 per cent in the 1990s—women remain disproportionately represented in vulnerable employment. Globally, on average, women earn 24 per cent less than men. In Norway the situation is better, with women's pay standing at 86.4 per cent of men's in 2014. One of the most significant structural barriers to women's economic empowerment is the disproportionate burden of unpaid work carried by women, which impacts on their ability to pursue paid work and/or education. This also has implications for economies as a whole. Using conservative assumptions, the McKinsey study estimates that if women got paid for the household chores and family care they provide, it would add an additional $10 trillion per year to the global economy.

- Building strong partnerships across all segments of society, including civil society and the private sector. Here the vital role of women's civil society organisations cannot be overstated. Norwegian civil society is known as vibrant and has a strong voice. The Forum for Development and Environment co-ordinated the inputs of many Norwegian civil society organisations in the lead-up to the 2030 Agenda, and now actively advocates for SDG implementation. An important part of its advocacy has been to call for gender issues to be prominently reflected in the Agenda.

The Norwegian private sector has also demonstrated its commitment to the SDGs; indeed this year's Business for Peace Award Ceremony, to be held in Oslo City Hall in May, has the promotion of business support for the SDGs as its cross-cutting theme.

Resources are needed. While money isn't everything, big ambitions—like Agenda 2030—require big investments. The UN Conference on Trade and Development (UNCTAD) estimates that to achieve the

SDGs by 2030 in key sectors in developing countries will require the investment of between $3.3 trillion and $4.5 trillion every year. Development investments must include resources targeted for gender equality initiatives, including for the collection, analysis and use of gender-disaggregated data which are essential to inform policy-making and planning.

Norway has been a generous contributor to international development co-operation in general, including to UNDP. It is one of very few OECD countries to have reached the target of 0.7 per cent of GNI being committed to ODA, and indeed has exceeded that target. The empowerment of women consistently remains a top priority in Norwegian development assistance policy.

The promotion of gender equality and the empowerment of women is central to the mandate of UNDP and intrinsic to its development approach. Reflecting this, our Strategic Plan takes a similar approach to Agenda 2030, by including gender equality as a specific outcome of and a key factor across all pillars of our work. For instance, as part of our efforts to end poverty, we support countries to develop pro-poor strategies which focus on the empowerment of women and girls, and address the barriers women face in accessing and controlling assets, resources and services.

This includes support for women farmers, which has a direct impact on ending hunger and improving food security. For example, in India UNDP worked in partnership with the Ministry of Rural Development to address rural poverty and social exclusion, especially for women. This resulted, among other things, in more than 970,000 rural women getting improved access to credit.

Our work on governance includes promoting women's participation, leadership and access to justice, including in conflict mitigation, mediation and peace-building. In Sierra Leone, for example, UNDP supported the establishment of Saturday Courts to supplement weekday court sittings and ensure swifter adjudication of sexual and gender-based violence cases.

Gender features prominently in our work on the environment. We support partners to mainstream gender equality into national policies, strategies and planning for climate change, and to make sure that climate finance equally benefits women and men. We also offer support to ensure that disaster risk reduction policies are developed with the participation and leadership of women, and take into account how disasters impact differently on women. In Honduras, for example, UNDP supported government efforts to integrate gender perspectives into national disaster risk management policy, including in early warning systems for potential flooding and landslides on the Choluteca River.

Looking ahead, UNDP is committed to promoting gender equality and women's empowerment across all areas of our work. We see this as a key component of our contribution to the achievement of the 2030 Agenda.

The 2030 Agenda is an unprecedented opportunity to address the challenges faced by women and girls. Keeping gender equality and women's empowerment at the centre of development efforts is also one of the best ways to advance this ambitious agenda for people and our planet. The SDGs can't be achieved if the tangible and intangible barriers faced by so many women around the world are not addressed.

As one of the most prominent champions of gender equality and women's empowerment, Norway is at the forefront of these efforts. UNDP is committed to working with Norway on ensuring that the 2030 Agenda makes a difference with and for women. Today, International Women's Day, is a very appropriate day to celebrate our partnership to that end.

Power of Parity—
Parity of Power

New York, United States of America
14 March 2016

*Helen delivered the following speech as part of 'Power of Parity—
Parity of Power: Why and how to increase the number of women
in political leadership', a side event held at the UN Headquarters
Building and hosted by the Women in Parliaments Global Forum
(WIP) and the Permanent Mission of Germany to the UN. The
theme of the event was gender equity in political leadership. WIP is
one of a number of communities functioning under the umbrella of
the Women Political Leaders Global Forum (WPL), which focuses
on demonstrating the impact of women in political leadership and
is comprised of members who are women in political office.*

––––––

Many thanks for the invitation to speak on a subject close to my heart:
increasing the number of women political leaders. But first, thank you to
the Women in Parliaments Global Forum and the Permanent Mission of
Germany to the United Nations for hosting this event. I also congratulate
the Women in Parliaments Global Forum for their leadership campaign

on our theme today. It is refreshing and powerful to see men also speaking out on why women's political leadership matters.

In 2000, I attended the UN's Millennium Summit as Prime Minister of New Zealand. Mary Robinson, then UN Human Rights Commissioner, convened a side event of women heads of state, heads of government, and UN organisations. I regret to say that we could all have fitted into two telephone boxes. Today, we would fill quite a lot more telephone boxes, but needless to say at top leadership level in most fields, women are far from achieving parity. In parliaments worldwide, for example, women make up under 23 per cent of the membership.

So why does this matter?

First and foremost, having women in political leadership is a matter of both equity and logic. It is a basic human right for women to enjoy full legal equality and equality of opportunity, and for any girl born today, in any country, to have the same life prospects as any boy. As well, the international community stands little chance of achieving the new Sustainable Development Goals if half of the world's people and their potential and talents are not able to make their full contribution. Women must have equal opportunity across all spheres of life.

Second, having women in leadership positions sends a powerful message—about what it is appropriate for women to do and about what they can achieve. It changes societies' perceptions of gender roles, inspires other women to aspire to lead and encourages girls to believe that no door is closed to them.

Third, having a critical mass of women in decision-making also has an enormous impact on what issues are addressed. Time and again, we have seen how women bring to the political agenda issues of critical concern to women and their progress—from childcare to parental leave, equal pay, sexual and reproductive health and rights, and gender-based violence. In Algeria, for example, women make up 31.6 per cent of the legislature. Might this critical mass of representation be linked to last month's decision to make it an explicit obligation of the state to promote parity between men and women in the labour market, and to the decision to have a new law criminalising all forms of domestic violence against women and girls? Another example: in 2006, Rwanda passed a far-reaching law to combat gender-based violence. At the time, women comprised 49 per cent of the country's parliamentarians, a number which since then has climbed to 62 per cent—the highest proportion of women parliamentarians in the world.

To complement women's leadership in political decision-making, we need women at high levels of public administration, where, in effect, many political choices are made. We need women in the police, prosecutors' offices and the judiciary as leaders in enforcing laws which uphold women's rights and security. We need to ensure women's participation across peace-making, peace-building and post-conflict processes, as is set out in UN Security Council Resolutions 1325 and 2242. We need women fully engaged in addressing climate change adaptation and mitigation and disaster risk reduction planning and recovery.

UNDP supports its partners to address the barriers to women's advancement in all sectors. We promote women's political participation by supporting women as candidates and voters, and by supporting women's representation across governance institutions, including constitutional committees, parliament, the judiciary, the police and public administration. We support the use of quotas for electoral office, including through political parties which are so critical for supporting women's rise in political systems. Political parties can be the greatest champions or the greatest opponents of lifting women's representation.

The challenges are great, but with the 2030 Agenda for Development— which addresses and incorporates gender equality more than ever before in global development agendas—we have an unprecedented opportunity to address the issues faced by women and remove the barriers which prevent them from fulfilling their potential. By doing so, we stand our best chance ever of eradicating poverty, realising human rights for all and leaving no one behind.

Women's Economic Empowerment for Sustainable Development in Rural Areas

New York, United States of America
18 March 2016

The Women Entrepreneurs Association of Turkey, or KAGİDER, is focused on developing entrepreneurship among women to strengthen their status economically and socially. Helen gave the following keynote speech at an event hosted by KAGİDER, drawing connections between the association's goals and the UN's recently adopted Sustainable Development Goals (SDGs) to end poverty, fight inequality and injustice and tackle climate change by 2030.

———

My thanks go to the Women Entrepreneurs Association of Turkey (KAGİDER) and the Vodafone Turkey Foundation for hosting this event. UNDP greatly values its partnership with both organisations, and we are keen to expand our collaboration around implementation of the 2030 Agenda for Sustainable Development.

I will speak today about the importance of women's economic empowerment both in general and in rural areas, and about the platform for this which the new global development agenda and the SDGs provide. I will also share some examples of how UNDP is working to advance women's economic empowerment around the world.

In the world of work, there continue to be significant inequalities between women and men in many societies, including in levels of formal participation in the labour market, income, entrepreneurship, access to credit, inheritance rights and land ownership. Note, for example, that:

- The gender pay gap is real and persistent—globally, on average, women earn 24 per cent less than men.

- An estimated 47.9 per cent of women are in work which is informal or precarious, limiting their access to social protection.

- In all countries, women are 'time poor', as they carry a disproportionate burden of unpaid care work. Women in developing countries work 73 more minutes per day than men; in developed countries women work 33 minutes more. Unpaid work is a particular burden for women in poor rural areas, where they bear the main responsibility for gathering firewood and water, and from where men often migrate to cities or abroad, leaving women as single heads of households with many more responsibilities.

- Laws and policies often deny or limit women's rights to inherit and own land. Even when such rights are enshrined in law, legal loopholes, poor enforcement and discriminatory practices can undercut the formal legal guarantees.

- In developing countries, women make up an average of 43 per cent of the agricultural workforce. Yet they have on average less access to resources, including to quality seeds, fertilisers and tools, agricultural extension services and to financial services. This makes women less productive—even though they work as hard.

Yet women's economic empowerment has significant multiplier effects. For example, increasing the share of household income controlled by women changes spending in the household in ways which benefit children. Strengthening women's economic opportunities is also an essential contribution to eradicating poverty.

Agenda 2030 and the SDGs have the potential to make a real difference for gender equality and women's empowerment. Gender equality is acknowledged in the agenda as a fundamental right, and as a driver of progress across all development goals. Reflecting this, it is both the sole focus of one of the new SDGs—Goal 5—and is also integrated into the other goals.

The SDGs address women's economic empowerment, including that of rural women. SDG 2 on Ending Hunger, for instance, includes a target to 'double the agricultural productivity and incomes of small-scale food producers, in particular women, indigenous peoples, family farmers, pastoralists and fishers, including through secure and equal access to land, other productive resources and inputs, knowledge, financial services, markets and opportunities for value addition and non-farm employment' by 2030.

To deliver on the new global agenda, we must address women's economic empowerment on several fronts.

We must close gender gaps in education, health and access to productive resources. This will contribute to lifting women's incomes, and in the rural sectors to lifting agricultural production—thereby contributing to the reduction of poverty and hunger. The UN's Food and Agriculture Organization has calculated that if women had the same access to productive resources as men, they could increase the yields on their farms by 20 to 30 per cent. That could raise total agricultural output in developing countries by 2.5 to 4 per cent per annum, and reduce the number of hungry people in the world by 12 to 17 per cent. Climate change, however, stands to have a disproportionate impact on rural women and girls. It is likely to add to the burdens of their traditional roles of growing food and gathering water. And because of structural barriers like unequal access to credit and land ownership, women are less likely than men to have the resources to adapt to climate change. Climate action policies must address these gender dimensions of the challenge of adaptation.

We must increase women's overall participation in the labour force.

A recent report by McKinsey Global Institute concluded that as much as $28 trillion, or 26 per cent, could be added to global annual GDP by 2025 if women participated in the labour force at the same rate as men.

We must remove the structural barriers to women's economic empowerment. For example, women must have the right to own and inherit land and property and to access credit. Women with strong property and inheritance rights earn up to 3.8 times more income than those who don't have those rights, and their individual savings are up to 35 per cent greater. Women with those rights are also up to eight times less likely to experience domestic violence. Families where women own more land devote more of their budget to education, and their children are 33 per cent less likely to be severely underweight and up to 10 per cent less likely to be sick.

We must intensify our efforts to prevent sexual and gender-based violence. This is an important factor in empowering women economically. The risk of sexual and gender-based violence can limit women's and girl's mobility, which in turn keeps them from accessing education, resources and services and engaging fully in entrepreneurship. It can impact on women's health, and keep them out of work, threatening their livelihoods and incomes.

We must invest in the care economy. A study of seven countries by the International Trade Union Confederation shows that investing just 2 per cent of GDP in the care economy could create over 21 million new jobs and lighten the burden of unpaid work on women.

Infrastructure improvements also play a critical role in reducing women's care burden, including through investments in access to water supply, sanitation, electricity, roads, safe transportation and healthcare, as well as in high-quality family care services, maternity and paternity leave policies, and flexible work arrangements. These issues are addressed in SDG 5, which has an explicit target to recognise, reduce and redistribute unpaid care work. It calls for public provision of services, social protection and infrastructure to address the care burden carried by women.

And we must make the invisible visible. Development investments must include resources targeted for gender equality. To achieve this, the situation of women at work and in the household and in the community must be made visible, through the collection, analysis and use of data which is disaggregated by sex, age and rural/urban status.

Some of these measures can be implemented quickly and show results sooner than others. Facilitating access to credit, providing targeted skills training and including women in agricultural training and extension services could have visible results in a relatively short time span.

To transform women's economic status, we must focus on addressing structural inequalities and entrenched biases. This calls for taking into consideration gender concerns across the board, so that all policies and plans are based on an assessment of how they impact both women and men. This is the integrated approach which UNDP pursues to ensure that our development efforts leave no one behind.

UNDP integrates gender equality and the empowerment of women and girls in all its efforts to end poverty. We support countries to develop pro-poor strategies which address the barriers women face in accessing and controlling assets, resources and services. This includes support for the empowerment of women in rural areas—which in turn has a direct impact on ending hunger and improving food security. For example:

1. Employment generation

In Turkey, UNDP is working in innovative ways to empower rural women to make a living. In Misi, a village near Bursa, UNDP provides women's organisations with guidance and resources to contribute to the sustainable tourism sector, and to facilitate partnerships with public and private institutions.

In Southeast Anatolia, UNDP and the GAP Regional Development Administration teamed up to establish the fashion brand Argande to train rural women to manufacture clothes and accessories which are sold online and in retail stores.

UNDP is now building on this experience to reach out and provide opportunities to Syrian women in Southeast Anatolia. Such initiatives also foster connections between migrants and their Turkish peers thus contributing to social cohesion in this difficult situation.

2. Access to land and credit

In India, UNDP supported a network of civil society organisations aiming to enhance women's ownership of land. As a result, more than 5,300 women claimed land rights. In Gujarat, issues of women and land ownership are now integrated into the training of government officials, including those holding land records, and fifteen Land Legal Literacy Centres have been established in twelve districts.

UNDP also supported the first-ever active involvement of women in decision-making bodies related to land use and rights in the North Eastern Indian State of Nagaland. Women there now own and lease land on a long-term basis from village councils for agricultural and horticultural production. This has increased the average annual income of the women by 20 to 25 per cent, and has improved their social standing in their communities.

3. The care economy

UNDP has also focused on the care economy. In Uruguay, for example, UNDP partnered with other UN agencies, the government, civil society and the private sector to integrate early childhood, disability, old-age and care services in the government's social protection agenda. Subsequently, a national system of care was established.

In Turkey, UNDP, along with UN Women and the ILO, has supported independent research by Istanbul Technical University Women's Studies Centre. It showed that investing in early childhood and education and care would create almost 720,000 new jobs directly.

Keeping gender equality and women's empowerment at the centre of our development efforts will be key to the success of Agenda 2030 and the Sustainable Development Goals. Central to this is addressing the rights and needs of women living in rural areas who must not be left behind in development progress.

At UNDP we firmly believe that there can be no sustainable development if the tangible and intangible barriers which hold back half the population are not addressed. Women are powerful agents of change—and empowering women benefits whole societies. We look forward to working with all partners on this important agenda.

Candidate for UN Secretary-General

New York, United States of America
14 April 2016

In April 2016 Helen officially submitted her nomination as New Zealand's candidate to become Secretary-General of the United Nations, and delivered the following statement to the UN General Assembly during an informal dialogue. If she had won, she would have replaced Ban Ki-moon upon his retirement at the end of 2016, and she would have become the first woman to hold the United Nations' top post. In October that year, following a series of straw ballots, the Security Council chose António Guterres as the candidate to recommend to the UN General Assembly as the next Secretary-General. The following January, Helen announced that she would step down from her role as UNDP Administrator at the conclusion of her second four-year term in April 2017. Of her experience running for Secretary-General, Helen told The Guardian *in June 2017, 'I hit my first glass ceiling at the UN,' adding, 'I think younger women have felt that the war is won, and then they see something like the Secretary-General contest . . . and they think, "Hang on, there's something going on here that's standing in the way of my gender going that next step."'*

I welcome this opportunity to present my vision for the United Nations, to engage with members of the General Assembly, and to tell you why I believe I have the experience and the leadership skills required to serve as Secretary-General.

I am greatly honoured to have been put forward as New Zealand's candidate, with the full support of the government and of parliament. First, however, let me tell you a little about my story. I grew up on a backcountry farm in New Zealand. There I learned from my parents values which I believe are essential to leadership: being ambitious, but also realistic; and being hardworking and resilient when times are tough.

Many in my family and local community fought and were killed in World Wars One or Two. So, like other New Zealanders of my generation, I was raised with deep respect for the United Nations—and for the important role it was given to save succeeding generations from the scourge of war. I am proud that New Zealand was a founding member of the United Nations and has a long tradition of support for it.

I also grew up in a society which prioritised opportunity and fairness for people. Throughout my life, I have done my best to find ways to overcome injustice and inequality wherever I have encountered them. The first cause I became actively involved in as a young person was the movement against South African apartheid. Apartheid was a unique, pernicious and systematic form of discrimination which stripped people of their dignity. Its end, to which the United Nations contributed a great deal, was a major achievement of the late twentieth century.

My commitment to social justice at home and abroad led me to a 27-year parliamentary career which culminated in nine years as Prime Minister of New Zealand. Since then, I have been in New York these past seven years as Administrator of UNDP. I have met and worked with many of you in this room. In my different capacities, I have been welcomed in many of your countries. I have met many of your presidents, prime ministers and ministers over many years, and I have listened to and learned from them.

I have also visited many communities struggling with poverty and conflict. Everywhere, I have been inspired by the determination of people to strive for a better life for their families, no matter how steep the odds against them are.

But their determination alone cannot produce progress.

So, let me talk about the importance of tackling the serious challenges of our times. Around our world, many people look to the United Nations with hope and expectation that it will strive to help overcome conflict, achieve sustainable development and reduce inequality. We look to the UN to bring us together around the common cause of building a better, fairer and safer world.

Seventy years on from the UN's creation, however, serious challenges are testing its capacity to deliver. The problems are getting harder to solve, and the opportunities to do so are more difficult to grasp. Yet we must strive to do our best through closer collaboration, dialogue and broader partnerships.

I see the years ahead as vital for renewing the UN's capacity to deliver. Without doubt, the UN has contributed to largely ending conflicts between nations. It has supported development and prioritised the eradication of poverty. It has deepened respect for human rights, including for gender equality. It has helped to rein in the nuclear arms race. Of course there have been failures and bleak moments, but we should acknowledge the organisation's strengths and build on them.

All my life, I have been deeply committed to the ideals of the UN Charter. I see them as enduring. But since they were drafted, the nature of the challenges the United Nations must confront has changed a great deal. The responsibility to adapt and modernise our organisation to ensure that it is fit to tackle the issues of today and tomorrow falls to member states and to the Secretary-General.

I am optimistic that, if the United Nations does adapt, its unique convening power and global coverage will enable it to be both relevant and more effective.

In my vision statement, I have set out some of the challenges we face: the perpetuation of extreme poverty, the protracted conflicts, the terrorism and the violent extremism, a displacement crisis across continents, the pandemics, the impacts of climate change and the resource shortages.

The list could go on. We all know what is happening.

Now, we need to focus together on what we do about it. We must shift the focus from solving problems after they have arisen to helping to prevent them occurring.

So, how to deliver results for future generations?

You as member states have agreed on the visionary and ambitious 2030 Agenda and Sustainable Development Goals (SDGs), the Paris Agreement on Climate Change, the Addis Ababa Action Agenda on

Financing for Development and the Sendai Framework for Disaster Risk Reduction. I am strongly and personally committed to driving progress on these. Particularly urgent action is needed on implementing the Paris Agreement on Climate Change. Poor and vulnerable countries need support to build resilience to the changing climate, including to the severe weather events they are already facing. We face worsening weather for decades.

Whatever the problems we are seeking to solve, our chances of succeeding are better if we can harness our collective strengths. All my life I have fought for gender equality and women's empowerment. As Secretary-General, I would ensure that the United Nations prioritises the full and equal participation of women in decision-making, economies and societies.

I am a long-time advocate of the importance of harnessing the potential of youth as a huge force for good in our world when given the opportunity to contribute and engage.

To deliver results in all these areas, the UN must be practical and effective. The incoming Secretary-General will need to update the administration, and make full use of new technologies in doing so. The United Nations must become more effective in delivering to member states, and be a better place to work. It must be transparent and frank about what it can and cannot do. It should work closely with member states to ensure that the resources entrusted to it are prioritised around activities where the United Nations can make the most difference.

Transparency should be a guiding principle for the way in which the Secretary-General relates to the Security Council and the General Assembly and engages with member states. I have led UNDP to its current ranking as the world's most transparent development organisation. I want to bring that approach to the whole United Nations.

All parts of the UN need to embrace open, modern management practices and governance. And I believe in investing in our staff. They are the UN's greatest asset, and we must reward talent to get results. As well, the UN must get better at both anticipating and responding to the serious challenges arising in our world. My UNDP experience has given me many insights into how the UN's impressive response machinery— across peace operations, humanitarian responses, human rights, peace-building and development programmes—could be better co-ordinated.

If you elect me as the next Secretary-General, one of my first priorities will be to enhance partnerships with regional organisations which are playing an increasingly important and complementary role. I would also seek to include the unique contributions of the private sector, academia and civil society.

The UN can bring many diverse players together around one table. Together, we can mobilise great knowledge, networks, and strengths around tackling the world's most difficult problems and around responding more promptly to negative trends and warning signs of instability or conflict.

The UN needs a proven leader who is pragmatic and effective. I have demonstrated those qualities during those nine years as a prime minister and seven years as Administrator of UNDP. I am skilled at bridging divisions and getting results.

Coming from New Zealand shapes who I am and what I have to offer. My country is highly culturally diverse in a region of great diversity, the Asia-Pacific. Throughout my career, I have shown my ability to build unity amidst diversity. As your Secretary-General, I would commit to upholding the United Nations Charter, and to listening to and working with every member state.

I am acutely aware that what the United Nations does or does not do affects the everyday lives of countless millions of people. This is a responsibility which we all share. In New Zealand there is a Māori proverb which says, 'He aha te mea nui o te ao? What is the most important thing in the world? He tāngata, he tāngata, he tāngata. It is people, it is people, it is people.'

We owe it to people everywhere to make the United Nations the best it can be. We owe it to all of us to work together to build a better, fairer and safer world.

In that spirit I look forward to engaging with members of the General Assembly today and responding to your questions.

The Role of Women in Transforming Societies

Marrakech, Morocco
16 November 2016

In 2016, the United Nations Climate Change Conference brought together political leaders and activists from around the world to discuss environmental issues, and incorporated COP22, the twelfth meeting for the Kyoto Protocol, and the first meeting for the Paris Agreement, which aimed to prevent the rise of global temperatures. The Women Leaders and Global Transformation Summit, at which Helen delivered the following keynote speech, was a COP22 session with the aim of facilitating co-operation between women to support the implementation of the Paris Agreement.

It is a pleasure to join this discussion on the role of women in transforming our societies so that they become more inclusive and sustainable. Tackling climate change and achieving the new Sustainable Development Goals (SDGs) are huge tasks. Climate change itself is a huge threat to development as it increases the scarcity of resources like water. I just came from the Tafilalt oasis region of Morocco where climate change threatens the elaborate ecosystems which have made human life and food production possible in drylands.

Women and girls typically face higher risks and greater burdens from climate change, particularly when they are living in poverty. The unequal participation of women in decision-making and their unequal access to resources and information compounds existing inequalities. Often women are not included in climate-related planning, policy-making and implementation. Yet the evidence is clear: women's participation in leadership, decision-making and community representation are vital for delivering successful climate action and achieving sustainable development.

Supporting women's leadership and engagement has been central to UNDP's commitment to climate action. We worked closely with many countries as they developed their Intended Nationally Determined Contributions (INDCs), and support countries to mainstream gender in their policies and actions. Women must be active participants in responding to climate change, and gender-responsiveness must be incorporated throughout NDC planning and implementation.

UNDP's goal is for all NDCs to integrate gender fully across adaptation and mitigation. Women must have access to the resources necessary to build resilience to climate change. As well their roles as consumers and suppliers of energy, and in key sectors such as transportation and livestock management must be recognised—each of these is an important entry point for emissions reductions.

In Morocco, UNDP worked with the government on training for more than 200 women on the development and requirements of the Nationally Appropriate Mitigation Actions (NAMAs) and the Third National Communication to the UN Framework Convention on Climate Change. In Niger, our focus on building women's resilience to climate change has resulted in greater female participation in decision making. And in Bhutan, UNDP's Low Emission Capacity Building Programme built women's decision-making capacity and promoted low-emission, gender-responsive development strategies.

UNDP is committed to working with national governments and all other partners to promote gender equality and women's empowerment in climate action. By recognising, advocating for and supporting women's leadership at all levels, our joint efforts can ensure that the good intentions of the Paris Agreement actually lead to gender-responsive—and ultimately, successful—climate action.

Speech at the Opening Session of the World Assembly for Women 2016

Tokyo, Japan
14 December 2016

Helen returned to Tokyo to attend the World Assembly for Women 2016 (WAW! 2016), where she delivered this speech as part of the opening session, which also featured speeches by Katsunobu Kato, Japan's Minister for Women's Empowerment and Gender Equality, Mayor of Yokohama Fumiko Hayashi, and Akie Abe, the wife of the Prime Minister of Japan.

———

It is a pleasure to participate in the World Assembly for Women in Tokyo once again. This is my third time at WAW, and I am delighted to be back. I commend the government of Japan for its commitment to gender equality and women's empowerment—we need voices like Japan's more than ever.

We are at a pivotal point on these issues—and also a precarious one. Gender equality, both as a human right and as a driver of development, is more entrenched in the 2030 Agenda and the Sustainable Development Goals (SDGs) than it was in any prior development framework. Yet progress towards gender equality is uneven and slow—and in some areas is sliding backwards. This requires urgent attention.

In the past 20 years, the proportion of women in parliaments has nearly doubled—yet this translates to women comprising only 22.9 per cent of parliamentarians worldwide. In 39 countries, fewer than 10 per cent of the parliamentarians are women. If we continue with business as usual, it has been estimated that closing the gender gap in parliaments will take another 82 years. That is intolerable.

Women are also poorly represented at the decision-making level in public administration globally. Across G20 countries, for example, women represent 48 per cent of the overall public administration workforce, but are in under 20 per cent of the decision-making positions. Yet these top jobs play a critical role in ensuring access to services for women and men.

In economies, the challenges in achieving gender equality are also great. Women earn on average 24 per cent less than do men, and are only half as likely as men to have full-time waged jobs with an employer. Women are over-represented in vulnerable work, and are therefore often without social protection. They are also under-represented in senior management in the corporate sector, holding only 22 per cent of senior business leadership positions. Worldwide, women hold just 12 per cent of the seats on corporate boards—and only 4 per cent of the chairs on those boards.

Even more alarming, over the past four years, the economic gender gap is estimated to have worsened, reverting to where it stood in 2008. According to the 2016 World Economic Forum's Global Gender Gap report, at the current rate of progress, eradicating gender disparities in pay and employment opportunities will take 170 years—until 2186.

It is against this backdrop that we must step up our efforts to put gender equality at the centre of development efforts. We must invest our time and resources in proven interventions to empower women and drive gender equality.

We must promote women's participation, including through quotas which remain the most effective way to increase women's participation in leadership and get issues of importance to women on the table. We have seen quotas increase women's participation in parliaments and political parties, and on corporate boards, and we have evidence of the positive impact this then has on women's lives.

Discriminatory laws which are holding women back must be repealed. It is shocking to read that, of the 173 economies covered in the World Bank's 2016 report on women, business and the law, 155 have at least one law which creates a barrier for women seeking opportunities which does not exist for men. In many countries women face discrimination in family matters—such as on the right to divorce and inherit property—and do not have the right to own land, assets or access credit.

The disproportionate burden of unpaid care work done by women also needs attention. Women do as much as three times more unpaid work than do men, from caring for children, the elderly, the ill and the disabled to preparing food and gathering water and fuel. This unpaid work deprives women of time for earning money, upskilling and engaging in public life.

Addressing the unpaid-care burden in many countries requires making day-care and elder-care facilities available to working families, and providing paid maternal and paternal leave benefits to encourage the sharing of responsibilities. Japan has made significant moves in this direction.

We need to recognise the efforts of business leaders who have made a commitment to diversity and equality, and who recognise that their businesses and society do better when everybody's contributions are rewarded.

We also need to eradicate violence against women and girls—this is experienced by around one in every three women worldwide. This basic violation of women's rights is an outcome of gender inequality, and it perpetuates it. To stop violence against women, we will need a broad-based change in attitudes, beginning with education and reaching the media and the wide range of leaders across society.

Finally, we must ensure that all young people have access to comprehensive sexuality education and that women and girls have access to sexual and reproductive health and rights and healthcare. Without these, they will have neither control over their own lives, nor equal status.

The prioritisation of both gender equality and the empowerment of women in the 2030 Agenda and the Sustainable Development Goals is an achievement, but must not be cause for complacency. It must be regarded as a challenge and, even more important, as a call to action. I hope all attending this World Assembly of Women will take up this challenge.

Statement on International Women's Day 2017

New York, United States of America
8 March 2017

The year opened with the Women's March, a series of protests held on 21 January in cities all over the world in support of, among other things, women's rights. The protests, most of which were in direct response to the incoming US President Donald Trump, were an offshoot of the Women's March on Washington, which was held to, according to its organisers, 'send a bold message to our new administration on their first day in office, and to the world, that women's rights are human rights'. Against this backdrop, International Women's Day just over a month later served as a particularly potent reminder that, as Helen highlights in this statement, the quest for gender equality remains a work in progress.

———

This year, International Women's Day is devoted to 'Women in the Changing World of Work: Planet 50-50 by 2030'. Globalisation and technology change are driving that change. It's important that women are able to succeed in this new world of work. As it is, a global wage gap persists, with women earning on average 24 per cent less than men. Women are only half as likely as men to have full-time waged jobs with an employer. Women are over-represented in vulnerable and informal work, often without social protection, and are under-represented in management in the corporate sector, holding only 22 per cent of senior business leadership positions.

A disproportionate load of unpaid work is a constraint on women in the workforce. Women are estimated to do as much as three times as much unpaid work as men do, from caring for children, the ill and the elderly to growing and preparing food.

In communities lacking ready access to basic services, investments in water and sustainable energy would save women the time they currently spend gathering water and fuel. Changing gender stereotypes so that both men and women contribute to care work is also important in achieving gender equality.

Access to new technologies is important for women in all societies for access to information and to services, including for banking. Girls should be encouraged to study science, technology, engineering and maths—subjects which open up many opportunities—and more corporate effort is needed to promote women's participation and advancement in the technology sectors.

In the 173 economies covered in the World Bank's 2016 report on women, business and the law, 155 have at least one law which discriminates against women. There are still countries where women do not have the right to divorce, inherit property, own or rent land, or access credit. This is a huge constraint on women's economic empowerment.

The time is now to resolve to clear away the barriers to gender equality in the world of work and all other spheres. The 2030 Agenda for Sustainable Development urges that no one be left behind. That means leaving no woman behind—anywhere.

The Leadership We Need: Sustainable development challenges

Canberra, Australia
18 June 2017

The theme of the 2017 Crawford Australian Leadership Forum was 'Global Realities, Domestic Choices: Responding to a digitalising, deglobalising, post-truth world'. Helen delivered the Crawford Oration that preceded the Forum. Sir John Crawford (1910–84) was a noted Australian economist who was knighted in 1959 and named Australian of the Year in 1981.

Let me begin by thanking the Chancellor of the Australian National University, Honourable Gareth Evans, for the invitation to deliver this year's Crawford Oration, named in honour of Sir John Crawford, an outstanding public servant, economist and university leader.

I have titled this lecture 'The Leadership We Need—Sustainable development challenges'. Over the next two days, the Crawford Australian Leadership Forum will focus on the need for leadership in many spheres—from economic policy, trade and investment to global governance and security, migration, the disruptive impacts of technology and more.

All of these spheres are encompassed in the big and bold 2030 Agenda for Sustainable Development agreed by world leaders at the United Nations in 2015. It seeks to eradicate poverty in all its forms and to create a more peaceful, inclusive and sustainable world.

That short description alone makes it clear that the global sustainable development agenda is a very large one. My lecture today will cover the new development-related agendas which the UN's member states have launched, the challenges in the way of realising the aspirations of those agendas, and the leadership and actions required to move us towards achieving the Sustainable Development Goals (SDGs) at the heart of the 2030 Agenda and other targets set across the agendas.

1. The new global agendas

I have referred to agendas plural, as the 2030 Agenda is complemented by a number of other ambitious global agreements reached over a remarkable two years in 2015 and 2016. The best known of those is the Paris Climate Agreement reached in December 2015. It was a major milestone reached in the global effort to fight climate change, and took less than a year to enter into force.

Other agreements from that biennium include the Sendai Framework for Disaster Risk Reduction, the Addis Ababa Action Agenda on financing for development, the outcome of the World Humanitarian Summit in Istanbul, the New Urban Agenda from the UN Habitat III Conference on Housing and Sustainable Development, and the New York Declaration from the UN Summit on Refugees and Migrants.

Taken together, these agendas call for transformation in the ways we think about and do development.

First, there is a significant lift in ambition. The 2030 Agenda is about 'getting to zero' over fifteen years—including by eradicating poverty and hunger entirely, and by ending the epidemics of AIDS, tuberculosis and malaria. The Millennium Development Goals (MDGs) which preceded the SDGs did not dare to be so ambitious, but they did show that determined action to meet targets in key areas like health and education gets results. It remains to be seen whether significant progress can be achieved across the much broader canvas of the SDGs—with their seventeen Goals, 169 targets, and, at last count, 232 indicators comprehensively covering economic and social development, protection of the environment, and peace and governance.

Second, increasing resilience to shocks is at the core of the new agendas. Those shocks could be economic, social, health, disaster or conflict related. All such shocks can drive people back below the poverty line. Yet, in many cases, much can be done to limit the risks of shocks occurring, and to limit their effects if they do. Investing up front in broad risk reduction and conflict prevention is a high priority in the new agenda.

Third, the global development agenda is clear that achieving sustainable development requires peaceful and inclusive societies, justice for all, and effective, accountable and inclusive institutions at all levels. The 2030 Agenda says, 'There can be no sustainable development without peace and no peace without sustainable development.' This is the first time a UN development agenda has set goals and targets around the governance and capacities needed for such societies to be built.

Yet clearly goals in this area, as across all the SDGs, will be especially challenging for the 1.4 billion people living in contexts which can be described as fragile. That number was forecast in the UN Secretary-General's Report to the World Humanitarian Summit to grow to 1.9 billion by 2030, and that bleak outlook has to be overcome to meet the vision of the 2030 Agenda.

Fourth, meeting the goals of all the new global agendas requires the mobilisation of unprecedented levels of finance. All sources will need to be drawn on—as the Addis Ababa Action Agenda points out, public and private, domestic and international, and developmental and environmental finance are all needed. I shall return to the theme of the leadership and partnerships required to realise these goals later in the lecture.

2. Challenges in the way of realising the new agendas—to name a few

A) Eradicating extreme poverty will be extremely challenging. As of now, more than three-quarters of a billion people, mostly in South Asia and sub-Saharan Africa, continue to live in such poverty, defined as living on under US$1.90 a day. Ending that will require tackling persistent inequalities and discrimination. It will require growth which is inclusive of all—women, young people, people with disabilities, indigenous people and members of minorities of all kinds. It also requires peace and stability. All that speaks to the size of the challenge.

B) Global economic uncertainty—this seems to be the new normal. The latest UN World Economic Situation and Prospects Report estimates that the world economy expanded by only 2.2 per cent last year, the slowest rate of growth since the global financial crisis. A pickup is forecast over the next couple of years, but a range of uncertainties and downside risks remain. Without steady growth at higher levels, it is not possible for low-income countries to achieve the ambitions of the new agenda, and the progress of middle- and upper-income countries would be constrained too.

C) The employment challenge—the global economy is just not generating enough jobs and livelihoods. The International Labour Organization (ILO) expects global unemployment to rise to a total of 5.8 per cent this year—adding another 3.4 million people to the ranks of the jobless.

The jobs deficit is particularly acute for young people—at 1.8 billion strong, the current cohort of adolescents and youth is the largest the world has ever known. Most of these young people live in developing countries, where their aspirations, energy and innovation could result in significant demographic dividends—if serious investments in their capacities and in opportunities for them are made. The converse is also true: unemployed, alienated and disengaged youth are not a recipe for peace and harmony anywhere.

Nor can we entirely predict the disruptive impact of current technological change on the job market—including the scale of replacement of human labour by robots. Past waves of technological innovation were also greeted by concerns about what work people would do in the future—to a large extent, new areas of work kept emerging. But are there limits to that, and will societies need to rethink how to ensure minimum basic incomes for all? Already Finland is piloting a universal basic income, with the stated goals of cutting red tape and reducing poverty and unemployment, as are provinces and cities in some other developed countries.

D) The impact of natural disasters, including climate change. The scale of weather-related disasters of recent years is the face of the foreseeable future as climate change intensifies. Even if the high ambition of the

Paris Agreement is realised—that is to keep the global temperature rise to below two degrees, and ideally to below 1.5 degrees Celsius, above pre-industrial levels—we can expect worsening weather for decades to come.

So, everything possible must be done to support countries to adapt to this outlook, especially the poorest and most vulnerable. In extremis, dramatic weather events bring severe dislocation and death—whether from flooding and cyclones or years of drought. Take Hurricane Matthew in Haiti last October, when more than 1,000 people died, or the 260,000 who died in the famine which hit Somalia from 2010 to 2012, half of whom were children under five years of age. Greater resilience to such adverse conditions must be built.

Urbanisation also compounds disaster risks, both by concentrating more people together, and because the poor live in the most vulnerable locations within cities. I shall always remember my visits to informal settlements cascading down the steep hillsides of Port-au-Prince in Haiti. Those at the bottom of the ravine are the first to be flooded, and with a major earthquake, like that of January 2010 in which close to a quarter of a million people died, the poorly constructed homes of the poor literally fall down the slopes.

E) The number of violent conflicts generating massive displacement and creating high levels of need. When I arrived at UNDP as Administrator in 2009, my briefing notes routinely told me that the number of armed conflicts in the world had fallen. From around 2011, however, that changed. Uprisings and protracted conflicts in the Arab States region account for some of the increase. As well, on the African continent, Mali and Central African Republic descended into deadly conflict in 2012, and South Sudan in 2013. Elsewhere, the insurgency in Afghanistan continues, as does deadly conflict in eastern Ukraine.

That long list of troubled countries could be added to, and we must also take into account others which are experiencing waves of terrorism fuelled by violent extremism, and still more which are experiencing deadly crime waves. Late last year, for example, I visited El Salvador and Honduras, which are both experiencing a scourge of armed violence. Criminal gangs there make the lives of people miserable and dangerous in many places. Persistence of poverty at scale is a significant problem.

Earlier this year, the UN drew attention to the threat of famine in four countries: Somalia, Yemen, South Sudan and North-East Nigeria. Those four have one deadly attribute in common: protracted conflict which has seen many people displaced, and unable to produce their own food or earn the incomes they need to buy it. In Somalia, the crisis of conflict has been compounded by three years of drought, producing dangerous levels of food insecurity even in relatively stable areas.

All of these settings generate significant displacement—indeed we are currently witnessing the world's largest ever forced displacement crisis. At over 65 million people, that represents a larger number than at the end of World War Two. Twenty-one point three million of these are refugees—the far greater number is of the internally displaced.

Meeting the humanitarian needs of the displaced is putting huge pressure on aid budgets, but the greater pressure still is on the societies caught up in these events whose economies and human development can be set back for many years. The impacts are felt not only by the country which is the source of the conflict, but also by neighbours. The economies of Jordan and Lebanon, for example, have struggled since the Syria crisis began, and their public services are under strain.

F) The geopolitical environment in which we are trying to advance sustainable development and build the solidarity it requires. These are times of both significant geopolitical polarisation and of mixed support for multilateralism and official development assistance. Deep divisions on the UN Security Council prevent it from acting decisively in ways which might bring a number of deadly conflicts to an end. Thus, the peace required for sustainable development remains elusive, and hopes of realising the global goals and agendas in the countries at the epicentres of these events are largely a pipe dream.

Elsewhere in some countries, national interests are to the fore, and the easiest budgets to cut are those for development assistance. Within those budgets, the easiest to slice are those for the UN agencies, as for the most part they do not have significant domestic constituencies, but rather depend on governments placing a high value on multilateral action. These adverse trends combine to make the UN a less effective force than it needs to be to give global leadership on the big agendas.

3. The leadership and actions required to meet the sustainable development challenge

Leadership is required at every level: global, regional, national, local and individual. It must encompass the public and private sectors, NGOs and civil society. The role of national governments must be complemented by those of local governments and other stakeholders.

A) At the global level, the multilateral system must be fit for purpose in order to lead on the global agendas. The UN's development system undergoes continual reform, and is regarded as a key partner by developing countries in mainstreaming the global agendas into national plans and budgets, bringing expertise and innovation, building capacities and advocating for the resources required.

The peace and security work, however, of the UN needs a lot of rethinking if it is to make a meaningful contribution. A current focus of discussion in UN circles is how to prevent conflict and sustain peace—both so critical to sustainable development. Clearly that is not a short-term endeavour—achieving peace and stability needs rather more than investments in early warning systems for spotting tensions and the dispatch of mediators and peace-keepers when peace has broken down.

For it is surely no accident that many states which lapse into deadly internal conflict have high levels of poverty and/or inequitable distribution of wealth, governance which is not inclusive and/or does not reach all corners of the land, and/or an absence of the rule of law. These are development challenges and they require both long-term attention and investment in change.

More holistic thinking and action across the UN system would help address the nexus between these issues. This, however, is not uncontroversial among member states, with a number unwilling to see more linkages built between the development, humanitarian, human rights and peace, political and security pillars of the system.

B) No amount of leadership at the global level, however, can substitute for that required at the national level. Governments need to take the sustainable development challenge seriously and implement the measures required for transformation. The new global agenda is markedly different from the Millennium Development Goals. It is a universal agenda, applying to countries rich and poor. Many countries across all income categories are giving priority to implementing it. Some of the most inspiring actions are coming from the countries which face the most challenges—like Somalia, which has been preparing its first national development plan in more than three decades, and is aligning it with the SDGs.

It goes without saying that the Paris Climate Agreement, now in force, is also a universal agenda, with all parties to it expected to make national commitments to climate action, and implement them. In this respect, it is unquestionably disappointing to see the United States disengage from the Paris process, but it is also inspiring to see individual states, cities, businesses, NGOs and local communities in the USA stepping up to the challenge.

I am under no illusion as to how difficult leadership on these issues is. In my time as New Zealand Prime Minister, it was a simple matter to ratify the Kyoto Protocol in 2002. The hard grind lay in implementation. Most people agreed that the government should do something about climate change, but many objected to having to change to energy efficient light bulbs or pay more for petrol. The agriculture sector, which generates around 50 per cent of New Zealand's greenhouse gas emissions, was particularly resistant. But leadership requires putting the case over and over again, and endeavouring to take the greater number of people with you.

Leadership by governments on sustainable development must be based on 'whole of government' thinking: the objective is to build models of growth which are inclusive and don't wreck the environment. Ideally these efforts need to be led from the top of government—to put weight behind ensuring that all ministries and sectors pull in the same direction.

In the course of implementing the much less ambitious Millennium Development Goals in developing countries, such cross-silo and cross-sector approaches were vital for making progress. For example, what presents as a health crisis, like maternal mortality, may well have its roots in forced early marriage, girls being withdrawn from school, lack of transport to health facilities and/or an inability to pay for care. All those issues need to be addressed to drive maternal mortality down.

Another example: we can't preserve forests if agriculture and logging are allowed to intrude on them at will. Protected areas need to be enforced, capacities for that have to be built, and support for small holders to intensify production on already cleared land is important. Getting broad agreement from companies to deforestation-free supply chains is vital. Broad groups of policy-makers and stakeholders have to come together to find and implement solutions to complex and interlinked problems.

At the domestic level, all governments can prioritise designing policy and regulation which will steer investment towards sustainability. Phasing out fossil fuel subsidies and making renewable energy investment attractive are good examples of what is required. And so is the establishment of the rule of law which gives citizens and other stakeholders confidence in the future of their investments—whether they be those of the smallest micro-entrepreneur or those of major investors. Catalytic funding to support building these capacities should be a priority for ODA (Official Development Assistance).

Leadership at the sub-national government levels matters too—often that is where the planning powers and the funding to make a difference lies. Australia as a federal state knows that well. The various international organisations for local government work hard to bring their memberships up to speed with what is needed—the work of the Commonwealth Local Government Forum is a good example.

C) Leadership and action on financing for sustainable development. Achieving the SDGs and implementing the Paris Climate Agreement requires domestic resource mobilisation and private investment on a very large scale. International public finance like grant aid can help, particularly if it is used to catalyse other investment. This and other aspects of the case for Official Development Assistance needs to be put much more forcefully in donor countries. This requires leadership. We need more countries to step up on international development, and not step out.

The United Nations Conference on Trade and Development (UNCTAD) has estimated that in order to achieve the Sustainable Development Goals in key sectors by 2030, annual investments made in developing countries would need to total US$3.3 to $4.5 trillion per annum. They calculated that the current funding gap was $2.5 trillion per annum. Clearly public funding would be far from sufficient to bridge that gap.

The Addis Ababa Action Agenda emphasised that financing for development must draw on all available sources—domestic and international, public and private, and, I would add, developmental and environmental. Indeed, environmental public funding, including that being mobilised for climate action, could quickly outgrow the volume of traditional official development assistance.

International public funding can be catalytic in supporting the development of institutions, capacities, good policy, and enabling environments, all of which facilitate access to other funding. Support for developing tax assessment and audit capacity, for example, helps countries collect the taxes they are due. ODA continues to matter, especially for least developed and low-income countries, fragile states and Small Island Developing States.

It has been encouraging to see the leadership shown by the international and regional financial institutions—the IMF, the World Bank and the myriad of regional development banks—in aligning their investment strategies with the SDGs and the Paris Agreement. They have been instrumental in showing how to leverage from the billions they have traditionally invested to the trillions required for the new global agendas.

The development finance landscape is dynamic and fast evolving, with many new finance providers—public and private—emerging. South–South co-operation is growing in importance, across concessional financing and grants, and is complemented by trade and investment. A mega-initiative from the South is China's Belt and Road. It has the potential to accelerate development in the countries within its scope, but also needs to be consciously designed for human and sustainable development impact.

A number of developing countries are exploring and using new financing instruments, such as green bonds, blue bonds, diaspora financing schemes and development-oriented venture capital.

D) The leadership of the private sector on sustainable development is indispensable—how business does business and the scale of its investments will make or break the global agendas. There are tremendous examples of such leadership. For example, on climate action where commitment to zero-deforestation supply chains for palm oil is estimated to cover up to ninety per cent of global procurement. Many other businesses see their future in sustainable practice and investment, preferring to be on the right side of history and doing the right thing by society and the environment.

E) Leadership should also come from parliaments and all levels of civil society—voice is important in advancing global agendas. Parliaments scrutinise and approve budgets and government priorities. Civil society has an advocacy role. The media have a duty to inform. Universities and other research institutions have expertise—their voice counts too.

In conclusion

The challenges to achieving sustainable development include entrenched poverty and inequalities, protracted conflicts and forced displacement, economic and political volatility, a major jobs deficit, an urgent need to adapt to demographic trends and the severe exposure of many countries and communities to severe natural disasters—including those exacerbated by climate change.

These challenges call for bold approaches to building a more just, peaceful and sustainable world. Thanks to the far-reaching global agreements concluded in the past two years, there are good roadmaps for inclusive and sustainable development. The alternative to following them is to have a world characterised by even more turmoil and instability than the one we know today. That is avoidable—or at the least can be mitigated—with resolute action. That is why it is imperative for leaders to build support for the steps required to meet the sustainable development challenge.

Achieving Gender Balance in the Saudi Arabia Civil Service

Riyadh, Saudi Arabia
25 September 2017

In 2017, Saudi Arabia's Ministry of Civil Service invited Helen to attend a major workshop on achieving gender balance in the civil service. The workshop sought to meet the expectations of Saudi Arabia's Vision 2030 and National Transformation Plan, which set specific targets with respect to the advancement of women—namely increasing the participation of women in the workforce, including in the civil service, and ensuring that the representation of women increased at the highest and most influential levels of the civil service.

I am honoured to serve as a special advisor to this initiative on achieving gender balance in the civil service of the Kingdom of Saudi Arabia. I understand that the initiative has arisen from Saudi Arabia's Vision 2030 and the National Transformation Plan.

Vision 2030 seeks to increase the participation of women in the labour market from 22 to 30 per cent. Achieving gender balance in the civil service would help achieve that goal. But it is not only a question of lifting the numbers of women in the civil service—it's also a question of ensuring that there is movement towards gender balance at all levels of that service. Saudi Arabia is not alone in having few women in the top ranks of its public administration. The National Transformation Plan has a target for lifting those numbers.

The direction set in the important national vision and plan seeks to empower all citizens to fulfil their potential and thereby contribute, in the words of Vision 2030, to 'a strong, thriving and stable Saudi Arabia that provides opportunity to all'.

The civil service is a significant contributor to the design of government policy and to its implementation. That makes gender balance in it at all levels important—women need to be well represented wherever decisions are being made and implemented. The voices, perceptions and concerns of the female half of the population need to be incorporated.

So, the question is how to move towards achieving gender balance in the civil service. This workshop can consider concrete proposals for that.

First and foremost, though, leadership is critical: the highest authorities and officials must want gender balance in the civil service to be advanced. With that direction from the top, as we have already seen in the Vision and Plan, progress can be made.

I make the following suggestions on what could be helpful, drawing on my years of experience as a Prime Minister and Minister, and as UNDP Administrator. UNDP for several years has had a significant programme on Gender Equality in Public Administration, and has compiled case studies and gathered evidence on what works and best practice.

I propose that the Saudi Arabia civil service focus for now on practical actions which do not need more decrees and regulations. These actions would largely be in the fields of recruitment and promotion practice, mentoring and nurturing female talent, and addressing workplace culture to ensure that it is welcoming of women.

On recruitment

Language in advertising of all posts from entry level up should encourage women and men to apply. If women are not coming forward in sufficient numbers, targeted recruitment drives should be undertaken. Qualified women are out there, but for a range of reasons they may not see themselves in civil service positions, especially at senior levels.

Competitive examinations at entry level have been seen to boost the numbers of women in public administration elsewhere. Recruitment and selection panels need to be given gender-sensitisation training in order to avoid inappropriate questioning.

Women should be represented on all shortlisting and selection panels. Where a shortlist of candidates is to be interviewed, at least one woman should be on that shortlist, and ideally more.

Where a woman and a man candidate are judged equal on merit, appoint the woman candidate—this is not unusual practice internationally where organisations are striving to achieve gender balance.

I offer some practical examples of these kinds of actions.

When I was New Zealand Prime Minister, we wanted to ensure that more women were appointed to government boards and advisory bodies. We expected ministers to bring forward recommendations which included women's names. The Ministry of Women's Affairs maintained a Women's Appointments File with many names on it of well-qualified women who could be considered for such positions. We drew on this file and other sources of information to gather women's names for consideration. Our experience was that it you look for the women, you will find them.

At UNDP when we were recruiting for the senior management positions there had to be women on the shortlisting panels, and the interview panel had to have women on it. In my time as Administrator we were at gender parity at the level of Assistant Administrator/Bureau Director Level and above, and at the Deputy Bureau Director level two-thirds were women. Our organisation had a gender strategy and was achieving its targets down through its levels.

For appointments of UN Resident Co-ordinators/UNDP Resident Representatives, I worked with Secretary-General Ban Ki-moon to boost the numbers of women appointed, and am pleased to say that those positions are now close to gender parity, rising from well under 40 per cent just a few years ago.

On nurturing female talent up through the ranks

There can be active programmes to mentor women in the civil service and to provide targeted talent development. An example: in UNDP's

Africa Bureau, there have been leadership development programmes for talented female staffers. Over the years, women from those courses have risen to senior levels in the organisation.

Peer-group support should also be encouraged. For example, women's networks across the public administration can be formed.

On workplace culture and practice

The civil service workplace must be women- and family-friendly. There must be zero tolerance for harassment and bullying of any kind. The culture must be one which encourages everyone to believe that they will be treated fairly and have equal opportunity.

Women in most societies carry a heavier burden of family responsibilities than do men for the care of children and support for older, frail and/or disabled family members. The workplace needs to be sensitive to that, ensuring that there can be flexibility around when hours are worked to accommodate family circumstances.

In general, advancing the numbers of women in the workforce will require both more childcare provision and more elder care and disability support services. It is very helpful to women to have childcare facilities at or near their workplace.

Other societies have also grappled with how to ensure that women have a viable choice to enter the workforce. In my time as a prime minister, we noted that one reason for our country's lower Gross Domestic Product per capita than Scandinavian countries with which we compared ourselves was our lower level of female workforce participation.

This led us to address barriers to workforce participation, and to introduce:

- 20 hours' free childcare as of right for all three- and four-year-old children

- a legal entitlement to a period of paid parental leave

- and extended annual holidays to give parents more scope to take breaks during school holiday periods.

In Japan, Prime Minister Shinzo Abe has been introducing a range of such policies to boost female participation in the workplace.

In New Zealand for many years, an Equal Employment Opportunities Trust has promoted best practice in the workplace on advancing gender equality. It holds annual awards to recognise workplaces across sectors which have reformed themselves to be women- and family-friendly, supportive of people living with disabilities, and to practice zero discrimination in all respects. The way in which the award winners operate offers solid models of best practice for others to emulate.

Many of the measures I have suggested above can be introduced by the civil service in the near term without formal decrees and regulation. Over time, as gender balance is pursued, the need may emerge for national policy statements and new laws. But I believe that if one was to start there, action now would be delayed.

For the most part, the law here does not appear to pose particular barriers to achieving gender balance in the civil service. The challenges are more about overcoming stereotypes of what positions women should hold. It will be important to reaffirm continually that achieving gender balance is a priority for the country.

Complementing that, gender considerations need to be mainstreamed into public policy and into government budgets. There are a range of different practices within governments around the world on where advice on gender equality is driven from. My own country established a Ministry of Women's Affairs in 1984 for that purpose. Others may have women's policy units within presidential or prime ministers' offices. All departments may be required to have strategies to achieve gender equality.

In conclusion

I believe that a series of practical actions taken in the civil service now can see the numbers of women at all levels rise rapidly. Saudi Arabia has many female graduates who have struggled to find work. A welcoming civil service can embrace such women and women with appropriate skills and qualifications below degree level.

It will be important to have clear action plans and timelines, to stick to them, to monitor progress regularly, and fine-tune targets and approaches continually. There may be a need to review the amount and quality of data available to do that. The National Transformation Plan has time-bound targets which need to be met in lifting women's participation in the workforce at large and in the civil service in particular.

With concerted action now, those targets can be met, and exceeded. That will contribute to shifting Saudi Arabia up global gender equality indices. Its current ranking is very low, and I understand that there is disquiet about that. I wish the Ministry of Civil Service well in its initiative to achieve gender balance in the civil service and hope that these suggestions will be of assistance.

The Importance of the 2030 Agenda for Sustainable Development

Oxford, England, United Kingdom
30 September 2017

*Helen visited Green Templeton College at Oxford University in
2017 to give the following address to the Foundation Dinner.
Founded in 2008, Green Templeton College specialises in subjects
relating to human welfare and social, economic and environmental
well-being, so was therefore, as Helen noted afterwards, 'an excellent
opportunity for me to speak on the importance of the 2030 Agenda
for Sustainable Development for all countries—rich, middle
income and poor—and to comment on how university communities
can support its implementation'. On the same visit, Helen was
also a guest at Oxford's annual Women of Achievement event, in
conversation with Moira Wallace, Provost of Oriel College.*

———

Thank you for the invitation to address this annual Foundation Dinner.
Your College Principal, Professor Lievesley, wrote what, for me, was

a compelling letter of invitation to come tonight. She told me that improvement of human well-being in the twenty-first century is core to the college's educational mission, and that many of the college's activities address how to build more equitable and just societies. That was music to my ears, because it resonates with what has driven me throughout a long career in public life at the national and global level.

But I would add one extra component to my mission—that is, sustainability. Over many years I have been convinced that unless we live, work and develop in ways which keep us within the earth's planetary boundaries, we will not succeed in achieving human development for all. The world's poorest and most vulnerable people are on the front lines of climate change and other forms of environmental degradation. There is no way to a better future for them without global solidarity and action around tackling those challenges.

In all truth, our world faces rather a lot of profound challenges. They fill our television screens, columns of newsprint and Twitter feeds every day. There is no need to rehearse the problems: we know what they are, and we know that they are crying out for solutions.

In the quest for solutions, there is a role for everyone. Clearly the fellows and graduate students of Green Templeton College with their expertise across medicine, management and applied social sciences have contributions to make. In my comments tonight, I will refer to a number of areas where action is needed and conclude with some words on the role of university communities.

At the level of global agreements, we have advanced a long way from the era when development and environment were addressed in separate silos. The importance of holistic approaches was recognised 45 years ago at the landmark UN Conference on the Human Environment in 1972, and again at the Rio Earth Summit of 1992 and the World Conference on Sustainable Development in 2002.

Then in 2012, as attention was turning to what might succeed the Millennium Development Goals (MDGs), the Rio+20 Conference on Sustainable Development called for the next generation of global goals to be Sustainable Development Goals (SDGs). A lot of progress was made in developing countries on poverty eradication, health and education, which were targeted in the MDGs, but there was a growing interest in a more universal and transformational agenda.

Just over three years later, and following wide consultation, world leaders formally agreed on new global goals, the SDGs and on the 2030 Agenda for Sustainable Development, which is visionary, bold and universal.

All societies will face challenges in meeting the SDGs. They call, for example, for the eradication of poverty. Can my country, New Zealand, or this country, the United Kingdom, or any other country say hand on heart that that is not a challenge for them? I don't think so. All our countries need to take the new agenda to heart and work with the widest possible range of stakeholders to reach its objectives.

We must tackle the multidimensional poverty which denies full access to education and to health and other services. We must tackle hunger—and that challenge is growing. Last year, for the first time this century, global hunger levels rose to a total of 815 million—or 11 per cent of the population. In a world as wealthy as ours and with so much food waste, that is scandalous.

The new agenda calls explicitly for a significant reduction in equalities. That too is a challenge for countries rich and poor. Markets will not deliver greater equality—the way they function produces winners and losers. But in our societies, we need everyone to be winners, fulfilling their potential, whatever it is, and having equitable access to opportunities and services. We have work to do on this in the Global North—as does the Global South.

Inequality has many dimensions, of which income is just one. Gender inequality remains pervasive. Disabled people face many challenges. Whole communities of people suffer disadvantage because of ethnicity and/or faith. Indigenous people are often marginalised. To be LGBTI in many societies is to face repression. The new global agenda should be a rallying cry to all nations to live up to the vision of the Universal Declaration of Human Rights of 1948—it never envisaged that some would be permanently denied their rights. Its seventieth anniversary next year would be an opportunity for all UN member states to reaffirm their commitment to its values, and to resolve to act against inequality and discrimination at home.

The SDGs set targets across the environmental challenges—climate change and the threats to our marine and land environments. We have to meet these head on—or pass a toxic legacy to future generations. From the more frequent and intense mega-tropical storms and flooding to the severe droughts which see millions abandoning their land in the Horn of

Africa now, the case for action to adapt and mitigate is clear. The poorest and most vulnerable countries cannot fund that action themselves—the rest of us must step up.

Another fundamental truth recognised in the new global agenda is that progress on sustainability requires peaceful, inclusive and just societies based on the rule of law. What hope for progress can there be right now in Syria, Yemen, Libya, South Sudan and a long list of other countries wracked by conflict? We need wars to end and new constitutional settlements to be put in place for the people of conflict-stressed countries to be able to realise their aspirations.

My message to all in this college and to university communities at large is that you have a role to play in the implementation of the new global agenda. That role encompasses action on the education goal, SDG 4, which calls for universal access to affordable and quality education, and has many specific targets. But it goes well beyond that—achieving sustainable development requires joined-up action across sectors. Advancing cross-disciplinary research is crucial to that. Operating in silos won't get us to where we need to be.

Around the world, policy-makers are looking for evidence of what works. University research and analytical communities are among those who contribute to creating the knowledge base against which policies and their implementation can be evaluated.

As well, universities can be powerful advocates for a more just and sustainable world. In all societies, universities and their staff have status and are respected for their contribution. Do not underestimate the power of your voices when you speak out. Advocacy is important in encouraging governments to do what they must to progress the global agenda to which they have all subscribed.

I speak tonight as both a realist and an optimist. Over close to four decades in public life, I have held many positions where I could work to change things for the better. That wasn't ever easy, but persistence pays off. That's why I am an optimist—if enough of us are determined to build a better world, we can make a difference. The fruits of that are the legacy we must leave for future generations. I am encouraged that the educational mission of Green Templeton College seeks to help make that difference and to contribute to building more equitable and just societies.

Forced Displacement: Responding to a global crisis

Canterbury, Kent, United Kingdom
29 October 2017

Founded in 1945, the United Nations Association UK (UNA-UK) is a charity devoted to building support for the UN among policy-makers, social influencers and the public. Each year, UNA-UK in Canterbury holds a service for world peace at Canterbury Cathedral in support of promoting peace and understanding throughout the world.

———

I am honoured to speak at this annual United Nations Peace Service at Canterbury Cathedral on 'Forced Displacement: Responding to a global crisis'. I am delighted that the proceeds of tonight's collection will go to UNHCR, the UN's refugee agency, which works so hard on behalf of us all and with its partners to meet the needs of people fleeing from war and persecution.

We live in times of unprecedented forced displacement—by the end of last year, 22.5 million people were refugees, 40.3 million were internally displaced and 2.8 million were asylum seekers. That adds up to a total of 65.6 million people forced from their homes by circumstances beyond their control, and dependent on whatever solidarity the international community can muster.

The countries generating displacement are to be found from the Sahel to Central Africa and the Horn. They are to be found from the Maghreb to the Middle East and to Afghanistan and Myanmar in Asia. They are to be found in Europe itself—most notably currently in Ukraine. They are to be found fleeing from autocratic rule and repression in an even wider range of countries.

This is a crisis with global implications—and one to which the international organisations leading the response are struggling to respond, despite great generosity from a number of governments and from citizens around the world.

There is no end in sight to a number of the crises which have generated the forced displacement, and high levels of response will be required for the foreseeable future. Sadly, some of the crises have gone on so long, or are of such little geopolitical importance, that the suffering of the displaced is scarcely reported.

In my eight years leading the United Nations Development Programme (UNDP), working with the UN's humanitarian and development agencies and with governments committed to supporting our efforts, I saw the response to displacement expand beyond the provision of relief to embrace enhancing the resilience of the many millions of people affected. Each of the displaced people is a human being just like us—any one of us could have been born into the circumstances the displaced face. We need to look beyond the numbers to the human face of this crisis.

The provision of shelter, food, water and sanitation is vital, but displaced people have many more needs which must be met to uphold human dignity. For example, there are children and adults seeking to continue their education—access to a wide range of health services is vital. And people want work. Most households displaced have been self-sufficient in the past, with skills and livelihoods. To face a future in a camp without a home of one's own or a livelihood is bleak. People may be displaced for years—if not for generations as Palestinians and others have been.

So, the quest has been to find sustainable solutions for displaced people, acknowledging that their predicament may be a long-term one. That means going beyond relief to using the tools of development to create opportunities for work and livelihoods for refugees and the internally displaced. I have seen countless heart-warming examples of how this is done by UNDP and other agencies: supporting microenterprise to start up, supporting skills training, with a focus on displaced women and youth, and ensuring that people with disabilities are included.

This work is supported day in, day out in, for example, Syria, among the internally displaced and their host communities, and in the countries neighbouring Syria which have borne the brunt of the refugee crisis arising from that deadly conflict. Turkey led the way in enabling refugees to work in designated sectors. Jordan and others are also making that possible. If refugees can contribute to growing the economy of their host country, everybody wins.

As well, if the displaced can stay economically active, they are better equipped for the day they all dream for—the day they can go home.

I am pleased to say that the United Kingdom has been at the forefront of those who recognise the worth of the 'beyond relief' approach, and the need to support the creation of work opportunities. It has also recognised that host communities and countries need support too. Great as the refugee flow into Europe has been in recent years, it is but a small fraction of the flow into countries neighbouring those in crisis in Africa, the Middle East and beyond.

The UN refugee agency has the major challenge not only of providing protection for refugees, but also of endeavouring to find more permanent homes for many. The numbers of developed countries accepting annual quotas of refugees is not great, and the numbers seeking resettlement vastly outnumber the places offered.

That being the case, it is vital that sufficient support is given to host countries which are neighbours to the countries in crisis and are the place of refuge of first resort. Lebanon, for example, has, for some years now, hosted a refugee population equivalent to around one-quarter of its population. It cannot do that alone. That has increasingly been recognised by donor countries and the international financial institutions.

But that same level of support needs to extend to countries like Uganda, which has received more than a million refugees from South Sudan since July last year, and to those neighbouring Central African Republic which are accommodating 450,000 people who have fled the violence there in the past four years.

The factors contributing to forced displacement are obvious, lying variously in injustice, absence of the rule of law and denial of rights, autocratic governance, and an inability or unwillingness to mediate conflict which results in the spillover of tensions into outright conflict. All these causes are preventable—if ruling elites have the will to develop inclusive governance based on the rule of law and fostering cohesive societies, and if conflict between nation states can be averted.

It is no accident therefore that the new global agenda for sustainable development, the 2030 Agenda and the Sustainable Development Goals (SDGs), places emphasis on the importance of inclusive, fair and just societies based on the rule of law. As the agenda says, there can be no sustainable development without peace, and no peace without sustainable development.

The United Nations was founded as World War Two came to an end. An imperative for its founders was to build an organisation capable of succeeding where its predecessor, the League of Nations, had failed—in maintaining peace and averting war. The UN is struggling to respond to today's conflicts, which are very different in nature to those which preceded its formation. Its effectiveness now and in the future will depend on how it steps up to these challenges. The big question is—will its structure and ways of working mandated by its 1945 charter enable it to do that?

Meanwhile the UN's humanitarian and development agencies will keep on doing their best to respond to circumstances on the ground, and to bring hope to people caught up in conflict and repression, and to those seeking to rise out of poverty. Those organisations need our sustained support, and UNHCR will greatly value the solidarity of the congregation here tonight.

Gender Equality for Inclusive Development

Republic of Mauritius
6 November 2017

On her first visit to the Republic of Mauritius in the Indian Ocean, Helen delivered the following public lecture on why gender equality matters for development. Notably, this speech fell just eleven days after the Sixth Labour Government took office in New Zealand, helmed by Prime Minister Jacinda Ardern, the country's third female and second youngest Prime Minister.

I am delighted to be visiting Mauritius for the first time, and I thank all those who have facilitated my visit to this beautiful country: the Office of the Prime Minister, the Ministry of Foreign Affairs and the Ministry of Gender Equality, Child Development and Family Welfare. It has been a great pleasure for me to meet with the Prime Minister, the Deputy Prime Minister, the Speaker of the National Assembly, the Minister for Gender Equality, Child Development and Family Welfare, and with business leaders, non-governmental organisations dedicated to environmental protection, and social enterprises. I also greatly appreciate the support of outgoing UNDP Resident Representative, Simon Springett, and his staff for my visit. It has been of particular interest to me to visit initiatives supported by the Global Environment Facility Small Grants Programme administered by UNDP, and to see the difference which the projects make for local communities and the environment.

My topic today is 'Gender Equality for Inclusive Development'. This covers a range of issues which I have worked on throughout my life, both as a parliamentarian in New Zealand and, more recently, as Administrator of UNDP, which works around the world to support the empowerment of women and gender equality.

But, first, let me say a little about me and my country. I am a former long-time New Zealand Prime Minister, and in that capacity attended four Commonwealth Heads of Government Meetings with Mauritius Prime Ministers. On this visit I have been pleasantly surprised to learn that there is considerable knowledge in a number of quarters in Mauritius about my small country on the other side of the world.

People here have expressed interest in our extensive public administration reform, our strict biosecurity measures to protect both our very important primary industries and our unique biodiversity, and in our environmental and conservation management. I find, for example, that Mauritius and New Zealand have learned a lot from each other over the years about how to bring rare bird species back from the brink of extinction. I saw yesterday the Mauritius kestrel—its population plunged to just four birds, but, thanks to dedicated conservation partnerships, it now stands at 52 breeding pairs. New Zealand has similar stories. For example, that of the Chatham Island robin population, which plunged to just five birds, but now stands at around 250.

New Zealand has been a pioneer in many things. In 1867 it established parliamentary representation for indigenous people. In 1894 it enacted the world's first industrial conciliation and arbitration legislation, and in 1898 the world's first old-age pension. It was one of the first countries in the world to establish comprehensive social security, free hospital care and free education to the end of secondary schooling—this happened in the 1930s. It also passed the most far-reaching nuclear-free legislation in the world in 1987, and has been at the forefront of advocating for nuclear disarmament for decades.

But, most relevant to my lecture today, in 1893, New Zealand became the first country in the world where women won the right to vote—

legislation enfranchising women was enacted in 1893. Next year marks its one-hundred-and-twenty-fifth anniversary.

It took quite some time, however, for women to become established as Members of Parliament. The first woman was elected in 1933—40 years after the passage of the legislation. When I entered parliament in 1981, there were eight women MPs out of a total of 92 MPs—or under 9 per cent. At that time, very few women had ever been ministers, and having a woman prime minister would have been seen as a very remote possibility. Indeed, I can never remember it being discussed as a possibility at that time.

A lot has changed since then. New Zealand now stands out as the only nation state which I can identify which has had three women Prime Ministers. The latest one, Jacinda Ardern, took office just eleven days ago at 37 years of age. For the second time in our history, three of the top four constitutional positions within New Zealand are held by women, as the Governor-General and the Chief Justice are also female. For close to a year in 2005–06, all four of the positions were held by women with the election of a new Speaker of Parliament before the retirement of the serving woman Governor-General. As well, in those times, the Cabinet Secretary was a woman, along with the head of the country's largest company, and professional associations like those for medicine and law were headed by women. In the New Zealand parliamentary elections on 23 September this year, the proportion of women elected rose from the 34.2 per cent of the previous election to 38.3 per cent.

Does this mean that all is well for women in New Zealand? Not exactly. The law does not discriminate against women, but the proportion of women in cabinet and parliament stays below parity, there is a gender pay gap in median hourly earnings of around 12 per cent, and gender-based violence persists. Overall, however, the Global Gender Gap Report of the World Economic Forum ranks New Zealand in ninth best place, and it stood at thirteen on the Gender Development Index in the UNDP Human Development Report on 2015 data.

What this demonstrates is that New Zealand, like all countries, has work to do on gender equality. Despite significant progress and good law and social provision, inequality persists.

Why does this matter? Quite simply because as Hillary Clinton once famously said: gender equality 'is not only the right thing to do; it's the smart thing to do'.

Gender equality is a right enshrined in the 1948 Universal Declaration of Human Rights, and it is advanced through what countries do to implement the United Nations Convention on the Elimination of Discrimination Against Women. But it also stands to reason that if the full contribution of women to economies and societies isn't realised, countries won't realise their full potential.

Last year UNDP published a Human Development Report for Africa titled 'Gender Equality and Advancing Women's Empowerment in Africa'. It revealed that, on average, a shocking $95 billion every year is lost to Sub-Saharan African GDP as a result of gender inequality. The loss peaked at $105 billion in 2014—equivalent to around 6 per cent of the region's GDP. It is simply a 'no brainer' for countries to address gaps of this size.

So, you may ask: Are the gaps reducing as we near the end of the second decade of the twenty-first century?

Sadly, they are not.

In the past week, the World Economic Forum has released its 2017 Global Gender Gap Report. It shows a widening gap on all four dimensions measured: educational attainment, health and longevity, and economic and political empowerment.

On current trends, it would take 100 years to close the overall gender gap, 217 years to achieve economic parity, and 99 years to achieve equal numbers of women and men elected to parliaments. The global economic gains from reducing gender inequality are considerable—projected at $5.3 trillion by 2025 even if there were only a 25 per cent reduction.

So how is Mauritius doing?

I've mentioned the global state of affairs at length so that the state of gender equality here can be put in its context. Mauritius has work to do—as does every country. The upside is that all countries can share experiences about what works for them. The experiences of others can then be considered for adaptation to a national context.

On women elected to the national legislature

Mauritius stands well below the current global average of 23.6 per cent. The proportion here is 12 per cent currently. This matters. A critical mass of women in parliaments is necessary for the perspectives of women to be well reflected in legislation—and even just to get issues on the national agenda as high priorities. International evidence suggests that when the numbers of women parliamentarians reach significant numbers, issues previously unaddressed will come to the fore.

On the participation of women in the economy

Here too, Mauritius has some significant issues to address. The proportion of women of working age in the workforce is 46 per cent—as against 74 per cent of men. I am told that the unemployment rate for women is around 11 per cent, and that the pay gap with men could be as high as 50 per cent. Overall this means that not only are women poorer than men, but that Mauritius itself has less income than it would have if women were in the workforce in the same numbers and with the same earnings as men.

So, what to do?

Mauritius has put in place important mechanisms and frameworks to advance gender equality. It has the Gender Unit in its Ministry for Gender Equality, Child Development and Family Welfare, and it has a National Gender Policy Framework. There is also a detailed and measurable National Action Plan for 2017–20 to end Intimate Partner Violence.

I was delighted to learn that a Parliamentary Gender Caucus has been established with the Speaker in the chair. The objective will be to sensitise MPs to gender issues in their important roles as legislators, advocates, and monitors of government policy and spending.

The most recent report I saw from the UN Committee on the Elimination of Discrimination Against Women identified a number of areas where Mauritius could usefully change its laws, policy and practice. I am sure that the government of Mauritius, like all governments, will have studied these carefully and been taking the Committee's recommendations forward.

Let me share from my own experience and knowledge some thoughts on what might be useful in the areas of increasing the numbers of women legislators and the participation rate in the economy.

On political participation

Five years ago, UNDP released the excellent *Guidebook to Promote Women's Political Participation*. It was based on case studies of what had worked around the world to boost the numbers of women elected. It took a 'whole of electoral cycle approach', looking at what could be done to boost the numbers of women selected and then elected, and then looking at support for women when elected, especially when the entry of women into such positions had been relatively rare.

There is little doubt that the nature of the electoral system can have an impact on the numbers of women elected. The First Past the Post, single member constituency system of, for example, the United States, the United Kingdom, and—until 1996—New Zealand seems to be the least conducive to electing women. This may relate to the traditional occupants of constituencies being male with their spouses playing a support role.

New Zealand changed its voting system in 1996 to a Mixed Member Proportional Representation System modelled on that of Germany. Now only half the parliamentarians are elected from constituencies; the other half come from party lists. In general, the parties have made efforts to ensure that their lists are more representative of women—after all, they do want women to vote for them. In the first MMP election in 1996, the proportion of women elected jumped from the 20 per cent of 1993 to 30 per cent. That was a 50 per cent increase in just one parliamentary term.

The UNDP Guidebook highlights the critical importance of political parties with respect to women's representation—without their support, the numbers simply will not rise, as most people are elected to most parliaments with the backing of a political party. So, the parties need to be convinced that boosting the numbers of elected women is the right thing to do. That becomes easier with party list systems, where women can be placed in electable positions. Some parties rank their lists by alternating the names of women and men on each list.

In other systems where women's representation has been slow to grow, legislation for quotas has been enacted. There are many examples of this approach in Sub-Saharan Africa—and it does work. Rwanda is the standout example, with 64 per cent of those elected to its House of Representatives in 2013 being women.

Women standing for election need ongoing support from their parties. In general, old girls' networks do not have the same financial resources as old boys' networks, so funding for women candidates is an issue. As well, in some countries, women are exposed to greater danger when campaigning, and need support for their physical security.

Post-election, cross-party groupings of women parliamentarians can ensure that women support each other. These become especially important where elected women MPs are either few in number, and/or where there are many new women MPs who are looking for support to do their job to the best of their ability. UNDP supports a number of such women's parliamentary caucuses.

On increasing the participation of women in the economy

I referred earlier to the potential to expand the size of economies by advancing gender equality in the world of work. In my time as New Zealand Prime Minister, we identified that one significant factor behind our country having lower GDP per capita was the lower participation rate of women. Prime Minister Abe in Japan has in recent years been tackling a similar issue—Japan's economy has struggled to grow, and increasing the participation of women in it has become an important government priority.

For Mauritius, it is a national aspiration to move out of middle-income status to high-income status. Many factors will play a part in that, including strengthening institutions and embracing a culture of growth through innovation. Mauritius has shown a remarkable capacity to reinvent itself in the face of economic shocks, and therefore can plan for and take the steps towards breaking out of the middle-income trap if it so determines.

Gender equality in the workforce will be conducive to that, so, the question is, what policies to follow to make it possible.

My own government took a number of practical steps to make paid work a real option for women, and in recent years I have observed Japan putting a number of similar measures in place. The model for my government was Scandinavia, with its excellent early childhood education and care services, paid parental leave for parents, and extended annual holidays enabling parents to have more time with their children during school vacations.

Accordingly, in New Zealand we made early childhood education available free of charge for 20 hours a week for all three- and four-year-olds, introduced paid parental leave as a right in law for the first time, and extended annual holidays an extra week to a statutory entitlement to four weeks.

Globally, three of every four hours of unpaid work are done by women.

These pressures will increase as our populations age, as it is women who do most of the unpaid elder care work, as they do for children and for family members who are ill or have disabilities. So, for women to be able to be in and stay in the paid workforce, our social services need to be operating well to lift the unpaid care work burden which is such an obstacle to participation for many women.

As well, there may be cultural barriers to women going outside the home to work. These may take time to overcome, but overcome they can be—and have been in many societies. Governments can also play a role in tackling the harassment and social norms which continue to exclude women from paid work.

Addressing the gender pay gap should also be a priority—and in Mauritius the gap is a large one. On average globally, women earn 24 per cent less than men do. Women tend to be disproportionately employed at lower levels of the workforce. Much can be done to ensure equal consideration for women to be employed at all levels of responsibility, not least through hiring and promotion policies.

Currently the world of work is subject to major disruption—as globalisation deepens, as the pace of technological change speeds up, and as the need to tackle climate change and prioritise the environmental sustainability of our economies and societies forces change in industry sectors, transport, and energy generation.

The transition from old economies to the new will require continual adaptation and innovation. Governments will need to prioritise upskilling and access to lifelong education, supporting the development of entrepreneurial skills, as more people will have to create their own jobs, and facilitating the movement of people from declining sectors to growth sectors.

In planning for the world of work of the future, it's important to plan with a gender lens—to ensure that the disadvantage women already suffer in the world of work is not expanded by the way we respond to today's challenges.

In conclusion

Gender equality is not just an idea whose time has come. It is long overdue in coming, and women, families and whole countries are not maximising their potential because of that.

Achieving inclusive development requires gender equality to be a top priority. It means removing the persistent and pervasive barriers to the full participation of women in all spheres of national life. These barriers may lie in law, policy, practice, custom and culture, and in a failure to provide the range of services which help lift the burden of unpaid care work from women.

Let us also acknowledge the heavy toll on women and their health, physical safety and self-esteem of domestic violence—that scourge must be tackled decisively.

All these issues are identified in the new global agenda—the 2030 Agenda and the Sustainable Development Goals (SDGs). There is a standalone goal on gender equality and empowering all women and girls: SDG 5. Gender equality is also mainstreamed through the other sixteen goals.

The new global agenda is universal, and all countries are expected to work to achieve it. That gives extra impetus to the efforts here in Mauritius, in New Zealand, and in all other countries to advance gender equality.

The Importance of Education in Achieving Sustainable Development

Nadi, Fiji
20 February 2018

*Helen gave the following keynote address at the opening session
of the Twentieth Conference of Commonwealth Education
Ministers, taking the opportunity to highlight the importance of
the Commonwealth, as a champion of education for development,
utilising education to contribute to achieving the UN's Sustainable
Development Goals (SDGs).*

———

My thanks go to the Commonwealth Secretary-General, Rt Hon.
Patricia Scotland, for inviting me to address this Twentieth Conference of
Commonwealth Education Ministers (CCEM) on the role of education
in achieving sustainable development.

I am delighted that the Conference is being held in Fiji, a country which
gives high priority to its participation in international organisations,
and where challenges at the heart of the global sustainable development

agenda are so pressing, not least those of building resilience to adverse events such as those brought about by climate change.

In this respect, let me acknowledge the severe impact of Cyclone Gita, which cut a swathe through the South Pacific in recent days. In Tonga and in Fiji's southern islands, it is described as the worst storm in living memory, and it caused widespread flooding and water damage in Samoa and American Samoa too. The peoples of the Small Island Developing States (SIDS) of the Pacific, the Caribbean and the Indian Ocean are very resilient—they have lived with extreme weather events throughout human history.

Climate change, however, is an existential threat to SIDS. It raises the level of threat from storms and sea water inundation significantly, and that requires building higher levels of resilience than ever before. Even if the full ambition of the Paris Agreement on Climate Change is realised, we face worsening weather for decades to come. The need for solidarity with the most vulnerable nations is great. They need support for adaptation—and in the SIDS support is needed for recovery from the powerful storms which wipe out infrastructure and livelihoods, and may cause loss of life. Tonga and Fiji's southern islands have needs right now; and in the Caribbean, Dominica and Barbuda both suffered huge damage last year during a very severe cyclone season.

Recovery must also mean building back better, in efforts to stop the same damage happening to infrastructure and in loss of life as happened before.

We must also acknowledge the ever more severe weather events affecting Africa. There, prolonged droughts, compounded by other factors, have brought some regions in some countries to the brink of famine in the past year, requiring major domestic and international responses. In the far south of the continent, Cape Town faces the prospect of becoming the first city in modern times to run out of water after three years of drought. Let us hope that the worst-case scenario for Cape Town can be averted, but, even if it is, the message is clear: governments at all levels must be better informed about all conceivable risks and put in place credible measures to manage them.

The theme for this Conference is 'Sustainability and Resilience: Can Education Deliver?'. The short answer is that, yes, it can—and it must. We live in an age of turmoil and uncertainty. We need education to play its full part in equipping current and future generations of citizens to rise to the challenges which face our world. That means that education has a role to play, not only in meeting the targets of the education SDG— SDG 4—but also in contributing to progress on all the other SDGs.

So, let's consider the task ahead! First, can I commend the Commonwealth Secretariat for its excellent work in preparing the papers for this CCEM and those which have preceded it. The Secretariat and its associated organisations were at the forefront of debate about the shape of the new global agenda for sustainable development—Agenda 2030 and its seventeen Sustainable Development Goals.

Back in 2012 in Mauritius, the eighteenth CCEM set up a working group to provide input on the place of education in the post-2015/post MDGs framework. Your nineteenth CCEM in the Bahamas agreed on an agenda to promote Education for Sustainable Development. Now this twentieth CCEM focuses on key themes to take the 2030 Agenda forward by: developing education as a key enabler for sustainable development, building resilience through education, and enhancing teaching, management and financing to meet these objectives.

Throughout, the CCEMs have grounded their work in the Commonwealth's values of equity, access and development. Your efforts are also mirrored in the work of the Commonwealth Local Government Forum, of which I am patron, and which has done so much to promote action on, first, the Millennium Development Goals (MDGs), and now the Sustainable Development Goals across subnational governments in Commonwealth Countries.

Many speakers at this CCEM will address detailed issues of education strategy, delivery and funding. I will therefore direct my comments to the overarching issue of how education can contribute to achieving sustainable development. I will address three interlinked objectives of the agenda: its fundamental premise that no one should be left behind in development, its objective of achieving high human development for all in ways which don't imperil our planet further, and the need to achieve peace as a prerequisite for sustainable development and sustainable development as a prerequisite for peace.

Leaving no one behind

Yes, our world is healthier, better educated and wealthier than ever before, but the inequalities between us are huge—within many countries and between countries. High inequality is never a recipe for peace and harmony at home or globally. Many strategies are available to fight inequality, and successful approaches will be comprehensive ones.

An indispensable component of those strategies will be quality education for all, enabling each human being to reach their full potential and contribute to society. In the Commonwealth, it's estimated that thirteen million primary school-age children are not in school, and 20 million of secondary age aren't either. Four hundred million Commonwealth adults are illiterate. Each of those people has been left behind by the society of which they are part. That isn't good enough. Each human being denied education is a human being denied opportunity—and is being denied the right to education enshrined in the Universal Declaration of Human Rights which has its seventieth anniversary this year.

While the world has made tremendous progress towards gender equality in education, the girl child still faces particular barriers. Each year some fifteen million girls are married before the age of eighteen—that's estimated to be 28 girls every minute, or one every two seconds. Many of these girls have not been able to finish their education. Early pregnancy is among the leading causes of death for girls aged fifteen to nineteen worldwide. And child brides face a significantly higher risk of contracting HIV.

But turn that around by enabling every girl to complete her education and make her own choices about her life. That helps to:

- Reduce poverty. UNESCO has estimated that each extra year of schooling is associated with increased earnings of up to 10 per cent.

- Reduce maternal deaths, and reduce child mortality too. A child born to a mother who can read is estimated to be 50 per cent more likely to live beyond the age of five.

- Turn the tide on HIV. Research suggests that women with post-primary education are five times more likely to be knowledgeable about HIV/AIDS than are women who are illiterate.

What these simple facts tell us is that education is a foundation for development. Invest in it, ensure everyone has a right to it, and we enable people to live better lives. Whole societies benefit too. That's why no one must be left behind. And for those who have missed out to date, investing in basic literacy and other skills will help transform lives.

There's another major challenge too. We are bombarded now with information about what is termed the Fourth Industrial Revolution and the potential for disruptive technologies to change the world of work and services as we know them. Technological change won't stop; the issue is how to enable people to take advantage of it and not be left behind in this new era.

We human beings have proved remarkably adept at adapting to previous periods of technological change. For this one, the contribution of our education systems needs to be at the forefront. People will need broad skills and high digital literacy, and their capacity for innovation and entrepreneurship will need to be developed further to create the world of work of the future.

When I was New Zealand's Prime Minister a decade ago, we used to say that 80 per cent of our country's five-year-olds would be doing jobs which had not yet been invented. That was before Snapchat, Instagram and Uber began, and Airbnb was just being founded. Now Uber drivers face the prospect of being made redundant by the driverless car, and lawyers, accountants, and service and manufacturing workers of all kinds will see many of their skills replicated by artificial intelligence.

Education will have a critical role to play in helping us ride the wave of these changes. Not investing in education for this new world will see not only individuals but also whole countries left behind. We owe it to our citizens to give them the best chance they can to be able to participate fully in the economies and societies of the future. We will also have to innovate in social policy and income distribution, but that's a topic for another speech!

Providing for people and planet

Achieving sustainable development requires us to think and act holistically. We can be proud of the significant human development gains made in our world, but they've been made at a terrible cost to our ecosystems. The health of our oceans, our forests, our water supply, our climate and our biodiversity are all at risk from the way we have developed.

The environment is not an infinite resource which just keeps on supplying the natural services we depend on—it can be damaged beyond repair. Of the nine recognised planetary boundaries, it's said that we have already exceeded two, and have passed the safe operating space of two more, including of our climate.

On the basis of commitments made to date by countries on addressing climate change, we cannot meet the ambition of the Paris Agreement. Indeed, the latest draft report of the Intergovernmental Panel on Climate Change suggests that the 1.5-degree-Celsius limit in global warming above pre-industrial levels would be exceeded by the 2040s. Other research suggests that on current trends there is only a five per cent chance that the Earth will limit warming to 2 degrees Celsius by the end of this century. Without urgent action to curb emissions, we are careering towards a 3–4 Celsius future. The consequences of that for cyclone- and drought-prone countries, and indeed for us all, would be catastrophic.

The harm we are doing to our ecosystems now threatens to undermine the human development gains we've made. That was recognised in the 2011 UNDP Human Development Report on Sustainability and Equity, which forecast that in a worst-case scenario, which is not improbable unless we take a radical change in direction, improvements in human development would slow to a crawl and likely regress in Sub-Saharan Africa and South Asia.

More recently, the Rockefeller-Lancet Commission on Planetary Health found that continuing environmental degradation threatens to reverse the health gains made over the past century. It stated that 'we have been mortgaging the health of future generations to realise economic and development gains in the present'. Development as we have known it is badly out of balance.

So, never before has the need been more urgent for education for sustainable development. This could take many forms. For example, the immediate past President of the UN General Assembly, His Excellency Peter Thomson of Fiji, advocated for the inclusion of the Sustainable Development Goals in education curricula. He is right—if we place the new global agenda at the heart of education, we have a chance of future generations avoiding the mistakes current and previous generations have made.

Learners should be enabled to understand our world as a complex ecosystem with finite resources, but also with infinite human capacity to rise to challenges and find solutions if given the opportunity and enabled to acquire the skills and means to do so.

Education can empower each of us and our societies to find ways of lifting prospects for all within the boundaries which nature has given us. If new generations can incorporate these ways of thinking and acting in their value systems, then our common future will become much brighter than it may seem right now.

Peace and sustainable development

The 2030 Agenda is clear: there can be no peace without sustainable development and no sustainable development without peace. Countries mired in conflict can't get ahead. Lives are lost. Services are curtailed. People flee their homes and communities. Often the environment suffers too as people turn to endangered wildlife for food and scarce tree cover for firewood. And there are spillover effects to neighbouring countries. Some members of the Commonwealth are experiencing these serious effects right now.

When everyday life is disrupted like this, schooling is one of the first services to suffer. Take the severe impact of Boko Haram on education in North East Nigeria. Children literally risked their lives to be at school. Some were kidnapped and some of those are now dead. Many, it seems, were forced into early marriage to Boko Haram fighters. These are heart-rending stories.

Think too of the toll of the so-called Lord's Resistance Army in Northern Uganda and other states on which it predated. Or think of the children of South Sudan right now—in over four years of violence, more than three million people have been displaced. Over a million have fled across the border—most to Uganda, a Commonwealth country which needs international solidarity to cope with the needs this creates. Seventy per cent of those refugees are children. All up, UNICEF tells us that half of South Sudan's children are not in school—the highest proportion of out of school children in any country in the world.

Our responses to these crises focus of necessity on the short-term needs, but that should not be to the exclusion of addressing the underlying issues. That is one reason why the global sustainable development agenda has a goal dedicated to achieving peaceful and inclusive societies based on the rule of law. This SDG 16 is sweeping in its reach, with targets ranging from promoting representative, responsive and honest governance to reducing all forms of violence and related deaths everywhere.

UNESCO from its outset has promoted peace through education. At its best education should promote tolerance, mutual understanding and respect, and inclusion. Those are building blocks for a more peaceful world.

As well, I suggest, we must engage young people in the search for solutions. Let's listen to what they have to say about how their societies could be made more peaceful and inclusive. Our schools are the places to encourage young people to think outside the box, to question, to challenge and to propose solutions. Governments may not always be comfortable with that, but in a world where 1.8 billion citizens are aged between ten and 24, we ignore youth at our peril.

Access to education and skills training can play a big part in building peace. Educated and skilled citizens form part of a virtuous cycle of development. Where people are marginalised and denied hope, education and opportunity, can we be surprised that negative options become attractive? Unfortunately, we can think of many circumstances where crime in the forms of terrorism and trafficking does pay and where legitimate livelihoods are limited. We need to address the fundamental drivers of these problems, and not just their symptoms. In achieving the peace required for sustainable development, education has a major role to play.

In conclusion

I am excited by the drive of the Commonwealth to work for sustainable development. I applaud the focus at a series of Conferences of Commonwealth Education Ministers on how education can contribute to that.

The challenges our world faces are great—and they can seem daunting. But we can't walk away from them. Each of us and each of our communities and countries can make a difference for a better world. Fundamental to making that difference is investing in education as a driver of inclusion and of human and sustainable development. The impacts of that will be felt far beyond measures of educational achievement, important as they are. The knowledge and skills gained will help all countries achieve the vision of the 2030 Agenda for a world without poverty and conflict, where no one is left behind, and where we achieve progress within nature's boundaries.

Breaking the Glass Ceilings: Reflections on the future of women's leadership

Manila, Philippines
16 March 2018

Helen gave the following keynote speech at the Asian Development Bank on the occasion of Gender Month 2018.

My thanks go to the Asian Development Bank for inviting me to be the Distinguished Gender Month Speaker for 2018. My topic is 'Breaking the Glass Ceilings: Reflections on the future of women's leadership'.

As you know, I come from New Zealand where women are used to breaking through glass ceilings: we have had three women prime ministers in the past two decades, three women governors-general in the past three decades, and for the second time in our history three of the top four constitutional positions located within New Zealand are currently held by women—that of Governor-General, Prime Minister and Chief Justice.

For close to a year in 2005–06, all four such positions, which include that of the Speaker of Parliament, were occupied by women. As well, women have been Cabinet Secretary, head of the country's largest company, and heads of government departments and professional associations. Role models for young women abound.

This year, New Zealand celebrates its one-hundred-and-twenty-fifth anniversary of women's suffrage—it was the first country in the world where women gained the right to vote.

The Global Gender Gap Report places us in ninth best place, and in the last UNDP Gender Development Index based on 2016 data, we stood at thirteenth. Thus, we in New Zealand have much to be proud of—but not all the gender battles have been won. We must continue to campaign for gender parity across politics, the economy and society. A gender pay gap of around 12 per cent in median hourly earnings persists, and a recent study showed that the proportion of women in senior management positions had fallen.

I will draw on the New Zealand experience in my lecture today, and on what I observed in my work leading the United Nations Development Programme for eight years—I was UNDP's first, and to date only, female leader. Breaking through glass ceilings is important, and women's leadership matters. In my address today, I will discuss why this is so, and how the remaining barriers can be addressed.

But first to the normative basis for gender equality. It is a right enshrined in the 1948 Universal Declaration of Human Rights. Thus, the United Nations took up the cause of women's rights as human rights from its earliest days, and has done outstanding work to promote these through major agenda-setting world conferences from 1975 to 1995 from Mexico City, Copenhagen and Nairobi to Beijing, the UN Convention on the Elimination of Discrimination Against Women and its reporting processes, the annual meeting of the Commission on the Status of Women, which is meeting in New York as we speak, the mainstreaming of gender in the programming of its development and humanitarian agencies, along with their many gender equality-specific initiatives, and the creation of a dedicated agency, UN Women, in 2010.

The UN's top position has remained closed to women—but I am very hopeful that the next and tenth Secretary-General will be a woman. After more than seven-and-a-half decades, surely it will be time. As Hillary Clinton once famously said, 'gender equality is not only the right thing to do; it's the smart thing to do'. It is clear that the global economic gains from reducing gender inequality are considerable. They've been projected at $5.3 trillion by 2025 even if there were only a 25 per cent reduction in the gap. Put simply, if the full contribution of women to economies and societies isn't realised, it's not only women who won't reach their full potential—whole countries won't reach their full potential.

The Asian Development Bank has long recognised this simple truth. It adopted its first official policy on the role of women in development in 1985 and expanded it in 1998 to incorporate considerations of gender in all aspects of its work. Ten years ago, it recognised gender equity as one of five 'drivers of change' to be stressed in all its operations.

Around the world, we see other development banks and the International Monetary Fund stressing the importance of gender equality. We see governments of all kinds recognising its importance. Saudi Arabia, for example, may be a late mover in this area, but it is now taking a number of important steps which even a year ago would not have been thought to be likely—for example, by promoting women's employment, and enabling women to drive and be at public events which were previously off limits.

So, you may ask: Are the gender gaps reducing as we near the end of the second decade of the twenty-first century?

Apparently, they are not. The 2017 Global Gender Gap Report of the World Economic Forum told a rather depressing story. It showed a widening gap on each of the four dimensions it measured: educational attainment, health and longevity, and economic and political empowerment.

On current trends, the World Economic Forum forecasts that it would take 100 years to close the overall gender gap, 217 years to achieve parity in the workplace (across wages, seniority and participation), and 99 years to achieve equal numbers of women and men elected to parliaments.

This is surely utterly unacceptable.

In the area of leadership, the numbers of women globally are very low. Women are only 7.2 per cent of heads of state, 5.7 per cent of heads of government, 23.3 per cent of parliamentarians, around 20 per cent of Fortune 500 company board members last year, around 15 per cent of corporate board membership according to the Credit Suisse surveys of some 3,000 global companies, and in under a quarter of senior management roles in the private sector. Information for the public sector is sketchy but appears to be not dissimilar. These inequalities are persisting in spite of the clear advantages of having women in leadership positions.

In the corporate world, study after study finds that companies with more women on boards get better financial results. That's hardly a surprise—those boards stand to be more attuned to the attitudes and behaviours of whole populations, rather than of just one-half of them.

In parliaments and in ministries, a critical mass of women is needed for the perspectives of women to be well reflected in legislation and decision-making—and even just to get issues on the national agenda as priorities. The international evidence suggests that when the numbers of women parliamentarians reach significant numbers, issues previously unaddressed, but of importance to women, will come to the fore—not least those dealing with access to public services and addressing violence against women.

So, what can be done?

There are proactive steps we can take to grow the numbers of women in leadership, but we also need to ensure that women are more fairly represented across all levels of the economic, social and political organisation of societies. Getting into leadership positions normally involves a progression up the ranks—but women may find it difficult to get on the first rung of the ladder, and when they do, they may find that some rungs are missing for them.

The World Bank's Women, Business and the Law Report in 2016 found that around 155 countries have at least one law which discriminates against women, 100 countries put restrictions on what work women can do, and women in eighteen countries cannot get a job without their husband's permission.

In research compiled for this year's report, the Bank found that 1.4 billion women lack legal protection against 'domestic economic violence', defined as 'controlling a woman's ability to access economic resources as a form of intimidation and coercion', and more than one billion women lack protection against domestic sexual violence.

Taken together, these factors amount to significant barriers to women getting ahead. Women need full economic independence, they need access to sexual and reproductive health services, they need to be able to determine if, who and when they marry, they need safety in their homes and communities, and they need the laws which are supposed to protect their rights upheld. Only then can we expect to see major progress on women's leadership globally.

For the most part in developed countries, the barriers set out above have been overcome. Yet others remain. There are, for example, persistent gender pay gaps between men and women. These are perpetuated variously by work in female-dominated occupations being remunerated less than that in male dominated occupations, the different life cycle patterns of women and men, which see more women taking time out for family responsibilities and then often not catching up in seniority with male counterparts who had continuous work service, and outright pay discrimination. Even as venerable an institution as the BBC stands accused of paying women presenters and others less than their male counterparts.

Thus, if more women are to rise to the ranks of leadership across all areas of economies, societies and politics, there is a wide range of structural factors to be addressed. This is as relevant to women rising to political leadership as it is to women rising to be top leaders in major public, private and non-governmental organisations.

I freely acknowledge that my career path to becoming New Zealand Prime Minister could not have been followed at the time I did that had I had family responsibilities. I am delighted that both social attitudes and social services have now advanced sufficiently for our new Prime Minister, Jacinda Ardern, to be expecting a baby and carrying on with her job. This is a powerful role model for young women in our country and further afield.

Let me now talk about some of the ways of tackling these challenges.

1. Making paid work a real option for women with children

First and foremost, there is a need to make paid work a real option for women with children. It's not a real option if affordable, accessible and quality childcare is unavailable, and if there is not an entitlement to sufficient paid parental leave in the time leading up to and after the birth of a child.

My government in New Zealand more than a decade ago took a number of practical steps in these areas, and in recent years I have observed Japan taking similar measures as it endeavours to retain more women in the paid workforce. The models for my government were from Scandinavia, with their excellent early childhood education and care services, paid parental leave when a new baby arrives, and extended annual holidays enabling parents to have more time with their children during school vacations.

Accordingly, in New Zealand more than a decade ago, we made early childhood education available free of charge for 20 hours a week for all three- and four-year-olds, introduced paid parental leave as a right in law for the first time and extended annual holidays an extra week to a statutory entitlement to four weeks.

More broadly, the burden of unpaid work done by women must be addressed. Globally, three of every four hours of unpaid work are done by women. These pressures will increase as our populations age, as it is women who do most of the unpaid elder care work, as they do for children and for family members who are ill or have disabilities.

So, for women to be able to be in and stay in the paid workforce, our social services need to be operating well to lift the unpaid care work burden which is such an obstacle to participation for so many women.

2. Addressing gender pay gaps

On gender pay gaps and the under-representation of women in senior management positions, a number of steps can be taken. For example, as New Zealand Minister of Labour in 1990, I introduced pay equity legislation which allowed remuneration in female-dominated occupations to be compared with that in male-dominated occupations with similar levels of competency requirements, and for determinations to be able to be made to lift pay in the former where the gap was attributable to gender. Sadly, that legislation did not survive the incoming government in 1990.

Over time, greater convergence between male and female patterns of working life in New Zealand, and no doubt elsewhere, narrowed the pay gap, but there remains a differential between pay in male- and female-dominated occupations.

An interesting development has been the acceptance by New Zealand courts that claims for equal pay for work of equal value in the care sector could be tested pursuant to the Equal Pay Act of 1972. The government of the day decided to resolve the issue out of court by negotiation, and then to legislate for the agreement reached. Last June, the Care and Support Worker (Pay Equity) Settlement Act was passed unanimously by parliament and has led to these workers in these female-dominated occupations receiving pay rises of between 15 and 50 per cent.

It should also be noted that Iceland has recently passed far-reaching legislation which makes it illegal not to pay women and men equally. This appears to goes beyond the normal equal pay legislation. Now Icelandic companies employing more than 25 people must receive official government certification to prove their equal pay policies.

Action can be taken to improve the recruitment of women in areas where they are under-represented and to support their promotion into higher levels of responsibility. Measures in these areas are well known to many employers. They include:

- On recruitment: gender-neutral job advertisements, targeted recruitment, gender-sensitive interviewing, having women on all shortlisting and selection panels, ensuring no all-male shortlists and, where male and female candidates have equal merit and the target is to lift the numbers of women employed, to opt for the female candidate.

- On retention: it's vital to have a conducive workplace culture and practice which is women- and family-friendly and has zero-tolerance for harassment and bullying. The #MeToo movement is bringing a lot of very nasty, and even criminal, behaviour into full public view, and should be a clear signal to all employers of what they must do to keep staff safe from predators.

- On promotion: mentoring of and targeted talent development for women are vital, and peer group support through women's networks should be encouraged.

The objective of all the aforementioned measures is to see women more equally represented across all levels of organisations and equally paid.

3. Overcoming the barriers that prevent women rising to positions of political leadership

Addressing the range of barriers which prevent women fulfilling their potential in the economy and in society will help lay the basis for more women to rise in political systems too. Globally these systems have long been male-dominated, with the stereotypical image of Members of Parliament, Cabinet Ministers, and Presidents and Prime Ministers being largely that of a male with a supportive wife. This takes some changing, even in democracies of long duration.

Six years ago, UNDP released the excellent *Guidebook to Promote Women's Political Participation*. It was based on case studies of what had worked around the world to boost the numbers of women elected. It took a 'whole of electoral cycle approach', looking at what could be done to boost the numbers of women selected and elected, and to support those elected—especially when the entry of women into such positions had been relatively rare.

There is little doubt that the nature of the electoral system itself has an impact on the numbers of women elected. The First Past the Post, single member constituency system of, for example, the United States, the United Kingdom, and—until 1996—New Zealand seems to be the least conducive to electing women. This may relate to the traditional occupants of constituencies being male and their spouses playing a support role.

New Zealand changed its voting system in 1996 to a Mixed Member Proportional Representation System modelled on that of Germany. Now only half the parliamentarians are elected from constituencies; the other half come from party lists. In general, the parties have made efforts to ensure that their lists are more representative of women— after all, they do want women to vote for them. In the first MMP election in 1996, the proportion of women elected jumped from the 20 per cent of 1993 to 30 per cent. That was a 50 per cent increase in just one parliamentary term. Women's representation in the New Zealand Parliament now stands at 38.2 per cent—and reaching parity no longer seems like a distant dream.

The UNDP Guidebook of 2012 highlighted the critical role of political parties in lifting the numbers of women elected. Without their support, the numbers simply will not rise, as most people are elected to most parliaments with the backing of a political party. So, the parties need to be convinced that boosting the numbers of elected women is the right thing to do. That becomes easier with party list systems, where women can be placed in electable positions, and where the absence of sufficient numbers of women may attract negative comment and have adverse electoral consequences. Some parties rank their lists by alternating the names of women and men on each list to boost the chances of more equitable representation.

In some political systems, legislation for quotas has been enacted. There are many examples of this approach in Sub-Saharan Africa—and it does work. Rwanda is the standout example, with 64 per cent of those elected to its House of Representatives in 2013 being women. Women standing for election need ongoing support from their parties. In general, old girls' networks do not have the same financial resources as old boys' networks, so funding for women candidates is an issue. As well, in some countries, women are exposed to greater danger when campaigning, and need support for their physical security.

Post-election, cross-party groupings of women parliamentarians can ensure that women support each other. These become especially important where elected women MPs are either few in number, and/or where there are many new women MPs who are looking for support to do their job to the best of their ability. UNDP has supported a number of women's parliamentary caucuses around the world.

To conclude

Despite much progress in many places, many glass ceilings remain, and women in leadership positions globally are still a rare commodity. Those glass ceilings have to be tackled head on—and there are many proven ways of breaking through them. Addressing the basic structural issues is a precondition—women can't even get near the glass ceilings if they are denied equality and protection under the law and are unable to determine their own destiny.

I acknowledge the efforts of the Asian Development Bank to recruit women to its international staff ranks, and for championing gender equality as a key driver of development. The Bank has walked the talk by incorporating stronger gender design elements in its projects, and has achieved that in 48 per cent of its lending—almost twice the rate of a decade ago.

The direct and ripple effects of what you do will have immeasurable impact on attitudes to and progress towards gender equality in the countries which you serve. May one of those consequences be the emergence of many more women leaders in all spheres of life across the Asia-Pacific region.

Allen & Unwin
Level 3, 228 Queen Street
Auckland 1010, New Zealand
Phone: (64 9) 377 3800
Email: info@allenandunwin.com
Web: www.allenandunwin.co.nz

83 Alexander Street
Crows Nest NSW 2065, Australia
Phone: (61 2) 8425 0100

A catalogue record for this book is available from
the National Library of New Zealand.

ISBN 978 1 98854 705 3

Design by Kate Barraclough
Set in Adobe Garamond Pro
Printed and bound in Australia by Griffin Press
10 9 8 7 6 5 4 3 2